Praise for Susan McDougal and the *New York Times* Bestseller,
The Woman Who Wouldn't Talk

"Every American who loves our Constitution and deplores the abuse of power by the far right should read this book."
—President Bill Clinton

"Anyone who believes that prosecutors can't abuse the American criminal justice system should read Susan's book, *The Woman Who Wouldn't Talk: Why I Refused to Testify Against the Clintons and What I Learned in Jail.* It's a chilling account of the abuse she suffered from Starr's crowd and a sobering reminder that protecting our freedom depends on guaranteeing the rule of law for everyone."
—Hillary Rodham Clinton in her bestselling book, *Living History*

"Still without anything to link the Clintons to Jim McDougal's chicanery . . . [prosecutor Hickman] Ewing put the screws on Susan McDougal. She refused to cooperate and was shackled and transported to the first of seven prisons. . . . In September, she telephoned *The Arkansas Times,* a weekly paper in Little Rock, to say that her former husband was preparing to support Hale's story. 'He told me he was going to lie, and he wanted me to lie too,' she said. She declared that she was determined to defy Starr. 'I'll never talk to the independent counsel,' she said. She refused to go before a grand jury because she was sure she would be indicted for perjury when she didn't say what Starr wanted her to. . . . Susan McDougal, down on her luck, became the woman he [Starr] imprisoned."
—Sidney Blumenthal in his bestseller, *The Clinton Wars*

"Prosecutor Kenneth Starr pursued Susan as if he were Javert in 'Les Miserables'. . . . Hellish days in seven jails was the result. Susan tells her story in wry, candid tones. Once you read it, you realize what a travesty federal justice can often be."
—Liz Smith

"It's a harrowing book—so exciting I got up in the middle of the night to continue reading."
—*Providence Journal*

"This book starkly shows what happens to people who stand up against government coercion."
—*Booklist*

"Susan McDougal, a modern-day Joan of Arc."
—James Carville

"She took on the most powerful prosecutor in the country . . . and fought him to a standstill."
                                                                    —*Fort Worth Star-Telegram*

"[The story's] merit is found in the courage McDougal summoned after being sent to prison, and in the grave warning of what could happen to anyone, any day, under a repressive government."
                                                                    —*Boston Globe*

"Engrossing, often funny . . . McDougal's dignity and courage . . . brought Starr's operation to a standstill."
                                                                    —Gene Lyons, *Arkansas Democrat-Gazette*

"The story of a heroine—someone who didn't ask to play the role, but stepped up to the plate when confronted with the Republican version of the 'axis of evil.'"   —*Buzzflash.com*

"Engaging . . . gossipy, insightful . . . [McDougal] comes across as a spirited and forthright person who does not hesitate to call Kenn Starr a liar who would ruin lives in order to implicate the Clintons. Despite harsh treatment . . . McDougal refused to sacrifice her principles."
                                                                    —*Library Journal*

"The standoff between [Kenneth Starr] and the brassy businesswoman rocked a presidency and helped shape the political landscape of the last decade. . . . [A]n emotional page-turner."   —*Philadelphia Inquirer*

"An emotional page-turner, fueled by outrage over a series of brutal, politically motivated prosecutions by [Ken] Starr's team. . . . The reader is left to wonder how such a thing could happen in the Land of the Free."   —Timothy Phelps, *Newsday*

"Never mind Starr and the millions he cost us, the story here is how and why . . . a girl from Camden, Arkansas found the sheer nerve to say no to a fleet of city-smart, determined lawyers. . . . Moving and compelling, composed . . . with dignity and compassion."
                                                                    —*New York Times Book Review*

THE WOMAN WHO WOULDN'T TALK

SUSAN McDOUGAL

WITH PAT HARRIS

Introduction by Helen Thomas

CARROLL & GRAF PUBLISHERS
NEW YORK

THE WOMAN WHO WOULDN'T TALK

CARROLL & GRAF PUBLISHERS
AN IMPRINT OF AVALON PUBLISHING GROUP INC.
245 WEST 17TH STREET
11TH FLOOR
NEW YORK, NY 10011

FIRST CARROLL & GRAF CLOTH EDITION 2003
FIRST CARROLL & GRAF TRADE PAPERBACK EDITION 2004

LIBRARY OF CONGRESS CATALOGING-IN-PUBLICATION DATA IS AVAILABLE.

ISBN: 0-7867-1302-X

PRINTED IN THE UNITED STATES OF AMERICA
DISTRIBUTED BY PUBLISHERS GROUP WEST

This book is lovingly dedicated in the memory of Alice Ann Harris, who passed away before it was published but who was an inspiration to all of those involved.

CONTENTS

INTRODUCTION
by Helen Thomas

Susan McDougal has written her life story in a book titled *The Woman Who Wouldn't Talk*. It could also have been called "The Woman Who Wouldn't Give Kenneth Starr What He Wanted."

It is an odyssey of betrayal and courage. It is also a powerfully gripping tale, distressing and disturbing at times, yet uplifting throughout, especially as it nears its climax.

Among the most moving chapters of this fascinating book are those in which McDougal tells of her childhood amid a big loving family in Camden, Arkansas; the most painful sections are her journey through seven different jails around the United States after she was found in "contempt of court." Her confinement included punishment which can only be deemed "cruel and unusual," especially the seven week stretch in Los Angeles's Twin Towers facility when she was held in 23-hour per day lockdown in a Plexiglas-enclosed soundproof cell. Her jailers claimed this was for her safety, although it is an absurd justification, as she had nothing to fear from her fellow inmates. This period of confinement led to such severe sensory deprivation that McDougal tells readers she was on the verge of seeing her mind become entirely unhinged as she spent day after day in her cell, watching the pod outside as if it were a surreal silent movie. It is the most harrowing part of her story.

McDougal paid this heavy price for refusing to nail former President Bill Clinton and his wife Hillary in the investigation of the Whitewater land deal, which had gone sour before the Clintons ever left Arkansas. She had no damaging information about the decades-old transactions, which had been handled through Madison Guaranty, a savings and loan owned by her husband Jim McDougal.

She also refused to go along with sleazy deals offered by the Office of Independent Counsel, led by Kenneth Starr, that would have saved her from imprisonment. Indeed, Starr is the villain of the piece, although Susan saw him face to face only once. We learn that Susan's anger toward Starr and his minions, who in several bruising conferences implied that any damaging information about the Clintons would remove her from legal jeopardy. Her revulsion at these tactics actually sustained her and strengthened her resolve.

The McDougals' marriage had ended in divorce in 1985, as Jim's bouts with bipolar mental illness and the indignities he heaped on Susan tore at their bonds. Jim fancied himself a *bon vivante*, but he was pathetic and quickly became a caricature in the Washington limelight as the conservative campaign against the Clintons intensified. Ironically, Jim, whom Susan bluntly describes as a "con man and a liar," made his own deal with Starr in hopes of avoiding an ignominious death in jail. Yet that would be his fate. Deal or no deal, Susan McDougal was a match for Starr; as relentless as he was in pursuit of Whitewater, and determined to expose Clinton's personal life, she was equally resistant to the coercion that the jail sentence was meant to exert.

Who can forget the attractive tall brunette woman handcuffed and shackled as she was led away by law enforcement officers? It was played over and over again on America's television sets. In the early days of her ordeal, after she had decided not to testify lest she contradict her ex-husband and Starr's other lead witness, David Hale and walk into a perjury trap, she went home to spend time with her family. Her mother, who as a Belgian pre-med student during World War II married an American army sergeant named James Henley, asked her daughter, "Isn't there anything you know about the Clintons that you can tell them?"

"Mom," she said, "I don't know anything they did wrong. Anything I would say would be a lie."

At this point, her mother understood, and told Susan: "It sounds like what happened during the war, families turning against families, children informing on their own parents so that they could live. . . ."

Susan had the strongest support from Pat Harris, her co-author, who at different points has been her fiance, her lawyer, her best friend, and always her confidant. In times when she panicked and began to lose hope, he was always there for her.

As I read Susan McDougal's chronicle, my admiration for her soared when I read the description of her twenty-one months of incarceration, and the seven different jails in which she was confined. She rolled with these punches and many others. The numbing hours in her cells; the interminable bus rides as she was continually shuttled from courts to hearings and back to jail; the vile abuse she had to endure from a male prisoner during one of those rides. Inquiring readers will probably want to pull at the threads of the same riddle I did: with Starr and his prosecutors determined to coerce Susan's cooperation, were the onerous terms of her imprisonment actually dictated by the Office of the Independent Counsel? Did it serve their purpose for her to never become too accustomed to any one correctional facility? Or make too strong a bond with any of her fellow inmates? She and Pat Harris are currently filing a subpoena with the courts for information on these questions, as readers will discover in Chapter Fifteen of this book.

Parading Susan in shackles was actually one of her adversary's biggest mistakes. As the pictures flashed around the country the public began to rebel against Starr and the judges who showed her no mercy, even as a lifelong back condition, worsened by prison, threatened to inflict permanent damage to her spine.

Like me, I believe readers will find Susan's depiction of her fellow women inmates—who told her their stories, and still were able to dance, sing, and celebrate during those lonely nights in jail—a truly redeeming part of the book. Her sympathy even extended to the jail matrons, some of whom turned out to be quite humane and understanding. It took a Susan McDougal to find a rainbow shining through it all.

The deteriorating back condition finally led to her release. Freed at last, she did not forget the friends she made in prison among her fellow inmates. On his last day in office, President Clinton gave her an unexpected pardon. For the last several years, she has lectured around the country, passionately describing the miserable conditions in which women prisoners are often confined and often suffer cruel treatment. This is a part of the book that she clearly hopes will be discussed as much as her role in the Whitewater story.

Throughout the entire ordeal, from the first questions about Whitewater to her release from prison, her compassion and sense of humor were her sturdiest armor. Susan McDougal has not only survived the turbulent times in her life, she has prevailed over them.

Author's Note

I wrote this book with the help of Pat Harris, whom I've known since 1982 and who has been my most solid supporter throughout difficult times. At various points in my life, Pat has been my fiancé, my lawyer, my best friend, and my confidant.

Because he was so involved in my life during the past twenty years, Pat appears frequently in this book. Though he helped me write it, he deferred to me on how to write about him. Any depiction of Pat and/or his actions are my words alone.

In the course of writing this book, Pat and I have relied on many sources in addition to our own memories. These include trial and testimony transcripts, newspaper reports, magazine articles, television clips, and books such as *The Hunting of the President* by Joe Conason and Gene Lyons.

We have also spent many hours revisiting events with one another, with my parents and other family members, and friends such as Claudia Riley. In this way, we've been able to reconstruct much of my life—a life that turned out to be far more eventful and unpredictable than I ever expected it to be. No one's memory is perfect, but with the help of all these sources, I have told my story in the fullest and most accurate way that I could. Any errors in the text are ours alone.

SUSAN McDOUGAL
October 2002

PROLOGUE

MY FIRST IMPRESSIONS OF FAULKNER COUNTY Detention Center in Conway, Arkansas confirmed my worst fears about life in jail. I was greeted by a prison matron named Zoe Ann Hudspeth, a heavyset, powerfully built woman who looked like she'd just walked out of a Hollywood B movie about women in prison.

Zoe Ann had been a matron for years, and had seen and heard it all—her cardinal rule was that she never took crap from anyone. A stickler for rules, she quickly made it clear that she would not suffer any foolishness on my account. When one of the guards suggested that I be taken to a private cell that Webb Hubbell had once occupied, she snapped, "She'll go in with the rest of the girls!"

A guard led me to the women's wing of the jail, and when I walked in, I saw a small group of women sitting near the television. They'd just been watching news clips showing U.S. marshals leading me away in handcuffs that morning. I took my first step into the jail pod, balancing my dinner tray in one hand, a sheet and blanket in the other, with my gym mat—which is what I'd be sleeping on—tucked under my arm.

As I walked in, there was a chorus of "Hey, Susan." I'd had no idea what kind of reception I would receive, but fortunately the women seemed happy to see me. As I searched for a place to put my stuff down, the clip of my leaving the courthouse came on yet again. This was the first time I'd seen it, and as I stared up at the tiny overhead TV, tears began to well up in my eyes.

Suddenly, a voice cut through my reverie. "I know you didn't *buy* that outfit!" shouted one of the women.

"What the hell were you thinking, wearing that thing to jail?" another taunted, and all the women started laughing.

"Well," I said with a smile, "this is the first time I've been arrested. I thought I'd wear something comfortable. Next time, I'll try to dress more appropriately." The women looked at each other, eyebrows raised. It seemed I'd passed their first test.

Your first night in jail is your worst night, but the women at Faulkner County Jail were determined to help me through it. There weren't enough beds to go around, so I'd been assigned to sleep on a gym mat on the floor. But my fellow inmates remembered what their first nights were like, and one who'd had a pretty hard time offered to give up her bed for me.

Several of the women gathered around me and started telling stories about their lives, which were alternately heartbreaking and hilarious. By late in the evening they were doing comedy sketches—imitating their pimps, acting out a paranoid crack cocaine high, pretending to catch their boyfriends with other women. Although they told their stories as outrageously as they could to garner the most laughs, I was amazed at how perceptive these women were. Not surprisingly, I ended up my first night in jail crying—but from laughter, not despair.

After the laughter had died down, someone explained that every new girl who comes through has to play a game called "How did you get here?" You start from when you were very young and explain how you ended up in jail. The game had only rule: no bullshitting was allowed—you had to be completely honest. I wasn't the only new prisoner in the women's pod that day, so the girl who'd come in earlier than I did was up first.

Listening to her tell her life story, I started thinking back on everything that had brought me to this point. How did a small-town

Arkansas girl with dreams of being a preacher's wife end up a nationally known felon? How could a simple real estate project that had failed miserably end up becoming the most expensive investigation in the history of the United States? How could a young girl who had grown up giving patriotic speeches to the American Legion about the greatness of the U.S. government end up in jail for defying that government? As I lay there on my bunk, I realized it wasn't such a simple thing to answer the question, "How did I get here?"

1

THE EVOLUTION OF A MARXIST HOLY-ROLLER

TO THIS DAY, MY MOTHER SWEARS MY father tricked her into marrying him. Laurette Mathieu was a medical student in Liège, Belgium, during the waning days of World War II when she first met Sgt. James B. Henley of the U.S. Army. He was riding up and down the streets of Liège on his army-issue motorcycle, looking confused and lost. The local newspaper had run a story the day before asking the citizens of Liège to please assist the Americans in any way possible and Laurette saw this as opportunity to help an American in trouble.

With the encouragement of her best friend, she yelled out, "Do you need directions?" Sergeant Henley took one look at the attractive young woman calling to him and immediately pulled over to the curb.

My mother recalls that she repeatedly explained the directions while my father feigned confusion, after which he said, "Just come with me and show me." She was reluctant, but like most Belgians, she was grateful to the American forces and wanted to help them in any way she could. So she hopped on the back of the motorcycle and pointed him in the direction of the base.

Once he'd gotten her on the motorcycle, Sergeant Henley had no intention of simply driving this pretty young Belgian woman to the base. He insisted on taking her home—which not only made him look chivalrous, but gave him the benefit of finding out where she lived. From that point on, he became a regular visitor in the Mathieu house, much to the delight of my grandmother, who worshiped the Americans. She was certainly not opposed to having her daughter entertain a Yankee, especially one as handsome and charming as Sergeant Henley.

For the next few weeks, Sergeant Henley came to see Laurette nearly every day, sometimes going AWOL from the base to do it. He told her all about his hometown of Camden, Arkansas, painting it as a perfect little town in the most picturesque part of the country. He also regaled her with stories about the beauty and glamour of America, most of which he'd stolen from the movies: before joining the army, he'd never been outside of small-town Arkansas.

Although she will admit to having been intrigued by my father's stories, my mother insists that she had no intention of marrying anyone. She was dating a fellow Belgian medical student at the time and had decided to wait until the war ended before deciding where her future might lie. But my father had already decided his future would include her.

"Laurette," he told her, "I've been told that I am being shipped out to the front any day now." His voice breaking, he told her how he'd gladly fight and give up his own life if it meant she could have a brighter future. In return, he just wanted one thing: the privilege of being her husband for a brief, shining moment.

Moved by his courage, Laurette was plunged into uncertainty. She told her two suitors that she needed time to think and made them both promise to leave her alone for a week while she tried to sort it all out. Her Belgian boyfriend honored her request and left her alone. My father also agreed to honor her wishes—and then proceeded to show up at her house for seven days in a row. On the eighth day he showed up at the house to find the Belgian boyfriend sitting in the dining room having dinner with the family. My father stormed out of the house and headed back to the army barracks.

To everyone's surprise—including my mother's—she jumped up

from the dinner table and went straight to the base to find him. Until that moment, she hadn't realized the depths of her feelings for him—and now he'd stormed out, perhaps for good. When she caught up with him, my father did not mince words. "I'm about to be transferred to the front," he told her. "I don't have time to waste." She could either marry him, he said, or he would probably never see her again.

Unsure of what to do, but knowing that she didn't want to lose him forever, she agreed to marry him. A few weeks later, after she'd already become Mrs. James B. Henley, she learned the truth—the mission my father was being sent on was actually a routine exercise with a degree of danger only slightly greater than an army barracks inspection. By the time she discovered the truth, however, she was safely ensconced in the local army housing for young married couples and scared out of her mind.

Sergeant Henley has a different version of the story. To hear him tell it, my mother was immediately taken with the debonair American serviceman who bore a striking resemblance to Robert Mitchum. She fell hard for him and was just waiting to come to the promised land, America. If given the opportunity, she would gladly serve as his dutiful wife and bear him many children, all the while never removing her transfixed, adoring gaze. The way he tells it, she would beg him to tell her stories of life in America and could not wait to get married.

As I grew older and began to realize that my father's stories were often more fiction than fact, I began to suspect that my mother's version was the more accurate one. However, one thing still confused me: how could a woman, especially a strong-willed, intelligent one like my mother, be pressured into marrying before she was ready. I remember promising myself that when my time came, I would hold out for true love on my own terms. God would later punish me for this bit of hubris.

My parents were married on October 11, 1945, and suddenly my mother found herself thrust into the role of American military wife. Over the next fourteen years, she packed up and moved with him every couple of years—from Brussels to Munich to Heidelberg, Germany (where I was born in 1955), to Fort Riley, Kansas. Then, in 1959, my father retired from the army and took his Belgian bride and growing brood back to the small town where he had grown up.

Camden, Arkansas was a far cry from the place my father had described when courting my mother. It was and still is like many southern Arkansas towns: quiet, friendly, devout, and mostly conservative, but with an underlying live-and-let-live attitude. When we moved there for good in the late fifties, the chief industry was timber and, thanks to the paper mills, you could smell Camden long before you could see it.

My father had had many years of distinguished army service in both Europe and Korea, but he never did advance past the rank of sergeant for one simple reason: he could not follow orders. Every time his career seemed to be on the rise, he would violate a curfew or go AWOL and soon find himself busted down a pay grade or two. Now that he was retired, his attempts at breaking into the private sector were not much better. Unable to follow directions from his bosses, he found himself wandering from job to job until he finally decided that his future would lie in that last-chance domain of the headstrong: he decided to become an entrepreneur. In the early sixties, he bought a gas station near downtown Camden and promptly became a part of the burgeoning American middle class.

My mother was keeping busy as well. My father might have had trouble sticking to one job, but there was another area in which he proved to have remarkable consistency: over the course of twenty years, my parents produced seven children—four boys and three girls. The three oldest, Danielle, Jim, and Bill, were all at least seven years older than the three younger children, Paula, David, and John. I was right in the middle, and my relationship with each of the two groups was very different. With the older set I was the kid sister, always trying to measure up. I never could quite succeed, as Danielle was a beauty queen, Jim was the brain, and Bill was the most popular teenager in town.

But my relationship with the younger kids was a different story. While Paula, David, and John were still very young, my mother took a job as a nurse to help provide for our family of nine. When that happened, I found myself responsible for getting the younger kids out of bed, making their breakfasts, and getting them dressed for school. Each night, I looked over their homework and made sure they brushed their teeth before bed. I seemed to fall naturally into the role of surrogate grown-up—and I took it very seriously.

I became aware early on that I was not like other kids. Instead of playing outside or watching television, I found comfort in reading about the world beyond Camden and imagining lives different from my own. In the third grade, we had a class project where all the kids were supposed to dress up as their favorite historical figures. Kids came to school that day dressed as Davy Crockett, Abraham Lincoln, and even Dorothy from the Wizard of Oz. I, on the other hand, asked my mom for a white lab coat so I could go dressed as Marie Curie. It was the first time I began to get the weird looks that would be the hallmark of my youth.

The rest of my brothers and sisters were relatively normal, which made my quirks stand out even more. My younger sister Paula, with whom I shared a bedroom and whose biggest concern was showing off her blond hair to its full advantage, used to bemoan what an oddball I'd become. "Susan!" she'd shriek. "Why can't you just be normal?" I would just laugh because I knew she was right. The evidence was everywhere, like the time in the fourth grade when I went to donate my used books at the school book fair. As my fellow ten-year-olds piled their Nancy Drew and Hardy Boys books on the table, I dropped off *The Rise and Fall of the Third Reich*.

I was always a daydreamer, and reading fed my imagination. On summer days, instead of going to play ball or hang around with other kids, I used to take Paula, David, and John to the library. I loved the library so much that we'd walk the two miles there even if it was 100 degrees outside—but then, when we got there, we had to do battle with the librarian. She was a cranky woman, and she would never let me look around anywhere but the children's section.

As soon as she'd turn her back, I'd sneak over to the history and biography shelves and conduct a hurried search for books about World War II. The most fascinating tales I'd ever heard were my parents' stories of wartime Europe, so I was forever trying to get my hands on as many books about Hitler, concentration camps, and the Russian front as I could. Not surprisingly, this alarmed the librarian, who once even called my father to complain when she caught me sneaking out of the children's section. Instead of getting me in trouble, she succeeded only in confusing my father, who couldn't figure out what the fuss was about. With seven active kids, my parents tended to reserve their worrying for times when someone was in danger of losing a limb, not when they were trying to read history books.

In the fifth grade I managed to sneak a copy of Karl Marx's writings out of the library. To an idealistic eleven-year-old, the concept of sharing the wealth among all people sounded wonderful. Excited at this new idea, I brought it up with my teacher, Mrs. Booker. "Under communism," I informed her, "everybody would be equal. There'd be no rich people, and no poor people." A look of bug-eyed horror crossed her face. "I work hard for my money," she said. "I'm not going to give it away to anyone." I argued with Mrs. Booker for a few minutes, trying to convince her that she would probably end up with *even more* money under a communist system, but inexplicably she remained unswayed.

My conversation with Mrs. Booker created something of a ripple in the community. A few of the other kids went home and told their mothers about our discussion, and the frightful prospect of possibly losing one of its young people to the lure of communism was too much for Camden to take. Some of the mothers notified the church leaders, and the following weekend, the whole Sunday school was asked to pray for my soul.

This would be a common thread throughout my early life: reading would usually get me into trouble. Having never traveled anywhere—save for a seemingly endless two-week, flu-ridden station-wagon trip to Jacksonville, Florida—reading took me out of Camden and into the world. I had always been a daydreamer, and reading took me a step further. The more I read, the more I became convinced that I was somehow being deprived of seeing the magnificent and fascinating places in my books. I'd had very little contact with the world outside Camden, but my love of reading convinced me of one thing: I decided early on that the quality I wanted most in a man was that he be able to "speak like a book."

For some reason, despite seven shots at it, my parents failed to produce even one shy wallflower of a child. I used to fantasize that our family was an Arkansas version of the Kennedys, conveniently overlooking the fact that we had no money, political clout, or Ivy League educations. Though we were a big, loving family, we were hardly the Kennedys—in truth, we were more like the Brady Bunch on amphetamines. We spent our evenings crowded around the dinner table, with each of the seven children vying to be heard over the shouting and each willing to offer opinions without the slightest provocation.

But one voice always rose above the tumult—that of my father. During the last ten years of his army service he'd served as a drill sergeant, shaping up young recruits with a two-step program of yelling and yelling louder. At home, he saw no reason not to raise his children in the same manner. Strict discipline was required in everything we did, from waking up at 05:30 every morning to making up our beds with hospital corners. We were to come directly home after school and, if there was a need to go out, we were given a rigid, nonnegotiable deadline as to when we were to return. Being late meant a whipping, which was accompanied by the inevitable lecture in which my father insisted he had to whip us because he loved us so much. During these times, he introduced us to the unique army vocabulary—words that might seem inappropriate at a dinner party but later came in handy for me during discussions about Kenneth Starr.

For my sisters and me, dating was pretty much out of the question. Even if we did happen to get a date with a local boy, the thought of having him meet Sergeant Henley was enough to dampen any romantic desire. But when she was seventeen, my oldest sister, Danielle, began seeing Bobby Jo Dickinson, a James Dean wannabe complete with ducktail, tight white T-shirt, and a souped-up '57 Chevy.

Because my father forbade any of us from going out on weeknights, Bobby Jo would drive his Chevy up and down our street honking his horn, and call Danielle at all hours of the night—all of which drove my father crazy. He'd hear that engine roaring by and begin cursing, "It's that damn boy again!" Before he ever met Bobby Jo, he'd already developed an intense dislike of him.

My father also didn't like for me to go for rides in the Chevy, because Bobby Jo was an amateur drag racer and must therefore be a dangerous driver. I, of course, loved to be invited along for rides, and I remember cruising along the streets of Camden, with the radio blasting Elvis songs and my sister and me singing at the top of our lungs. I was only eight years old, but I already felt the thrill of infatuation: I too was in love with Bobby Jo and his ducktail.

The eventual meeting between my father and Bobby Jo happened when, one afternoon in downtown Camden, my father accidentally rear-ended a car in front of him. As he stepped out to the curb, he looked with amazement to see that the car he'd just hit was a souped-up '57 Chevy. When he looked at the young man who'd just emerged from the driver's seat, my father exclaimed, "You're the kid who's been driving up and down our street!" Bobby Jo extended his hand and said politely, "Don't worry about the damage, Mr. Henley. I can get it taken care of." From that day on, my father quit complaining about Bobby Jo. A year later, Danielle married him in a ceremony at our house, and thirty years later they hate to spend even one night apart. Ironically, Bobby Jo has also become one of my father's favorites and his chief defender in the household; whenever political arguments arise in the house, Bobby Jo is often my father's only ally.

Though my father was strict, he could also be softhearted, especially if he felt someone was being mistreated. He also possessed the Irish blarney for great storytelling and outrageous acts—from the minute he would arrive home, the house would come alive. My father loved to hug his children, tell us how much he loved us, and then pledge his undying devotion. "If you ever get locked up in a Mexican jail," he'd shout, "I'll get you out—even if it costs me my life!" We'd laugh while he wildly mimicked tying on a bandanna, clenching a knife in his teeth, and storming through the jungle to find us. I accepted these promises unconditionally, never questioning why I might someday end up in a Mexican jail.

When my father wasn't around, my two older brothers, Jim and Bill, would provide the entertainment by trying to outdo each other in every category. Their arguments always went the same way: Bill would make some grand pronouncement that he knew would irritate Jim. Unable to abide such ignorance, Jim would retort, "That is so stupid! Take it back!" The ensuing argument would last for hours—sometimes even days—while everyone in the house would beg Jim to just let it go. But Jim never would. He'd harangue Bill, shout at him, even sit on him—anything to get him to admit he was wrong. Their arguments were epic, and Jim was so stubborn that I don't recall Bill winning a single one.

I spent most of my youth dying to get home to watch the nightly entertainment show that was our family. In fact, growing up, I never could figure out why people liked watching TV. I didn't know what other people's families were like, but at our house, family dinners were a lot more interesting than any episode of *Leave It to Beaver*.

With seven outspoken children and a drill sergeant, our family discussions were complete free-for-alls. Many of them revolved around politics, and they usually started in the same way—with my father erupting about something he'd seen on the news. A lifelong Republican, my father was growing increasingly disenchanted with the party for nominating liberals like Barry Goldwater. When the Beatles came to America, my father marched my two younger brothers down to the barbershop and demanded buzzcuts for them. Poor David and John were the only two little crew-cut boys in primary school that year.

My father was extremely vocal about whatever didn't please him. One of his favorite exercises was complaining about our country's "coddling" of everything from criminals to hippie youth to third-world countries. During these rants, he tended to overlook the fact that he was famous throughout town for personally coddling anyone with a hard luck story who needed a cup of coffee or a meal. To my father, what the country really needed was a president who was a blend of George Patton and Joe McCarthy. He finally became somewhat satisfied with Ronald Reagan, although he remained suspicious of those Hollywood types Reagan hung around with.

Political discussions were made all the more entertaining by the fact that my brother Jim was at the furthest possible extreme of the political spectrum. My father's namesake and chief tormentor, Jim was a slender, thoughtful boy who loved to follow politics and, by the time he was ten, was writing earnest letters to newspapers. He also was a liberal's liberal who couldn't fathom my father's inability to see obvious truths.

As he grew older, Jim ratcheted up the level of his provocation and began to challenge my father on virtually every one of his basic beliefs. I would watch in dread as these arguments escalated, and jump in to beg them to stop. Jim eventually joined the Peace Corps, a vocation that seemed to have been designed to irritate my father. But later in life, Jim finally took a profession my father could approve of: he became a minister. He did, however, end up with the affectionate label of the Red Priest for his socialistic sermons.

My brother Bill also liked to agitate my father, but for entirely different reasons. Bill had inherited my parents' good looks, and that, combined with a wild streak, made him the teenybopper idol of Camden. By the time he reached high school, Bill was known as the local Lothario.

Like Jim, Bill chafed under my father's rigid rules, and he bent and broke them at every opportunity. The result was a lot of yelling, a few whippings, and a singularly unchastened Bill. Although my father's temper might have frightened Bill at times, his fears were largely trumped by his greater desire to meet girls.

By the time he reached high school, Bill was the local heartthrob and one of the most popular kids in school. In sharp contrast, I slid through school largely unnoticed by my classmates. I knew I was socially awkward, but for the most part I didn't care how I was perceived—for me, the members of the Henley family were the coolest people I knew, and the only ones I really cared about getting along with. I was a little bit curious about how it would feel to be part of the hip crowd but, despite the fact that Bill tried to help me fit in, I seemed incapable of achieving any degree of coolness myself. The futility of my efforts was confirmed by the fact that no one ever seemed to remember my name; I was known to everyone as Bill Henley's little sister.

Bill took note of my failed efforts to emulate him with classic teenage-boy sensitivity. One day as we were walking to school together, a speeding car whizzed within inches of me, very nearly running me over. As we walked on, he turned to me and said, "You realize that if you'd been hit, the newspaper headlines would read 'Bill Henley's Sister Hit By Car!'" This became a running joke between us. Years later, on the day after CNN broadcast pictures of me being dragged off in handcuffs, I called Bill from jail. "I just had a look at *USA Today*," he told me. "The headline says, 'Bill Henley's Sister Taken to Jail'!"

Growing up, I was forever trying to keep the peace between my father and my brothers. I was my father's favorite and was rarely the object of his wrath, so I had a hard time understanding why everyone always seemed to be angry and picking fights with him. It was so easy to get along with him—if you just didn't do the things that you knew would anger him, then he wouldn't get mad. It often seemed to me that Jim and Bill were deliberately provoking him—which, of course, they were. Whenever arguments would start heating up, I would beg them to stop provoking him and let the rest of us just enjoy the evening. This was the beginning of a philosophy I would adhere to the rest of my life: I've always turned to appeasement as the easiest solution to any problem.

In virtually every way, my mother was the exact opposite of her husband. She had been a medical student, and he had almost no formal education. She grew up in a European city; he was raised in an Arkansas agriculture town during the Depression. He was a difficult, stubborn man, and she was calm, the patient voice of reason. I don't know how in the world my parents ended up married—but I know that once they did, they argued for the rest of their lives.

For most of the early part of their marriage, my mother simply acquiesced to my father's wishes. In truth, she had little choice: she was a stranger in a strange land with young children to raise. Besides that, she came from a generation in which a marriage commitment was a lifetime commitment. She had married James Henley and, for better or for worse, that was that. She was willing to overlook his temper—and a lot of other things—to keep the peace.

But it wasn't a good idea to push Laurette too far. She had a strong will of her own, and a very clear sense of right and wrong.

Growing up in Belgium during the war had given her a definite sense that not everything in life was some shade of gray; she saw things as black-and-white and was prepared to stand up for what was right, regardless of any personal sacrifices involved. During the early sixties, for example, she invited my younger brother John's whole class to his birthday party. Because his school had just integrated, that meant the neighborhood white kids would be going to a party with black kids—most of them for the first time in their lives. Some of the neighbors came by to inform my mother that that just wasn't "the way things are done around here," and to suggest she rescind the invitations for some of the kids. But my mother wouldn't hear of it. She wasn't trying to be heroic—she just made no distinction between the kids she'd invited, and she was not about to turn some kid away.

The war had affected my mother in ways large and small but, unlike my father, she didn't like to talk about it (other than occasionally thanking him for personally saving Europe). On the rare occasions that she would talk, she told us about seeing the death camps just after the war, and described how the Nazis had made lampshades of human skin and pillows out of hair. She spared us none of the gruesome details and told us about how our father had been ordered to guide the leading citizens of one German town through a nearby death camp. "We didn't know," they told him. "Well, you're going to know now," my father had responded. "Because I'm going to walk you through and show you."

My father loved to tell my mother that "if it wasn't for me and the American army, you'd be goose-stepping down the Champs-Elysées right about now"—but she didn't need him to prod her about it. My mother loved America for what it had done in the war. "This is a great country," she would tell us. "This is a place where people put their lives on the line for people they didn't even know." She missed her family and certain things about Belgium, but she was by far the most patriotic American in Camden.

We were, of course, greatly affected by our mother's professions of love for this country. I was proudly patriotic, even as a teenager;

during my sophomore year of high school, I entered an oratorical contest at the American Legion, delivering a speech entitled, "Who Knows How Many Men Have Died to Preserve America's Freedom?" I won all the way to the state level with my speech, to the delight of both my parents. However, my father became less thrilled when shortly thereafter I announced that I was a Democrat. It would have been much easier on my father if I had just told him that I was pregnant with Satan's child.

Although my mother spoke English well, nuances unfortunately escaped her. Because she had learned English by studying books, she had an impressive vocabulary—far better than that of the average American—but no grasp of ordinary slang at all. As a result, she ended up in numerous conversations where neither side could understand what in the world the other was saying. Compounding the problem was her foreign accent, and her self-consciousness about it.

As a result, practically every time my mother had a conversation— with neighbors, store employees, repairmen and the like—she was sure she was being insulted. When a store clerk would ask, "Can I help you find something?" she saw it as an affront to her intelligence. Nor did she understand or appreciate Southern congeniality. Whenever anyone asked how her children were doing, she would always come home and complain that *she* didn't pry into *their* family business, so why did they go snooping into hers? She was a private person who saw no reason to discuss her affairs with anyone other than family, and no reason to indulge in the time-honored Southern tradition of meaningless pleasantries. Not surprisingly, Camden society didn't go out of its way to socialize with her.

Her socializing was further reduced by my father's insane jealousy. Because she was a very attractive woman and, coming from Belgium, very exotic, my father was certain that every man in Arkansas wanted to run off with her. She rarely left the house for anything other than basic errands—and even then, he usually went with her. Despite the fact that she spent nearly every moment either at home with children or within my father's sight range, he was still somehow convinced she was carrying on numerous affairs. Sadly, neither time nor age has mellowed his emotions; my mother is seventy-seven now, and my eighty-one-year-old father is still convinced that she has something going on with the termite man.

I spent the first seventeen years of my life at school, at home, or at church. My father pretty much limited my social life to youth group outings through the First Baptist Church—one of the few social activities my father assumed was not fraught with sexual longings run amok. In my teenage years, I began spending a lot of my free time at the church, partly because I was becoming increasingly interested in religion, but mostly because it was my only social outlet.

Boys never expressed much interest in me in high school, largely because I was socially inept, and partly because I was scrawny, so underdeveloped that my brothers nicknamed me the Stick. Paula, who was four years younger than I, had her first kiss before I did—and when a boy finally did kiss me, backstage during the senior play, I was so shocked that I turned and fled.

My first "date," at age sixteen, was with a college student who was a minister. This suited my needs perfectly: he was a gentleman, he'd read a fair number of books in his life, and he was dedicated to the church. Our evenings together consisted of praying and going to various religious revivals—but then, after a few months, we began to struggle with the temptations of the flesh. Before long, we'd start our evenings off by holding hands and praying the same prayer: "Let the words of my mouth and the meditation of my heart be acceptable in thy sight, O Lord, my strength and my redeemer." This, we hoped, would give us strength to endure the temptations that befell us with increasing frequency.

When it came time for me to choose a college, I decided to attend Ouachita Baptist University—largely because my minister boyfriend was a student there. By the time I enrolled, however, he'd already graduated and gone on to preach somewhere else in Arkansas, so our romance—what there was of it—never fully blossomed. But my short time dating a minister had led me to decide that being a minister's wife would be the ideal life for me. And Ouachita was the place to find one. Ouachita would never be confused with Berkeley: it was a Southern Baptist college where religion was a major part of the required curriculum.

In the fall of 1972, I went to Ouachita with a full-ride scholarship to study Latin—hardly a major rife with job possibilities, but a subject I loved studying. I had it all planned out: I could continue my religious studies while helping my husband preach to the flock. Eventually, we would start our own family. In the end, I would live happily ever after as a mother, minister's wife, and community volunteer.

All I needed to do was find a nice, clean-cut young man from a good home who was looking for a wife and someone to raise his children. Instead, I met Jim McDougal. It was not unlike going to the movies to see *The Sound of Music* and ending up watching *The Exorcist*.

2

THE BRIDE OF MCDOUGALSTEIN

MY FIRST ENCOUNTER WITH JAMES BERT McDougal would set the stage for the next twenty years of my life. In the span of about three minutes, I was introduced to everything that was maddening, thrilling, and entertaining about Jim all at once.

It happened in July 1975, during the summer between my junior and senior years at Oauchita. I was doing some work for one of my professors in the Old Bookstore—the wooden building with a front porch that served as the college's political science office. One afternoon, I somehow managed to lock the professor's keys in his office while he was away. That was bad enough, but this professor was also known campuswide for his temper—and one of the things that got him particularly upset was his phone going unanswered during office hours. Having locked the keys in, I stood helplessly outside the door, listening as the phone inside rang loudly and incessantly. I knew I was in trouble.

After frantically looking through my purse and pockets, I stumbled over to the next office, looking for anyone who might be able to help me. The door to that office was open, revealing a slender, balding man seated primly behind a desk. I knew his name—Jim McDougal—and I'd even said hello to him while passing in the hall, but I didn't really know him, and this was no time for introductions. "I've locked the keys in the office next door," I blurted. "Have you got an extra key to it?"

Jim didn't miss a beat. Without saying a word, he rose from his desk, strode down the hall, and planted himself in front of the door to try his own set of keys. When that failed, he lifted one foot waist-high and promptly kicked the heavy wooden door in, splintering the frame and breaking the lock. As I stood there, staring in disbelief at the remains of the door, Jim smiled at me, turned on his heel, and walked back to his desk. In that one moment, Jim had perfectly illustrated his philosophy of life: kick the door down, worry about fixing it later.

Jim McDougal was like no one I had ever met. Then again, he was like no one anyone had ever met. Growing up a skinny, bookwormish only child in the tiny town of Bradford, Arkansas, Jim had chosen politics as his ticket out of town. As a young man, he'd dropped out of college to go work in Washington, D.C., for Sen. John L. McClellan. Over the course of the next decade, he worked his way up under the patronage of McClellan and Congressman Wilbur Mills—the legendary chairman of the House Ways and Means Committee. After a few years, Jim became a senior aide for the world-renowned senator from Arkansas, J. William Fulbright.

Not only was Jim bright, ambitious, and politically savvy, he had also charmed the Washington elite with his irreverent wit and dead-on impersonations of Winston Churchill and Franklin Roosevelt. This latter skill was especially useful when, after one of his numerous alcoholic binges, Jim would call the White House and demand—in Churchillian tones and an extremely irritated manner—to speak to the president.

By 1967 Jim recognized that he was an alcoholic and became an active member of Alcoholics Anonymous. When he arrived at Ouachita to teach political science in 1974, at the age of thirty-four, he hadn't had a drink in seven years. Although being sober may have calmed him down some, it did nothing to tame his irreverence. Years later, when Whitewater made him a nationally known figure, Jim was often described as flamboyant and eccentric—a characterization he loved to play for all it was worth. But the caricature so often drawn by newspaper reporters was not the Jim McDougal I met in 1975. Jim was unusual, irreverent, and charming—but never the one-dimensional eccentric he was later portrayed to be.

Jim was far from a handsome man. Already balding by the time he was thirty, he wore thick-framed glasses and had a narrow, somewhat drawn face that tended to make him look sickly. In fact, his health was never good, as he suffered from numerous actual allergies and a broad range of imagined ones. By the time Jim arrived at Ouachita in his mid-thirties, he could easily have passed for a man in his mid-forties. If there was one man a young, sheltered, devoutly religious girl from small-town Arkansas would never think twice about, it was Jim McDougal.

Then he opened his mouth. Despite growing up in a family where talking was the chief recreation, I had never heard anyone talk like Jim. When he spoke, the things he said seemed to come right out of the books I'd grown up reading—and his experiences rivaled those of the characters I'd always dreamed of meeting. Jim sensed that I was fascinated by the way he talked, and he would lay it on thick when I was around. Listening to him made me realize that there really were people out there living like the books I read. Looking back, perhaps I'd have been better off illiterate.

Ouachita Baptist University, with its emphasis on religion and its strict curfews and rules, was not the kind of place you'd expect to find a man like Jim McDougal. In fact, Jim came to the school during a difficult time in his life. He'd lost his job working for Senator Fulbright when the senator lost his reelection campaign in November 1974, he'd recently gotten divorced, and he was feeling lonely and adrift. When his friend Bob Riley, who was then the head of Oauchita's political science department, offered him a job, he gratefully accepted. He moved into the "guest house" on the Rileys' property—a trailer down the hill from their house—happy to be closer to Bob and his wife, Claudia, who were two of Jim's favorite people.

Bob Riley was a true World War II hero, having enlisted in the Marine Corps as a teenager, fought at Guadacanal, and been seriously wounded when he threw himself on a gun turret to protect his fellow marines. After he'd been evacuated, Bob spent months in military hospitals, finally emerging at a frail ninety pounds and almost totally blind. For the rest of his life, little pieces of shrapnel would still occasionally fall out of various places on Bob's body, clanging to the floor.

Believing that Bob could never get a normal job again, the Marine Corps sent him to massage school to learn a trade that didn't require vision. But Bob had other plans. He enrolled in college, and studied by getting friends to read his textbooks aloud to him. He was as ambitious as he was smart, and in the coming years he built a political career, getting elected lieutenant governor of Arkansas in 1970 and very nearly winning the governorship in 1974. Upon his defeat, he retired to Arkadelphia to head up Ouachita's political science department, and settled in to become a mentor to generations of political up-and-comers.

Bob was a man of boundless charisma, topped off by an ability to make you feel like he was thrilled just to be having a conversation with you. A born storyteller, he loved spinning tales with just enough "flavor" stirred in that you were never quite sure if he was gently pulling your leg. Whenever someone told him where they were from, he would often respond, "Really? I'm from there, too." Bob's trademark was a black eye-patch, worn over his empty eye socket. By wearing the one patch, he gave most people the mistaken impression that he could see out of the other eye. He was so good at hiding his near-total blindness that only his close friends knew about it—and some of them only learned after years of knowing him. Claudia served as his eyes, and she did it with a grace and ease that seemed to come naturally to her.

Bob Riley mentored dozens of young Arkansas politicos, but he loved none more than Jim McDougal. Like so many before and after him, Bob found himself taken in by Jim's sense of humor and his ability to match anyone story for story. Bob and Jim could talk for hours, each trying to outdo the other with the most outrageous—or simply the most outrageously told—story. I remember sitting on the Rileys' porch once while Bob told the funniest story I had ever heard—an hours-long epic involving a French guide on a hunting trip. We all laughed so hard and so long that Bob finally had to go to the emergency room. He couldn't stop laughing and feared he was having a heart attack.

For Jim, teaching a political science class or two at Ouachita was a perfect solution to his sudden unemployment. What better job could there be for him, after all, than getting paid to stand in front of a group of people and tell stories? And because his teaching duties wouldn't require too much time, he could continue to work on the burgeoning real estate business he'd started on the side. Years later, it occurred to me that there was another reason the Ouachita job was perfect for Jim: in his mid-thirties and recently divorced, he would have a chance to find a new wife among a group of impressionable young girls—Jim's favorite type. As I would discover later, this search for interested young girls was a pattern he would repeat for the rest of his life.

Although Jim enjoyed teaching and flirting with coeds, that was a mere pastime compared to his great love: real estate development. While still a young aide for Senator Fulbright, he'd begun investing small amounts of money in tracts of Arkansas land, subdividing them and then selling the smaller lots. He found success almost immediately, and after a few years he'd built a track record as an accomplished small developer. Although his projects were profitable, none of them made him a fortune, which was fine with Jim. He was in real estate for only one reason, and it had nothing to do with money. Jim desperately wanted to be perceived as a success. As such, he focused not on the profit margin of each project, but on how quickly he could sell it out, tell his friends about the success and move on to the next one.

Nothing brought more joy to Jim than being able to brag to Senator Fulbright and others about how he'd just bought three hundred acres, divided it into fifteen twenty-acre parcels, and sold it all within six months. Details weren't important; what mattered was that Jim could show his political friends—most of whom were business neophytes—that while their knowledge was limited to the political arena, he was brilliant enough to succeed in both business and politics. His real estate business was something he could control—and then invite his politically successful friends in when he wanted. It was obvious that money was a secondary concern when Jim convinced Senator Fulbright to invest some money with him on a parcel of land near Conway, Arkansas—even though he had more than enough money to finance the project himself and reap all the rewards on his own.

In a state like Arkansas, a man like Jim—who had absolutely no interest in sports and couldn't drink beer because of his alcoholism—was pretty much relegated to oddball status. But with his real estate ventures, Jim was able to cultivate a mystique about himself. It didn't matter anymore that he wasn't one of the boys—he was something even better. He was the brilliant, slightly off-center genius, an enigma even to those who knew him well.

Jim embraced and enhanced this reputation, even dressing the part for good measure. While most professors the wore standard-issue corduroy pants and fading blazers, Jim was always turned out in three-piece Brooks Brothers suits, carefully matched neckties, and the most perfect shoes I'd seen this side of a Cary Grant movie. He paid close attention to every detail about his clothes, a mannerism that oddly enough never applied to any other area of his life. But he never looked perfectly put together, thanks to a peculiarity I've never known anyone else to have: Jim couldn't stand to have his clothes touch his skin. They had to be made of quality materials—all cotton, all silk, or all wool—but he always wore them in a way that made him look rumpled. Years later, a reporter would write that Jim looked like he'd gotten dressed by standing still while people threw clothes on him.

Following the door-kicking incident, Jim and I began to have short conversations whenever we saw each other. I had been equal parts shocked and intrigued by his impulsiveness that day and, like most of the students at Ouachita, I didn't know quite what to think of this charismatic, slightly peculiar professor. Then one day he sauntered up to my desk in the political science building and asked me casually if I would like to go to lunch.

"I can't today, but maybe some other time," I told him, surprised to have been asked.

Jim stood for a moment in the doorway, then lifted his chin and stated in a haughty voice, "I never ask twice." He then turned and walked back to his office. I was amused, and as I sat at my desk, I remember smiling and thinking, "We'll see."

By the time I got to Ouachita, I had outgrown my adolescent nickname of the Stick and now had my share of boys asking me out. So I wasn't thrown by Jim's request to take me out—in fact, I was looking forward to seeing whether I could convince him to break his own rule and ask me again. Over the next two weeks, I dropped by his office several times to make small talk and flirt as obviously as I dared. I never stayed long, but the message was always clear: if he was still interested in having lunch with me, I could be persuaded. Sure enough, one day soon thereafter, he again managed to find his way to my desk. Hands in his pockets, sizing me up, he said, "I'm going to give you a second chance."

This time I accepted, rather smug in the knowledge that I'd been up to the challenge. Besides, what could it hurt? If there was anyone on campus who appeared to be harmless, it was Jim. Over the last three years I'd spent my share of evenings fighting off football players and future preachers in the front seats of their cars. From the looks of Jim, I was pretty sure I could take him in two rounds. Unfortunately, like George Foreman in Zaire, I was way too confident. I was about to be knocked out by the dating version of the rope-a-dope.

From the beginning, I never treated my relationship with Jim as having any serious potential. He was simply a nice change from the college boys I had been dating, most of whom seemed to think Winston Churchill was a cathedral in Europe. Nor did Jim seem to take our dating very seriously. He was always very laid-back, the quintessential Southern gentleman. I suspected he was only interested in a short fling with a coed, a conquest that would enhance his reputation.

Most of our early dates consisted of driving around Arkadelphia and the surrounding countryside in Jim's convertible, talking about anything and everything imaginable. I can't count the times I ended up in tears from laughing so hard at Jim's stories—I loved his outrageous sense of humor, and he played to his audience perfectly. I could tell he was surprised that I was familiar with most of his literary and political references, and I in turn was surprised when he asked my advice about his real estate business—including the deal he was doing with Senator Fulbright. When I offered my opinions he swore he would do exactly as I suggested. For a twenty-year-old girl who had spent most of her life shrinking under the glow of her better-looking, more popular older siblings, it was thrilling to have a college professor ask my opinion.

Jim would ask me where he should place ads, what I thought customers were looking to buy, and why and how he could make his projects more marketable. Though at first I was flattered by his faith in me, slowly it began to dawn on me why he so readily trusted my judgment—Jim knew he was like a space alien: he lived here among the rest of us, but he had no idea what most normal people were thinking, because he was the furthest thing from normal himself. By comparison, he saw me as the very symbol of apple-pie Americana. Because I'd grown up in a God-fearing, flag-waving family, Jim viewed me as someone who could translate for him the thoughts and dreams of ordinary Arkansans. It was but one of the numerous errors in judgment Jim made about me before we married.

Although the attention Jim was giving me regarding business matters was interesting, the real head-turner was the parties. On a fairly regular basis, Jim would make the one-hour drive to Little Rock to attend some political fund-raiser or campaign kickoff. Sporadically at first, then with increasing regularity, he began taking me with him. On these trips, he'd introduce me to the high society of Arkansas politics—congressmen, current and former governors, and assorted state representatives.

At one such event, Jim introduced me to the Arkansas attorney general, a young Harvard graduate with the timeless Southern name of Jim Guy Tucker. With his liquid blue eyes, perfectly dimpled chin, and a chiseled jaw that Superman would have envied, Jim Guy was so handsome it hurt to look at him. He wore nothing but expensive Sulka starched white shirts, perfectly tailored and so crisp that he always looked like he'd just come from a photo shoot. In 1976, the girls at Ouachita had more posters of Jim Guy Tucker hanging in their dorm rooms than of Robert Redford.

Jim had met Jim Guy through his sister, Carole Tucker Foreman (who was later appointed secretary of agriculture under Jimmy Carter), and the two men had become close friends, even owning a house in Little Rock together for a time. Jim had a profound respect for Jim Guy's intellect—especially because he, like Jim, was interested in business as well as politics. And he admired Jim Guy for another reason: although a physical limitation had prevented Jim Guy from serving in Vietnam, he had chosen to go anyway, working as a journalist and later writing a book about the men he met there.

At the parties in Little Rock, I loved to watch Jim as he worked the crowd. At first, he'd hang around the fringes of the gathering, a bit aloof. Then, when the mood struck him, he'd suddenly launch into stories about his days in Washington, mesmerizing the guests with anecdotes about everything from going drinking with Robert Kennedy to giving Senator Fulbright lessons on how to be more "down-home." Jim would lean against a fireplace mantel, strike a David Niven pose—complete with cigarette and limpid gaze—and reduce everyone in the room to helpless fits of laughter. Then, just when his command of the audience was at its peak, he would announce that we had to be going, motion to me to fetch his coat, and then swagger to the door with the gaudy confidence of a man who knows how to go out on top.

That same fall, Jim introduced me to another up-and-coming Arkansas politician: Bill Clinton. Bill was gearing up to run for Arkansas attorney general at that time, and Jim called me one afternoon with a request. "Listen," he told me, "my friend Bill Clinton is supposed to speak at Henderson State University in about an hour. Can you get some friends together and go over there?" Apparently Bill was concerned that, barring a miracle, the only people who would show up at the student union for his speech would be a handful of students either looking for their mail or enticed by a last-minute offer of free pizza.

At the time, I was auditing a speech class at Henderson, which was right across the street from Ouachita. Bill was scheduled to speak at the same time my class was meeting, but I promised Jim I'd see what I could do. I went to my professor and told him the situation. "We could go listen to this guy speak, and then critique him in our next class," I said. "Or maybe he could talk to us about how it feels to deliver a speech in front of a large audience." The professor was still not swayed, so I said, "Listen, they're kind of worried no one will show up. I'm sure the class can get something out of this, and it would mean a lot to this guy."

To my surprise, the professor agreed, and he took the whole huge class—an auditorium full of people—down to the student union. We jammed into the common area, and when Jim walked into the room, his eyes lit up. It was a standing-room-only crowd! No matter that these shining young faces reflected nothing more than relief at being rescued from the normal class day. When Bill took the podium, his reaction was much the same. To a politician like Bill Clinton, having a crowd of captive young college students willing to listen to his vision for Arkansas was as good as it got. Bill thanked me for bringing that crowd practically every time he saw me for the next ten years.

My first impression when I saw Bill walk in was that he looked incredibly young. He'd already been a Rhodes scholar, finished law school, taught law at the University of Arkansas, lost a bid for Congress, and was about to run for Arkansas attorney general—and he looked like he could still be in college. He had a baby face, with chubby cheeks and a happy, aw-shucks grin. Although he was tall, he didn't have the broad shoulders or barrel chest of an athlete—but he did project intensity. Even his hair was intense: a great mop of thick, wavy brown hair that unfortunately looked like he'd tried to trim it himself.

By far his best asset was the complete ease with which he carried himself; he was obviously a man who was comfortable in his own skin. As he spoke that day, he moved around the room, talking to us rather than at us and connecting with anyone who'd give him eye contact. He spoke of a "new" Arkansas, a place that could improve on its past and build a hopeful future. He was definitely good, but he struck me as a young man who was teaching a class, not as a serious politician on the rise.

When Bill finished speaking, Jim went up to talk with him, and I soon joined the two of them. Bill wasted no time getting to business: almost immediately he hit Jim up for a campaign contribution, and

Jim obliged by writing a check right there for $1,500, the maximum allowable amount. Then Bill turned to me.

"How about you?" he asked. "Can you do the same?" I laughed. I was just a student, living on the little stipend I got from my scholarship and help from my parents! I was amazed that this guy thought I could just write a check for $1,500—and even more amazed at how easy it was for him to ask. I couldn't imagine having to go around asking people for money, but for Bill it seemed second nature. In fact, when I told him I didn't have any money to give him, he didn't miss a beat—he turned to Jim with a smile and said, "Why don't you help her out? You could give her that amount to donate."

I don't remember much else about Bill from that day, but over the next few weeks Jim began talking more about Bill and his campaign, and soon we were seeing more of him. One evening, Jim made plans for us to meet Bill for dinner in Little Rock. We were supposed to meet him on the corner of Asher and University Avenues at 6 P.M., but by six-thirty, there was no sign of him. Finally, by a quarter to seven, Jim was fuming. "Come on," he barked, and stormed off toward nearby Bowens Restaurant.

Just then, a dark blue convertible with an attractive redhead behind the wheel came speeding up, lurching to a stop out in the Bowens parking lot. Bill jumped out of the passenger seat without opening the door, then came loping up to us, grinning all the way. He obviously hadn't wanted us to meet the redhead, who pulled out of the parking lot as soon as he'd hopped out of the car.

"You fuckup!" Jim yelled at Bill, who responded by enveloping Jim in a big bear hug. "This is the last time I stand outside anywhere and wait for you!" I stood to the side, unable to believe that Jim had just shouted such an obscenity on a public sidewalk—and at Arkansas's next attorney general, no less. But Bill just smiled, put his arms around both of us, and walked us into the restaurant.

Once we got inside and sat down, Jim began to question Bill. "Okay, what's the deal with the girl?" he needled. "You didn't even let us see her face! Who is she?" But Bill just mumbled something about her being in a hurry, and being a friend of a friend who just offered him a ride. "Aha, another friend of a friend," laughed Jim. As we sat there in the booth, Jim started to tease Bill about the parade of big-haired, big-breasted women he used to bring around Senator Fulbright's office. "Looks like your tastes haven't changed," he said.

Bill's big grin made it obvious that he enjoyed hearing Jim expound on his growing reputation—especially with me sitting there to provide an audience. But after a few minutes of listening to Jim's teasing, Bill rested his chin in his hands and got a wistful look on his face. Gazing off dreamily, he said, "Jim, I think I might get married."

For the next twenty minutes, Bill told us about a woman he'd dated off and on since they met back in law school at Yale. She was different, he said, from the other girls he'd spent time with. She was engaging on every level—and she wasn't afraid to challenge him. I didn't know Bill well at this point, but I thought to myself that if he was truly in love, he had an odd and detached way of expressing it. He'd cock his head to one side, squint into the distance, and say, "She's so different. She's a really intriguing woman. I think I'm going to marry her," as though he'd found some rare specimen of flower and had no choice but to pick it. As he spoke, I felt a little sorry for this woman, whose name, he told us, was Hillary. I remember thinking that whenever I got engaged, I hoped my future husband would talk about me in a more romantic way than this.

Anyway, how serious could Bill be about this woman? We'd just seen him ride up in a convertible driven by a beautiful redhead whose favors he'd apparently just enjoyed. Now here he was talking in a kind of clinical way about the woman he supposedly wanted to spend his life with. I found it hard to take Bill seriously, but on the way home after supper, Jim said, "I think the boy might be serious. I've never heard him talk about anyone like that."

I had trouble pinning down who Bill Clinton really was and I certainly wasn't the only one. As I got to know him better, I saw that he had an amazing ability to be whoever he wanted to be. He was one of the most intelligent people I've ever met, but he was always able to make people feel he was just like them. He was a Rhodes scholar in a state where the unofficial motto is "Thank God for Mississippi"—the only state in the Union that routinely scores worse than Arkansas in education rankings. He was incredibly ambitious, and aspired to the national spotlight early on—yet he came across as the kind of guy you'd meet any day of the week, any place in Arkansas.

There were times, however, when he couldn't quite keep a lid on his brilliance. Jim liked to tell the story about when Bill, as a student intern, had been assigned to drive Senator Fulbright to a campaign rally in a rural area of Arkansas. Senator Fulbright was the kind of man who didn't like people chattering away at him. In fact, he was so protective of his time and attention that there were people who'd worked in his office for years whose names he never knew. When the senator found himself stuck in a car with Bill Clinton, it was like he'd suddenly been sentenced to his own personal circle of hell. By the time they got back to Little Rock, hours later, Senator Fulbright was fuming. "Keep that boy away from me," he angrily told Jim. "He never quits talking! He's just got to show everybody how much he knows!"

When Bill was with Jim, he always had a gleam of fun in his eye. He loved Jim, and because he was six years younger, he was always asking Jim's advice. "What do you think I ought to do?" he'd say, then watch with a look of intense interest as Jim spoke. Bill was better than anyone I've ever seen at faking that kind of interest, but with Jim I believe it was genuine. Bill was charming: like Bob Riley, he had the gift of knowing exactly how to make anyone feel special, important, listened to, or loved.

These were all things the whole world would come to know about Bill Clinton. But there was one other, odd thing about him I remember from those times. He always smelled kind of earthy, like a farmer who never could wash the aroma of soil out of his skin. Jim always thought Bill smelled funny, and once, when he lent Bill a coat, he wrinkled his nose when he got it back. "Susan!" he complained. "I can't ever wear this coat again. I'll never be able to get that man's smell out of it."

Not long after our evening at Bowens Restaurant, we received an invitation to attend Bill and Hillary's engagement party in Hot Springs. This would be the first time we met Hillary, and as we drove to the party, we entertained ourselves by speculating on what she might be like. Bill had told us she was different—but still, we figured she'd be bouncy and pretty, like most of the women he'd dated so far. "But apparently, this one can at least put two sentences together," said Jim, laughing.

As we walked up to the apartment for the party, Jim said, "Now, listen. She probably doesn't know Bill's Arkansas friends, and she's going to be nervous. Let's try to make her feel comfortable." With that, we rang the doorbell and walked in.

The apartment was small, and as we entered the foyer, I could see into the living room. Bill sat in a chair right in the middle of the room, and a young woman was sitting half on the arm of the chair and half on his lap. I knew this must be Hillary, but she looked absolutely nothing like I had expected. With huge owl-like glasses, a mane of frizzy hair, and almost no makeup, she looked like she'd just hitch-hiked in from Greenwich Village. While the other women at the party were dressed in their finest *Saturday Night Fever* fashions—bright polyester blouses, slit dresses, and stacked platform shoes—Hillary was dressed for comfort in a modest, plain outfit.

There couldn't have been a starker contrast between Hillary and the rest of the people at the party, but she wasn't at all nervous or self-conscious. She and Bill just seemed happy and in love, and they held court there in the middle of the room as the guests milled about around them. I don't remember them moving out of that chair once the whole night. In fact, they looked like they might never move out of that chair for the rest of their lives.

After I got to know Hillary, I realized that her calm confidence at that party was one of her defining traits. She'd lived in Washington and worked on the Congressional impeachment inquiry staff during the Watergate affair, and now here she was in little Hot Springs, Arkansas, hanging out with Bill's down-home buddies. She conversed with everyone pleasantly enough, but she didn't seem to really connect with anyone but Bill. Then Jim walked up.

Jim and Hillary hit it off right away. For someone who was used to spending her time with East Coast intellectuals, Jim's eloquent observations, with quotes from Whitman and Emerson thrown in, were a welcome relief from the party chatter. Though she never left Bill's side that night, Hillary spent a fair amount of time talking with Jim, and they both clearly enjoyed it.

At one point, Bill called me over. "So, how about you and McDougal?" he teased. "When are we going to hear those wedding bells?" I laughed and said, "Don't hold your breath."

"All right, Child Bride," he said, laughing along with me. "We'll see." From then on, that was Bill's nickname for me—Child Bride. Though I'd seen him a few times with Jim, it wasn't until that night that Bill and I began to be friends. I think he could tell that I felt a little out of place at the party—I was only twenty, after all, and everyone there was at least a few years older than I. Besides, I didn't drink, and anytime I found myself in a crowd where people did, I always felt a little uncomfortable. It's interesting to look back now and realize how, at that party, Jim was focused on making Hillary comfortable, while Bill was looking out for me.

On the ride back to Little Rock, I could tell Jim was impressed with Hillary. He also seemed to have a newfound respect for Bill for having the courage to marry a strong, intelligent woman. His only criticism was of her clothes. "Why don't you take her shopping?" he said to me. "She could use a little help." He thought for a moment, then said, "I think you two could become friends."

When Jim suggested that Hillary and I could become friends, he said he wanted me to "help her fit in. You could help soften her up." Looking back, I suspect he also knew I could learn something from her. She was a woman who wasn't afraid to show her intelligence, and that was a rare thing in Arkansas at that time. Jim knew the side of me that loved books and the life of the mind and he saw that I deliberately hid this from most people. If Hillary and I became friends, he reasoned, we could both learn something from each other.

But as I spent more time with Hillary, it became obvious quickly that that would never happen. Whenever I was alone with her, I could tell she viewed me as a lightweight—Jim's cute coed piece of fluff. Irritated at this condescension, I perversely decided to embrace it. Before long, I began purposefully bringing up topics I knew Hillary disdained, like shopping and hairstyles, just to show her that this hick

Arkansas girl didn't care what Eastern intellectuals thought of her. For her part, Hillary seemed uncertain how to respond. Sometimes she would politely engage in my inanities, but other times she did little more than look at me quizzically.

But although Hillary made it clear to me that she felt superior to the people she met in Arkansas, I remember feeling sorry for her. She just seemed so gawky, and had trouble relating to people. She was, unlike me, a fully formed adult, sure of herself and her opinions—but she lacked warmth, and as a result she had very few friends in Arkansas. Jim would say, "Why don't you invite Hillary to the movies?" and I'd think, "Okay, I'll try one more time to break through the ice." But I never could.

However lukewarm the bond might have been between Hillary and me, her relationship with Jim continued to flourish. People who knew the Clintons in those years tended to make a big point of playing to Bill's ego; he was, after all, a rising political star. But Jim took the opposite approach. He praised Hillary nonstop, becoming one of her chief defenders at a time when she'd already begun to attract the kind of criticism and vitriol that would follow her all the way through the White House and into the Senate. Knowing that Hillary continually got flak about her appearance, he also took every opportunity to compliment her on how she looked. Despite her feminist leanings, Hillary wasn't above a little Southern flattery—and Jim McDougal was a man who knew exactly how to dish it up.

As we came to know the Clintons better, I was fascinated by the way they interacted with each other. I never wondered whether theirs was simply a marriage of political ambitions—it was obvious to anyone who knew them that they were truly in love. The more germane question for me was how these two people, whose personalities and backgrounds were so different, were able to make their marriage work. Bill was a guffawing, back-slapping, natural-born politician at ease with everyone and everything. Hillary, on the other hand, was quiet and bureaucratic in her approach to things. She was so deadly earnest about everything: whenever someone disagreed with her, she would eagerly engage them in debate, convinced she could persuade them of her point of view by the sheer force of her own convictions.

In the past ten years, amateurs and experts alike have spent thousands of hours trying to analyze the Clintons' relationship. Reporters have speculated about screaming matches in the White House, the lack of sexual attraction between them, and their supposed sham "marriage of convenience." It's been a long time since I had any contact with the Clintons, but I can say for certain that when I knew them, very early in their married and political life, their marriage was nothing like the media has portrayed it. Their relationship struck me as no more volatile or unusual than that of any two highly intelligent, emotionally charged people struggling to balance ambitions with the mundane difficulties of making a relationship work.

As for Clinton's infidelities, it always struck me that it likely had nothing to do with sex and everything to do with approval. Hillary gave him everything he needed in a wife: intelligence, ambition, character, and, I believe, a great deal of love. But the one thing she did not give Bill, at least when I was around, was the constant approval that he craved. I have never known another human being who needed to be told all the time how great he is. If Bill is not being praised in sufficient quantity, then he practically begs people for it. Hillary, however, was not interested in Bill's emotional neediness. As a strong, confident woman, she did not need other people's approval and could not understand Bill's need for it. She simply refused to give it to him and he was desperately looking for it. I am sure that the adoring women he had sex with were more than willing to fulfill that need. Whenever I heard about Bill having an affair with someone, I always speculated that the sex probably lasted for five minutes and the discussion about how good he was at sex lasted for thirty.

Jim and I dated somewhat sporadically for a few months, and in the meantime I continued to see other young men. Ouachita frowned on professors dating students—in fact, they frowned on pretty much anything but Bible-reading and studying—so we had to keep our dates low-key and out of sight. Ours was not what you'd call a sizzling romance, but I always enjoyed my time with Jim, and I found him a far more interesting companion than the college boys I went out with. Most of my other dates at Ouachita were pretty much interchangeable: some earnest twenty-year-old would take me to dinner and perhaps a movie—or maybe, if he had a wild streak, we might go parking at the dam.

Not only was Jim far more engaging than any student, he also was well beyond the kind of game-playing that characterized so much of college dating. Jim was absolutely straightforward about everything, and easy to be around. When we weren't driving to Little Rock for parties, we'd take leisurely drives all over Arkansas to look at potential land deals. Though I was always pleased to be included, there soon came a point for me when every pine tree began to look pretty much alike. Not to Jim, though. He loved the art of the deal, and he attacked new projects with an enthusiasm and energy that most men reserve for sex or football. I'd usually get caught up in his excitement and, even when I didn't, I always enjoyed listening to Jim talk on our long drives together.

By the winter of my senior year, Jim and I had been seeing each other casually for about six months. When plans were made for him to chaperone a student trip to Washington, D.C., he asked me if I'd like to come along. I didn't really want to—I never felt comfortable being around fellow students while I was with Jim, and it seemed a little much to be joining him when he was supposed to be a chaperone. Besides, I didn't think my father would let me go—he especially wouldn't have let me go if he'd known I was dating Jim. Though I'd told my mother early on about our relationship, I'd been afraid to tell my father about it.

I told Jim I didn't think it was a good idea for me to come to Washington. But as he always did when he really wanted something, Jim persisted. "I really want you to meet Senator Fulbright," he pressed. As I would so often do in the years to come, I relented under Jim's persuasive pressure.

We arrived in Washington in the midst of a bitter cold snap, only to find that our hotel rooms were equipped with ancient, paint-peeling radiators that gave off less heat than a secondhand toaster oven. The hotel's one redeeming feature was a cozy Irish pub off the lobby, and for the next week, Ouachita's renegade band of Bible-thumping political science students routinely spent evenings gathered at the bar. Though he never drank, Jim routinely urged others to treat themselves to a few drinks, and almost everyone spent a fair part of that trip inebriated.

In my case, that didn't take much. Not only had I never drunk alcohol in my life before that week, I also was a real lightweight. This was a trait I inherited from my father, whose nickname during his army days was One-Beer Henley. I had a drink or two at that Irish pub, and the next thing I knew, I was in the elevator telling Jim I was Mata Hari. Alcohol made me further lose the inhibitions that I had begun losing anyway, and as the elevator creaked upward, I remember feeling sexy and happy and telling Jim how good-looking I was while he grinned.

Three nights before we were scheduled to return to Arkansas, Jim arranged for the two of us to have dinner with Senator Fulbright and his wife, Betty. "The senator can be somewhat formal," Jim warned me that afternoon. "And he doesn't suffer fools gladly. He's perfectly capable of dressing down anyone if he sees fit—man or woman."

The one thing that worried me about meeting Fulbright was a seemingly unbreakable habit I've had since I was a girl: whenever I'm nervous, I get more and more talkative and frenetic. Like a desperate comic unable to milk a laugh out of a dead crowd, I just press harder when I feel things aren't going well. It's almost like an out-of-body experience—I sit there and listen to myself rattling on, fully aware that I am making an ass of myself, but totally incapable of shutting up.

At the dinner, Senator Fulbright immediately put me at ease. "You remind me of my wife when she was a girl," he told me. "Betty always wore white eyelet dresses." I was flattered and charmed by the senator, who had a laughing, self-deprecating manner that would have made him a huge hit at the Henley household. He quite obviously went out of his way to make me feel comfortable, complimenting me at every opportunity and telling Jim on several occasions what a lucky man he was. He also quizzed me at length about my background, my politics, and my ambitions, but he did it in such a relaxed manner that I felt totally at ease. To this day, I'm not quite sure why the senator was so kind to me that night, but I've never forgotten it.

The Woman Who Wouldn't Talk

At the end of the evening, as we took a taxi back to the hotel, I could tell that Senator Fulbright's attentions had had an effect on Jim. He confided that after dinner, the senator had taken him aside and whispered to him, "She's a keeper. Hang on to that one." Jim was so surprised and pleased by the senator's reaction that he talked on and on about the conversation, all the way to the hotel. I was elated that I'd made Jim proud, and happy to see him so excited. I was not, however, prepared for what came next.

When we arrived back at the hotel, Jim escorted me to my room and paused dramatically in front of my door. "I'd like to speak with you, if I may," he intoned. He spoke this phrase in such a formal, detached way that I half expected him to tell me he'd just been diagnosed with an incurable disease. A few hours later I would have been happier if I had been diagnosed with an incurable disease. We entered my room, and Jim turned to face me.

"Susan," he began. "I think it's time we had a talk." In later years, I would recognize this as a clear signal to run and hide, but I didn't know it then.

"I think we should get married," he said.

Although I'm best known for refusing to talk, my friends and family will tell you that I rarely lack for words. But that night, in a cheap hotel room in Washington D.C., I stared silently ahead for what felt like an eternity, unable to say a thing. When I found my voice, I blurted the first thing that came to mind: "You have got to be kidding!" Of the million different responses you can give a man who's just asked you to marry him, "You have got to be kidding!" ranks as possibly the one they are least expecting.

But Jim was definitely *not* kidding. As I sat on my bed looking at him in disbelief, he proceeded to bare his soul and emotions in a way I'd never expected.

"Susan," he began, "I want to be completely honest with you. I want you to know that I've been an alcoholic, and I've done some terrible things in my life. But I'm sober now. I go to AA, and its main precepts require honesty in all things. I want to be honest with you, and want to tell you everything about me."

I still could not speak. Jim went on.

"The biggest downfall for an alcoholic is not living honestly. If I'm not absolutely honest with you, I'll end up drinking again and ruin my life. I want to live my life honestly, and I want you to share it with me."

I was overwhelmed by this sudden outpouring of emotion. No man had ever spoken to me with such sincerity and such depth of feeling. But still, I knew I couldn't give him the answer he wanted.

After taking a moment to catch my breath, I told Jim, "I'm not ready to get married." I was twenty years old—I'd never lived on my own, balanced a checkbook, or held a full-time job. My life so far had consisted of two phases: growing up sheltered in a big family in a small town; and then spending a few years at a rigid, conservative college in another small town. I hadn't even begun living yet—I didn't even know what opportunities were out there for me. Besides that, Jim and I had only been dating for six months. I knew him well enough to know that I loved him, but certainly not well enough to marry him.

Having laid himself on the line, Jim was not about to take any answer but yes. "Baby," he insisted, "I am thirty-five years old. I'm not interested in just dating anymore. This isn't a game for me." Seeing I was still unconvinced, he said, "I'm tired of having to keep this relationship a secret. I'm a professor and you're a student! If we get engaged, we won't have to sneak around anymore."

And so it went for an hour. We went back and forth on why we should or shouldn't marry, each of us holding stubbornly to our positions. After a while I suggested a compromise: "Why don't we live together for a while," I said, "and see how it works out?" But Jim's response was adamant. He would not, he declared, introduce me to his friends as his live-in girlfriend. It was marriage or nothing.

After a few more minutes of arguing, Jim gave me his final word on the matter. If I would not marry him, he said, he never wanted to see me again. Whether he meant it or not, this got my attention. Jim was unlike anyone I'd ever met. He had introduced me to more exciting people, places, and ideas in the span of our courtship than I'd met in my entire life to that point. In spending time with Jim and the Rileys, I'd found a family for myself away from my own family in Camden. I wasn't ready to marry Jim, but I certainly wasn't ready to lose him forever, either. I'd been filled with emotion earlier in the evening when Jim had spoken so beautifully and sincerely; if I let him get away, would anyone ever talk to me like that again? Would I ever feel this way about anyone but Jim?

As the night wore on, Jim could sense that I was softening. Summoning all his considerable oratorical power, he drew a picture of the extraordinary life we'd lead together. He talked about the beautiful house we'd buy, the sophisticated parties we'd throw, and the fabulous trips abroad we'd take. He seemed to have a much better vision of what our lives would be like than I did, and I was drawn to that vision. A life with Jim might be many things, but it certainly would never be dull.

As my resolve weakened, I kept coming back to one fact: not only did I trust Jim, I also believed he knew even better than I did what was good for me. This was a trait I would end up exhibiting more than once in my life—usually with disastrous results. I found myself swayed by another factor: after six months of dating Jim, his kick-the-door-down philosophy had begun to wear off on me. I could just say yes to Jim right now to stop this argument, I reasoned, and then fix it later. Once we got back to Arkansas and were in a less pressurized atmosphere, I could sort things out. With that in mind, I finally gave Jim the answer he was looking for. "Okay," I told him, "I'll marry you."

Not only was Jim an exceptional salesman, he also knew how to protect himself from buyer's remorse. He knew he had to close the deal completely, lest I wake up in the morning and tell him I'd changed my mind. So despite the fact that it was now ten o'clock at night in Arkansas, he picked up the phone and called my parents to tell them of our engagement. They were less than thrilled that their daughter was marrying a recovering alcoholic sixteen years her senior, but they told me they trusted me and the decisions I made.

The next day, Jim continued to spread the word. He called Senator Fulbright, who graciously offered to invite Jim's old friends from the Hill and throw us an impromptu engagement party at the Capitol Press Club that very night. Jim then took me to one of the most exclusive jewelry stores in Washington, where he instructed me to pick out any ring I wanted. When we'd settled on one, he slipped it on my finger. He was so happy he almost had tears in his eyes. "I want to give you something else," he told me, "something you can put on and wear today. You just made me the happiest man in the world." He picked out a gorgeous necklace that matched the ring, clasped it around my neck, kissed me gently, and said, "This is the first of your wedding gifts."

When I walked into the engagement party that night, wearing a black satin dress with a scalloped neckline and my new jewelry, Jim gallantly took my hand and led me to the dance floor as the band began playing "Satin Doll." This would have been a touching moment, except that no one dances like Jim McDougal. It was always a showstopper when he took to the floor—he looked like a marionette with a caffeine junkie pulling the strings. You couldn't get too close to him without risking a black eye or broken limb, but it was the funniest thing in the world to watch. This was the first time in my life I'd danced with any man other than my father, and I kept my distance, laughing at his antics and realizing that even if I wasn't ready to marry him, I truly did love him.

This was the kind of romantic evening every girl dreams about for her engagement party. That night, I let myself believe that the fairy-tale life Jim had described might actually turn out to be real.

3

THE YOUNG AND THE RESTLESS

THE FIVE MONTHS BEFORE THE WEDDING went by in a blur. At first, I was still sure I could convince Jim to postpone any ideas of marriage, but soon enough it became clear that my fate was no longer in my hands. Jim had taken control of my life and was running the show.

One afternoon soon after we were engaged, Jim was driving us from Arkadelphia to Little Rock when he suddenly veered off the freeway and headed for the countryside. Thinking he wanted to look at some new potential land project, I didn't ask where he was taking us. He pulled into the driveway of a tiny house with a large veranda, a rock garden in the front lawn, and a fresh coat of bright yellow paint.

Jim got out and strolled toward the house. When he stopped at the front step, pulled a key from his pocket, and proudly threw the door open, it suddenly dawned on me why we were there. This was where we were going to live—Jim had, without saying a word to me, chosen our future home and fixed it up in inimitable McDougal style. "Welcome to the love nest," he said with a smile.

I walked into the house, and all I could think was, the funniest little place I'd ever seen. The living room had silk wallpaper, the carpet was six inches thick, the rooms were filled with odd antiques, and the bathroom walls were covered with reproductions of some famous artist's drawings of huge naked people. Jim had apparently spent $20,000 fixing up a $5,000 hut—and there was nothing left for me to do but tell him I loved it. So I told him I loved it. I couldn't believe Jim had made this decision without asking me, but I figured I ought to just let it pass.

I didn't find out the most extraordinary thing about our little shack until after we were married and had moved in. One evening, as I was lying on the living-room floor reading the newspaper, I suddenly began to wonder if I was seeing things. The carpet seemed to be moving! As I squinted closer, I could suddenly make out an army of tiny insects marching every which way across the floor! I shrieked and leapt up, brushing my arms and legs and hopping toward the next room. "Jim!" I yelled. "This house is infested!" That was when Jim revealed the truth about the "love cottage."

The house was actually a converted goat shed, and Jim had simply slapped the six-inch-deep carpet down right on top of the floor where the goats had lived, died, been fed, given birth, and done all manner of other things. The tiny insects I'd seen were goat mites. I couldn't believe it when Jim broke this news to me—we were living in a converted goat house!

Though I'd agreed to marry Jim, I had always expected I'd be able to wiggle out of it. But through the early spring of 1976, as I drifted along toward my graduation from Ouachita, Jim threw himself into the wedding planning. He was in something of a hippie phase at the time— reading a lot of *Mother Earth News* magazine and growing his sideburns long—and he decided that we should get married outdoors, where we could be one with each other and nature. The week before the wedding, when I remarked that the May heat had turned the grass in the front yard brown, Jim responded with characteristic overkill, ordering that the lawn be watered all week. By the day of the wedding, it resembled a mud-wrestling pit.

On May 23, 1976, Jim McDougal and I were married in the mud-slicked front yard of the little goat house in the country. I wore a huge wedding dress that made me look like an ice-cream cake, and Jim outdid his usual sartorial splendor by donning a mint-green Yves Saint

Laurent silk suit with flared legs. In attendance were Arkansas attorney general Jim Guy Tucker and his wife Betty, and Bill Clinton and his wife, Hillary Rodham.

The wedding was a bizarre affair. The mud pit made it impossible for me to wear the *peau de soie* white heels I'd bought to match my wedding dress, so I ended up walking barefoot while the hem of my dress dragged in the mud.

Because we'd invited Bob Riley to preside, the ceremony took about three times as long as it should have. For some reason, it hadn't occurred to either Jim or me that, because Bob Riley was blind and couldn't read a printed text, he might have trouble leading a wedding service. And Bob, being Bob, was not about to admit there was anything he couldn't do—especially something Jim McDougal had asked him to do. As we all waited patiently in the late-May sun, Bob muddled through the lines he'd been able to memorize; whenever he got stuck, he would simply call on someone in the audience to pray. More prayers were offered at our wedding than on any *700 Club* broadcast.

With the wedding over, Jim and I couldn't wait to get away for our honeymoon. Despite the fact that he intensely hated traveling—another thing he'd conveniently failed to mention when he'd described our future life together in that hotel room—Jim had gone to elaborate lengths to arrange a honeymoon that would please me. The trip was to last a full month and included stops in some of Europe's most beautiful destinations.

First, Jim had arranged for us to stay in the Algonquin Hotel in New York, the site of so many of the Dorothy Parker stories I loved to read. Then, we'd fly to Belgium so I could visit with my relatives in Europe for the first time (I had seen them when they'd come to the United States, but I'd never gone there for a visit). Our itinerary would also take us to Switzerland, Italy, and Spain, and included a stop in the city I'd always dreamed of visiting—Paris. This might truly have been the dream honeymoon for a young couple just beginning a new life. Unfortunately, I would never find out. Within two weeks, we were back in Arkansas and firmly ensconced in the goat house.

Jim was angry from the first day of our honeymoon until the time we

43

came home. In New York, he hated the taxis, the food, the crowds—everything that makes New York what it is. I was learning very quickly that Jim got very annoyed when he lacked control over his environment. And when you travel, of course, you have almost no control over your environment. We hadn't even left before we left New York, and I was already dreading the rest of the trip.

On the flight to Europe, Jim sat in the smoking section while I sat several rows in front of him in nonsmoking. Those few rows gave me enough space from him to seriously contemplate what I'd just done. The more I thought about the fact that I'd just married Jim—despite the fact that I'd been so convinced I could get out of it—the more scared I became. I began to cry softly, and before long my heart was beating so loudly I could feel it in my eardrums. I couldn't get my breath. This was the first panic attack of my life, and I had no idea how to handle it. All I knew was that at age twenty, I was suddenly married, on my way to Europe with a strange man, and very much alone.

Although Europe was as beautiful as I had imagined, the novelty of it couldn't prevent our honeymoon from veering quickly toward disaster. We visited my Belgian relatives, whom I hadn't seen since I was twelve, and, after suffering through their poorly disguised looks of surprise at my older groom, we headed for the promise of romantic France. On a whim, we decided to take a detour to Versailles before arriving in Paris—but after a day-long train trip, then a thirty-minute walk from the station during Europe's worst heat wave in decades, we discovered the palace was closed for renovation work.

When we arrived in Paris, I wanted to go immediately to the top of the Eiffel Tower so we could take in the full breadth of the city—and hopefully get our honeymoon back on track. Once we reached the top, I asked Jim for a coin so I could look through the telescope, but he flatly refused. "There's nothing to see," he said with irritation. Tired of bearing up under the stress of his moods, I snapped, and for the next twenty minutes we stood at the top of the Eiffel Tower and argued in front of strangers from all over the world. That night we walked back to the hotel in silence, and for the second time I was overcome with the crushing feeling that I'd gotten in way over my head.

We continued to try and salvage the honeymoon, but one final indignity pushed Jim over the edge. We'd taken a train to the south of France to spend a couple of days on the Riviera relaxing among the beautiful people. God alone knows why we decided on this, as Jim hated the idea of lying on a beach under a glaringly hot sun and was spending the entire train ride grousing about why anyone would want to lie in the nasty sand sweating for hours. We suffered through a sweltering train ride, then found on arrival that we'd apparently made a mistake in connections and had gotten off at the wrong stop. For the next hour, we sat outside in the midday heat, our luggage piled at our feet, waiting for another train.

Just as our train came into sight, I heard a cartoonlike "splat!" emanating from Jim's direction. A pigeon—and a rather large one, by the looks of it—had flown over Jim's head and apparently mistaken him for a statue. Seeing a huge, gooey mess running down Jim's bald pate was more than I could take—I burst out laughing.

That was it. For the rest of the day, the silence between us was unbroken, save for periodic interjections of Jim saying, "That wasn't funny!" and me saying, "Yes it was!" When he was ready to speak again, Jim said, "I think it's time to go home." I started shaking my head in disbelief, unable to accept that we couldn't even make it through our honeymoon. And yet the suggestion was almost a relief. "Let's go home," I told him, "but you have to swear you'll never tell anyone." The next day, we flew back to Arkansas, and for the two weeks after that, we hid out at the goat house. With the exception of a single four-day jaunt to Mexico a few years later, that honeymoon was the last vacation we would go on during our eight years of marriage.

I had learned a lot about Jim on our European trip, and now that we were back it was time for him to learn something about me—namely, that I couldn't cook. The first morning we spent at home as a married couple, he gently woke me up, smiled, and asked "What's for breakfast?"

"You want me to cook?" I asked him sleepily.

"You're a wife now," he responded. "That's the deal."

I thought about that for a minute, then said, "How about we go to the diner down the road instead?" He laughed and said that sounded good to him, and from that point in our marriage, we ate every single meal out. Whenever I would apologize for my ineptitude in the kitchen, Jim would just smile. "Baby," he'd say, "I didn't marry you for your cooking."

I was relieved that Jim wasn't looking for a June Cleaver wife, but soon it became obvious that he wasn't really looking for a wife at all—at least not in any conventional sense. What Jim was looking for was a twenty-four-hour personal assistant, someone who could do all the things that he was incapable of doing. That was how Jim defined love: finding someone who would gladly take care of him and make sure that things around him didn't go wrong. This was something I'd done for my little brothers and sister all my life, so I was definitely suited for it. In the beginning, I even enjoyed it. I was just glad that I had some purpose in life.

Jim had left his job at Ouachita the day I graduated, and now we began to work together on the real estate business. We settled easily into a division of labor: he handled the financial and development matters—buying the property, obtaining the necessary loan funding, and subdividing the property—while I focused on selling, marketing, and running errands. Though Jim controlled the details, he did often take my advice on marketing and sales. He could excitedly talk business day and night, and he was constantly coming up with new ideas. Many of them were off-the-wall, but some were brilliant—and I began to realize that one of my jobs would be to try and differentiate between the two.

Every morning, Jim would go down a list of things we needed to accomplish, and then I would set out to do them—either with or without Jim, depending on how he felt. Some days he'd stay indoors because his allergies were acting up, and other days the heat might be too much for him. There seemed to be no end to the environmental elements that could prevent Jim from functioning properly. "As Winston Churchill used to say," he'd tell me, "I've got a 'delicate cuticle.' "

I was also having some health problems around this time, especially with my back. Ever since I was a girl, I'd had chronic back pain, but I always just thought it was something everyone had. I had pretty much just put up with the pain, but in my early twenties, soon after marrying Jim, I'd had a frightening episode that led me to discover what was really wrong with my back.

One morning, I woke up and could barely move. I couldn't get out of bed, and I couldn't move my arm; it was as though I was paralyzed. I struggled to roll out of bed, scared half out of my mind, and when Jim realized what was going on, he got me into the car as soon as he could and took me to the hospital. When the doctor took an x-ray of my back, I couldn't believe what I saw. My spine looked like an "S." He told me I had scoliosis, a condition where the spine curves, then recommended that I get a steel rod implanted in my back.

I didn't want to have surgery, even though I was worried about the pain and temporary paralysis I'd suffered. The doctor gave me a series of exercises to do, and told me how I might be able to keep my back from worsening through proper care. I decided to take that route, and see how things went. Though I continued to suffer pain, I was able to go on and do the things I always had done.

For the most part, our daily list consisted of simple chores relating to the real estate business—things like returning phone calls to potential customers, meeting clients at our various properties, taking checks to the bank, or writing newspaper ads. None of it was very demanding, which suited me fine. In the beginning, Jim tried to talk with me about the financial side of real estate development, but he could tell that I would quickly lose interest. Jim would get all excited telling me about price-per-acre and amortization rates, and then he'd notice that although I was nodding my head in agreement, I was more than likely staring blankly out the window at the same time. He realized quickly that I had no interest in the financial side, and soon he stopped bringing money matters up altogether.

In the first two years of running the business together, every project we touched seem to succeed. Just as soon as we'd buy a tract of land, we always seemed able to sell it out faster than even Jim's most optimistic projections anticipated. With each success, Jim felt increasingly infallible in his business acumen, and he'd boast to his friends about his string of successes. Even better than bragging, however, was being able to let his friends in on a deal, making them a quick profit, and then listening to them sing his praises to everyone around. He'd done it for Senator Fulbright, he'd done it for Jim Guy Tucker, and he'd even done it on a much smaller scale for Bill Clinton. By getting his friends involved in his sure-fire real estate schemes, Jim knew they'd continue to spread the growing legend of Jim McDougal, political genius and real estate developer extraordinaire.

One day in 1978, Jim received a call from Ozarks real estate broker Chris Wade. Knowing that Jim could turn around desirable acreage more quickly than anyone else, Chris was calling to tell him about a piece of land in default—a tract that overlooked the Buffalo River in the rapidly growing retirement area of northwest Arkansas. To Jim, the parcel sounded like a true winner: beautiful land that he could sell relatively cheap to retiring middle-class Yankees looking for their own slice of Southern heaven.

The next weekend, we made the four-hour drive to see the land. On the way, I expressed concern about how far from Little Rock it was—but any fears we had about the project's eventual success evaporated when we got there. This was a virgin forest, a place of almost otherworldly beauty. We stood silently on a bluff, surrounded by towering trees and looking down at the rushing river as the water crashed into spray on rocks.

I turned to Jim and said, "We should call this Whitewater."

Not long after we'd seen the parcel of land by the Buffalo River, Jim and I bumped into Bill and Hillary Clinton at the Black-Eyed Pea, a Southern-style eatery with wide wooden booths and checkered tablecloths. The Pea operated according to one basic culinary rule: fry anything that moves and then slap a mound of gravy on it. Dinner there meant heaping portions and washtub-sized glasses of iced tea, and it was one of Jim's favorite places to eat. It also wasn't surprising to run into Bill Clinton—or anyone else in Arkansas politics, for that matter—wedged into one of the Pea's booths.

We sat with the Clintons that evening, talking as usual about Bill's political career—he was now running for governor—and the state of things in Arkansas. Near the end of the dinner, Jim brought up the land we'd just been to see. "We've just gotten back from up around Flippin," he began. "The most amazing piece of land is for sale up there. You and Hillary ought to come up with us and have a look at it." Having already broached the idea of a partnership with the Clintons, he told them, "I think this is the place."

As with all of Jim's partnerships involving political friends, this project was not about making money. But unlike the others, this one involved more than just trying to impress the Clintons. The way Jim told it, our Whitewater partnership would be equal parts good politics, good business, and good fun. In Jim's grand scheme, we'd buy the land and spend weekends going up with the Clintons to plan and manage the project, and just have a good time. And Bill would get some political benefits out of it, as Little Rock politicians rarely made trips to this part of Arkansas.

Even better, Whitewater could become a destination for the rest of the Arkansas political elite too. The key to this plan was a place called Gaston's. The Whitewater land was located in a part of Arkansas so remote it was the hinterlands, but there was one establishment nestled nearby. Gaston's was a rustic hotel overlooking the water but, more important, it had a small airstrip beside it. Jim envisioned all our political friends buying pieces of Whitewater, flying their planes up on weekends, and gathering for fun and political talk. Jim would be the real estate genius who'd make it all happen, the suave proprietor of his own nineteenth-century-style salon in the wilderness.

As Jim began describing his vision for the land, both Bill and Hillary seemed excited. In Bill's case, this did not necessarily mean much—he seemed upbeat all the time. But Hillary—unlike Bill—wanted to know all the details. It wasn't that she was nervous about it—in fact, I don't recall either of them asking a single question about what would happen if the lots didn't sell. Why should they have? This was beautiful land at low prices and, according to Jim, the project would be easy, something we only had to worry about on weekends.

The parcel of land wasn't large—only about 240 acres. Jim planned to split it into twenty to thirty plots between 5 and 10 acres in size, then sell them each at a price of about $10,000. In addition to Little Rock movers and shakers looking for a getaway, the location would appeal to retirees from the Northern states: Arkansas had the third-fastest-growing retiree population in the country, after Florida and Arizona, and these were people who wanted privacy and a place to hunt and fish. For $1,000 down and $99 a month, anyone could own a 10-acre tract in the lush, unspoiled countryside overlooking the beautiful White River. There seemed to be no way Whitewater could fail. Everything was set to go—all Bill and Hillary needed to do was say the word, and they were in. Our discussion about the project lasted about twenty minutes, and within two weeks, the papers were signed. We were partners in an obscure, but financially certain real estate investment.

In November 1978 Bill Clinton was elected to his first term as governor of Arkansas. I was thrilled for Bill and Hillary and, of course, excited that friends of ours would be occupying the governor's mansion. That said, I didn't expect that Bill's ascension to the state's highest office would have much effect on Jim and me, other than getting a few more invitations to parties.

But a few weeks after Bill's victory, Jim suddenly had an idea. "Why don't we find a house in Little Rock?" he asked me one night. "It might be nice to live closer to our friends in town." On the surface, this suggestion made sense: Jim and I worked together on our real estate projects all day, then went home to our little goat house in the country to spend our evenings—it was only natural that he might want some new social outlets. But I saw something more troubling in his idea. I had already begun to suspect that Jim was growing restless with our life, and this sudden suggestion seemed to confirm it.

A few days later, the real bombshell hit. Somewhere between "Pass the salt" and "What's for dessert," Jim broke in with an announcement. "I've agreed to go to work in the governor's office," he told me. "Starting next week, I'm going to serve as the governor's economic development liaison."

I couldn't believe what I was hearing. There were two problems with this announcement. One was that Jim had presented it to me not as a possibility or a topic for discussion, but as a fait accompli. No matter that I was not only his spouse but his business partner as well, Jim had again unilaterally made a decision that would have a dramatic impact on our lives.

The second problem was that I had no earthly idea how I'd be able to run our real estate projects on my own. Business was booming, and because we were the only two employees, we had to work late into the evening seven days a week to keep things under control. My two years assisting Jim with marketing and sales were the only work experience I had, and although I was good at organizing what Jim wanted done, there was no mistake as to who was in charge. Jim spent every waking hour thinking about the business—and now he'd just announced that he'd be turning it over to me so he could focus on something else. How did he expect me to suddenly know how to run things?

"Don't worry, baby," he said soothingly. Even with his new full-time job, he said, he could continue to run the financial side of the business— and I could handle the development side. "Remember," he said with a smile, "I'll always just be a phone call away. Don't worry! It's gonna be fun!"

As I would soon find out, the pursuit of fun was Jim's new avocation. He'd always been moody, sometimes swinging from darkly melancholy to cheerful and back in the course of a day. But the phase he was entering now was something different. Jim was about to embark on a manic high. It would be years before we would learn that he actually suffered from manic depression.

Since meeting Jim, I'd tried to make myself into the person I thought Jim wanted me to be: a pretty, bouncy wife who dressed for attention, knew how to charm a room, and lived to assist Jim in his personal and professional life. In the beginning of our relationship, I'd always been able to be myself with Jim, and I could let him see the sides of me no one else saw. But as our marriage progressed, my life became more about playing a role and less about being myself. Soon I was having trouble differentiating between the two.

Now, just two years into our marriage, Jim was already bored with me. Not only did he want to get away from our full-time work together, but his interest in sex had suddenly dropped off completely. Some of this was due to his manic phase, but I had no way of knowing that. All I knew was that, at age twenty-four, I had made myself into Jim McDougal's wife, love, Girl Friday, and business partner—and now, having completed that transformation, I found it still wasn't enough to keep his attention. Very soon after Jim began working at the governor's office, I slipped into a severe depression of my own.

Jim's job at the governor's office paid almost nothing, but he didn't care. He was in his element: here was a whole new audience of important people who'd never heard his stories—and now that he wielded a degree of power, they had to at least pretend to be interested in listening to him. In addition, the Capitol offices were filled with young, attractive staffers and interns looking for mentors to guide their budding careers. For a man who loved the attention of young women, a twenty-three-year-old wife couldn't compare to an eager nineteen-year-old intern.

The more excited Jim got, the worse I felt. During the winter of 1979, my depression was so bad that I often couldn't get out of bed. I cried much of the day, paralyzed by the thought that my marriage was failing and unable to cope with the real estate business, which was rapidly failing. There were too many bills, too many loans, too many details I didn't know how to deal with—and Jim was away all day, leaving it in my hands. At first I called him frequently, but after a while he stopped taking my phone calls at work.

One night, I stood at the back door, waiting for Jim to come home after a long meeting at the governor's mansion. Jim had never been a late-night person—when we lived in the goat house, he was always in bed by 9 P.M.—but in any Clinton administration, late nights are the norm. And in his manic state, Jim was able to log more hours than he could ordinarily have done. I had already spent the entire evening peering out the windows, watching for Jim's car, and now I stood at the back door looking out into the darkness, tears spilling down my face.

Finally Jim pulled up the driveway. He got out of the car, and looked at my tear-stained face. "I can't stop crying, Jim," I said miserably. "I feel so depressed."

"Get over it," Jim replied, and walked past me into the house. My depression was casting a pall over the party.

Jim would have his share of days when he suffered from depression, but when he was manic, he had no patience for anyone else being depressed. "Don't be such a downer," he'd say irritably, frustrated that I couldn't just snap out of it and have some fun. "You have two choices when you wake up," he'd say. "It can be a good day, or it can be a bad day. You make your choice."

At some point, when my depression had begun to abate somewhat, I did make a choice. The real estate business was already going to pieces, so I decided not to obsess over how to maintain it. Instead, I decided that if the governor's office was really so much fun, I'd start going down there myself. If you can't beat 'em, join 'em, I figured—so I went shopping, bought a bunch of new clothes, and tried to remake myself once again.

The first Clinton gubenatorial administration has become legendary in Arkansas political folklore for a number of reasons, most of them negative. Like any new governor, Bill wanted to surround himself with a staff of friendly faces and people he trusted. But Bill was just thirty-two—the youngest governor in the country at the time—and most of his friends were around the same age. When he began making his appointments, it seemed to many in the political establishment that Arkansas was being handed over to a bunch of people who still got carded in bars.

The Clinton youth movement did not play well with the Arkansas press, and reporters quickly began harping on the arrogance of the governor's staff. That observation had some merit: many of the young reformists in the governor's office didn't even try to disguise their contempt for other state officials—many of whom had been elected back in the fifties and sixties. These old-style politicians had a certain way of doing things, and they weren't especially enamored of having twenty-something up-and-comers urging them to reform. There was no love lost between the two factions, and things got testy quickly.

These were heady times for the governor's staff, many of whom were college and law school friends of the Clintons who'd never set foot in Arkansas until taking a job at the statehouse. They tended to see Arkansas as a kind of liberal laboratory, a place where they could try out new programs and ideas before introducing them to the nation. Never mind the fact that this worked far better in theory than in practice; whatever the Clinton staffers lacked in experience and pragmatism, they more than made up for in enthusiasm.

Nor was their enthusiasm limited to work-related projects. The motto around the governor's office was "Work hard, play hard," and just about everyone did his best to live up to it. Discussions on budget compromises tended to run a poor second to discussions on who was sleeping with whom, and more important, who could possibly be slept with. This was the late seventies, the giddy peak of the sexual revolution, and the last few years before the advent of AIDS would change the rules of sexual behavior. In addition, these young people possessed the aphrodisiac of power—and their boss, who set the tone for the office, certainly made no secret of his own sexual appetites.

The result of all this was that during Bill Clinton's first term, the governor's office gained the reputation of being a continual fraternity party. In truth, most fraternity parties were much less juvenile. I still remember when Miss Arkansas came to the governor's office in 1979, and how the men on the staff seemed unable to keep from drooling as they peered down the corridors to try and catch a glimpse of her. Bill reveled in the fun, but Hillary was obviously uncomfortable with the level of testosterone in the air. In the beginning, at least, she didn't make a huge effort to crack down on it—though the jokes and comments tended to get hushed whenever she was around.

Once, when Jim and I were at the governor's mansion for dinner, the men at the table began talking about a new secretary who'd just been hired. She was very young, and a complete knockout—and she'd been given what sounded to me like a completely made-up job. All day she sat at a desk right in front of the governor's office, and occasionally she'd take visitors on tours. That was it.

The men at the table just couldn't stop talking about what a looker this girl was, commenting on and rating every part of her anatomy. They were like sailors on shore leave, but with less decorum. I looked across the table at Hillary, who sat absolutely stone-faced, and suddenly interjected, "Hey, Hillary. Did you hear that Kevin Scanlon, the University of Arkansas football player, is working in the governor's office now?" All eyes at the table turned to me. "Yeah, I saw him down in the mailroom. What a body on that guy! You have got to come down there with me to have a look at him."

For one of the few times I ever saw, Hillary burst out laughing, grateful that somebody had taken care of the situation without her having to play the role of the shrew.

Looking back, it's easy to criticize the atmosphere that permeated the Clinton statehouse. But at the time I was part of the problem, not the solution. In my effort to win back Jim's attention and approval, I began wearing my skirts shorter and my blouses lower-cut. With Jim's encouragement, I also took part in the sex talk and endless flirting. As the wife of the economic liaison, I sometimes approached legislators about certain issues, and I had no compunctions about hugging them or recounting the latest dirty joke making the rounds. Anxious to show Jim I was no longer a rube, I was happy to engage in a little risqué talk if it would sway some sixty-five-year-old state senator into supporting whatever the governor's position was.

I was rapidly becoming what I despised. I remember being outside the state Senate chamber with Jim one day, schmoozing a senator from eastern Arkansas about one of the governor's latest proposals. Hillary came by and accosted another senator about the same bill. For twenty minutes, she logically laid out her position, pointing out the good aspects of the measure and urging the senator to do the right thing. After she left, Jim and I began to make fun of her naïveté and how she would never get it. Here I was, the great radical believer, and now I was making fun of someone for standing up for their beliefs.

I was out of my depression, but not out of the woods. Even though I'd transformed myself, and Jim was no longer avoiding me, I still felt lonely, and upset at how our relationship had changed. We were no longer even having sex together.

Soon enough, the atmosphere in the governor's office, which I'd once thought was so sophisticated and urbane, just seemed oppressive to me. The jokes no longer seemed funny, and the giddy excitement of Clinton's first year as governor had worn off. Press coverage of Clinton's office was becoming increasingly critical, with reporters singling out staffers for various screw-ups. For the most part, Jim escaped unscathed, but it was hard to see our friends pilloried in the newspapers every day. The pressures of governing took their toll on the whole staff, and the camaraderie of the previous year had given way to a bunker mentality, as people hunkered down and blamed everyone else for what was going wrong.

When I stopped to think about it, I could hardly believe what my life had become. I had dreamed of having a loving husband, raising a family, and living a quiet life in the country. Instead, I was fighting depression, flirting with half the Arkansas legislature, and scared to death that my marriage was failing. I had been raised to believe that you get married once and that's it—there was no history at all of divorce in my family. I needed to find a way to fix what was broken, but I had no idea how to start.

The one thing I wanted was to somehow get Jim away from the governor's office. Things had spun out of control when he went to work there, and all I could hope was that getting him out would help us get things back to normal. But I knew Jim wouldn't leave unless he had a good reason to.

Then, one afternoon, we happened upon the Bank of Kingston.

4

YOU KEEP MANHATTAN, JUST GIVE ME THAT COUNTRYSIDE

ONE SUNNY SATURDAY MORNING, JIM AND I decided to make the three-hour drive from Little Rock to Fayetteville to join some friends at a University of Arkansas football game. Since Jim hated football, his willingness to drive that far just for a game would have been nothing short of astonishing. But there was, of course, an ulterior motive: Jim had heard about a piece of land for sale near Huntsville, which was on the way to Fayetteville. Though our real estate business had largely stagnated while he was working in the governor's office, he never tired of looking at whatever piece of land might be the "next big deal."

It was a gorgeous fall morning as we slipped off Interstate 40 and onto the "pig trail"—the back-road route to Fayetteville. With its numerous twists and sharp turns, the pig trail made for a slow journey, but it was the height of leaf-changing season and the scenery was spectacular. New England might be famous for its foliage, but the brilliant red, orange, and yellow hues covering the Ozarks in the fall rival the best the Northeast has to offer. We were almost to Huntsville when we found ourselves passing through a small town square consisting of a feed store, the Valley Café, a garage, and a sturdy one-story brick building with a gold-lettered sign out front. The sign read BANK OF KINGSTON.

Jim suggested we stop for a minute to get a Coke and pulled the car over. We went into the café, ordered two Cokes to go and then strolled back outside. Jim walked over to have a closer look at the bank.

The Bank of Kingston was small, but it had a kind of quaint, early-twentieth-century architectural charm to it. Because it was Saturday, it was closed, so we walked up to the large plate-glass window that ran the length of the front and peered in. It was obvious Jim was intrigued, but I wasn't sure what he was thinking. That wasn't unusual, since I rarely knew what Jim was thinking. Jim walked around the whole building several times, pretty much ensuring that he'd draw maximum attention to himself in this small town. Sure enough, the owner of the feed store eventually walked over.

"Are you looking to buy the bank?" he asked Jim.

"You mean it's for sale?" Jim replied, looking suddenly like the kid who's just been handed the keys to a candy store.

"Yep," the man said. "It's always for sale."

That was all Jim needed to hear. As we pulled out of Kingston, all he could talk about was buying that bank. Ever since he was a boy, when his classmates would dream of being the next Stan Musial or Joe DiMaggio, Jim had dreamed about being a banker. He'd instantly liked Kingston, which was about the same size as the town where he'd grown up, and he was ready to trade in the craziness of Little Rock politics for small-town life. Buying the Bank of Kingston would allow him to do all these things at once.

Besides that, buying a bank would satisfy Jim's insatiable need to have a new thing to work on. When he'd gotten bored with our real estate business, he'd taken a job at the governor's office. Now that he was bored with that, he wanted to buy a bank. It didn't matter that he had no idea how to run a bank—as he always did, he could just kick the door down and figure out how to fix it later.

I wanted to get out of Little Rock even more than Jim did, but I had a hard time believing that this was the way to do it. Owning a bank was something wealthy people did, and I certainly didn't consider us wealthy. The whole idea seemed far-fetched, and I figured Jim's excitement would pass. After that day, I put the notion out of my mind and didn't discuss it with him again.

Of course, Jim didn't need to discuss it with me—he would do what he wanted to anyway. A month later, I found myself packing everything we owned and moving to Kingston as the proud co-owner of the Bank of Kingston. Jim quickly renamed it Madison Bank & Trust, which he chose partly because Kingston was located in Madison County, and partly just because he liked it.

One of the first things Jim did was approach Steve Smith and his wife, Julie Baldridge, to go in with us as partners. Steve worked in the governor's office and, like Jim, he seemed fed up with the atmosphere there and ready for something new.

Steve, an old-time liberal anarchist, had been elected to the Arkansas legislature at age twenty-one. He became friends with Bill Clinton in 1974, when Bill ran unsuccessfully for the U.S. Congress in Arkansas's Third District. When Bill had been elected attorney general in 1976, he'd appointed Steve to run his office, and Steve had been with him ever since. He was one of Bill's closest advisers, and he enjoyed working with him—but he never stopped hating the banalities of day-to-day politics. Steve also regularly drew the wrath of the press corps, partly because he didn't suffer fools and made no secret that he considered most of the press corps to be fools.

In the governor's office, Steve also took a lot of heat from another angle, namely Hillary. He and Hillary were different in just about every way, and Steve was one of the people in the office who didn't take things as seriously as Hillary would have liked—or, at least, he didn't give the appearance that he did. Hillary and Steve clashed often, and as the end of Clinton's first term as governor drew near, Steve was as anxious as Jim was to get out. When Jim proposed going in as partners at the Bank of Kingston, it was the ideal solution for Steve, who'd grown up less than thirty minutes away from Kingston and still had relatives nearby.

A burly, bearded man who could have passed for Luciano Pavarotti,

Steve was an American original. He was possessed of a truly impressive intellect, which in most people would have been their defining characteristic. But Steve also had a perverse sense of humor. He's the kind of person who could easily whip up a serious issue-oriented editorial for a major publication—but would much prefer writing a subversive, sarcasm-laced article for an underground weekly. He took particular delight in writing about the drinking and sexual habits of moralistic right-wing politicians.

Steve had one other impressive skill: a knack for understanding immediately what people were thinking in any situation. For Jim—who we had called E.T., because he seemed to come from another planet—this skill was invaluable. Before we married, Jim had mistakenly thought I could help give him insight into the world of ordinary people. Gradually he discovered that, despite my middle-class, small-town upbringing, I was not exactly a great barometer for normal thinking. Now, with Steve, he'd finally found someone who could fulfill that role for him.

During their time working together at the bank, Jim came to have a great fondness for Steve Smith. The two were as close as friends and business partners can be, and they spent inordinate amounts of time together. At the bank, Steve was the president, Jim was the chairman of the board, and I was the general flunky. Unfortunately, I was pretty much fulfilling that same role at home as well.

I had hoped that moving to Kingston might help resurrect our failing marriage. I imagined it would be just like the old days in the goat house: we'd work together every day and then retire to our small house at night. Away from the atmosphere of the governor's office, living the simple life in a small town, I thought we could get things back to normal. It became clear all too soon that my hopes were misplaced.

It was true that life was much simpler in Kingston than in Little Rock. The bank, for example, had just one telephone, which hung on the wall near the tellers' lines. Whenever anyone in the bank got a call, they'd have to walk around the counter and stand next to the window while they talked. Shortly after our arrival, we installed a three-line phone system that was not only much more efficient, but proved to be a major tourist attraction.

Kingston (population 238) was primarily made up of farming families that had lived in the area for generations. Ironically, some of the farmers had become millionaires in the early seventies when the government had bought their land to become a part of a protected area along the Buffalo River. Yet that influx of money didn't change their lifestyles in the least—for the most part, they still drove older model pickup trucks and rarely traveled outside a 30-mile radius from the town. Unfortunately, the vast majority of the farming families were not well off at all: the annual median income in the valley was less than $10,000. What the people of Kingston lacked in financial wherewithal, however, they more than made up for in kindness and basic human decency.

As kind as they were to us, it was clear that they still eyed us with a certain amount of wariness, and an even greater degree of amusement. And we did not disappoint. As soon as we bought the bank, Jim started doing business in his own trademark style. He decided we should paint every building in the town square—for free. We picked out classic Victorian colors, and he sent me around to ask people which color they'd like for their building. "When people drive into Kingston," he'd say, "they won't believe how quaint it is!" Jim also bought a piece of land right next to the bank that had a large barn standing on it. "I've always wanted to own a green barn," he claimed, and quickly hired painters to turn the barn green. Our first couple of months in Kingston, we put a coat of paint on pretty much anything that wasn't moving.

Shortly after we arrived, Jim bought a small two-bedroom white-frame house around the corner from the bank. The house needed a lot of work and Jim was forever promising to get it renovated. After a month of those promises going unfulfilled, I began to get irritated.

"Jim," I said, "we have been living here for over five weeks and we still don't have running water. On top of that, the roof is leaking on the rugs and the flies from the pasture out back are starting to take over the house."

"Don't worry, baby," he promised, "When I am finished this place will be the Taj Mahal."

"It's hard to be patient, Jim, when I haven't had a shower in three days and I'm wearing the same clothes for the fourth day in a row," I whined.

"You can quit complaining about bathing," Jim answered. "I just had the workmen bring up several buckets of water. Go heat them up on the stove and you can enjoy a nice, hot bath."

I stripped out of my clothes, put a towel around me and headed for the bathroom. As I pushed open the bathroom door, I was treated to the sight of five large buckets of water placed on the cracked linoleum floor. Also in the bathroom was the neighborhood dog we had recently befriended who was balancing precariously on the edge of one of the buckets, loudly lapping out the contents.

Very quietly I went back to the bedroom, put my clothes back on, and grabbed the car keys off the kitchen counter. As I headed out the door, I yelled back at Jim, "You can reach me at my mother's."

Shortly after the bathing fiasco, Jim made good on his promise to renovate the house and I returned from Camden.

We completely renovated the bank as well, bringing in a well-known Little Rock architect to help us. We fixed up the pressed tin that covered the ceiling and repainted the front an almond color with burgundy accents. When we found the bank's original scrolled brass teller windows in a storage room, we sent them out to be repaired and then reinstalled them over the tellers' windows. We also found a sketch of the original tile floors and found a local artisan to replicate it. On the old ball safe, the bank's most distinctive feature, we repainted the original fourteen-karat gold lettering and re-brassed the fittings. By the time we'd gotten everything fixed up, you felt like you'd walked through a time warp when you walked into that bank. It was now a beautiful relic from a bygone era.

Although Kingston was tiny, the town square became a center of activity for the bank's grand opening. People came from miles around to see the elephant Jim brought in to give rides around the town square, and the hot-air balloon he hired to float over the town. Jim loved to think up promotional deals that no one else would ever come up with. Of course, there was usually a good reason why no one else ever came up with them.

But we didn't need gimmicks to get people talking about us and the bank—our customers seemed to get a kick out of just seeing what Jim and I would wear each day. They'd come in wearing dungarees, work shirts, and baseball caps, and Jim and I would be dressed in our best eighties fashions. I'd be wearing colorful jackets with big *Dynasty*-era shoulder pads, while Jim always had on Brooks Brothers suits with regimental ties.

We might never have gained acceptance in Kingston if it hadn't been for Gary Bunch, who served as our ambassador to the rest of the town. Gary's family had owned the Bank of Kingston for years, and Jim had been smart enough to keep him on when we bought the bank. Gary was a "good old boy" through and through—he'd come to work every day, sometimes hung over, dressed in checkered shirt, blue jeans, cowboy boots, and a huge black cowboy hat. He spoke with a strong drawl, and his conversations were always peppered with colorful sayings involving possums and cow patties. Gary knew he was a walking stereotype, and he played the part to the hilt.

But to assume Gary was just a dumb hick with no business sense was a mistake. On more than one occasion, I witnessed the result of people underestimating Gary, and they always regretted it in the end. He had real insight into people's character, like Steve Smith did, but Gary also had the advantage of having been a member of the Kingston community for years. As such, our customers knew he was approachable and trustworthy. We would never have gotten very far in Kingston if we hadn't had Gary on our side.

Fortunately, Gary had taken an instant liking to Jim when they met, and it was returned in kind. They established their own special rapport quickly: Gary poked fun at just about everything Jim did, and Jim retaliated by unleashing a string of curse words in various combinations that would put Gary in stitches. Jim could curse like no one I've ever heard before or since—he cursed the way some people sing, with perfect rhythm and inflection. It was like listening to poetry. Wherever Jim and Gary went together, they were the ultimate odd couple: Garth Brooks in boots and jeans, and Don Knotts in a Polo shirt and Bally shoes.

Gary also went out of his way to befriend me and make me feel welcome. After figuring out that I wasn't some stuck-up banker's wife, he decided there might be hope for me in the Kingston community. "My wife goes to the local women's county extension club," he said to me one day. "Why don't you go with her to a meeting?"

I was excited at the prospect. I wanted to fit in with the women of Kingston, and here was the perfect way to get to know them. I had been reading about women all over the country getting together in small meetings to celebrate their common bond and to talk about issues relevant to them. At my first meeting, I took my seat as someone led a roll call, then the pledge of allegiance, followed by a reading of the last meeting's minutes. I couldn't believe it. Here I'd thought I'd be getting into a warm, loose gathering of women talking about the issues affecting them—and this little group of six or seven women were running their meeting like a legislative session. Then we got to the subject of the meeting: cow birthing.

The next meeting focused on spring canning and the one following that dealt with the problems involved in crop rotation. I had not really expected a hotbed of feminist theorizing in Kingston but I had hoped that our conversations would focus on a broader range of topics.

After a couple of meetings, I spoke up. "Maybe we could all read a book and discuss it next time we meet?" A disapproving hush fell over the room. "Or we could get some films and show them down at the bank, if anyone's interested." Again, silence.

As I glanced around the room, I began to get an oddly familiar feeling. Where had I seen these looks before? What was their message? Suddenly it hit me: These were the same stares I'd get in Camden after I had suggested yet another socialistic reformation. It was a look of genuine confusion as the bearer of the look tried to determine if I was dangerous or just clueless. Fortunately, the women of Kingston appeared to settle on the latter.

Before long I found myself feeling terribly lonely in Kingston. Jim, excited as always by a new project, spent all his time focused on the bank. He was forever hatching new schemes with Steve and figuring out what new promotional stunt he could pull off. Once again, he was on a manic high while I became, in his eyes, the "downer." For Jim, every day was like going to Disneyland—and if you weren't ready to go Disneyland with him, you were bringing him down.

Just as he had with the interns in the governor's office, Jim reveled in the attentions of the young women of Kingston. He never held a single business meeting in the bank, preferring always to go over to the Valley Café, where he could chat up the high-school-age waitresses in skintight blue jeans. What Jim wanted was a pretty young thing who'd agree with everything he suggested, and I could no longer be that for him, so he continued to seek it elsewhere.

But the problems in our marriage can't all be laid at Jim's feet. As I became more lonely and felt more detached from Jim, I added to our troubles by inviting my brothers and sisters for extended visits. I missed the camaraderie of my family, and having few if any friends in Kingston, I reached out to my family to fill the void. Jim wanted little more than some peace and quiet when he came home—and the Henley family was as loud as ever. In our tiny house, Jim would get more and more irritated as my brothers and I would howl with laughter over stories from our childhood. During these times, it began to seem like whatever made Jim happy made me unhappy, and vice versa.

Though I'd hoped our life in the country might restore some romance to our marriage, that didn't happen. But Jim had always been more interested in having a business partner and assistant than a real wife, anyway—he wanted to come home to someone who'd be more excited about the bulls and bears than about the birds and the bees. I could probably have fulfilled that role, but I just didn't care about business in the way Jim did. Like he'd done with the real estate business, Jim at first tried to explain the financial workings of the bank to me. He'd excitedly begin telling me about stock market investments he was making to bolster the bank's holdings—and I'd just turn the TV on. Not surprisingly, he soon stopped trying.

There was, however, one way that I tried to help out on the financial side of the business. Paperwork at the bank had always been done by hand, and with the dawning age of the personal computer, I decided we should computerize our records. This was a considerable departure from the kinds of things I'd been doing—things like helping to decorate the bank's offices and running errands. But my efforts only resulted in more strife between us. Jim did not understand computers and he hated having to deal with them or hear about them. More and more, we had less and less in common.

All I could think was, "I have got to get out of here." I was so tired of fighting the same fights with Jim every single day. I was twenty-six years old, and I was spending my life working in a bank, practically friendless, and enduring an unhappy marriage. The only fun I had during the week was talking with customers when they came in—but even then, I felt more like an exhibit in the McDougal sideshow than I did a part of the community. On the weekends I was lonely and even more unhappy. I soon began leaving town whenever I could find an excuse to go somewhere.

At first, I'd find reasons to spend the weekends away—I'd go home to Camden, or to Little Rock. But then, the weekends stretched out to include Fridays and Mondays, and soon I was in Kingston only three or four days a week. We'd get a brochure in the mail for a conference on marketing and I'd sign up right away—anything to get me out of Kingston. Looking back now, I realize there were many things I could have done to make my life there more bearable. But I had no perspective at all. My entire adult life had been spent with Jim: being his wife and business partner, and getting involved in projects he'd dreamed up. I didn't know how to make a choice for myself, or how to create opportunities for myself. The only thing I could think to do was run away. So I did.

By the time our one-year anniversary of living in Kingston rolled around, Jim and I were arguing constantly and ready to kill each other. One weekend, Jim had a solution: "Baby," he said one afternoon, "let's go to Tulsa." Tulsa may not rate with Venice or Paris as a romantic get-away, but I was glad Jim had at least suggested something. At this point in the marriage, I was willing to try anything—and besides, I had been the one nagging him that we never went anywhere together.

I made reservations at a nice hotel, and that Friday morning we put our bags in the car and started the three-hour trek to Tulsa. We weren't even to the Oklahoma border before I realized we were in trouble. "It's so damn hot!" Jim said. "How in the world are we going to do anything in this kind of weather?" And that was just the beginning of a litany of complaints. "I don't know why we're going to Tulsa anyway," he said. "There's no good restaurants there." And "It's gonna take us hours to get there in all this damn traffic." And "I don't know why we're going to all this trouble just to spend a couple of nights in a hotel room."

At last, we arrived in Tulsa. "Let's get something to eat," Jim said. We had been told about a couple of very good Italian restaurants in Tulsa so I suggested we go to the hotel first to check in and get directions. Jim had other ideas. The first Denny's he saw, Jim wheeled the car into the parking lot and proceeded to get out. To Jim, there really was not any reason to blow $80 on linguine in clam sauce when a Denny's Denver omelette could be had for $6.99.

By the time we got to the hotel and checked in, my hopes for the weekend had faded—but it was now or never for us to try and turn things around. "What should we do for the rest of the day?" I asked him, then began reading aloud a list of sights and attractions in Tulsa. Nothing appealed to Jim—not the museums, historical sites, parks, or places of political interest.

He finally decided that all the tall buildings of Tulsa were creating a wind tunnel and made a draft in the street. He said it was making him sick.

Ten minutes later, we were in the car driving back to Kingston.

After the Tulsa trip, there was no pretense that we could salvage some sort of happiness out of life together in Kingston. Then, a few weeks later, Jim came home with an idea that he thought might put us both out of our misery.

"A friend was telling me about a savings and loan in Augusta that's for sale," Jim said. "It's gone bankrupt, and we could buy it for less than what you'd pay for a Buick." Jim's idea was that we'd buy the S&L, and he'd send me to Augusta to oversee it. The idea of Jim trying to run an S&L was already a stretch, but the idea of sending me to oversee it was really absurd. Buoyed by the relative success of Madison Bank & Trust, however, Jim decided that the need to actually know how to run a financial institution was highly overrated. An M.B.A. was nothing, he believed, compared to good old common sense and country know-how.

There were also additional benefits to owning an S&L. With the recent deregulation of the industry, S&Ls could soon be used to finance the type of activity that Jim knew best—real estate develop-ment. If we bought Woodruff County Savings and Loan, then Jim would truly be the proprietor of his own financial empire—he'd have a bank, an S&L, and a real estate business that would presumably be fueled into a major resurgence by the other two institutions.

Jim truly had the heart of an entrepreneur. I've never met anyone so completely unafraid to take risks, and so willing to go out on a limb to achieve what he wanted. He always seemed to have an answer for any situation—even though it was usually an answer nobody else would ever have seriously considered. No matter what happened between us in the personal side of our marriage, I never stopped trusting him on the business end.

Even though I knew that the idea of me running an S&L was absurd, I believed that Jim knew what he was doing. Besides, he was planning to keep the same staff in place at the S&L, so all I'd really have to do each day was show up, nod a lot, and greet people warmly. In other words, it would be a lot like the Reagan presidency.

Augusta was a five-hour drive from Kingston, and very close to Bradford, where Jim had grown up and where his parents still lived. It was agreed that I would live with his parents while working at the S&L. This wasn't a money-saving venture on my part; I wanted Jim to know that although he might have gotten me out of Kingston, he hadn't gotten rid of me. We were still a married couple, and by living with his parents rather than establishing my own independent home, I wanted to demonstrate that I was still committed to our relationship.

If I'd thought our situation might have been improved by putting some distance between us, I was soon proved wrong. Jim had said, "Just call whenever you've got a question about anything. I'll be here." At first, he was available when I needed him. But as the weeks wore on, he returned my calls less and less frequently. We only spoke when I could catch him by chance, or the few times he decided to call.

I was just as unhappy in Bradford as I'd been in Kingston, but now I had to deal with watching Jim's parents grow more and more worried as they realized their son's marriage was in trouble. Two salt-of-the-earth people who were as grounded as Jim was mercurial, Leo and

Lorene McDougal treated me with incredible kindness while I lived with them. Though they couldn't understand why Jim and I had chosen to live apart, they were unfailingly supportive. But it upset them that Jim would never come to Bradford—to see either me or them.

On one occasion I overheard Lorene pleading with Jim to come visit me, but by now there was no chance of that. Jim was riding high, sitting astride a burgeoning business empire—and very happy to be rid of me. There didn't seem to be any reason why he'd ever need me back in his life. But as usual, Jim had a surprise in store.

During one stretch in February 1982, almost two weeks went by without any word from Jim. Then one afternoon he called me at the savings and loan. "Susan," he said, "I've just announced that I'm running for Congress. I need you to get dressed and meet me in Little Rock as soon as you can, because we're getting ready to have a press conference."

I was floored. In the nearly seven years I had known Jim, I'd never once heard him express a desire to run for political office. Now he'd suddenly decided to run against a sixteen-year Republican incumbent, John Paul Hammerschmidt. Annoyed and amazed that Jim had once again managed to completely blindside me with a major decision, I quickly got ready and drove to Little Rock. I don't remember much about the press conference, but the photo in the statewide newspapers the next morning told the story. There was Jim McDougal, perhaps the least photogenic candidate in Arkansas history, beaming at the camera with an ear-to-ear grin. Beside him stood the candidate's wife, looking for all the world like she had just been run over by a bulldozer.

Though Arkansas was a largely Democratic state, Republican congressman John Paul Hammerschmidt was considered all but unbeatable—in fact, he'd defeated Bill Clinton eight years before in Bill's first run for elective office. Hammerschmidt was unassailable mostly because he provided a level of constituent service unrivaled in Congress. Any letter received by his office had to be followed by a reply within twenty-four hours or a staffer would be looking for work. While most congressmen craved media attention, Hammerschmidt had turned maintaining obscurity into an art form. About the closest thing to notoriety that he'd achieved was becoming close friends with an up-and-coming conservative congressman—George Bush.

It would have seemed all but futile to take Hammerschmidt on, but these were the 1982 midterm elections, and voter discontent with Republicans was running high. So Jim decided the time was ripe to challenge Hammerschmidt, and he enlisted his now-constant companion and alter ego Steve Smith to run his campaign. The bank and S&L were left to drift on their own.

Campaigning with Jim was a truly eye-opening experience. Much to everyone's surprise, especially mine, Jim proved to be a dynamic, crowd-pleasing speaker. After listening to other speakers deliver their ponderously dull speeches in monotone, Jim would walk to the podium and, within minutes, have the crowd on its feet applauding wildly. Running as an unabashed, old-fashioned Roosevelt Democrat, Jim tore into the fledgling Reagan administration, railing against the pain Reagan's policies were inflicting on the poor and the "widder-women," a phrase Jim had picked up from reading about William Jennings Bryan's speeches in support of elderly widows. Then he would rail equally loudly against the conservative Democrats for being wimps and finish up with a call for a return to the days when Democrats stood proud. "We should never be ashamed," he'd shout, "of the principles that led this country out of the Depression and turned it into the greatest democracy known to mankind!"

Speaking at largely Democratic functions, Jim was an enormous hit. That same year, Bill Clinton was starting his comeback after having lost the previous governor's election, and our old friend Jim Guy Tucker was opposing Bill in the Democratic primary. This was a hotly contested primary fight between two charismatic candidates—yet almost everywhere they went, Jim McDougal would steal the show.

Running for public office was perfectly suited to Jim's short attention span. He could sweep in to a rally, shake a few hands and give a rousing speech, then bask briefly in the applause and leave almost immediately afterward, citing other campaign duties. Unlike Bill Clinton, Jim didn't revel in hanging around to talk with each person and trying to connect. Jim hated the small talk—his campaign style was basically twenty minutes of stage glory and then out the door. And he absolutely loved it. During his campaign, Jim was the happiest I'd seen him in some time—and the happiest I would ever see him again.

And a funny thing began happening between the two of us. I now began seeing Jim in a whole new light. The caring, impassioned candidate who stood up before crowds and talked about lending a helping hand to the less fortunate was nothing like the blasé, politically sophisticated governor's aide who'd been so willing to compromise any belief for a vote. When he spoke publicly, Jim beautifully articulated the very things that I believed growing up. Not only did the candidate Jim McDougal become my hero, but I fell in love with him all over again. I believed every word he said, and often during his speeches I found myself fighting back tears.

I couldn't believe the resurgence of feelings I had for Jim. In private he was still keeping his distance but I just figured he was under pressure and had other things on his mind. He was the one campaigning, and he knew what was right. If I ever got down, all I had to do was listen to him on the stump and I'd get swept away again.

After two months of hard campaigning, Jim won the Democratic nomination over three other formidable candidates. As we headed into the Democratic state convention in Hot Springs that summer, I felt incredibly proud of him, and of the way he seemed to be rising to the challenge. When we arrived at the convention, Jim was in great demand. Word had reached political activists around the state that he was a rabble-rousing speaker, and there was great anticipation surrounding his upcoming speech there.

Jim did not disappoint. He spoke eloquently and with great intensity of a Democratic party that needed to return to its roots, not run away from them. He tore into the Reagan policies of division and the patrician nonsense of "trickle-down" economics. By the time he wound up his speech, thousands of delegates were on their feet, offering a thundering standing ovation. It may well have been one of the highlights of Jim's life.

But that night turned into one of the lowlights of my life. To celebrate the speech, we went to dinner with a group of lobbyists and political consultants Jim knew from his days in the governor's office. Jim was absolutely beaming through the whole dinner. Surrounded by admirers, basking in the afterglow of his speech, he was as animated as I'd seen him in years. He was really connecting with the people at that table, in a way he seemed to connect now only with Steve Smith and Gary Bunch. It was, I suddenly realized, the same way he once used to connect with me—but didn't anymore, and hadn't for years.

Sometimes in life, you have a sudden moment of clarity, when you can step outside yourself and really see what's going on. Sitting at the table that night, I had one of those moments. I suddenly realized that Jim could not have cared less whether I was at that dinner or a million miles away. I simply did not exist for him anymore. Worse yet, I saw what my life had become: for the last seven years, I had followed Jim around, done what he wanted to do, made myself into what he wanted me to be. That had been my whole purpose in life, and it was all for nothing, as Jim was completely indifferent to me, and had been for a long time.

The realization was too much for me. I went over to Jim's chair, leaned down and said, "I'm tired. I'm going up to the room."

"Go ahead," he said, and turned back to the table.

I took the elevator up to the room in a kind of daze. I went in, shut the door behind me, and proceeded to tear the room completely apart—I tore the sheets from the bed, yanked Jim's clothes from the hangers. I turned over the suitcases, threw shoes, and screamed with frustration. All I could think of was, *What did you think you were going to accomplish by following him everywhere?*

My fit of anger was short but fierce, and the room soon looked like a rowdy rock band had been staying there. When Jim came up after the dinner, he let himself into the room, took one look around, and then walked right back out. When I saw him the next morning, he didn't mention the state of the room—and we never once talked about it. I continued campaigning with Jim, but things had changed. And now, for the first time, I understood that they would never change back.

With a few more weeks to go in the race, the margin between Jim and

Hammerschmidt had narrowed to ten percentage points according to our private polling. Jim had the momentum, and everyone was feeling upbeat. But we were brought crashing back to Earth soon enough by two unrelated events.

We learned of the first during a fund-raiser at a Fayetteville restaurant. The mood was upbeat and the crowd was cheering when a surprisingly subdued Steve Smith came by. He pulled Jim to one side and whispered something in his ear, and Jim's face literally turned pale. "What's wrong?" I asked him. "I'll tell you later" was all he would say.

When the fund-raiser ended, we got into the car to head back to the hotel. Jim looked at me, his face still pale and now looking more drawn than usual. "Susan," he said. "We've had a loan go bad at the bank."

A couple of months previously, he explained, Madison Bank and Trust had made a large loan to a local farmer. Because the farmer was somebody Steve Smith knew and trusted, Jim had gone ahead and made the loan without getting any real collateral. The farmer had used the money to pay off some debts—and then, earlier today, he'd declared bankruptcy.

That didn't sound good, but I was still confused. We'd had loans go bad before—that happened at banks all the time. "What's the big deal with this particular loan?" I asked Jim. "Why is this one so different?"

"This one was really big," Jim quietly replied. "The bank is wiped out. Everything we worked for is gone."

I couldn't believe what I'd just heard. Jim had always told me the bank was doing well. How could one single loan put us under? Had Jim misled me about the state of the bank, or was this loan really so enormous that it could sink a financially healthy bank?

Jim was devastated. The bank's failing didn't become public before the election, so it had no direct impact on his chances. But for two weeks after getting the news, Jim fell into a deep depression. He could hardly get out of bed, much less put on the kind of push he'd need in the last two weeks of an uphill campaign. He did manage to give a few speeches, but even the enthusiastic response of the crowds wasn't enough to pull him out of the state he was in. Seeing the race slip away from him, he decided to make one last-ditch effort. He told Steve to use what money we had left on a radio saturation campaign.

This might have been a decent idea, but unfortunately its execution turned it into the second major damaging event of the campaign. Desperate to turn the momentum somehow, Jim turned to a Little Rock political consultant named Jerry Russell—a man he'd long despised—to draft the ad. Russell specialized in negative advertising, a relatively new concept in 1982, and he immediately began selling Jim on the importance of tearing down Hammerschmidt if he hoped to win. A positive campaign against an incumbent can only get you so far, he told Jim—essentially to the level Jim had already reached. By the end of the conversation, Jim was sold on the idea, and he commissioned Russell to do a radio jingle that would personally attack Hammerschmidt.

Russell may possibly have been right about negative campaigning offering our only real chance to win. But the radio spot he produced for the Jim McDougal campaign will go down in the annals of Arkansas history as the worst single radio commercial ever created. The ad was relatively mild compared to today's slash-and-burn negative ads, but still, voters in 1982 didn't respond well to hearing their popular incumbent congressman ridiculed.

The real problem, however, was the jingle itself. It was the *Macarena* of radio jingles—a grating little tune that refused to leave your head if you were unlucky enough to hear it. Over and over, an annoying singsong voice proclaimed, "John . . . Paul . . . HAMMERSCHMIDT! Doesn't deserve to be re . . . e . . . lec . . . ted. . . . John . . . Paul . . . HAMMERSCHMIDT! He doesn't work for you!" All over Arkansas's Third District, people would lunge for their radio dials in an effort to change stations whenever the jingle was on.

The jingle began running one day about two weeks before the election. At McDougal campaign headquarters, you could pinpoint the times it ran, because the phone lines would immediately light up with irate people calling from all over the district. It wasn't just Republicans who didn't like it—even hard-core Democrats would call to complain, saying they weren't sure they could support Jim now or in the future. It's hard to overstate how horrible it was—after hearing it four or five times, I was ready to vote against Jim.

We pulled the spot a few days after it began running, but by then the damage was done. By election night, no one was under any illusions about what the result would be: Hammerschmidt 66 percent, McDougal 34 percent.

That night, Jim and I had planned to head back to Kingston, but when we got in the car he said, "Do you have any reason to go back there?"

I had no idea what I wanted at that point, but I knew that I didn't want to wake up in Kingston the next morning. Nor did I want to go back to Jim's parents' house in Bradford.

"I don't care where we go," I told him. "But I don't want to go back to Kingston." With that, he turned the car onto the interstate and headed for Little Rock. So long, Green Acres.

5

THE BRIDGES OF MADISON GUARANTY

WE ARRIVED IN LITTLE ROCK WITH no place to live, no real jobs, and most of our money tied up in stagnant real estate projects. Following the loan debacle at the Madison Bank & Trust, we'd agreed not to draw salaries there anymore, and now there was just a skeleton staff fulfilling the most basic bank functions. The S&L was still afloat, but there wasn't really any reason for us to move to Augusta, as the staff could run it. Until we figured out what to do next, the steady flow of monthly payments we received from our past developments would at least allow us to pay the bills.

It was time to start over again. After spending two weeks in a hotel, we moved into a second-floor apartment in a building that catered mostly to retirees—Jim and I were the youngest people there. Our two-bedroom apartment was bland and uninspiring, and it overlooked a parking lot and garbage cans. Though this apartment was originally supposed to be a temporary residence, we ended up spending almost our whole time in Little Rock living there, paying a monthly rent under $400.

Since the apartment was meant to be a temporary solution, we put most of our furniture in storage, leaving us with a sparsely furnished living space. Every night Jim would retire to the large leather recliner he'd positioned directly in front of the big-screen television, and either read or watch TV until he fell asleep. One day not long after we moved in, we found a cute little stray cat and took it in. Jim loved that cat, which he named Kitty, and he'd carry on conversations with it in baby talk. Other than these activities, Jim had little desire to do anything else.

Our first few months in Little Rock were as quiet as any I ever spent with Jim. He started going back to AA meetings, which he'd quit doing in Kingston because there hadn't been any nearby. Jim Guy Tucker offered us free office space in a building he owned downtown, and Jim and I carried stacks of paperwork down there to try to sort out the chaos of our business dealings. We'd go down there and spend hours working, trying to catch up with all the things that had fallen by the wayside during the last frenetic year or two.

One of the things I loved about Jim was that he was rarely without a plan, and this was no exception. The new plan involved our S&L. Under new rules in the recently deregulated industry, an S&L could wholly own a real estate subsidiary and also finance the sales in any real estate development. Jim envisioned a perfect cycle in this: First, he could find a piece of land and have the S&L subsidiary finance its purchase. Then, he could sell the land off in smaller pieces to customers—who would then finance their purchase by taking out loans through the S&L, using the land as collateral. If any customer defaulted on payments, the S&L could simply take back the land and resell it again. It seemed foolproof.

We opened a subsidiary of the S&L in Little Rock, then petitioned to change it to our main branch. In our application, Jim stated that we were real estate experts, and as such would rely heavily on investing in real estate rather than making loans or playing the stock market. Because the Woodruff County Savings and Loan was losing thousands of dollars daily, we asked for and received an expedited answer. Our request was approved, and we opened the Little Rock branch almost immediately. We named it Madison Guaranty. Though Madison Bank & Trust in Kingston had gone bad, Jim still loved the name.

I was absolutely amazed at how easy it was to suddenly own an S&L in Little Rock, especially when neither Jim or I had any expertise in running one. This pretty much summed up the attitude toward

S&L ownership in the '80s. They required a ton of documentation for a person to get a loan or to wire money, or even to open a checking account, but any idiot could own and run an S&L.

Jim had definitely hit on a profitable real estate niche, and it was one that appealed to his Democratic values. We would buy a piece of land, break it up into smaller pieces, then sell it off by offering low down payments and financing over a lengthy period of time—which kept the monthly payments low. Under Jim's system, anyone earning a decent middle-class income could afford to own several acres of land—to build a house, have a horse, start a farm, whatever they liked—all that within easy driving distance of Little Rock. And the rules governing Madison Guaranty meant he could expand this business by putting the sales and financing under one roof.

But there was one major drawback: Jim had no desire or ability to keep up with the mountains of paperwork and bureaucracy that came with owning a federally backed institution. To Jim, paperwork was simply tedious and unnecessary, and requirements like project studies and business plans were nuisances. Jim always went by his instincts—not by what some accountant was going to tell him.

Madison Guaranty got off to a promising start with the purchase of a twelve-hundred-acre parcel of land located twelve miles south of Little Rock. The land was far from beautiful, as it consisted mostly of scrub pine trees and had a nasty tendency to flood whenever the weather even looked like rain. But it had the twin advantages of being both centrally located and cheap. Jim envisioned cutting a few roads through the property, slapping down a layer of blacktop, and offering the public the chance to own five unrestricted acres within ten minutes' drive of Little Rock for just $15,000. We decided to call it Maple Creek Farms.

Jim had high hopes for the property, but even he didn't expect the response we got. One weekend in March 1983, before the land was ready to be shown, I placed a small ad in the *Arkansas Democrat-Gazette* to gauge the reaction. From the first morning the ad ran, the phone rang off the wall.

The Woman Who Wouldn't Talk

For many Arkansans, Maple Creek holds a special place in their hearts, right next to their love for Texans and transplanted Northerners who constantly refer to the Civil War. After the big initial response to Maple Creek Farms, Jim decided we had a winner on our hands and needed to get the word out. We filmed ads for the development and bought huge advertising packages on every local station, thereby ensuring that whether you watched TV at three in the afternoon or three in the morning, you could not avoid the barrage of Maple Creek ads. Since Jim surmised that sports fans and country boys were born of the same ilk, he arranged for the ads to reach total saturation during sporting events. Anyone watching a three-hour football game could well expect to see anywhere from three to six Maple Creek ads during the game. People were writing letters to the TV stations complaining about the frequency of the commercials, but Jim didn't care because the commercials were having the desired effect—Maple Creek was booming.

The star of these ads was a blue-jeaned, cowboy boot-wearing country girl from Camden: me. Though my only experience in front of a television camera was making one ad for Jim's congressional campaign, he insisted I had the right wholesome look. We rented a beautiful white stallion, I climbed on top of it, and we filmed me trotting around the property, gesturing toward the beautiful countryside and saying, "Just a twelve-minute drive from downtown Little Rock."

At the height of the ad campaign, people would stop me on the street in Little Rock, asking, "Aren't you the Maple Creek Farms girl?" Others would recite my lines verbatim—you could hardly help but memorize them, as the ads were on continuously. Everyone wanted to know if I really knew how to ride that horse, as in the ads I was always either standing next to it or riding very slowly in the woods.

The property began selling faster than we could build roads to show it. Within two months, customers were just walking through the woods and putting down stakes where they would buy a piece of land once it was developed. From dawn to dusk, we worked on Maple Creek with a small team Jim had hired: R. D. Randolph, a road contractor friend who'd worked with Jim in Senator Fulbright's office, and two salesmen—my brother Bill Henley and Pat Harris, who'd worked on Jim's congressional campaign.

Flush with the success of Maple Creek, Jim decided to expand his real estate empire. First up was a large land project called Goldmine Springs, in the town of Possum Grape near where Jim grew up. The project's name was derived from the fact that, as rumor had it, gold had once been struck in two large caves on the property. I was relatively sure that the source of the rumor was Jim, but whenever I asked him about it, he just smiled. We also initiated other projects throughout Arkansas, and nearly all of them met with quick success.

Soon, Jim and I found ourselves very much in the public eye. Local newspapers ran numerous articles about the real estate tycoon who was taking Little Rock by storm, and my Maple Creek Farms ads were ubiquitous. Jim loved the publicity and attention, and he enjoyed quoting his favorite article, which compared him to a junk dealer—someone who takes properties no one else wants and makes them profitable. In just a few months after moving to Little Rock, we were suddenly enjoying both business success and peer recognition, and Jim was ecstatic. In fact, though, he was veering into a new manic phase.

I was excited about our business upswing, and also happy that once again, Jim and I were working together as a team. We still argued, but at least now we were arguing about things that mattered—how the ads should look, or what our marketing plan should be—rather than just for the sake of it. Steve Smith was gone and Gary Bunch had remained in Kingston. To my relief, it seemed that Jim needed me again.

At first Jim didn't want to add additional staff, because he only wanted people he could trust and whose loyalty was unquestionable. As a result, too few people were trying to do too many things, and Madison suffered the usual disorganization and craziness that accompanied a McDougal enterprise.

On one occasion, Jim hired a crew of local workers to clear an area at Maple Creek. He wanted the work done carefully, so he'd specified that they should use chain saws rather than bulldozers. But when R. D. drove Jim over to look at their work, Jim became furious at how the workers seemed to be just cutting randomly and not following his orders. He rolled down the window in the air-conditioned truck and called one of the workers over.

"What kind of half-assed job is this?" he shouted. "I told you to be careful when you were clearing this area!"

The worker, sweating in the midday heat, filthy from his labors, revved up the chain saw and reared back as if to throw it through the window onto Jim's lap, clearly aiming to emasculate this ranting man in a suit. It was only R. D.'s quick action on the gas pedal that saved Jim. From that point on, Jim was a great deal more circumspect with all the laborers.

On another occasion, a local landowner dropped by to express some concerns about one development. Jim listened patiently and agreed to try to work with the existing landowners on any relevant issues. But after hearing several veiled references to "school problems," Jim realized what the real purpose of the visit was. Near the end of the conversation, the visitor made it even clearer. "Of course," the man said casually, "you realize this is an all-white school district, and we'd hate to see that change."

The visitor was a good six-foot-three and about 250 pounds, and he could have snapped Jim McDougal in two parts quite easily. But Jim leapt to his feet and got right up in the man's face—close enough so that when he began to rant, his saliva sprayed him.

"You tell all your KKK buddies to go fuck themselves," he shouted. "If we want to, we'll turn this into Harlem South." The man began backing out the door, with Jim trailing him and screaming until he was gone. It was times like this that I remembered what I loved about Jim. He might have been from another planet, but he could sure rise to an occasion.

As business continued to boom, Jim ruled over Madison as a sort of benevolent dictator. He wanted to make sure his employees were well taken care of, but he didn't want any one person to do too well. So although Pat and Bill, who were working eighty-hour weeks, were making thousands in commissions weekly, Jim limited what they could withdraw from their commission accounts. He then went a step farther and began investing their money for them. Whenever they griped about this system he loved to repeat the old joke, "If I give you the money you will just spend it on wine, women, and song—the rest you will squander." Soon, Pat and Bill took to referring to the S&L as the Madison Bank of Socialism.

In fact, Jim wouldn't have minded having his own little socialist empire. One afternoon, when we passed a huge antebellum mansion just down the street from the bank, Jim said, "We ought to buy that house and move everyone in." He was having fun, and ready to start a commune so that Pat, Bill, and R. D. could be with us all the time. I laughed and said, "There's no way I'm living with everyone from Madison." By the next day Jim had forgotten about the house—which was part of a consistent pattern. As with most of Jim's ideas, if I could keep him from acting on something for twenty-four hours, he'd forget about it and soon be on to something else.

With the revenue coming in from Maple Creek and our other projects, Jim began to envision running a real S&L, complete with loan officers, tellers, and high-interest CDs. To do that, we'd need a legitimate place of business—somewhere other than the small office building we'd been operating out of.

After looking at dozens of buildings in all sections of Little Rock, Jim and I finally decided on a large abandoned laundry in a deteriorating part of downtown. The location had great appeal to Jim: not only did it fit in with his "junk man" persona, but it also fit well with our Democratic principles. Jim was always bemoaning the fact that lower economic classes had no access to financial institutions or to the kinds of business and personal loans that others had. With our new location, the people in the surrounding depressed area would certainly have easy access to us, and we could make sure they were given opportunities.

Renovating the laundry building became my new job. With the help of a design team, we turned it into Little Rock's first Art Deco bank. The teller stations had big, comfy chairs with padded arms, and we bought period artwork and furniture at a market in Dallas. We also commissioned a huge sculpture for the bank, to be made of old stained glass that had once adorned other buildings in downtown Little Rock. All the offices were glass and brass, in keeping with the style of the time. The floor was solid ebony, and the walls were pale blue, and the exterior was pink—which led R. D. to dub it the Pink Palace, a name that stuck with it for years. Though the design team did much of the work, I was proud of my part in helping renovate the bank, which went on to win several architecture and design awards.

Less than a year after its inception, Madison Guaranty was a booming success. We now had several dozen people working for us, multiple successful developments, and an award-winning office building. Jim was in a full-swing manic episode, and the more quickly we grew, the more he wanted us to take on.

With so much happening so quickly, my job became trying to keep things to a manageable level of hysteria. When Jim would come up with some off-the-wall idea, I'd say, "That sounds great," then follow with, "I sure wish we had the time to do it." I spent much of my time trying to put a gentle kibosh on his ideas, without provoking his anger. I wasn't always successful, especially whenever some new thing captured Jim's imagination—like the project that caught his eye one morning in 1983.

It was a Sunday morning, and Jim was sitting at the kitchen table reading the ads in the *Wall Street Journal*. Some people enjoy jigsaw puzzles or crosswords, but this was what Jim did for fun—he always loved seeing what real estate was available, no matter the location. Suddenly, he stood up from the table in excitement. "Susan," he said, thrusting the paper at me, "look at this!"

It was an advertisement for twelve hundred acres of land for sale on Campobello Island, off the coast of Maine. Not only did the ad promise spectacular coastline and beachfront views, but as Jim knew well, Campobello Island was where Franklin Roosevelt spent his boyhood summers, and where he'd contracted polio. The island offered both history and beauty, and there had even been a popular movie made in the fifties called *Sunrise at Campobello*.

"We've got to buy that land!" Jim exclaimed. "This is the project of a lifetime!"

I didn't even have time to wonder whether this would prove to be a passing fancy or the real thing, as Jim immediately booked himself a ticket to fly up to Campobello the very next day. Worried that somebody might buy the land out from under him, he called the number on the ad and made them promise not to sell it until he could get up there.

Sure enough, Jim put a bid on the property within twenty-four hours of seeing it. Once the financing came through, we would own all the land on the island that wasn't protected by the Campobello trust. FDR's grandson even sat on the trust's board, a fact that excited Jim even further.

I wasn't sure what to think about Jim's sudden purchase of a chunk of Campobello Island. On one hand, we barely had enough staff to keep up with our projects in Arkansas, and now Jim was initiating our biggest project ever—off the coast of Maine! I knew what this meant. As he'd done when he went to the governor's office—and again when he sent me to Augusta, and again when he ran for Congress—he was now going to disappear from the day-to-day running of the business he'd grown bored with. Jim was a one-project man, and now that he was in love with Campobello Island, everything else would get short shrift.

On the other hand, it did seem like we were getting Campobello Island for a great price. I went up there shortly after Jim did, taking a camera crew to shoot an ad for it, and as we drove around the island in a jeep, I was stunned at how beautiful and wild the land was. It was absolutely breathtaking. While I knew we were already stretched very thin, I trusted Jim to know what he was doing. And Jim saw Campobello Island as the biggest, most exciting opportunity of his life. He was convinced we would make millions of dollars on it.

We had a huge party in Little Rock to kick off the Campobello Island project. With the who's who of Arkansas business and politics in attendance, we showed the footage we'd taken of the island—and right away we got inquiries about buying lots from some of Jim's friends and associates. It looked like we were on our way to yet another heady success. By the summer of 1984, Madison Guaranty was the hottest financial institution in Little Rock, and Jim was again basking in his reputation as a financial genius.

Then for Jim, the bottom fell out. For the first time, one of his manic swings gave way to a crushing depression, the likes of which I'd never seen him suffer before. He'd had mild downturns, but nothing like this.

It happened so suddenly that I didn't realize at first what was going on. Everything had been moving at top speed, and Jim was having the time of his life. Then, one morning, he said to me, "I just can't go in to the office today. I'm going to stay at home for a bit."

Jim's allergies were as bad as ever, and his overall health had never been good, so I didn't think much about this pronouncement. But then he said the same thing the next day, and the next. Before I knew what had happened, he'd stayed at home every day for a week—and then two, and then three. I started making excuses for Jim at the office, explaining that he was running errands or visiting his parents when in fact he was at home in his pajamas, smoking cigarette after cigarette and staring blankly into space.

Jim got steadily worse. One morning, as I got ready to go in to the bank, he said, "I don't know if I'll be alive when you get home." Frightened, I tried to reassure Jim that everything would be okay, and that he'd feel better soon. "Why don't you just leave me?" he said, his voice heavy. "You don't deserve this. Just get out."

For the most part, Jim was unable to do anything but lie around the house during this period. But I remember one heartbreaking occasion when he tried to pull himself out of his depression. He was trying to convince himself that he didn't need to feel so crushed by responsibility.

"I don't have to take care of the world," he said. "I only have to take care of you and Mother." Jim's father had recently passed away, which possibly added to his feelings of depression.

"That's right," I told him. "Don't worry so much. Just take care of yourself right now."

After a minute, he spoke again. "No, wait," he said, "I also have to take care of Jim Guy and Pat. And Bill Henley too." That began the spiral—pretty soon Jim was listing the names of dozens of people who he believed depended on him. And he just couldn't bear the weight anymore.

I worried that I had done something to bring this on. Jim had been calling me a downer for so long, and had been frustrated with me so many times for questioning his ideas, that I began to believe he was right. Worried that I was ruining both his health and my own, I decided to secretly see a psychiatrist.

At the psychiatrist's office, I began describing my home and work life, and explaining how I feared I was ruining my husband's health.

At the end of the session, he handed me a book, saying only, "You might want to read this." I looked at the title: *Mood Swings.*

I went home and started reading the book, which was about manic depression. And I was absolutely floored: this book had been written about Jim McDougal. It was as if the authors had witnessed Jim's life for the last decade and described it. I was frightened by what I'd read, but also relieved. For the first time, I began to understand that Jim was ill and that I was not to blame for all the problems in our marriage.

Before that day, I had probably heard the term *manic depression,* but it had never registered in my consciousness. But now I couldn't read enough about it. The illness, I learned, is caused by a lack of lithium in a person's system. It could make a person believe he can conquer the world one day—and then render him totally unable to function the next. And in severe cases, manic behavior could be accompanied by hallucinations and paranoia.

As I looked back on my life with Jim, I suddenly began to see the patterns of his behavior. In all the years of his frenzied business dealings and visions of grandeur, it had never dawned on me that he might have some kind of mental illness; I just assumed it was part of the package that came with Jim's quirkiness. I'd seen a lot of people have frequent mood swings, after all—I just thought that Jim's were a more severe case.

Left untreated, manic depression is a very difficult and dangerous illness. But fortunately, lithium pills have been found to effectively mute the highs and lows—and in some sufferers they cause the symptoms of the illness to disappear entirely. But the problem was, Jim didn't know he was manic depressive. He was never going to listen to me about what was wrong with him.

I wanted Jim to get help, but he was never going to agree to listen to me. And he would never agree to see a doctor. "What are they going to tell me?" he'd say. "I'm smarter than they are." And I always just let it go, somehow convincing myself that Jim still knew best. In truth, it was really hard for me to imagine any psychiatrist in Little Rock being able to figure out Jim, who was the smartest man I'd ever met. So instead, I just kept covering for Jim at the office, until gradually his depression would ease on its own.

For the most part, I was able to hide what was going on with Jim from most of the employees and business associates of Madison. But there was one person who wasn't fooled: Pat Harris. Pat had been at Madison from its inception, and he was used to getting ten or twelve phone calls a day from Jim, who always wanted a blow-by-blow account of what was happening on Pat's projects. As soon as the calls quit coming, Pat knew something was up.

One night in late August 1984, while Jim was still depressed, I went to Madison to pick up some documents he had to sign. I'd started going to the office late at night, hoping to avoid employees' increasing questions about Jim. I picked up the papers and, as I turned to leave, I noticed a light on in a back office. I walked back to find Pat working on a memo for Jim.

Pat and I had gotten to know each other during Jim's congressional campaign, when we often drove long distances together to attend rallies or hand out campaign literature. He was always easy to talk to, sensitive and smart, but his best quality by far was he really knew how to listen. I quickly grew to trust him almost as much as I did my family, and not long after I'd gotten to know him, I remember telling people, "If Pat Harris says it, it's the truth."

I loved to tease Pat about the constant stream of young coeds coming to the campaign headquarters to see him. With dark hair and hazel eyes, and an athlete's build, he was considered one of the more eligible bachelors in Little Rock. Our friendship deepened during the early years at Madison, but got derailed when he began to date a young secretary at the S&L named Diane. Diane had an open and intense dislike for me (which I reciprocated), and during the time Pat dated her, he and I stopped having the long talks we'd enjoyed. When I ventured to tell him at one point that Diane wasn't worthy of him, he not so kindly let me know I should butt out. Since then, they'd broken up but Pat and I had not quite recaptured our earlier friendship.

Now, though, sitting with Pat in the darkened offices, I found myself opening up to him. "Pat," I said. "Jim is sick. I don't know what to do."

Then I burst into tears. Pat told me he'd known something was up, as he hadn't heard from Jim in weeks. Then he sat quietly across the desk from me, just listening as I poured my heart out to him.

I'd never talked about Jim's problems to anyone—not even my family. I'd always felt it would be disloyal to him to discuss our private life. And I also feared that people would misconstrue some of Jim's eccentricities as signs of meanness. But Pat was different. He knew Jim well, and he understood that Jim had a good heart—even if his actions sometimes indicated otherwise. Pat had seen every side of Jim. He knew the plain-talking campaigner, the banker who wanted to take care of everyone, the explosive boss who'd scream at people for no apparent reason, and the control freak who kept his fingers in every aspect of every project. Because Pat knew Jim so well, he was the perfect person to open up to. I knew he wouldn't be judgmental, and I trusted that he'd keep what I told him in confidence.

For two hours I told Pat everything I'd ever wanted to say about Jim, Madison, and my fears for the future. Pat hardly said a word, but he never stopped looking at me with those kind eyes. He also didn't express any surprise or shock, but just let me talk until I was done. For the first time, I did not feel so utterly alone with my secrets and my unhappy marriage. But the next day, I worried that I'd overstepped. I felt disloyal to Jim, and upset that I'd broken the bond of silence that surrounded our unhappy marriage.

Yet once the dam was broken, there was no stopping the water from continuing to trickle out. Hoping to further sort out what was going on, I began attending Al-Anon meetings for people with loved ones who are alcoholics, until I realized an unsettling fact. The more I listened to women describe their alcoholic husbands, the more I realized that Jim was far more out of control than any of them—and he wasn't even drinking anymore. I found the meetings more depressing than helpful, and soon stopped going.

But over the next several months, I continued to confide in Pat. As I did, it slowly became clear that I was seeking him out for more than just discussions about my life with Jim. I had begun to fall in love with Pat.

This was all new territory for me. Whenever people had asked me whether Jim and I were in love—even in the earliest days—I had always answered, "Sure, whatever that means." I'd never felt the thrill of truly falling in love, so I'd always believed that romantic love must be little more than a figment of great writers' imaginations. I loved Jim deeply, but I loved him like a member of my family.

With Pat, it was different—I had fallen head over heels for the first time. I sought him out at the bank and felt giddy at the thought of spending time with him. But Pat was difficult to read, and despite all the time we were spending together, I didn't know whether he felt the same way about me. He paid a lot of attention to me whenever I was around, and he always listened intently to what I had to say—but Pat seemed to be that way with everybody. I found myself wondering more and more whether Pat was just being nice to me because I was the boss's wife—or worse yet, because he felt sorry for me, and secretly dreaded our "chance" meetings.

By now, Jim had swung back out of his depression and he was headed for yet another manic high—the one that would prove to be the final roller-coaster climb for Madison Guaranty. Despite the fact that he hated to travel, Jim was now flying to Campobello Island for a week or two every other month. He once again ratcheted up new projects, investing in six new developments within a space of three months. Madison Guaranty was adding new employees and new services so fast that when I walked into the building, I wasn't sure who were the customers and who were the employees. At its peak, Madison would employ almost a hundred people.

The business wasn't the only thing changing rapidly. Having swung back out of his depression, Jim decided to change his look to suit his new mood. He traded in his wire-frame glasses for colored contacts, and changed his clothes from Brooks Brothers to the Gap. Worst of all, he joined a Hair Club for Men and was now sporting a toupee that looked like a dead squirrel had been flattened and placed on his head. One of Jim's charms had always been his level of comfort at not having movie-star looks; his confidence and charisma had always come from his intelligence and sense of humor, and he was comfortable with that. Now, all of a sudden, Jim wanted to be Tom Cruise.

With Jim riding high once more, he again became dismissive and critical of me. At the morning staff meetings at Madison, he would curse and berate me nearly every time I opened my mouth. "Susan," he'd yell, "you don't know what the fuck you're talking about!" I always tried to laugh it off and give back as good as I got. But he'd never berated me like this in public, and now he was doing it every day.

We began having angry scenes both at work and at home. He just seemed irate with me a large part of the time, and he no longer tried to control his rage. I'd always been willing to accept a certain amount of craziness that went along with being Jim McDougal's wife, but now he was going too far. At one point, after he'd screamed at me for about ten minutes, he stared at me and said, "You'll never be anything without me."

I looked back at him and said, "I think being nothing would be easier than this."

"Then get the fuck out," he said.

Finally, I decided that I would. I began seriously considering moving to Dallas, at least for a few months. But first, I decided to tell Pat how I felt about him.

I drove to Maple Creek one afternoon in May 1985 when I knew Pat was working there, and when he walked over to the car I said, "Do you want to go for a drive with me?" He got in the car, and after we'd gotten a ways down the road, I told him what I'd been feeling. "I can hardly breathe when I'm around you. I think about you all the time," I said. "And I don't think I can hide my feelings anymore."

Pat wasn't surprised, and he confided that he'd been struggling to hide his feelings as well. He knew that my marriage to Jim had basically become a business arrangement—but still, it was impossible to imagine that Jim would countenance having one of his employees date his wife. But I told Pat I'd made a decision—I was planning to leave Jim and move to Dallas, at least for the summer. Once I was there, we decided, Pat would come down and we could sort things out.

When I packed my bags later that month, Madison was at its peak of success. Jim was full of manic energy and glad to see me go. I was about to turn thirty, and for the first time in my adult life, I was ready to consider life without Jim. I had not expected a lot of tears from Jim about my departure, but it would have been nice if he could have at least hidden his elation. I could hear him humming in the other room as I packed, and when he helped me load the car, it was less out of kindness than a desire to expedite my departure. He'd agreed to continue to cover my expenses and pay my bills while I was in Dallas, but it was clear that he felt separated from me in every other way.

With a packed car and nowhere to live, I took off for Dallas on Memorial Day weekend 1985. Dallas was close enough so that I could get back to Arkansas quickly, but far enough away that I wouldn't have to face anyone I knew. Scared to death of being on my own for the first time in my life, I convinced Pat to fly down and help me find a place and get settled.

One flight turned into another, and then another, and before we knew it, Pat was flying to Dallas every day so we could be together. Each day after work, he'd catch the 4:30 flight to Dallas, spend the night, and then get up at 6 the next morning to catch the 7 A.M. flight back to Little Rock. We'd go shopping or catch a play or drive out to the ballpark to watch the Texas Rangers play. During the day, I'd lie by the apartment pool and read while waiting for Pat to arrive. It was the best summer of my life, and the happiest I had been in a decade. I had forgotten what it felt like to live a normal life. That's what makes my decision to return to Little Rock after the summer so inexplicable.

Whenever people ask me whether there's anything I would have done differently in my life if given the opportunity, I think back to that summer in Dallas. I was living a dream life—no worries, no expectations, and wildly in love for the first time. Of all the poor decisions I have made in my life (a list of no small proportions), the decision to return to Little Rock after that summer was the worst.

6

JUST ANOTHER MANIC MONDAY

THE FALL OF MADISON GUARANTY WAS every bit as rapid as its ascent. At the beginning of 1986, Madison was featured in an Arkansas magazine as one of the fastest-growing financial institutions in the South. Six months later, the bank examiners announced we were close to insolvency.

It would be an oversimplification to say that Madison Guaranty collapsed as a result of Jim's ever-intensifying manic depression. There were other contributing factors, such as too-rapid growth combined with the employee inexperience and poor organization. Yet it's impossible to understand Madison's downfall without relating it to Jim's mental illness, for one simple reason: Jim McDougal was Madison. From day one, he'd had total control over everything that went on in the S&L. He once sent a memorandum to the various real estate projects stating that no decision was to be made without his approval—including when the grass would be mowed. Similarly, although he claimed he was delegating the banking duties to others, they all reported to him daily about every detail.

One of the biggest problems at Madison was that Jim tended to hire people who were young and inexperienced. Part of this was because

93

he knew he could control them better and they wouldn't question him. But there was another reason. Jim had always been intimidated by mainstream banking types—the kind who had M.B.A.s from top-tier schools and belonged to the local country club. He never felt like he was good enough to have them work for him. Then, when Madison became increasingly successful and the elite of the Little Rock banking community began calling about jobs, Jim was so flattered by the attention that he began hiring people for jobs that didn't even exist.

Jim's insecurity about this issue ran so deep that for several months he refused to work in the specially designed and elaborately detailed president's office in the Pink Palace. Instead, he worked in a small cubbyhole office underneath the stairs, right next to the employees' kitchen. Despite all his successes, Jim's own insecurities wouldn't allow him to envision himself seated in an office befitting a proper CEO.

Even if Jim hadn't been manic depressive, he still didn't have either the business acumen or the temperament to run a multimillion-dollar operation. On the one hand, he wanted to control every facet of the business, always wanting to know every detail about what was going on. On the other hand, he didn't want to be bogged down with minutiae. His fiery explosions of temper—especially when employees countermanded his decisions or seemed to be setting a course of their own—were legendary. But worse than his explosions was the alternative: total silence. Whenever an employee became too independent or started to question Jim, he'd simply cut that person out of his inner circle. He'd refuse to answer or acknowledge any request and generally make the person's job more difficult, if not impossible. The predictable result was a group of upper-level management employees unsure how to do their jobs and scared to make their own decisions. Not surprisingly, chaos ensued.

After the fall of Madison, it was widely assumed that it was a corrupt institution and, like many of the S&Ls that failed, the owners had been using it as their own personal piggy bank. That was simply not true with Madison, a fact the Whitewater investigation would actually confirm ten years later. Despite spending over $60 million on the investigation and having FBI experts go through every transaction at

Madison, Kenneth Starr and his investigators managed to come up with exactly one felony conviction partially related to Madison and one misdemeanor conviction that involved an appraiser who was not even an employee of Madison. A lot of very good people got tainted by the accusations surrounding Madison, people who had worked extremely hard and had sacrificed to help Madison succeed.

But what Madison may have lacked in criminal intent, it more than made up for in stupidity and incompetence, particularly at the top. Over the course of the past fifteen years, Madison has been investigated by almost every government agency imaginable including the Resolution Trust Corporation, Federal Home Loan Bank, the Department of Justice, and of course the Independent Counsel (OIC). They all reached the same conclusion—we were idiots. They could have saved the taxpayers a lot of money and time if they had just asked me. I could have told them that.

When I returned from Dallas at the end of the summer of 1985, Jim was still in full manic bloom. Although we were now separated, I was still making periodic appearances at the S&L and handling some random marketing projects. During my absence, Jim had brought in a whole new group of partners for new projects, some of whom were part of the Little Rock banking establishment. The very people who he felt had once shunned him and looked down on the "junk man" were now wanting to work with him.

And there was someone else who was ready to jump back on the McDougal bandwagon—an old friend who'd made a political come-back to once again become governor of Arkansas, Bill Clinton. When Jim had left the governor's office to move to Kingston in 1980, there had been some hard feelings on both sides. Jim and Hillary, who had always enjoyed a good relationship, were particularly on the outs, and Jim had begun blaming her for all of Bill's problems.

The main source of the friction, however, was a subject that went largely undiscussed—Whitewater. When Jim had approached the Clintons about Whitewater, he had envisioned it as a kind of Camp

David for Arkansas politicians, a place where the McDougals, the Clintons, and others could fly up for weekends of relaxation and political talk. But the reality had turned out to be quite different. Bill was now a hot topic on the national scene and spent many of his weekends out of state—he sure wasn't interested in sitting around at some isolated lodge in the woods on the weekends. Similarly, Bill's top aides—most of whom were already suffering culture shock from having left cities like New York or Washington, D.C.—had no desire to get even further away from civilization.

After some early sales had seemed to lend credence to the Whitewater project's viability, the next two years saw sales come to a virtual standstill. We had obviously misjudged the level of interest in property that was so remotely located, but the real death of Whitewater came with the sudden surge in interest rates in the late seventies. Jim's past success in real estate development had always come by following the same formula: get a moderate down payment (usually $1,500) and keep the buyer's monthly payments low. The way to keep payments low was to finance the property ourselves and charge a low interest rate over a lengthy period of time (fifteen or thirty years).

The problem was that now we were having to borrow money at 21 percent to cover the mortgage and development expenses—but under Arkansas law, we could only charge 10 percent to the customers. Unless we could sell the property very quickly, we were constantly having to refinance at higher and higher interest rates—losing money at every turn. Not only Whitewater, but every property in Arkansas, was subject to this law, making it more difficult to turn a profit on such projects.

Jim's solution to the Whitewater problem was to throw money at it and hope it would go away. Before Whitewater, he'd never had a project fail, and he didn't know how to handle it. Worst of all, he'd brought in the man who was the current governor of Arkansas as his partner, creating the one thing Jim hated most: speculation among people whose respect he sought that he was not the infallible real estate genius he was touted to be. Jim couldn't bear that, so he just continued to use money we made in other projects to cover the growing Whitewater losses.

Many people would later speculate that we'd given the Clintons a sweetheart deal on Whitewater, because Jim and I put far more money into it than Bill and Hillary did—yet we remained 50–50 partners. The truth was much simpler: Jim was just highly embarrassed about Whitewater's failure. He had two options. He could either sit down with the Clintons, admit we'd been wrong, and ask them for more money (something he'd already had to do once). Or, he could just cover the losses with money from other projects and avoid any direct discussion with the Clintons. For a man like Jim, this was a very easy choice to make.

For their part, the Clintons didn't appear too eager to address the situation either. Their focus was on Bill's political future and Hillary's law practice—Whitewater was never more than a blip on their radar screens. Although we weren't aware of it, Hillary had apparently done quite well in the cattle futures market, so they weren't under any great financial pressure.

Bill in particular would have been reluctant to confront Jim about Whitewater. Not only did he not want to alienate someone who was so well-connected in the Arkansas political realm, but Bill—like most of us—was at least a little intimidated by Jim. Whenever Jim was around, Bill tended to defer to him more than he did to others, and he always seemed to be leery of disagreeing with him. I was never sure why, but I assumed that when Bill worked for Jim in Senator Fulbright's office back in the early seventies, he'd probably been subjected to more than one of Jim's screaming fits. Whatever the reason, Jim was just not someone that Bill Clinton would confront if he didn't absolutely have to.

Furthermore, there weren't that many occasions when we had the opportunity to talk about it. Though we'd seen them a fair amount during the three years from 1977 to 1980, we hardly ever saw the Clintons from then onward. Our paths did cross sporadically in the eighties—primarily when Jim was running for Congress at the same time Bill was running for governor. Our conversations were generally cordial but tentative, as both sides danced around our cooled friendships. After that campaign year, I could count on both hands the number of times I saw Bill or Hillary. The idea that we were close friends with the Clintons for a long time was a myth propagated by Clinton opponents when Jim and I got in trouble and they wanted to taint the Clintons with our problems.

In 1986, both the McDougals and the Clintons were riding high. Bill was again governor, rolling along after being reelected and already being mentioned as a possible future presidential contender. Hillary was a star attorney at one of the state's oldest and most prestigious law firms. Jim was being praised as one of the biggest success stories of the Little Rock business community. As for me, I was so in love with Pat that I was oblivious to anything else around me.

The rapid collapse of Madison Guaranty began one bright spring day in 1986 when the federal bank examiners pulled into the S&L's parking lot and were surprised to see a number of Mercedes, Jaguars, Porsches, and even a Bentley parked in the employee parking spaces. According to the testimony given by one of the examiners before the Senate Whitewater Committee almost ten years later, they knew as soon as they saw the row of expensive cars that there was something very wrong going on—and they were determined to find out what it was.

But instead of investigating whether there was a simple explanation behind the cars, the examiners jumped to the conclusion that the management of Madison Guaranty must be looting the S&L to use as a personal piggy bank. The savings and loan scandal of the eighties was just beginning to heat up, and each day brought new stories of S&L executives with private jets, Cayman Island hideaways, and numerous sprawling mansions.

When the examiners saw our small parking lot filled with exotic cars, they assumed they'd stumbled onto a local version of the nation-wide S&L epidemic. If they'd bothered to ask the obvious questions, they not only would have realized that that wasn't the case, they would also have gotten some valuable insight into Jim McDougal and the operations of Madison Guaranty.

The great exotic car scheme was Jim McDougal at his most creative and most dangerous. Jim decided that Madison needed to establish a solid base of high-income depositors—the kind of people who'd be willing to take out high-interest loans that would make the S&L tons of money. Since most of the wealthier citizens of Little Rock already had long-established relationships with older institutions, Jim hatched a scheme to catch them when they were young. His solution was classic Jim: theoretically it was logical, but it was the kind of off-beat thing that nobody else would ever seriously think of doing.

He established a program to recruit students in medical schools to become loyal customers of Madison Guaranty. The basic concept was this: if we provided house and/or car loans to young medical students while they were still struggling to make ends meet, they'd be so grateful that they'd continue to be loyal customers throughout their lifetimes as wealthy doctors. Additionally, Jim figured out the perfect bait to entice them into this relationship—a nice new Mercedes, Porsche, or Jaguar. Madison would loan the med students the money for these cars, and then let them make minimal payments until they graduated and set up their practices.

And that wasn't all. Jim didn't want them buying just any old Mercedes from any dealer. To complete his scheme, Jim loaned a local upstart car dealer the money to go overseas and purchase a number of exotic automobiles—with the understanding that Jim would arrange to have them all purchased by the future physicians.

In theory, the idea was actually one of Jim's more enlightened ones. In practice, it was a disaster. After Jim treated the medical students to a lavish dinner at a French restaurant, they looked at him with justifiable skepticism while he laid out his proposal. It was a spirited performance, but not one student bought into the idea. Unfortunately, Jim had already ordered the cars—and now he was left with approximately a dozen expensive cars he'd promised the dealer he would sell.

As always, Jim had a plan. He sat down with several of Madison's top employees and told them that, based on their performance, he was going to arrange for them to have really nice cars. "These cars," he told them, "are a reward for your hard work and loyalty." Of course, there was one small detail that Jim swept over rather quickly. The company wasn't giving the cars to the employees; they were buying them. Most important, they were buying the cars at prices greater than the blue-book value, thus making the upstart car dealer a handsome profit. And they would purchase the cars with loans from Madison

Guaranty—at interest rates above the prime—thus making Madison a profit as well.

The exotic car scheme was Tom Sawyer and the white picket fence all over again. By the time Jim had finished stroking the "lucky" employees' egos and presenting them with their new cars, they were supposed to feel grateful for the opportunity. It was Jim McDougal at the top of his game.

Because he was the one person who oversaw every facet of Madison's operations, Jim was the only one who really knew how screwed up everything was. From the time the bank examiners arrived, Jim seemed aware that we might be ousted from the bank—a possibility he chose to hide from the rest of us.

The first sign that something was wrong came when Jim vacated his office at the S&L and began working in a small pre-fab home on one of the properties. Then he began to regularly lament the passing of the good old, simple days. "It would be great to get away from all this red tape," he'd say. "It sure would be nice if we could do what we used to do—just cut up a piece of land and sell it without having to create ten documents."

It seemed every time I saw Jim, from whom I'd been separated for almost a year, this was his lament—he wanted to get back to basics. Sure enough, a few weeks later Jim called me and asked me to drop by his office. When I arrived, he was in one of his truly manic moods.

"Baby," he said, "I've found a piece of land that's going to make us more money than Maple Creek and we don't even have to involve the S&L." He went on to say that he was arranging to purchase the land and was already dealing with the financing. Then came the kicker—this was to be my project. Jim would arrange for me to take out the loan to buy the land, and then make sure I had money to develop it. This would be my chance to strike out on my own and to have money to build a future. "It'll take no time at all to develop it," he said excitedly, "and then the money will just roll in."

As I sat there listening to Jim, it slowly began to dawn on me—this was to be my divorce settlement. Jim was going to help me with this new project in return for me turning over my stock in the S&L and my part of the payments that were still coming in on the previous real estate projects.

For me, I was in favor of anything that would make Jim happy and perhaps calm him down. Although he was having a good time dating nineteen-year-olds, I still felt guilty over the dissolution of our marriage and I wanted to make sure he was okay. Besides, I wasn't bitter—I was happier than I'd ever been, and just wanted out of the marriage so I could go on with my life. "Do whatever you feel is right," I told him.

Jim was ecstatic. He was in the process of arranging financing with a local businessman—a former municipal judge by the name of David Hale. Hale operated a Small Business Investment Corporation (SBIC), which was authorized by the government to loan federal funds to start-ups or struggling businesses. Although not required by law, the clear intent of the legislation creating the SBICs was for the money to go to companies operated by women and minorities. Hale had already agreed to loan Jim the money for the property in my name. Jim told me that he just needed to clear up a few details and then I could go in and sign for the loan.

A few weeks passed, and I'd almost completely forgotten about our discussion. Then Jim called to say everything was ready. I was to go by David Hale's office the next day, sign the loan papers, pick up a check for $300,000, and bring it back to Jim.

The next morning I had a tennis lesson not far from Hale's office. After I finished the lesson, I debated for a moment whether I should go home and change out of my tennis dress before dropping by his office, but decided that I was only picking up a check and formality was probably not required. When I arrived at his office, David Hale introduced himself and we had a brief moment of small talk. After that, Hale pulled out the loan papers that he had already prepared and showed me where to sign. After I had signed in the appropriate places, Hale handed me a check made out in my name for $300,000. I made some comment about how easy this was and laughed about how we should do it again sometime. I then left the office and headed downtown to Madison to give Jim the check.

The entire process lasted less than ten minutes, but it was ten minutes that would change my life forever. Six years later, it was this check and this brief encounter with David Hale that led to the Whitewater investigation—and ultimately to Bill Clinton's impeachment.

A few months after I'd signed for the loan at David Hale's office, Madison Guaranty finally came crashing down. In July 1986, when the bank examiners had finished their investigation, Jim and I were summoned to a meeting with Madison's board of directors, our attorneys (Jim Guy Tucker and his law firm), and the examiners.

After a brief recitation of the S&L's many problems—in particular, the consistently shoddy record-keeping—everyone in the room, including our own lawyers, agreed that Jim and I should no longer be involved in Madison's operations. Since I wasn't really involved in the operations anyway, this would have little effect on me. Nevertheless, it was devastating to be told that I could no longer be a part of the company I'd helped to build. I was furious at the accusations of criminal behavior. I didn't want to run the S&L but I knew we had to fight to clear our names. We couldn't take this lying down.

But Jim did take it lying down—literally. After the meeting, he went straight back to his apartment and did not emerge. I would drop in to check on him, but he was always either lying in bed or sitting in his recliner in his bathrobe. Whenever I tried to bring up the subject of Madison, he drifted off and refused to engage in any kind of meaningful discussion.

Then, one day when I stopped by, something even more serious was wrong with Jim. Shortly after I arrived, he had a seizure of some kind, after which he ran out of his apartment into the parking lot of his building. Frightened, I called an ambulance, which fortunately arrived quickly. Jim was loaded in and taken to a hospital.

Doctors at the hospital determined that Jim had suffered a stroke and that his carotid artery was dangerously blocked. Jim's health had been declining for several years, so the diagnosis may not have surprised him. But what did surprise him was another diagnosis the doctors made. They told Jim he suffered from manic depression.

A year and a half after I'd first read the book on manic depression, I found myself sitting with Jim in the hospital as he struggled with the news. "It's not true," he snapped. "Look at me! Do I look bug-eyed? I don't drool on myself, do I? Then why are they saying I'm mentally ill?" Though he would later come to accept the diagnosis, Jim simply couldn't accept it when he was first told. Being told he was depressive didn't seem to bother him. But he just couldn't stand the idea that he was manic.

For the next few months, I tried to help Jim come to terms with his health issues, while at the same time I hired a lawyer to fight the decision to oust us from Madison. But six months and several thousand dollars later, it was obvious that we were getting nowhere. There was no way I could afford any kind of real fight against the government— especially since I didn't know enough about Madison's operations to know for sure what I was fighting about.

Over the next year or so, Pat and I stayed in Arkansas and tried to make the best of things. With the collapse of Madison Guaranty, I was struggling, but there were still a few real estate projects that brought in some money. It didn't take long for us to realize that we wanted—and needed—a fresh start.

After talking it over with my lawyer and my family, I made the decision I should have made during that summer in Dallas. I decided to completely let go of Madison and Jim McDougal and get on with my life. In the summer of 1988, Pat and I packed our things and left for California.

7

THE BRENTWOOD HILLBILLIES

AFTER SPENDING THE PREVIOUS THIRTEEN YEARS trailing along with Jim McDougal's traveling circus, I was ecstatic to be starting a new life with Pat in California. The craziness that had characterized my twenties was, I believed, behind me—and I'd managed to emerge relatively unscathed.

Our plan was simple. Pat and I would live in California for one year, get stress-free jobs, and rest and recuperate in the sunshine. Pat would apply to law school for the 1989-90 academic year, and when he was accepted we would move near the school for the three years it would take to get his degree. We'd start our lives over from scratch, and, we hoped, start a large family. Though we weren't officially engaged yet, we didn't really need to discuss it because marriage and a family were what we had been aiming for from the very beginning of our relationship.

We'd picked California partly because Pat wanted to spend at least one year near the ocean, and partly because we'd taken a vacation there the year before and had loved it. Also, some friends of Pat's parents had offered us an unoccupied condo they owned near Los Angeles for thirty days until we could get our bearings. We soon discovered that we were perfectly suited for the California laid-back lifestyle. We spent the entire thirty days going to the beach, malls, and movie theaters. At the end of it, neither us had even interviewed for a job. So it was that we ended up at a mall one Sunday afternoon, newly homeless and desperately looking for a place to rent. We found an ad for a room in Brentwood, in a quiet, beautiful neighborhood not far from the freeway.

The owners of the house, Jan and Dick Forbath, were a warm, hospitable couple who hosted a cooking show on a local radio station. Despite their hospitality, it didn't take long to realize that we weren't in Arkansas anymore. On Thanksgiving they invited us for a traditional dinner with all the trappings of a down-home Southern turkey and dressing feast. As we gathered around the table, however, one of the other guests began talking about how the aura of the "green spirit" was upon us. She then went around the table reading each of our auras, commenting on what the "green spirit" had in store for us. In the South, talk of green spirits is limited to senile relatives and Ross Perot. Here, though, everybody seemed to be taking it very seriously.

With our savings rapidly diminishing, and the newspaper want ads proving a dead end day after day, I took my résumé to an employment agency and told the recruiter that I desperately needed to find work. She took a look at my résumé, which focused primarily on my marketing responsibilities at Madison Guaranty, and told me I could forget it. She immediately dismissed it as the marginally useful experience of a big fish in the small pond of Arkansas.

"You can forget about getting any marketing work in Los Angeles," she said. "But if you need something fast, there's always work for secretaries, especially executive secretaries. How are your typing and computer skills?"

At the recruiter's suggestion, I took a few typing and computer tests—and I aced them all. The recruiter told me that she would have no problem placing me in a decent job very quickly.

One problem still remained—my résumé was geared toward marketing jobs. The recruiter took my résumé into another room and came back an hour later with a rewritten version that focused on my secretarial and computer skills. The companies and dates were unchanged—but my duties had been changed across the board from marketing to secretarial. I then sat down with her and added another couple of lines stating that I had been a top-notch secretary for a real estate mogul named Jim McDonnell—I didn't want to put "McDougal," as I figured it would look suspicious if I had the same last name as my boss. I also changed the name of the real estate companies that I had worked on with Jim and omitted any mention of Madison. I knew the résumé was false. But, I also knew that I could perform all the duties on the résumé and that I needed a job.

It only took about an hour to make all the changes on the document, but it was an hour that would come back to haunt me ten years later. Prosecutors would introduce it at two trials and a sentencing hearing as conclusive proof that I was a con artist and liar. It was the single constant throughout the entire criminal process—every time the prosecution was slowed down by a lack of evidence at one of my trials, they'd whip out the résumé and talk about how I had lied to get a job.

As the recruiter had promised, a week after my appointment at the employment agency I had a job. I was hired as the executive secretary to Michael Hammer at Occidental Petroleum. Hammer was the grandson of Armand Hammer, the renowned philanthropist and legendary founder of Occidental. At age thirty, and the future heir to a huge family fortune, Michael Hammer was determined to show that he wasn't a lightweight skating by on his family name. As a result, he was a total perfectionist about every detail of his work—a fact that had apparently led to the departure of three previous secretaries in the past year.

In general, I don't respond well to perfectionists; in fact, I've never understood why people so often view that label as a badge of honor. I tend to equate the term with compulsive psychopath. But with Michael Hammer, I was determined to adjust and pay attention to every small detail. Succeeding in this job meant more to me than just the money: before Occidental, I'd never held a full-time job working for anyone other than Jim McDougal. As soon as I took the Occidental job, speculation began among my family and friends as to whether I had the requisite work ethic to last. Bets were being placed, with the over/under at thirty days.

As corporate secretary and heir apparent to the company, Michael held a simple but important job: he was responsible for the corporate minutes and all written communication with the board of directors. Even though the work seemed menial, I was given to understand that even the smallest error could result in major problems with the SEC. Thus, our days were regularly consumed with the correct location of commas and the proper amount of indentation for signatures. On one occasion, we spent three days on a two-paragraph letter that simply stated the time and place of a board meeting.

In between the numerous meetings on punctuation, the corporate secretary's office served as an outpost for various dignitaries who made the pilgrimage to see Armand Hammer. Everyone from politicians to athletes to movie stars would cool their heels in our office while waiting to have an audience with the great capitalist. One of those celebrities was an up-and-coming young senator from Tennessee, Al Gore Jr., who had just completed an unsuccessful presidential bid in 1988 and was rumored to be embarking on another run in four years.

I remember Gore's visit specifically because I was asked to escort him down the hall to show him where the men's rest room was. Having not made a habit out of visiting that particular rest room, I became confused and managed to point him toward a janitorial closet, which he duly attempted to enter. I instantly realized my error and, given the tight guidelines at work was fairly sure that I would be fired. Somewhere in the massive corporate handbook there had to be a rule stating that directing a United States senator to a janitorial closet was grounds for dismissal. Gore, however, took it in stride, joking good-naturedly about the incident. He did, however, ask someone else for directions when exiting the building.

Shortly after I began work at Occidental, Pat went to a job interview at another house in Brentwood, where a wealthy couple was looking for a personal assistant/property manager to take care of several houses they owned in the upscale west Los Angeles areas. He was supposed to call me as soon as his interview was finished, but after almost two hours I had heard nothing. Finally, the receptionist buzzed to let me know that Mr. Harris was on the line for me.

Pat was on a pay phone near a busy intersection, so it was difficult to hear him over the traffic noise. I was able to make out that he thought the interview went well and that the woman who interviewed him seemed particularly pleased that her dog liked him. Not sure I'd heard him correctly, I tried to get him to explain the part about why the dog was participating in the interview, but he assured me he would tell me the whole story later.

Of greater interest to Pat was the fact that his prospective employer was someone he recognized from the B movies he'd watched every Saturday as a child. Having grown up in a small Arkansas town with only one movie theater, Pat had spent his early years watching the double features there—and he had an uncanny ability to recall the names of even the most obscure actors and actresses who'd been in them. I had learned early on in our relationship to never question Pat when it came to recalling useless trivia. If there was a question about a sports figure, movie personality, or politician, Pat could not only tell you who the person was but their batting average, box-office numbers, or vote percentile they received in the last election. On the other hand, he could not remember the name of the person he had met an hour earlier.

"I swear she's the same woman from an old Tarzan movie I saw about twenty times," Pat said, laughing. "She also looks like the actress from one of my old favorites, *Jason and the Argonauts*. And I think she may have played Darrin's old girlfriend on *Bewitched*."

The concept that someone he'd seen on-screen as a child had now turned up as a potential employer had Pat laughing and talking a mile a minute. "I'll tell you more when I pick you up tonight," he said. Then, just before he hung up, he threw out as a casual aside, "By the way, I think her husband is a conductor of some kind. Maybe an orchestra conductor."

"What's his name?" I asked him.

"I don't remember," Pat said. "Something like Ruben Menta."

There was a long pause as I tried to make sure I'd heard him correctly over the traffic noise.

"Are you talking about Zubin Mehta?" I asked.

"Yeah, that sounds right," he said. "I think that's it. I take it you've heard of him?"

"My God!" I shouted. "He's the most famous conductor in the world. I can't believe you can pick out an obscure movie actress, but you don't know Zubin Mehta!"

"Yeah, well," he said, "we didn't get a lot of symphonies in Clarksville. If he'd been in a bad movie, I would probably have known him and I'd be a lot more impressed."

I had to laugh as I hung up. Pat was the only human being on the planet who could go to Zubin Mehta's house and think his wife was the star.

A few days later, Pat went to work for Ruben Menta—or Zubin Mehta, as he was known to the rest of the world—and his wife Nancy. His job was to manage the series of homes Nancy and Zubin owned in the ritzy Brentwood, Bel-Air, and Malibu areas of Los Angeles. Since Zubin was on the road most of the time (he was usually in Los Angeles for only two or three weeks every year), he didn't take an active interest in the business, leaving Nancy to run things as she saw fit. Because they rented these homes to wealthy clients—such as Tom Hanks and Dina Merrill—for amounts ranging from $5,000 a month up to $20,000 a month, Nancy aimed to run her properties like a world-class hotel. If a washer broke down, a repairman was to be quickly dispatched and met at the house. If a lightbulb burned out, it would be replaced immediately.

For the first few months, Pat would come home at night raving about what a nice woman Nancy Mehta was. She was exceedingly polite, he said, and always seemed to be concerned about his feelings and how he was doing. She insisted that he go home each evening at five o'clock—regardless of what they were in the middle of—because, as she repeatedly told him, she didn't want to disrupt his life.

Pat and Nancy worked out of the Mehtas' house, an Italian villa–style home on top of a hill in the middle of Brentwood. Although the house itself was not enormous, the property encompassed several acres and, depending on the smog level, offered gorgeous ocean views. The house was previously owned by Steve McQueen—a mark on one inside wall was allegedly made when he rode his motorcycle in the house—and it was a stone's throw from the home of one of Brentwood's many famous residents, O. J. Simpson.

I didn't meet Nancy for a few months. Then, one afternoon, Pat and I were driving up Sunset Boulevard when a stark white, older-model Rolls-Royce came swinging around a corner. A middle-aged, attractive blond woman was at the wheel, chattering away on a car phone—a real rarity back then—and a large, furry white dog sat with its head poking out of the passenger side window. If ever there was an exaggerated, stereotypical image of Southern California's rich and famous, this was it. I started laughing and pointed at the car, saying to Pat, "Would you look at that!"

Barely cracking a smile, Pat nonchalantly replied, "Try not to make fun of my boss."

As the weeks went by, Nancy began expressing an interest in meeting me. While at work, Pat would often talk about what I was doing and how my job at Occidental was going, and Nancy always seemed genuinely interested. After a couple of months, the three of us arranged to have lunch in Westwood at a restaurant near Occidental.

At lunch that day, I was struck by two things. First, although she was heavy, Nancy had one of the most beautiful faces I had ever seen. Immaculately put together, with perfectly manicured hands, lots of makeup, and a regal bearing, she reminded me of those Norse goddesses who adorn the prows of ships.

The second thing that struck me was how intensely interested she was in our lives. She asked questions about every detail, no matter how mundane. At the time I felt flattered: here was a woman who'd been all over the world, meeting with heads of state and foreign dignitaries—and yet she was genuinely interested in our lives. I saw this as a sign of how down-to-earth she was.

As we were leaving, Pat asked me what I thought of Nancy. I had to admit that she was every bit as charming as he had described her. Later that evening we talked about inviting Nancy to go to the movies with us. Pat and I generally went to the movies two or three times a week, and we knew that Nancy, who was a voting member of the Academy of Motion Pictures, Arts & Sciences, also loved going. So we asked her to join us the very next night to see the Tom Berenger/Debra Winger movie *Betrayed*—a title that would later prove to be ripe with irony.

That night I sat between Nancy and Pat at the theater. Nancy considered movies to be interactive events: from the opening credits, she began a running commentary about on-screen events, whispering about everything from the performances to plot points. Pat, on the other hand, regarded movies to be just short of a religious experience, with total silence being essential. I could tell he was increasingly perturbed by Nancy's constant talking, but he was not about to say anything—especially since it seemed that Nancy and I were getting along well.

As we left the theater that night, Nancy turned to me and said, "Do you want to come shopping with me this weekend?" Since she was Pat's boss, I would have said yes under any circumstances. But that was not why I accepted. Having been in Los Angeles for only a short time, I'd made very few friends—and I saw Nancy as someone who could be a friend. Though she moved in the circles of the rich and famous, she seemed to have few of the pretensions of newfound wealth. I liked her almost immediately, and I could tell the feeling was mutual.

Nancy is a woman of many talents—none greater than her ability to tear through a department store at hurricane speed, leaving enormous devastation in her wake. As we swept through the store, she peppered me with questions about each outfit. "What do you think of this?" she'd ask, before directing me to the dressing room with a terse "Go try this on!" I declined as politely as I could, and Nancy's attention was always quickly drawn elsewhere. We covered most of Neiman's, Saks, and I. Magnin's in a whirlwind ninety minutes before sitting down to eat lunch.

As the morning had progressed, Nancy's attitude toward me had changed dramatically—and not for the better. Now, picking at her lunch, she was clearly sulking, and I was racking my brains trying to figure out what I'd said or done to upset her. Finally, I worked up enough courage to ask, "Nancy, have I done something wrong?"

Her response was immediate and accusatory. "You have taken away all the joy of this day for me," she said "I would *like* to buy you some clothes that are appropriate for a corporate atmosphere like Occidental, but you *refuse* to even try anything on!"

"Nancy," I protested, "I thought we were coming here to go shopping for you!" Panicked at her visibly rising anger, I hurriedly added, "I couldn't possibly let you buy me anything. I came to spend some time with you, not to buy clothes for myself."

This only made things worse. "You're ruining the whole day for me!" she said, her voice brittle. "If you're not going to let me buy you any clothes, then let's just go home!"

Stunned at her outburst, I had no idea how to react. On one hand, I just couldn't let a person I barely knew buy me clothes—no matter how much money she had or how noble her intentions. On the other hand, if I continued to refuse, it looked as though she might explode with anger. Suddenly, I could see myself going home and having to explain to Pat how I'd managed to infuriate his boss by turning down her gift of free clothes.

I did the only thing I knew how to do—I started groveling. "Nancy," I said, "this isn't personal. I really appreciate your offer, but I just can't accept such a lavish gift." I didn't want to make a scene, I just desperately wanted to find a way to restore her good mood. I explained that the way I was raised just wouldn't allow me to accept such generosity. But my words had no effect on Nancy; there was one thing she wanted to do, and she was determined to do it. No other outcome was acceptable.

That day, I learned lesson number one about Nancy Mehta: no one ever told her "no." When she decided she was going to do something, she wasn't merely stubborn about it—it became a crusade of monumental proportions. Nothing on heaven or earth could dissuade Nancy from her mission, and hearing the word *no* only made her more determined to accomplish her goal. For years, I'd prided myself in my ability to persuade people to go along with me. But that day in Beverly Hills, I'd met my match in Nancy Mehta.

After picking at my chicken salad for a few moments, I finally realized that this was a battle I was not going to win. "Okay," I told her. "Let's go try some stuff on." Like some Dickensian street urchin, I was going to be outfitted by the benevolence of the upper class. Nancy's mood changed as quickly as if I'd injected a dozen Prozacs directly into her bloodstream. The sullen, simmering Nancy of lunch was once again the sunny, sweet Nancy who had picked me up that morning. After lunch, we flew through Saks and Neiman's again, with Nancy sending me to the dressing room with outfit after outfit.

That afternoon, I watched in a daze as a woman I barely knew bought over $2,000 worth of clothes for me. Even worse, she insisted on buying me the kind of women's business suits that I regularly made fun of as "stewardess costumes"—suits of the type that invariably adorned the frames of women with eighteen-inch waists, little pug noses, and their hair pulled back in buns so tight that it left stretch marks on their faces. I tried very hard to act enthused as the store clerk rang up the selections, but Nancy had to know I was distraught. When she dropped me off at home, I hugged her and thanked her for everything, and promised we would do it again.

But I was not out of the woods yet. I could not even imagine Pat's reaction when he found out that his boss had just bought me an expensive new wardrobe, so I quickly devised a plan. I marched into the apartment and, before Pat could say a word, I made an announcement. "Nancy has just bought me two thousnad dollars' worth of clothes," I said. "And I'm never going to wear any of them." I then dumped the clothes onto the closet floor with great fanfare and plopped down in front of the television.

Pat was stunned. He started to feign indignation, but the fact that I'd dumped the clothes ceremoniously on the floor pretty much defused that. Unsure of exactly what type of emotion was called for, he settled on curiosity and began asking me about my surreal day. By the time I reached the end of the story, he was supportive of my decision to let her buy the clothes—and to dump them in the closet. I never did wear a single piece of clothing bought that day.

Despite the fact that I hadn't wanted the clothes, I still felt an obligation to express my gratitude. At one point during the shopping fiasco, Nancy had mentioned once seeing an address book of Cary Grant's that was a true work of art. It had a burnished leather cover and had been painstakingly filled in with innumerable details. For people in Hollywood social circles, an address book is a complicated thing—you've got to organize information not just on friends' phone and fax numbers, but assistants' names, vacation home addresses, telephone numbers for private jets, phone extensions down at the stables, and so on.

In the years that had passed since she'd seen it, Cary Grant's book had stuck in Nancy's mind as something she'd someday like to make for herself. That night, as I talked to Pat about what we could do to repay Nancy, I decided that I could help her put one together.

The next morning I called Nancy and broached the idea with her. "This is the greatest gift you could ever possibly give me," she said, clearly touched. So I arranged to rent a computer and take a day off from work, and Nancy and I started what would eventually become a three-year endeavor. (Finding the perfect cover alone took us nine months.) The address book project marked the beginning of a friendship that would bring Nancy and me as close as sisters—and end in the most bitter acrimony imaginable.

While my friendship with Nancy was heating up, the honeymoon between Pat and Nancy was beginning to fade. One night he came home with a story that seemed to contradict everything he had previously told me about her.

A minor boundary dispute had arisen at one of the rental properties, and Nancy had approached the neighbor about the problem. After a few minutes of pleasantries, Nancy suggested a solution that she felt was fair. The woman said thanks, but since the amount of land involved was so miniscule, perhaps it was better to just forget about it and leave things as they were. Having broached the subject, however, Nancy was not about to leave it alone. She continued to insist on her solution as the best way to proceed.

After several minutes of listening to Nancy's harangue, the exasperated neighbor remarked, "You must not have much of a life."

At this point, Pat said, Nancy lost her temper. "She threw an absolute tantrum," he told me.

"So what?" I said. "Everyone loses their temper on occasion."

"I don't think you understand," he replied, raising his eyebrows. "We're not talking about a person just losing her temper. This was the most out-of-control screaming I have ever heard." What made it even more remarkable, Pat continued, is that she sustained this full-volume rant for almost fifteen minutes.

Although Pat had clearly been affected by the intensity of Nancy's rant, the story had very little effect on me. I had witnessed tirades from two of the best—my father and Jim McDougal—and I was relatively sure Nancy was an amateur compared with those two. Pat, however, was becoming increasingly wary of Nancy. She'd always had little idiosyncrasies, but in the past he had brushed them off as the general quirkiness of California's rich and famous.

As evidence, Pat described to me the strange relationship Nancy had with Taras, her full-blooded borzoi dog (a breed related to Russian wolfhounds). Not only did she spoil him completely by feeding him expensive rib eyes, T-bones, porterhouse steaks, and other red meat on a daily basis, she also talked to him as though he was human. As tall as a Saint Bernard, but lithe and elegant-looking, Taras tended to lumber slowly about the house, teetering to one side like a drunken sailor. Yet he was deceptively quick: in a flash, he could leap to his feet—or lunge at a person—with cobra-like speed.

The problem with Taras was that he was the canine version of Sybil—the most schizophrenic dog you could imagine. One minute he'd be lovingly nudging you to pet him—and the next minute, he'd rip the flesh off your arm. Over the years, the Mehtas had paid out thousands of dollars in damages, including a considerable sum in plastic-surgery costs for a onetime best friend of Nancy's. It wasn't that Taras bit people often; sometimes he went months without chomping on anybody. But he was so unpredictable that everyone was forced to tread very lightly around him.

No matter what the circumstances surrounding Taras's attacks, Nancy always suggested it was the victim's fault for somehow provoking her poor, helpless dog. One night, Pat came home livid after

Taras bit a teenage boy who was helping his mother deliver plants; the wound would likely leave a permanent scar on the boy's face. "There must have been some reason why Taras did that" was all Nancy said. She simply couldn't see it any other way.

When Pat had taken the position with Nancy, he had told her it would only be for a year, as he planned to start law school the next fall. By the time April 1989 rolled around, he had been accepted to several law schools and had been wait-listed at his top choice, Stanford. Confident that he'd eventually get in at Stanford, he gave Nancy notice that his final day would be July 1, giving her plenty of time to find a new assistant. Although they were still cordial with each other, neither Nancy nor Pat was particularly heartbroken about his leaving.

That same spring, my career at Occidental was soaring. Coming up on my one-year anniversary there, I had just received very positive evaluations, and Michael Hammer and I were getting along well. In some ways, we were very good for each other—he had loosened up around me, and I had become much more attentive to detail. Several people in the office congratulated me on being his longest-surviving secretary in recent memory. Michael even called me into his office to reiterate the evaluations and tell me how pleased he was with the way things were going.

Then, toward the end of April, Michael asked to speak to me privately. I walked into his office, and he calmly informed me that I could no longer work with him. If I wished, he said, he could get me transferred somewhere else in Occidental at the same salary—or I could choose to leave and receive a reasonable severance package.

I was completely stunned. For what seemed like several minutes, I just sat there silently, with no idea what to say. Finally, Michael began tearing up and his hands began shaking. "The work just isn't getting done," he said, his voice quavering.

Having just discussed my positive evaluations a few weeks before, I was about to ask what had changed—but I could tell Michael was emotionally distraught, and it seemed as though there must be something else he didn't want to talk about. A few more awkward moments of silence went by, and then I suddenly apologized to him. "I'm sorry this is so hard for you," I said. I then stood up from my chair, walked downstairs, and called Pat to come get me. Later on I ran into Michael Hammer. He apologized to me and explained that he had needed to ratchet his work up a few notches. Thank God I missed it.

Word of my Occidental demise quickly reached Nancy who was half a world away, in the remotest jungles of Africa communing with gorillas. Earlier that year, Nancy had seen the movie *Gorillas in the Mist*—the story of anthropologist Dian Fossey—and she'd decided that she and Zubin should follow in Fossey's footsteps for their vacation. But after a few days in Rwanda, she grew restless (there are only so many things you can say to a gorilla) and called Pat at the office. After first talking to Taras on the phone—a feat accomplished by having Pat put the receiver up to the puzzled dog's ear—she asked Pat what was new in his life. "Susan's left Occidental," he told her. "Well, don't let her do anything until I get back to California!" she said.

As soon as she got back from Rwanda, Nancy had me over to the house to ask what I planned to do next. "I've got interviews set up with a couple of law firms," I told her, to which she shook her head. "I want you to take over Pat's position," she said, "and I'll match any offer you get from another company." I told Nancy that I appreciated the offer, and that I'd let her know shortly.

The idea of working with Nancy was very appealing. I saw her as someone I could be friends with, and I respected her for her strength and determination. Besides, she was a lot of fun to be around; not only was she usually upbeat, but she was always willing to poke fun at herself. And she was very complimentary of everything I did, constantly offering me the kind of approval I've always sought and needed in life.

I genuinely liked Nancy and enjoyed her company, and whenever we were together, we pretty much spent the whole time laughing. In addition, I'd developed something of a Mother Teresa complex—I was sure that I could help solve everybody else's problems, despite the fact that I'd never been able to solve my own. The only thing Nancy needed, I believed, was just a little more support and patience than Pat had been able or willing to give her.

I was aware, of course, that Nancy had her eccentricities. Not only had Pat's stories given me pause, but the more time I'd spent around her, the more I'd been witness to her erratic behavior. But Pat told me that even Nancy's strangest habits were relatively harmless and that she did seem to be a lot more normal when I was around. He told me that what Nancy needed more than an assistant was a friend and that I was someone that Nancy was already close to. If I wanted to take the job, he thought it would probably work.

For the next three and a half years, I served as Nancy's assistant, marriage counselor, psychiatrist, workout partner, movie companion, and best friend. Life with Nancy was exciting, sometimes absurd, and often exasperating. The one thing it never was, however, was boring. Just like Jim McDougal, Nancy Mehta never lacked for ideas or the chutzpah to implement them. She would suggest some half-baked idea and I would go along for the ride—much like I had with Jim. We were like a modern-day Lucy and Ethel, always careening from one ludicrous scenario to the next, and usually laughing ourselves silly along the way.

In the beginning, most of these schemes revolved around weight loss. I'd been working with Nancy for only a short time when we stopped in the shopping district of Beverly Hills one afternoon for a quick lunch. As Nancy and I walked toward the restaurant, we saw a homeless man sitting against a wall. Instead of asking for money, he shouted to us, "Is it Mardi Gras?"

Confused by the question, we stopped for a moment. "What do you mean?" I asked him.

"I thought it must be Mardi Gras," he said, "because you two look like you're headed for Fat Tuesday."

Neither Nancy nor I responded—and in fact, she and I never spoke of it afterward. It was too painful and embarrassing. But after that day, we embarked on a series of weight-loss plans.

Our first plan was to get back to basics. We decided to eat healthier foods and begin each day with a vigorous run. Early on the first morning of our training regimen, her houseman Ronnie dropped us off on San Vincente Boulevard, a tree-shaded street lined with numerous shops and restaurants and frequented by hordes of L.A. joggers.

Nancy took off like a bullet as soon as she stepped out of the car. No stretching, no warm-up, no pacing—she seemed intent on making up for years of inactivity in the space of a few minutes. I took off after her, managing to catch her after a couple hundred yards because she was already running out of steam. After a few more yards, we both bent over in agony, gasping for breath. Seeing a small bakery across the street, I suggested we walk over to get a bottle of water and rethink our plan. Once we hit the bakery, however, the smells of fresh-baked bread and pastries overwhelmed us, and our order of Evian water expanded to include two croissants and an apple strudel.

Reinvigorated, we returned to the jogging strip and took off at a much more reasonable pace. After covering about a mile, Nancy and I were both exhausted, and we decided we'd done enough for one day. Ronnie wasn't back from running errands yet, so we wandered over to a small outdoor café to wait for him. Figuring we ought to order something, we requested a couple of desserts to reward ourselves for the morning run. By the time Ronnie arrived, we were recovered from our exhaustion and thinking about hanging around for lunch.

With our jogging regimen adding pounds by the day, we decided to try something different: Nancy hired a personal trainer to come to the house every morning and lead us in a tough workout. I found an ad for "trainers to the stars," and the next morning a pair of Ken and Barbie look-alikes showed up at the door.

After we assured the trainers that we were in reasonably good physical condition, they put us through an hour of rapid-calorie-burning aerobic exercises. I struggled through the first half-hour, then spent the second half-hour on the floor of the bathroom after crawling there to vomit. Nancy, to her credit, managed to get through the entire workout. Unfortunately, she was then unable to walk down the stairs for the next two days. I called Ken and Barbie. "We're going out of town," I told them. "We'll call you when we get back." When I hung up, I threw away their number.

Later that year, Nancy read that ballet was a great aerobic exercise, and she promptly decided that ballet lessons would improve both our minds and our bodies. I had major reservations about this scheme, but Nancy forged ahead and hired a former Russian premier ballerina to give us private lessons at her studio. She was a lovely woman, and even allowed us to lock the studio door when we worked out, so no one could walk in and see us in the skintight leotards we'd bought. Despite the fact that most of her students were under the age of fourteen and weighed less than a hundred pounds, she pretended as if it were the most normal thing in the world for two women who could not raise their legs above their kneecaps, to be taking ballet lessons. But despite her patience and our efforts, we continued to resemble the dancing hippos in the old Disney animated film *Fantasia*. As a result of the instructor's kindness, ballet lessons lasted longer than the personal trainer, but only by about a month. During that month we each gained approximately five pounds courtesy of the ice-cream shop abutting the ballet studio.

Our weight-loss schemes were comical at best, but the issue behind them was serious. Nancy's figure had gone from trim to matronly since she had married Zubin, and I always felt that her weight played a significant role in her loneliness.

In many ways, Nancy was the quintessential Los Angeles insider: she was wealthy, status-conscious, ambitious, generous, and outgoing—the kind of person who fits right in at parties and fund-raising events. But she had long ago lost one necessary ingredient of Southern California social success: the size-4 figure. Many of the women whose friendship she desired—such as Nancy Reagan—were notoriously weight-conscious, and Nancy Mehta had come to feel like an outsider among them. Partly as a result, she and I continued to grow closer.

When I first started working with Nancy in the summer of 1989, everything went along quite smoothly. Pat was still in Los Angeles, as despite his optimism, he hadn't made it off the waiting list for Stanford's law school. Now he was looking for a temporary job while he prepared to apply again for the following year. Nancy was respectful of my relationship with Pat and made sure that I finished work by five o'clock each day so I could get home in time for dinner with him. She was on the road with Zubin a lot during this time—conductors are rarely in one place more than a few weeks—so I didn't see all that much of her. And on the rare occasions when Zubin was in town, it was nice to have him around—he was one of the most charming, kind men I'd met in a while.

But things changed in the fall of 1989, for two reasons. First, Pat was offered his dream job: he agreed to spend the year before law school working for major league baseball's Texas Rangers. Because the team (whose managing partner was an affable lightweight named George W. Bush) was located near Dallas, Pat would have to relocate. We discussed whether I should go with him, but decided that since it was just a short-term job, I should stay in my secure position with Nancy—at least until we knew where he'd be going to law school the following year.

The second reason had to do with Nancy and Zubin's relationship. In October of my first year working with Nancy, she came home rather abruptly from one of Zubin's concert tours. It was obvious that something had happened, but she refused to say what; in fact, she refused to come out of her room for several days. Finally I asked her lawyer what was going on. He told me that Zubin wanted to divorce Nancy.

Nancy had no intention of going along with the divorce. In an effort to save her marriage, she enlisted the help of an envoy. She flew a member of the local Christian Science church to New York to talk with Zubin. Nancy was a lifelong, devout member of the Christian Science church, the small but powerful sect best known for its doctrine that all illness is in the mind and can be cured by prayer and will. The man Nancy chose as her envoy was a church "practioner," which is roughly equivalent to a minister or pastor in a Protestant church.

The practioner's trip to New York was a success: he returned to announce that Zubin had withdrawn his request for a divorce. Later, I learned Zubin's decision came with a number of conditions, foremost of which was that Nancy would no longer travel to Israel with him during the three months every year he spent as conductor of the Israeli Philharmonic.

With Pat having just left for Dallas, and Zubin withdrawing from Nancy, she got it in her head that she and I were in similar straits—left alone in Los Angeles by men out gallivanting around the world trying to recapture their adolescent years.

On my own in Los Angeles, with no real friends other than Nancy, I slipped easily into an increasingly close relationship with her. We shared the same interests—especially movies, shopping, and multiple desserts. Initially, we did social things together two or three times a week. That soon became four or five times a week, and then almost every day. A typical weekday now involved doing the following things together: working in the morning, having lunch, shopping in the early afternoon, having an afternoon snack, going to a late-afternoon movie, having dinner, seeing an early-evening movie, and having a late snack before I would at last head home. By the time I reached the first anniversary of working with Nancy, the line between employee and friend had disappeared completely.

The beginning of that first year had lulled me into a false sense of security. Nancy had been on the road with Zubin for several months, in an attempt to rescue their marriage. Then, whenever she was in Los Angeles, she was on her best behavior. She'd pushed her eccentricities below the surface, and even when some did pop up, they seemed relatively harmless—if not occasionally charming.

Once, when we were running late for a movie, Nancy pulled her Rolls-Royce up in front of the movie theater, flapped a $100 bill out the window, and promised to give it to anyone who would park the car for us. "Nancy!" I yelled. "You're going to go down in history as the only person ever to pay someone to steal her car!" Similarly, whenever we were at a restaurant, she would toss whatever bills were handy onto the table as a tip, as it was too much trouble to dig out her glasses to see the denominations. At one small bistro in Brentwood, she once left a $200 tip on a $52 bill, something we never would have known except for the fact that the next time we came to that restaurant, the waiters began fighting one another to serve us.

Nancy's quirks seemed amusing and harmless at first, but at the end of the first year they began to turn a corner to something more troubling. My lease had run out on my apartment and I had mentioned to Nancy that I needed to start looking for a new place. One bright, beautiful Saturday morning, just as I was waking up, she showed up unannounced at my apartment with a moving van and two workers ready to move my things into storage and me into her house.

As always with Nancy's unsolicited acts of spontaneous generosity, I didn't want to seem ungrateful. But I knew I needed a place to go home to, away from the uproar of the Mehta household. I began listing for her the reasons why I couldn't move in, but I might as well have been talking to myself. Oblivious to my protests, she directed the workers to load my furniture on the truck and take it to storage. At this point, I had two options: either start a screaming match with Nancy, or give in. I gave in.

From the day I moved into Nancy's house, I had almost no privacy. None of the inside doors in the Mehtas' home—including the bathrooms—had locks. It had been a long time since someone was in my face around the clock. During the last few years of my marriage, Jim had spent most of his time trying to get away from me. And although Pat and I spent most of our free time together, we were pretty low-key, usually reading, watching television, or going to the movies.

Now, all of a sudden, every movement I made was being planned, analyzed, or questioned. Mornings began with Nancy crawling into bed with me and talking about what the day would bring. After our full days of work, meals, movies, and shopping, we'd come home and fall asleep watching a video. At times I felt like I couldn't breathe. It wasn't that Nancy was mistreating me—on the contrary, she was upbeat most of the time. And I was still enjoying her company, for the most part. It was just that I needed some downtime.

And there were other things that troubled me about living with

Nancy. One was that I found the Italian stone villa motif of her home to be cold and unsettling. Nancy's taste in interior decorating—an odd combination of Hollywood chi-chi furnishings with Middle Eastern vases and rugs—didn't help. And the house's nonhuman inhabitants only added to the ambience. In addition to the killer dog, who seemed to lurk around every corner waiting to pounce, there was an even worse four-legged problem: rats.

I despise rats under the best of circumstances—and these were not garden-variety rats. At night, they would sneak into the small room containing Taras' daily ration of specialty steaks and chops, and they'd carry off as much meat as their little teeth could grasp. Eventually, word in the rat community must have leaked out, because by the time I arrived, Nancy's house was becoming the hot spot for rats all over L.A. Plied with protein and buffed up to enormous sizes, these rats possessed powers well beyond their wildest genetic imagination.

I'd been vaguely aware of the rat problem before I moved in, but now the reality of it was brought home in thoroughly disgusting ways. Late one night, for example, I went to the refrigerator to get a drink. Reaching blearily for the door, I noticed that the mop had somehow gotten wedged underneath the fridge. I bent down to pull it out—only to recoil, screaming, when I saw that the mop strands were moving. What I had assumed was a mop was actually a group of rat tails.

The next day I told Nancy that I couldn't stay another night unless the rat problem was solved. Her response was typical Nancy: offbeat, warmhearted, and the kind of thing no one else would do. Because she was anxious not to harm the rats, she bought a high-tech rat dispersal device. This was a small box that emitted a high-pitched screeching noise, undetectable to the human ear, but apparently designed to drive the rats to the edge of madness and hopefully out of the house. We installed the device near Taras' food and waited anxiously for the results.

Unfortunately, we had badly underestimated our enemy. As we saw the next morning, these were no ordinary rats; one of their finest had bravely taken on the role of kamikaze, and had gnawed through the electrical cord. We found his little fried rat body with the cord still in his mouth. He'd given his life, but his mission had been a success: the device was rendered inoperable. As much as I hated the rats, I had to admit a certain degree of grudging admiration for them.

8

TO THEE, I CLING

IN THE SUMMER OF 1990, AFTER I'd been working for Nancy for a year, Pat prepared to move from Texas to Ann Arbor, Michigan. He'd been accepted at the University of Michigan Law School, and we talked about me joining him there.

Pat and I had been living in different states for more than eight months, and we were tired of having to travel back and forth to see each other. On the other hand, I knew Pat's first year of law school would be difficult, and I figured he'd have to spend most of his time in the library, leaving me to fend for myself in a town where I knew no one. Because I was earning much better money working for Nancy than I could in Michigan, there was another option: I could stay and work for her one more year and send Pat money each month to alleviate the burden of his law-school loans. Since I had met Pat, we had always eschewed the practical solutions and based our decisions on just being together. But this time we decided to be responsible, so we agreed that I'd stay with Nancy for the next nine months, then join Pat in Michigan in the spring of 1991, at the end of his first year of law school.

Nancy was pleased that I'd decided to stay, and we continued our daily movie/shopping/eating routine and, if anything, pursued it with greater enthusiasm. She was traveling much less, which made her even happier. And I was enjoying myself too, having fun with Nancy and looking forward to Pat's visits whenever he had school breaks.

Things were going well, but soon enough there came a glitch. After years of leaving the family finances to Nancy, Zubin suddenly began to take an interest in them. Up until now, as long as he was able to charge things on his American Express card, he didn't really care how the bills got paid. To Nancy's dismay, he began asking lots of questions, in particular about how the rental properties were faring.

For Nancy, the rental homes were never just a bottom-line enterprise. The business gave her something to do with her time and an identity that was separate from just being Mrs. Zubin Mehta. She also enjoyed taking care of her renters and was forever trying to improve the properties. One month, for example, she spent more on gardening and landscaping for one house than the lease would bring in for the whole year. When Zubin started focusing on the bottom line, problems were bound to ensue. On one of his rare visits home, he walked into our office and saw five people scurrying around the small space, jumping at Nancy's commands. Zubin shook his head before observing sarcastically that Nancy seemed to need "more people than Exxon" to run the business.

The Mehtas' personal and business books were kept by a young accountant who worked from her home. With Zubin poking around, Nancy apparently decided she'd like to have a little more control over the books. When she heard about a computer program that would allow her to do her accounting in-house, Nancy jumped at the opportunity. It seemed the perfect solution, except that she had no idea even how to turn on a computer. That's where the second part of the solution came in: Nancy wanted to hire me to keep the books for her.

Getting me to do the bookkeeping would solve three problems for Nancy. First, she could keep the bookkeeping at home. Second, she wouldn't have to learn the computer program herself. And third, it would provide a way of convincing me to stay. Nancy knew that I planned to leave for Michigan at the beginning of the summer, and she'd already begun trying to talk me out of it. She and I spent nearly every hour of the day together, and it would be hard on both of us to end that. But the difference was that I'd be leaving her to be with someone I loved. And Nancy would simply be left alone.

Apparently fearful of that possibility, Nancy began trying to undermine my relationship with Pat. "Lawyers and doctors invariably dump the women who help them through professional school," she told me. "Once they've gotten what they need, they look for younger women. You're just setting yourself up for a letdown." I knew she was only saying these things because she was upset and wanted me to stay, so I didn't take her comments seriously. Pat and I had been separated for a year and a half, and our plan to finally live together again was already set.

But Nancy upped the ante. If I'd stay for just one more year and help her establish the bookkeeping system, she told me, she'd pay me the accountant's hourly rate for every hour I spent working on the bills—in addition to my normal salary of $3,200 a month. At $30 an hour for the extra time, that would add up to a lot of money.

It was quite an offer. Since I had virtually no expenses, I'd have plenty of money to help out not only Pat, but my parents as well. And then I'd have enough left over for things I'd always wanted to be able to buy for myself. For the first time in my life, I would be making a sizeable income of my own, and I'd be in total control of how it was spent.

I didn't know what to say. This was a very generous offer, and if I accepted, it would put Pat and me on far better financial footing. Yet my life with Nancy was beginning to suffocate me. For the past six months, I had been with Nancy almost every minute, and except for those now-rare times when she was on the road with Zubin, I spent every day of my life feeling crowded, with nowhere to go. I still enjoyed being around Nancy most of the time; by now she was like a sister to me. But I had long ago lost the ability to have my own life. Also, Pat and I had now been apart for more than a year, and I was growing tired of carrying on a long-distance relationship. Pat was anxious for me to get to Ann Arbor, and I was equally anxious to go.

When I told Nancy that I really wanted to be with Pat now, she raised the stakes even further. If I would stay and accept the new position, she said, she'd pay to fly Pat out to California whenever he could come. If the offer was tempting before, now it seemed almost impossible to turn down.

Pat and I talked several times over the next few days, and we went back and forth with the pros and cons of Nancy's offer. There was much to consider—financial concerns, our relationship, our future—and the decision wasn't an easy one to make. In the end, we decided that my staying with Nancy for one more year seemed the smart long-term plan. When I told Nancy of our decision, she was ecstatic. She revealed that she'd asked her church congregation to pray for my decision and she promised that everything would work out wonderfully.

If ever there was a project doomed from the start, the great in-house bookkeeping plan was it. Shortly after retrieving the accounting books, Nancy made the comment that the former accountant had forged several checks, and therefore must have been stealing from her, but I was sure the accountant was no thief. After Nancy told several people on the phone about her suspicions and began debating whether or not to call the police, I asked her to show me the evidence.

Nancy produced a series of checks, all bearing her signature, that she believed were forged. As I looked at the checks, I noticed two things right away. First, the signatures were a little different from Nancy's normal one, but they were close enough that they could easily have resulted from Nancy's signing checks in a rush. Second, and more important, the checks in question had been written to cover Nancy's own bills.

"Why would the accountant forge your signature to cover your expenses?" I asked Nancy. Though I tried to explain to her why this made no sense, I could tell it didn't matter to Nancy in the least. She only seemed able to focus on two things: that the signatures were not hers (though they almost certainly were) and that she was angry with her former employee. Fortunately, I was able to talk her out of calling the police and she soon dropped the subject.

This was not the first nor the last time that Nancy would accuse someone of stealing from her. A few months before the "forgery" incident, Nancy had "discovered" that Ronnie, the houseman, had stolen money by using one of her credit cards to purchase furniture for a friend of his. I found out about this accusation after the fact, when Nancy informed me she was deducting money from Ronnie's paycheck each month to pay off the credit card.

I had actually been present when Nancy had told Ronnie he could use the credit card for the purchase in question. Confused, I went to Ronnie and inquired what was going on, asking, "Did you remind her that she said you could use it?" Ronnie, who'd been with Zubin and Nancy for more than twenty years, just smiled wanly and shook his head.

"What good would it do?" he said. "Once she has something in her mind, nothing I can say will ever change it." Ronnie had been with Nancy long enough to know that arguing with her would only make things worse. "The best thing to do," he said, "is just shut up, pay it off, and she'll get over it."

Despite the fact that Nancy regularly seemed to falsely accuse others of stealing from her, I never seriously considered that she would do the same to me. For one thing, I told myself, she didn't treat me like she did the others. To Nancy, people like Ronnie and Kate were just employees—people who were beholden to her for their jobs. But I was not just Nancy's assistant; I was her best friend.

On another occasion, Nancy was reading an *Architectural Digest* article about a well-known L.A. decorator when she suddenly went into a rage: Two of the pictures on the wall of the decorator's home belonged to her! "I gave them to him years ago to be reframed," she shouted. "And he never returned them!" Indignantly, she demanded that I get the decorator on the phone that minute.

I watched as Nancy loudly berated the decorator, then suddenly fell silent. Even standing a few feet away, I could hear the man's voice through the receiver: he was screaming at Nancy, telling her where he'd gotten the paintings and offering to show her his proof of ownership. In the middle of his rant, Nancy quietly hung up the phone and calmly went back to work. She never brought up the "theft" again. A year later, when we were cleaning out the basement, Nancy and I found the allegedly stolen pictures.

The Woman Who Wouldn't Talk

Perhaps the ugliest incident of all occurred the summer after I took the bookkeeping job. I had traveled to Italy with Nancy and Zubin, and we were staying in a beautiful hotel in Siena. After returning from Zubin's concert late that evening, we said our good nights and went to our respective rooms. An hour later, in a dead sleep, I was startled awake by the phone. I picked it up to hear Nancy ranting on the other end.

The jewels she'd left in her room were missing, she said, and it was obviously the work of the cleaning woman. "You need to come help me get them back," she said, and hung up. A few minutes later, I met Nancy in the hotel lobby, where she'd already launched into a full-scale tirade. She screamed at the hotel manager that she wanted the cleaning woman brought to the hotel immediately and the police to come and arrest her. The manager, trying to remain calm, promised that he'd question the woman when she came in for work the next morning—but not sooner.

Outraged at this response, Nancy stormed back to her room to pack her things and leave immediately. As she angrily swept up her shoe boxes in the closet, she suddenly caught a glimpse of her "missing" jewels in one box—right where she'd hidden them. When Zubin reminded her that she often hid her jewels in her shoe boxes, she snapped back, "The maid must have moved them there!"

Almost from the moment I agreed to accept the bookkeeping job, I was miserable. If we'd been tied together too tightly before, Nancy and I were now practically conjoined. For a few months in the fall of 1990, I did manage to rent an apartment in Malibu, which at least gave me some relief from all Nancy, all the time, and allowed me to relax a bit. But it didn't last long.

Nancy harangued me constantly about the apartment—saying, among other things, that everyone in Malibu looked unclean—and insisted that I spend most nights at her house. This became such a constant source of contention between us that, when my brother David moved to California after college, I decided just to let him have the apartment. It just seemed easier to give in to Nancy than to fight with her over the apartment every day.

Nancy had been dependent on me for a while, but now it seemed that our relationship was crossing a line into something truly unhealthy. I began trying to pull away from her, but the more I did, the more desperately she clung to me. Things were spinning out of control, as evidenced by Nancy's behavior whenever Zubin was in town.

Zubin was only in Los Angeles for two or three weeks a year, and during those times the phone would ring incessantly with invitations to dinners and events. The callers were often members of the Hollywood glitterati—stars like Richard Dreyfuss, Gregory Peck, Walter Matthau, and Michael York. But increasingly Nancy began trying to convince Zubin that, instead of joining Gregory Peck for a fabulous dinner at Spago, for example, we'd have much more fun if Zubin, Nancy, and I (and Pat if he was in town) just went out together.

This odd compulsion reached the height of absurdity on the night of Zubin's New Year's Eve performance in Los Angeles. Following the concert, we went to a dinner attended by scores of celebrities, a star-studded affair on the most festive night of the year. At the dinner, Nancy insisted not only that I sit at the same table as her, but that I sat literally right next to her. It didn't matter that we'd spent almost every morning, afternoon, and evening of the past year sitting within several feet of each other.

As the months went by, Nancy continued to cling, but I tended to feel more sorry for her than upset by it. I rationalized her behavior, figuring that everyone was entitled to their quirks. Besides, we did have a lot of fun together. Still, I couldn't wait for the times when Pat would visit—not only because I missed him, but because his visits provided me a slight respite from being around Nancy all the time. Though she was becoming increasingly jealous of our relationship (and probably resented paying for the flights), Nancy honored my time together with Pat and, for the most part, she left us alone at nights. But now, even that was about to change.

Pat was coming for his spring break, and I couldn't wait. We'd get to have more than a week alone together, spending hardly any time at all with Nancy. But she had other ideas. Without telling me, she arranged to take me on a whale-watching expedition to Cabo San Lucas, Mexico, leaving Pat alone in L.A. for the last four days of Pat's visit. She told me about the plans the night before Pat arrived, excitedly describing our fabulous beachfront hotel and the special yacht that would take us whale-watching in the Pacific.

"You are losing your mind!" I blurted. "Pat's flying halfway across the country to see me, and you think I'm going to just tell him, 'Thanks for coming. There's food in the fridge. I'll talk to you when I get back from Mexico'?"

Nancy seemed surprised by my response, but she recovered quickly. "If it's that important to you," she said, "I'll pay for Pat to go with us too." No matter what I said, I couldn't convince her that that wasn't the point. I didn't want to go to Mexico; I just wanted to be with Pat and I sure didn't look forward to trying to convince him to spend half of his hard-earned spring break playing Jacques Cousteau in Mexico with Nancy. There was no way in the world I was going to be able to talk him into going.

Actually, there was one way: I begged. "If we don't go with Nancy to Mexico," I told him, "she'll make my life miserable for the next month." I swore I'd never again complain about being dragged to another sporting event if Pat would please do me this one favor. Eventually he softened, and before he knew what had hit him, we were winging our way to Cabo.

The entire situation was made worse by the trip itself. Though Nancy had raved about the luxury accommodations and the chartered yacht that would take us to see the whales, the reality was far different. The hotel was certainly nice enough, but when we went to the dock to meet our special boat charter, there was no one there but a fisherman standing by what is commonly known in Arkansas as a bass boat. For those unfamiliar with the term, this is a craft about the length of a canoe, and only slightly wider. Powered by a small outboard motor, a bass boat is used almost exclusively on small lakes and ponds. As it turned out, this was our special charter. We were about to go out on the Pacific Ocean in a boat I wouldn't have taken on the log ride at Disneyland.

I looked at Pat for assurance that he wouldn't let us out on the ocean in this death trap, but I should have known better. He lived for doing stupid stunts like this, and he was already plopping himself down in the little boat. I sighed and climbed in next to him, feeling relatively sure that I would not be returning. Fortunately, the captain of the vessel had no illusions about its seaworthiness. For the next three hours, he rode us up and down the shoreline, at a depth where we'd be lucky to spot a school of goldfish, much less whales. Not that I was complaining—every time we threatened to veer away from the shore, I would ask Pat whether he could swim that far back with me draped around his neck.

During the summer of 1991, Zubin had contracted to conduct in Florence for a month, and he had arranged to rent a villa during his stay. Nancy was planning on joining him—which meant that I'd have an entire month on my own to catch my breath. But once again, Nancy had a different plan.

One night at dinner, she surprised me with the news that she'd bought me a ticket to Italy—and that I'd be able to spend the whole month of June working with her in Florence. I never would have guessed that one day I'd be crushed at the offer of a free trip to one of the most beautiful cities in the world. But I was. Desperate for some time alone, I would have been thrilled to give up Italy in exchange for peace and quiet.

By the time I got back from Italy, I had decided how I'd spend the extra money I was making: getting therapy. After three years with Nancy, I knew that our relationship was unhealthy, and now I needed a neutral party to tell me how I could fix it.

Logistically, it was difficult for me to see a psychiatrist. Every time I left the house, even if it was to run a simple errand, Nancy insisted on going with me. If I declined, she suggested having someone else go, so I could stay with her. As a Christian Scientist, Nancy didn't believe in doctors—and especially not psychiatrists—so I couldn't simply tell her what I was doing. Eventually, I learned to sneak out by telling Nancy I was meeting my brother Bill for lunch so we could talk privately about family issues.

The therapist confirmed what I already knew. Nancy, he said, had made me her husband in every sense except sexual. She had come to depend on me as a spouse since Zubin was absent. I knew this assessment was correct, but that didn't make it any easier to hear. Besides, I already knew that she depended on me—what I wanted was advice on how to get out of this kind of relationship. When I brought this up to him, he just shook his head and told me that there were no easy answers.

It was the summer of 1991, and I wasn't sure whether Nancy's behavior was becoming increasingly erratic, or whether therapy was just helping me to be more honest in my appraisal of her. Whatever the case, it was a banner year for bizarre events.

The first occurred when Nancy was on one of her rare trips out of town. A few months before she left, Nancy had discovered that her dog, Taras, had a sister, Tasha, who was being abused by the man who had adopted her. Nancy arranged to get Tasha away from her owner, and she came to live with us. Sweet, gentle Tasha was everything demented Taras was not. I fell in love with her from the beginning, and used to lecture the jealous, skulking Taras on how to be more like his sister.

Both Taras and Tasha slept in Nancy's bedroom most of the time, even when Nancy was away. One morning I climbed the stairs to the bedroom to find Tasha lying prone, her breath stilled, her limbs already stiff with rigor mortis. I ran to the office, where I hurriedly called Nancy in Europe. "Nancy!" I screamed into the phone, "Tasha is dead!"

To my surprise, Nancy was very calm—far calmer than I was. "Darling," she said, "the dog is not dead. Please don't say that."

"Nancy, she's not breathing. I checked," I told her. "She must have died last night, because she's already stiff as a board."

But Nancy was insistent. "Susan, please," she said. "Tasha is not dead. I'm going to begin praying for her," Nancy told me. "Put me on hold, go back up to the room, and let me know if she starts breathing again."

I put down the phone and looked at Monique, a part-time assistant we'd hired just a few days before. Monique was part African-American, part Hispanic, and all hilarious.

"She's praying for the dog to come back to life," I said. "She wants me to go back upstairs and see if Tasha has started breathing." I started to go, then turned back and said, "Come with me."

Monique looked at me as if I'd lost my mind. "Let me tell you something," she said. "Black folks don't go for that hocus-pocus shit. I'll go with you, but if that dog moves, I'm out of here."

We nervously climbed the stairs, not knowing what to expect and, more troubling, not knowing exactly what we hoped to see. While I desperately wanted Tasha not to be dead, I shared Monique's feelings—if that dog somehow came back to life, I was out of there.

When we walked gingerly into the room, I noticed for the first time the sickening smell of decaying flesh. It was instantly clear there would be no resurrection; the dog was definitely dead. I picked up the bedroom phone and told Nancy that nothing had changed. "Tasha's gone," I said.

Nancy's calm vanished. She screamed at me, "Don't keep saying that! Don't say that! You're blocking my prayers with your negativity!"

Unsure how to respond, I suggested gently that perhaps we should call a vet to come look at the dog. Although Nancy didn't believe in doctors, she did for some reason believe in veterinarians, and so she agreed to have one come look at poor Tasha. When I found one who agreed to make a house call, it took him about two seconds to make the diagnosis.

"The dog is dead," he announced. What's more, he theorized, it looked like Tasha might have been killed by the bite of a poisonous snake. I called Nancy again, confident that this expert conclusion would close discussion on the matter. Again, I had underestimated Nancy's resolve: even in the face of death itself, Nancy refused to give in. "Call another vet!" she barked. I duly complied, and to no one's great surprise, the second vet offered the same diagnosis as the first: Tasha was dead. When I called Nancy again to tell her the news, she refused to talk with me.

Later that same year, Nancy and I were shopping in Beverly Hills when we heard reports of riots breaking out in South Central Los Angeles over the verdict in the policemen's trial in the Rodney King incident. We returned home, parked ourselves in front of the TV, and watched as helicopter news teams offered a bird's-eye view of rampant burning, destruction, and looting in the city.

Suddenly Nancy leapt to her feet and said, "Let's go!" Assuming that she was referring to our regular dinner and a movie, I followed Nancy out to the car. But as we headed out of Brentwood and cruised toward the freeway, I suddenly realized she had another mission in mind. "Where are we going?" I asked her.

"We're going to South Central," she replied, "Maybe there is something we can do."

In my early days with Nancy, I probably would have thought she was kidding, but by now I knew her well enough to know she was quite serious. I also knew that I only had one hope of stopping her: I had to turn the whole thing into a joke.

"Nancy, you've got to be kidding!" I exclaimed. "What do you think is gonna happen when they see two white women in a Rolls-Royce, cruising the scene?"

She turned to look at me. "What do *you* think will happen?"

"I can tell you," I said, "They're going to drag us out of this car and beat the hell out of us before you ever have a chance to explain whatever it is you're trying to do. And I'm going to turn on you in a heartbeat. I'll be screaming, 'She's the rich one! Here's the aristocracy, right here! Off with her head!'" I yelled. "'I'm just her poor servant girl!'" That broke the spell. Nancy was now laughing hysterically. More important, she turned the car around and headed back to Brentwood.

Nancy's increasingly bizarre behavior worried me, and our relationship continued to be impossibly stifling. But as hard as it seems to believe now, I never seriously considered just walking away. For one thing, I knew I only had to last a few more months before I could then join Pat in Michigan. Perhaps the more important reason, however, was that I truly cared about Nancy and I wanted to help make her life more enjoyable, which I felt I was doing. Although she had some strange habits, I believed her heart was in the right place—and that was enough for me. Even when she did nasty things or made harsh accusations, I chalked them up to knee-jerk reactions she made when she was angry. I justified them by focusing on the fact that she usually corrected them after she calmed down.

In addition, I felt genuinely beholden to Nancy. Not only had she given me a large salary and numerous gifts, she also did her best to take care of me, especially whenever she could see I was upset. There were many days when I wanted to leave, but there were also a lot of fun days when I felt very close to Nancy. And frankly, over the three years I spent with her, the good days outnumbered the bad by a considerable margin.

But my opinion of Nancy finally began to change after she hired Monique. Over the years we'd hired temporary assistants whenever we had a large project or were getting behind on paperwork. With the addition of accounting duties, I was falling behind on my regular workload, and we needed someone full-time just for data input and filing. From the first time I met with Monique, I knew she was an ideal fit for our office. Not only was she bright, hardworking, and flexible, she also had the sense of humor essential to surviving Nancy. We hit it off immediately.

At first Nancy also seemed to like Monique Osby. She started including her on some of our social forays and would laugh uproariously as Monique, who was recently divorced, described in hilarious detail the many faults of men. Several weeks into Monique's employment, however, Nancy's attitude began to change. At first she started making sarcastic comments about the way Monique dressed or talked, and soon the complaints were aimed at her job performance. Monique was very anxious to please Nancy and worked very hard to do things right. Nancy, in turn, began making it impossible for Monique to do her job.

On more than one occasion, Nancy sent Monique on errands she knew she couldn't fulfill. She'd send Monique to a particular store to pick up a certain item—knowing that the store didn't carry it. Or she'd describe some item she wanted in detail, but when Monique returned with it, she'd snap, "No, that's not the right one!" She seemed to delight in sending Monique out to run the same errands over again, at which point she'd come complain to me about how incompetent Monique was.

I couldn't understand why this was happening. As far as I knew, Monique hadn't done anything to upset Nancy—and yet Nancy seemed to dislike her intensely. I tried to restore Monique to Nancy's good graces by praising her and telling her funny stories about how Monique and I were terrorizing Brentwood whenever she was out of town. But the more I sang Monique's praises, the nastier Nancy got about her.

Finally I realized the problem had nothing to do with Monique—it had to do with me. Nancy was jealous of the fact that Monique and I had formed a friendship and that, for the first time since I'd known Nancy, I now had a friend other than her. By constantly praising Monique, I was actually making the situation worse every day.

Nancy's treatment of Monique marked the turning point in our relationship. Up until then, I had always excused her outbursts as spur-of-the-moment flashes of anger that didn't reflect her true nature. But Nancy was cruel to Monique, who desperately wanted to please her. And her cruelty wasn't a onetime temper tantrum—it was an ongoing campaign to hurt and humiliate another human being for no reason. From that point on, I began to lose respect for her.

The extra year I'd promised Nancy was almost up, and I suggested that we start training someone to replace me. Nancy acted as though she was amenable to the idea, but whenever I tried to actually move forward on it, she shot down my efforts. I'd been with Nancy nearly three years now, and increasingly it began to seem that I'd never get away from her. Being with Nancy was like a habit I couldn't break, and she had no intention of making it easy for me. As the weeks ticked by, I began to feel depressed and trapped.

The final straw came late one afternoon in the spring of 1992. I had become violently ill while at work, suffering a high fever and vomiting repeatedly. Because Nancy adhered to the Christian Science belief that illness is a sign of weakness and sin, I didn't want to alert her to my situation—and I also didn't want to spend the night at her house.

During a rare moment when we were out of Nancy's earshot, I quietly asked Monique to drive me to my brother David's apartment. Before we could escape, however, Nancy intercepted us. "You're just fine," she told me, when I informed her why I was leaving. "Let's just stick to the plans we have for tonight"—dinner and movie. At Nancy's insistence, I stayed another half hour or so, but finally I couldn't take it anymore. I explained to Nancy that, whatever her beliefs were, I believed I was sick and needed to go to my brother's apartment to lie down.

After much huffing, Nancy at last reconciled herself to the fact that I was determined to leave. But she refused to let Monique take me, insisting that, if I was going to cancel the evening plans and go to my brother's, the least I could do is let her drive me there. Grateful she'd finally given in, I climbed into the car—only to watch as we sped right past my brother's apartment and headed toward the movie theater in Westwood.

"Nancy, I'm sick!" I whined "I can't go to the movies!"

"You're not sick!" she shot back. "If I could just get your mind off of it, you'd feel better." And with that, we wheeled into a parking space and headed into the theater.

I escaped to the lobby during the movie and called Pat in Ann Arbor. "Get out of there, Susan," he said. "Take a taxi and go to the twenty-four-hour clinic! You need to take care of yourself!" But I was too feverish to put up a fight. Instead, I sat through the entire movie, drifting in and out of consciousness.

Pat's second year of law school was coming to an end, and though he and I had been separated for three years, I had no idea how I could extricate myself from Nancy and join him without incurring Nancy's anger. Feeling increasingly trapped, I unloaded some of my frustrations on the Mehtas' attorney, Grant Gifford. "I feel smothered," I told him, and asked for his help in finding someone to take over my position so I could get on with my life.

After listening to me pour out my heart, Grant made a very prophetic comment. "This is not going to end well," Grant said.

Despite Grant's pessimistic prediction, I forged ahead with something I hoped might be a solution. It had to do with Pat's summer plans in Dallas.

During the summer of 1992, Pat was working in a ten-week summer associate program at a large law firm in Dallas. The program involved numerous social activities at which the associates were expected to bring wives or dates. "I need to be there with Pat," I explained to Nancy, "to make sure he's presenting the proper image." My plan was to hire a temporary replacement, spend the ten weeks in Dallas, and let Nancy get used to not having me around. I could then come back at the end of the summer, spend a few weeks finishing training the new person, and leave Nancy with everything in good shape. When I told Nancy my plans, she just smiled and acted as if we were discussing some fictional event.

Although I continued making references to spending the summer in Dallas and then joining Pat at Michigan, Nancy simply ignored them. Periodically she'd bring up things she was planning for us to do together that summer—and in the future. She was already making arrangements for us to make a return trip to Italy, and she even volunteered to loan me the money for a house in L.A. It was as if she thought that the Dallas story was something I was just telling Pat in order to keep him happy. She seemed unable to believe I would actually want to leave.

As my departure drew nearer, it finally started to dawn on her that I was actually going to Dallas. So she began coming up with alternative ideas. She told me that, as soon as she returned from Italy, she'd rent a place in Dallas and come help me impress Pat's supervisors. Then, if Pat ended up with a job in Dallas, I could just continue to work with her in Los Angeles during the week and fly to see him on the weekends. I could go ahead and have a baby, as Pat and I planned to do, and she would help me raise it in L.A. By now I had no idea how to respond to Nancy. The entire relationship had gotten way out of hand. For someone who thought she could always fix everything, I was now painfully aware that this was not fixable. Grant was right—there was no way this was going to end well.

Around Memorial Day weekend Nancy left for a month in Italy, and I headed to Dallas for two months. It would turn out to be one of the most remarkable periods of my entire life, for reasons I never expected.

Pat and my family had been warning me for months that my relationship with Nancy had gotten out of control, but I'd never taken their concerns that seriously. When I was with Nancy—and I was *always* with Nancy—things seemed a bit wild but manageable. But now that I was away from her, living a "normal" life in Dallas, it was as though I could at last see the relationship for what it truly was.

I'd recently seen a documentary on how cults operate, and it shocked me to realize the similarities to my life with Nancy. One brainwashing technique cults use, for example, is to never leave new recruits alone but to hover around them at all times—keeping them from having normal relationships with friends and family. With no down time to reflect, and no real input from outsiders, the recruits don't realize just how strange everything is getting. That's what had happened to me at Nancy's. I genuinely loved and cared about her—but now that I was away from her, I realized how completely she had overwhelmed me.

With no Nancy, I now had nothing but time to reflect on what had happened over the last three years—and the picture that presented itself was a frightening one. Pat and I had moved to California four years earlier for some rest and relaxation time—and instead Nancy Mehta had, with my permission, commandeered our lives.

But I couldn't simply blame the situation on Nancy. This was the second time in my life I'd let myself be drawn in by a strong, controlling person. Sitting in the quietude of our apartment in Dallas, I slowly began to realize that perhaps my predicaments didn't stem entirely from Jim's or Nancy's emotional problems, but from my own as well.

While Nancy was in Italy I was able to avoid her phone calls for a couple of weeks by faxing her a message that we didn't have our phone installed yet. When that was no longer credible, I began offering excuses about the time differential to keep the calls to a minimum. But I knew I couldn't keep Nancy at bay forever. Before, when she was on trips, she'd thought nothing of calling me twenty-five times a day. Now we were barely talking at all, only once every two or three days.

When she asked me whether I'd prepared for her arrival in Dallas, I finally tried to level with her. "I don't think it's a good idea for you to come to Dallas," I said. "My cousins are coming from Belgium," I told her, "and I'm going to have to spend most of my time entertaining them. I'm sure you understand." She did not. From that point on, the frequency of our telephone conversations decreased even more dramatically and, when we did talk, our exchanges were much more formal. I dreaded going back to L.A. after the summer, but I consoled myself with the knowledge that it was only for a short time and that I now had a much better perspective on our relationship and knew better than to let Nancy dominate my life again.

The summer ended too soon, and it was time for me leave Dallas.

I flew back to L.A., confident that it wouldn't take long to train Nancy's new assistant and get out again. I had taught Nancy most of the computer programs she would need, and she had even begun doing some of the bookkeeping herself. The new assistant, a young woman named Cynthia Meister, was ready to take over. I knew Nancy was hurt that I didn't want her coming to Dallas, but I hoped that, with time, any hard feelings would be smoothed over.

When Nancy met me at the airport, we immediately fell into the same pattern as always. We went straight from the airport to—what else—dinner and a movie. Then she dropped me off to spend the night at one of her rental houses. She hugged me good night and said, "We've got a lot of work to get started on in the morning!"

The next morning Nancy surprised me by not calling first thing to wake me up. When 9 o'clock and 10 o'clock went by with no word from her, I began to wonder what was going on. By 10:30 A.M., I had a distinctly uneasy feeling. This was not like Nancy at all. But at long last, she sent Ronnie to pick me up, and we drove to the house.

I walked in the front door to find the Mehtas' accountant, Alan Byron, and their attorney, Grant Gifford, sitting with Nancy in the rarely used living room. There's an old saying in poker that goes, "There's always one sap at every table. If you look to either side of you and don't see him, then you must be the sap." That's about how I felt at that moment. It was obvious that something was wrong, and no one else looked distressed.

Grant wasted no time getting to business. Nancy had discovered a credit card that she hadn't authorized, he said, and it appeared that I had been using it for my own personal purchases, with the Mehtas paying the bill. His tone was more inquisitive than accusatory, as though he expected I'd have an explanation. And I did: Not only had Nancy known about the credit card but most of the charges on it were for her benefit.

"Nancy," I said, "you knew about this credit card. Surely you're not denying that."

"I never knew anything about it," Nancy shot back.

I would have continued to protest, but having dealt with Nancy for over three years, I knew it would be futile. You simply didn't disagree with Nancy Mehta, especially in front of others, as the only result would be launching her into a screaming fit.

After our brief exchange, Nancy stood up and strode into the kitchen to get drinks for everyone. While she was gone, I explained to Grant and Alan the way the credit card system worked. At Nancy's suggestion, she had arranged to pay me for my bookkeeping duties by giving me this credit card to use, with the idea that she'd offset the purchases against my earnings. If they'd look at the accounting records, they'd see two things: first, I'd never been cut a single check for my bookkeeping work. And second, my credit card charges almost exactly mirrored my earnings.

Alan had already gone over the books, and he quickly confirmed for Grant that he'd never seen any checks paid to me for bookkeeping. It was, therefore, entirely possible and rational that I might be getting paid through the use of this credit card. Both Alan and Grant seemed to breathe a sigh of relief.

But Nancy was not finished embarrassing me in front of them. She went on a rant about how she could no longer trust me. It would have been an Academy Award performance except that Nancy was no Sarah Bernhardt.

When Nancy finished ranting about how I'd betrayed her, and I still refused to do battle with her, Grant and Alan gratefully took the opportunity to leave. After they'd gone, Nancy led me into the kitchen, gave me a warm hug, and said, "Don't worry. Everything's going to work out." Ronnie would take me back to the rental house, she said, and we would talk again in the morning. She then handed me a gift-wrapped box.

"I hope you like it," she said. "It's a purse I saw in Italy. It reminded me of you."

I stood in stunned silence as Nancy walked out of the room. The whole thing had been an act. Now that she'd sufficiently chastened me, she assumed that I'd do anything to get back in her good graces—including coming back to work for her for good. I had seen her pull this stunt before, on people who depended on Nancy for a good portion or all of their income. There might actually have been a time when this would have worked on me. That time was gone.

I called Pat, who was still in Dallas, and told him what had just happened. Over the years I had come to depend on Pat's advice, as his instincts were generally good and he tended to be calm and rational in the face of adversity. But this time his temper took over. Already unhappy that I'd returned—even just for a month—to the cult, he said, "Go to the airport and get on a plane to Dallas. Get out of there right now." He was livid over Nancy's accusations and didn't want me staying there even a minute more. Unsure of what to do, still in shock from what had transpired that morning, I took his advice. When I got in the car with Ronnie to go back to the rental house, instead I said, "Take me to the airport."

Looking back, I've often thought that if I'd just stayed and talked things out with Nancy the next morning, the entire ugly aftermath would never have happened. But by getting on that plane, and leaving without a word, I had defied Nancy and even humiliated her. Ronnie had once told me, "Nobody walks out on Nancy Mehta." I had just become the first.

I flew back to Dallas, and Pat and I then went to Ann Arbor for his last year of law school. Just as we'd planned (and failed) to do four years earlier, we hoped to start a life together, free of the influence of any domineering third personalities. This time, we succeeded.

The next year of my life was a little like being in detox. It was also the most normal year I had spent since I was a sophomore in college. I got a job at the University of Michigan Law School working as an assistant to a woman I liked and respected, Roberta Nierson-Low. I loved the city of Ann Arbor, and even enjoyed the wintry climate, which made for good cuddling weather. Pat, however, with his unerring ability to kill a romantic ideal, wasn't nearly as fond of the cold, and kept turning the thermostat up to 85 degrees. Since I couldn't stand having the heat on and wanted the windows open full-time, we compromised by spending much of our time building fires in the fireplace. Unfortunately, neither one of us was particularly adept at the art of building a fire. In the space of nine months, we managed to burn up a footstool, set three small fires on the carpet, and set off the fire alarm approximately a dozen times. The tenants in the apartment above us eventually fled for their own safety.

After Pat graduated from law school in the spring of 1993, we moved to Nashville, where he had accepted a job with the local public defender's office. This was the perfect job for him, as he loved the excitement of being in a courtroom. And moving to Nashville was ideal as well, since Pat's brother, Ronnie, was a well-respected lawyer there and had a sizable house we could stay in until we got on our feet.

The only real drawback to staying with Ronnie was that the Harris brothers shared a demented fanaticism for anything related to the University of Arkansas football and basketball teams. Pat and Ronnie were the most polite, reserved Southern gentlemen you'd ever want to meet—until a Razorback game came on. Then they turned into raving lunatics. At times I swore they were foaming at the mouth. I also learned to cheer loudly for the Razorbacks because I soon learned that the entire atmosphere in the house for the coming week was going to be dictated by the outcome of the game.

The time we spent in Nashville was the life I'd been dreaming about for years. Nashville is a friendly, family-oriented town, and Pat's family took me in. For the first time since I'd left Arkansas, I felt like I had a real home.

I quickly became close friends with Ronnie's wife, Carolyn, who was down-to-earth, extremely well-read, and possessed of a quick wit. I used to love sitting around the kitchen with Carolyn, griping about the Harris boys. I also loved Ronnie and Carolyn's children, Charlie, Sarah, and Susan. The three kids had amassed numerous scholastic, athletic, and artistic awards—all without getting into even a hint of trouble (that we knew of, anyway). I once told Carolyn that she should quit her job and write a primer on how to raise perfect children.

For the first time, I was leading the kind of life June Cleaver would have envied. Pat would come home from his job, I would cook dinner, and then we'd go to see Sarah's school play, Susan's dance recital, or Charlie's basketball game—or maybe just sit around eating cheese dip and playing Trivial Pursuit. I worked sporadically at temp jobs when we needed extra income, but they were all very low pressure positions.

I desperately needed this downtime, and I loved seeing Pat so happy. We'd been through a long haul, but now—eight years after we'd begun dating—we could finally get married and settle down to start our own family. On weekends we began to look at potential wedding sites and make plans for our wedding.

At Thanksgiving of 1993, as I drove back to Camden, I remember thinking that I had more to be thankful for than at any time in recent memory. Pat was rising rapidly in the public defender's office, the wedding plans were progressing nicely, and I'd just started a new job working for a doctor at Vanderbilt Hospital. This was President Clinton's first year in office, and questions about Whitewater had created a few ripples—but the story had quickly died.

Cruising down I-40, I was singing loudly to country-and-western stations and thinking about how to coordinate all the Henley and Harris family members for our wedding. It had been an unseasonably warm fall in the South, and the crisp autumn weather we expected in October was just beginning to arrive in late November. This was truly the best of times. Within hours, my life would change forever.

9

THE REINCARNATION OF MA BARKER

I ARRIVED HOME FOR THANKSGIVING IN 1993, not only excited about the future, but thankful that, for the first time in several years, my entire family would be together for the holiday. When I walked into my parent's house, my father jumped up to greet me, but my mother seemed unusually reserved. At the first opportunity, she pulled me into another room and asked me what was going on.

"A man called here looking for you," she told me. "He said he was from the FBI. He wanted to ask you questions about Whitewater." Unsure whether the man was really an FBI agent, my mother had refused to tell him where I was or how to reach me. He'd continued to press her, but she wouldn't budge. Finally, he'd offered an inducement: if I would agree to contact him and answer questions, he said, he would see what he could do about the criminal charges filed against me in California.

On hearing the words "criminal charges" and "California," I felt like I'd had the breath knocked out of me. It had been a year and a half since I left California, but I knew instantly that all this had to be related somehow to Nancy Mehta. Suddenly nauseous, my head reeling, I tried to take in what my mother was saying without betraying the panic I felt. I knew that if I showed any concern, it would ruin the holiday.

"Oh, is that all?" I responded, grasping for something reassuring to say. "Don't worry, Mom. I got a speeding ticket in L.A. a couple of years ago that I must have forgotten to pay. They probably issued a warrant for my arrest for failing to pay it or for not showing up for court. I'll get Pat to take care of it after the holiday."

My mother knew me well enough to know I would hide bad news in order to protect her. And I knew her well enough to realize she was just pretending to go along with my explanation. After some of the other family members arrived, I snuck away to a phone and called a lawyer I knew in Little Rock, Sam Heuer. "Can you find out what's going on?" I asked him. A few minutes later, he called me back with the news: California authorities had issued a warrant for my arrest for embezzling $150,000 from Nancy Mehta. Not only was I being charged with nine counts of embezzlement, fraud, and grand theft, but the prosecution also included three counts of state income tax fraud for not having paid taxes on the income I had allegedly embezzled.

"This has to be a mistake," I told Sam. I just couldn't believe that nearly two years after I'd left California, Nancy would suddenly file charges—especially for something she knew I hadn't done!

"Don't do anything, and don't call anyone," Sam advised me. "Just hold off until I find out more about what's going on."

Though my mother was thrown into a panic by the FBI agent's asking about Whitewater, that was a secondary concern for me at the moment. A low-grade buzz about Whitewater had been going on for some time already, and because there was nothing to the story, I figured it would just die out. But the idea that Nancy Mehta had filed charges against me was devastating.

I decided to let Sam handle whatever needed to be done—if anything—regarding potential Whitewater questioning. The one thing I cared now about was getting a lawyer in California so I could find out what Nancy had done.

I didn't know any attorneys in L.A., but one of Ronnie's law partners recommended Leonard Levine, an attorney he'd met while working on the case involving the death of actor Vic Morrow on the movie set of *The Twilight Zone*. Pat called Leonard, who agreed to represent me—and, thankfully, gave me some time to raise the funds I'd need to pay him. Leonard made arrangements for me to surrender and have a bail hearing in Los Angeles the week after Christmas.

As Christmas of 1993 approached, and families across the country made plans to gather together for the holidays, Pat and I made plans to drive to California for me to be arrested. Since our car wasn't running well, I borrowed my sister-in-law Glenda's brand-new van. We set off for the long drive the day after Christmas.

When we arrived at the Santa Monica police station, I learned that, even though I'd turned myself in voluntarily, the police had no plans to make my arrest any less unpleasant. For the first time, I watched as an officer snapped handcuffs around my wrists. It was a surreal moment, arousing feelings of intense fear, humiliation, and frustration all at once. He then took me to a holding cell inside the courthouse while I waited for my hearing. A few minutes later, three or four more officers wandered into the area and he yelled at them to come over and "take a look at this one. She's all dressed up with nowhere to go."

When it came time for my bail hearing, I was led into the courtroom in handcuffs. I couldn't look at Pat—I was too ashamed. I'd been told that I would likely be released on my own recognizance, and a minimal bail was set. Pat and I paid it and got out of the courthouse as soon as we could.

I was free to return to Nashville as soon as the arraignment was finished, but instead of rushing right back, Pat and I stayed a few days with my brother Bill at his Malibu apartment. We made plans to go out with him on New Year's Eve, but when that evening rolled around, I didn't feel much like celebrating. I asked Pat if we could just head back to Nashville and he agreed. We packed up our things and got in the van to start the long drive home that night.

Driving across the desert, we found ourselves stuck in the heavy traffic headed to Las Vegas. It was depressing enough to be spending New Year's Eve in a traffic jam in the desert, but the situation was made even worse because, no matter how many times we promised not to discuss the Mehta charges, one or both of us would invariably begin talking about them. We were reliving the entire three years all over again. Suddenly, as we were stopped dead on the interstate, we felt a jolt and heard a sickening crash. We'd been rear-ended by a car driven by an uninsured drunk driver who spoke almost no English. Thankfully, the van sustained only moderate damage, but because it was borrowed—and brand-new—I felt miserable about the accident. "Great," I thought. "Now I can go home and tell Glenda that I've screwed up again."

At that moment, it seemed like everything I touched somehow managed to turn into disaster. In the course of just a week, I had been arrested, handcuffed, thrown into a holding cell, humiliated in a public courthouse, and, now, involved in an automobile accident in the middle of the desert. As I stood by the side of the highway, looking up at the vast universe of stars in the black night sky, I thought, "Things cannot get any worse." I wasn't even close.

Less than two weeks later, on January 12, 1994, President Clinton requested the appointment of a special prosecutor to investigate Whitewater. In truth, the announcement barely even registered on the outermost fringes of my mind. I was still reeling over the Mehta charges and was unable to focus on much else. When I did think about it at all, I thought the investigation would be a good thing. The rumors about Whitewater had been simmering for a couple of years already, and a true investigation, would quickly reveal that no one, including the Clintons, had done anything wrong.

But if it seemed unimportant to me, much of the country—and the media—felt otherwise. As soon as the special-prosecutor story broke, a few dozen reporters suddenly materialized outside our front door in Nashville. Both Pat and his brother Ronnie advised me not to answer any media questions unless and until I was called in by the special prosecutor. Yet the press continued to gather outside each day, in case I had a change of heart and wanted to talk.

The media has become one of the more reviled institutions in this country, but for the most part I found the press contingent to be very considerate and polite. Despite the fact that we've all seen footage of reporters crowding around their subject, screaming questions and thrusting cameras in their faces, the reporters respected my refusals to speak and didn't push the issue. In fact, I was always impressed by their dedication and professionalism: when I'd be sitting in our cozy house in Nashville, they were sitting in the freezing cold, waiting for hours on the off chance that I might suddenly have something to say.

For several days, one reporter in particular—Chris Vlasto of ABC News—cut a particularly sympathetic figure as he sat in the cold in a rented van outside our house. Even after all the others had given up and left, Vlasto would periodically trudge up to the front door and ask if I'd speak to him for "just one minute." My response was always the same: we'd give him a cup of coffee and send him back to his van. But Vlasto was so persistent and so very courteous that several times I came close to talking to him, even though I knew that I really did not have anything newsworthy to say. I simply did not know anything the Clintons had done wrong, but no one was interested in hearing me say that. A couple of years later, I would learn the hard way that Vlasto's driving motivation had less to do with getting the true story than with his intense personal hatred of the Clintons. The courtesy he was showing me in Nashville was the same as the snake showed Eve right before he offered her the apple.

For a while, I couldn't figure out why the press was so interested in me. Then a news producer who wanted me to appear on his show explained it to me. There were four people who knew what went on in Whitewater, he said. Two of them were in the White House, and they weren't going to be talking any time soon. The third one, Jim McDougal, was a self-described con artist and eccentric. That left me. Many reporters considered me the only person who could help them bust the Whitewater story, which, no matter how mundane, was the closest thing to Watergate they had going. So they camped out in our driveway, dreaming of becoming the next Woodward or Bernstein.

Despite the increasing media attention, I did everything I could to stay out of the limelight. Every day, our phone rang incessantly with calls from people urging me to tell my story—Diane Sawyer, Barbara Walters, Connie Chung, and other big-name TV journalists continually tried to get me on their shows. And I was also receiving calls from tabloid TV shows and magazines offering to pay me money to talk.

I turned them all down and asked them not to call back. I just wanted to be left alone and allowed to go back to the life I was building. Years later, after I had refused to cooperate with the Office of the Independent Counsel (OIC), Kenneth Starr accused me of enjoying the attention and appearing on every television show that would have me. I did use the media later on to fight back, but only after Starr had dragged me into the spotlight. In the beginning I did everything I could to stay out of sight.

Having the crowds parked outside my house was difficult enough, but a larger personal crisis developed when a CNN reporter tracked me down at my new job at Vanderbilt Hospital. The reporter came into the hospital, camera crew in tow, looking for an interview. The hospital management had no desire to have camera crews prowling around the corridors or the notoriety of having an employee who was the subject of a media scandal. Unwilling to put up with the media frenzy, they let me go.

Now unemployed, with my legal expenses in the Mehta case climbing daily, and a virtual prisoner in my own home, I found myself with a lot of time to reflect on my life. A year earlier, Pat and I had been living an idyllic existence, and we'd been ready to get married and start our family. Now I was accused of stealing money from a former employer in California and engendering the hatred of people I'd never met.

As the days went by and my life became increasingly surreal, I began to seriously question my own judgment, and I found myself wondering whether or not I was the person I had always believed I was. I began to consider whether I had serious emotional problems. There was, after all, one common denominator to all the messes I blamed on Nancy Mehta and Jim McDougal: me.

I also became increasingly anxious as the Mehta trial approached. If it came down to Nancy's word against mine, I realized that no jury would ever believe me. She was the rich wife of a world-famous conductor—and I was now seen by many people as a crooked accomplice to Bill Clinton's alleged crimes. Day after day, I sat in the house and brooded about how I had so completely screwed up my life. And the more I thought, the more afraid I became. Soon I found myself putting on a mask of sanity while dealing with others, while inside I was coming apart.

After a few weeks, the media frenzy died down, and later that winter Pat and I moved to a rented home in the Bellevue section of Nashville. One afternoon, the cable man was supposed to come and hook up our TV. As someone who watches sports religiously, Pat cared more about having working cable TV than he did about running water or telephones, so it was imperative that I make sure the cable guy got the job done. After waiting for most of the morning, I was happy to at last hear the doorbell ring. I opened it to find a pleasant-looking young cable installer standing on the doorstep.

The installation proved to be a complicated affair. The cable man was there for the better part of two hours, during which time we carried on a running conversation on topics ranging from finding affordable housing in Nashville to the best local place for Mexican food. Then, seemingly out of nowhere, the cable man blurted out, "Well, ol' Bill Clinton's really got himself in a mess with all this Whitewater stuff, doesn't he?"

I was not about to be dragged into a discussion of Whitewater, so I just smiled and made some offhand comment about not keeping up much with the story.

But the cable man went on, warming to the subject. He began rambling about "sweetheart deals" and then ventured that he thought Hillary had a lot more to do with the whole thing than any of us knew. All the while he kept trying to draw me into the conversation too, asking my opinion about the whole affair.

I continued to deflect his questions, then suddenly had a terrible thought: what if this guy wasn't really a cable man? What if he was an OIC plant, sent here to pry information out of me? After all, he seemed to be inordinately interested in Whitewater and my opinions about it. And from what I could tell, he didn't seem to know much about cable installation.

Then I had another thought: what if this guy was here to bug my phones? I'd recently read a book about John Gotti, and remembered the part describing how the FBI had sent fake "phone installers" to bug his house. Pat and I had just moved into this house. Had the FBI followed me here to bug it? As the cable guy chatted away, I wrestled with whether I should ask him to leave. But I knew Pat was desperate for his cable TV, and I could just see myself explaining to him that the reason we didn't have it yet was because I was sure the cable guy was an undercover FBI agent.

In the past I'd always made fun of conspiracy theorists. But now my mind was running wild with thoughts of telephone bugging, stake-outs, and tailings. I felt my panic rising and left the room to try and compose myself. *You're being ridiculous*, I thought. *So what if the cable guy is asking questions about Whitewater? It's in the news, after all.* After a few deep breaths, I returned to the living room, just as the cable guy said, "I'm sorry, but there's a problem with the wiring to the house. I'm going to have to get a special part and come back again."

That was it. Now I was convinced: this guy didn't know the first thing about cable installation! I just knew that when I called the cable company after he left, they'd say that the real installer was still on his way. As I opened the door to let the man out, I happened to glance down the street. I almost jumped out of my skin. Parked on the street, less than fifty yards from my house, was a van with a big satellite dish on top. This was obviously the communications vehicle.

In a panic, I slammed the door shut and tried to think of what to do next. I needed to call Pat—but now the phones were bugged! I had to get to a pay phone—or perhaps I could call him from here but somehow inform him in code what was going on. Frozen with fear, unsure what to do, I was paralyzed. I decided just to wait quietly until he came home from work.

A couple of hours went by, and the doorbell rang. I looked out the window to see the same cable guy standing on the front doorstep.

I opened the door. "I'm back to finish the job," he said. "I stopped by the office and got the part so you could have your cable by tonight."

While we were talking on the front step, I saw another man lock the door of the satellite van and begin walking toward the house next door. When he saw us, he turned and walked across the lawn to greet me.

"Hi!" he exclaimed. "You must be the new neighbor. Welcome to the neighborhood!"

We exchanged a few pleasantries, and I slyly got to the point. "I notice you have a satellite van parked in front of your house," I said. "Any particular reason?"

"Yeah," he responded. "I work as a broadcast technician for Channel 5 news here in Nashville. Sometimes I bring the truck home with me. I hope that's not a problem."

Taking a couple of steps out onto the lawn, I could see the bright red Channel 5 logo painted on the side of the van. "No problem at all," I said, then took the cable guy into the house to finish the job.

An hour later, after he'd left, having successfully hooked up the cable, I put my head in my hands and started laughing hysterically. I wasn't sure if I was demonstrating a good sense of humor or just cracking up.

The year 1994 is a total blur in my memory. Although I worked a few temp jobs here and there, for the most part I was sleepwalking through life. The press frenzy around Whitewater had subsided, and Pat and I were living quietly in Nashville. But about every two months or so, I was jarred back into reality by having to travel to California to make a court appearance for the Mehta trial.

Though things were moving forward to trial, I still halfway believed either that the charges would be revealed as having no merit or that Nancy would decide she'd extracted enough revenge and drop the case. The Mehta case was already a huge financial burden, and the longer it went on, the worse it became. We'd already borrowed money from both my parents and Pat's parents. And thanks to his brother's help, Pat was also able to take out a sizable loan that went a long way to paying Leonard Levine. But I didn't know how long we could keep this up. I couldn't get a full-time job with a felony trial hanging over my head, and Pat couldn't keep taking time off from work to go with me to California every couple of months. Something had to give.

Pat and I decided to talk to Leonard about making an unheard-of move for a criminal defendant: I would agree to an interview with the prosecutor if he would agree to investigate my assertions—and, if he determined that I was telling the truth, he would drop the case. Since whatever I said in an interview could later be used against me, this was a defense lawyer's nightmare. But I didn't care. I knew I was telling the truth, and I just wanted this fiasco stopped before Pat and I were completely broke.

Leonard was against the idea, but he agreed to approach District Attorney Jeffrey Semow. As a former D.A. himself, Leonard was quite confident that Semow would leap at the chance to have a "freebie" interview with the defendant. But to our surprise, Semow declined. This made no sense at all—we were offering Semow a golden opportunity with no downside, a prosecutor's dream, and yet he wasn't interested. For the first time we began to wonder exactly what was driving this indictment.

One explanation lies in the personality of Jeffrey Semow himself. Semow was a twenty-five-year veteran of the Los Angeles D.A.'s office who, despite his length of service, had never been assigned to any of the high-profile cases that regularly drift through the offices of that celebrity-laden city. According to people within Semow's office, this fact rankled him to no end.

While other L.A. prosecutors were becoming minor celebrities themselves, Semow had been left to toil in the mundane world of regular criminals. According to one person who knew Semow, he was especially upset that his name never even came up amid speculation as to who would prosecute the O. J. Simpson case. So when my case came up, he was not about to let it slip by him. Even Semow's own brother reportedly said that he regularly bragged at family holidays that the Mehta case would make his career.

Semow, who was in his early fifties, looked no older than thirty-five and could probably have even passed for being in his late twenties. Pat always insisted he was a dead ringer for Ned Flanders, the self-righteous neighbor on the animated series, *The Simpsons* ("Hididelyeo, neighbor!"). Either way, there was one thing we could agree on: Semow clearly had worked himself into a frenzy over this case.

Before one hearing, Semow and Leonard stood in the hall outside the courtroom discussing procedural details. Semow asked whether Leonard had talked to me about the possibility of waiving a jury trial and just letting the judge hear the case. "We discussed it," Leonard said. "But Susan won't agree to it."

Semow exploded. "You tell that fucking bitch that if she won't agree to it, I'm going to start fighting every motion for continuance!"

Semow obviously didn't realize that Pat was sitting nearby and could hear every word of the exchange. Pat was momentarily stunned. Having dealt with prosecutors for the past year, he understood that they sometimes become emotionally involved in cases—but no prosecutor in his or her right mind would start publicly cursing a defendant. The prosecutor's role in the judicial system is to seek justice, not to go after someone for personal reasons. Semow, with his profane eruption, had stepped way over the line.

Pat's moment of being stunned quickly gave way to anger. One of the things that I love about Pat is that he hates the idea of anyone being picked on or treated unfairly.

When Pat sat next to me in the courtroom as the hearing began, I could tell something was wrong, but he refused to tell me what it was. Then, when the hearing ended, Leonard and Semow went outside to discuss further details. Before I knew what was going on, Pat had broken up the meeting by getting up in Semow's face.

"Don't you *ever* call Susan a 'fucking bitch' again," he shouted. "Who the hell do you think you are? What kind of a prosecutor are you?"

Semow was totally taken aback. As a prosecutor, he was probably used to wielding all the power and being sucked up to on a regular basis—it's unlikely he had ever been confronted quite like this before. Also, Pat was bigger than Semow, and it appeared he was not in total command of his temper at that moment.

Caught off guard, Semow followed his gut instinct: he lied. "I never called her that," he retorted. But as soon as he'd said it, he looked sheepishly at Leonard, who knew it was a lie. Leonard stepped between them to avoid any further unpleasantness, but Pat stood his ground, demanding an apology. Instead of giving one, Semow turned on his heel and yelled back at Pat, "Don't you ever speak to me or come near me again." He stormed out while Leonard restrained Pat from going after him.

In the summer of 1994, it looked as though the Whitewater investigation would die the quiet death it deserved. Hearings in the House and Senate were winding down, Independent Counsel Robert Fiske hadn't been able to find any wrongdoing, and the furor in Washington seemed finally to be ebbing.

Then, on August 5, Fiske was inexplicably removed from his post and replaced by Kenneth Starr. I thought it was strange to remove Fiske—especially since he'd begun announcing his findings just a month before—but I was ready to give Starr the benefit of the doubt.

But from that point, the Whitewater investigation spun out of control. It seemed to be taking on a life of its own. Though I was still not involved in any direct way with the investigation, I did keep an eye on the hearings and various reports. But I was far more worried about the Mehta trial, as it continued to threaten our future.

By the beginning of 1995, Pat and I faced a painful decision. His career in the Nashville public defender's office had taken off—he'd been promoted to one of the plum assignments in the office and now was handling felony cases before one of the best judges in the county. He loved his work, his boss, Karl Dean, and the group of young lawyers he worked with. Within a year or two he felt he would be ready to establish his own practice and start making good money.

But despite what we had hoped, the Mehta case was not going to just go away. In addition to the expense of having to travel so often back and forth to California, we needed to raise another $50,000 to pay Leonard for the trial.

At the preliminary hearing, Leonard had done a terrific job of cross-examining the detective on the case, Ignacio Gonzalez. He'd uncovered numerous inconsistencies in what Nancy had told the detective (because of a recent change in California law, Nancy would not have to testify at the preliminary hearing herself, so Gonzalez's testimony was key.) These inconsistencies would later be a cornerstone of my defense at the trial. By then, Leonard would no longer be my attorney because we simply could not afford him, but his work was central to the defense we ultimately mounted.

On the way back from one of our California trips, Pat came up with a temporary solution. "Let's move to California until the trial's over," he said. He would ask his boss for a hiatus, and we could go to L.A. and put our full effort into fighting the charges. If we worked together, Pat reasoned, we could organize the case and do the majority of the trial preparation, thus saving ourselves tens of thousands of dollars. Although I hated to leave Nashville and the future we were building, it didn't seem like we had much choice. I was beyond making any decisions so I just agreed with whatever Pat suggested.

Before we got a chance to go, however, I found myself directly involved in the Whitewater investigation for the first time. Though my name had frequently been mentioned—usually in the context of Madison Guaranty, which was now being fingered as one of the most corrupt financial institutions in the nation—I had taken no active role in any of the proceedings. But in March 1995, the OIC invited me to come to Little Rock, meet with their attorneys, and answer questions.

One of the persistent misconceptions about my role in the White-water investigation was that I refused to cooperate with the OIC from the beginning. That was absolutely false. When I was invited to Little Rock to meet with their attorneys, I actually looked forward to it. I had seen some of the Whitewater hearings on television and I felt that there were a lot of false statements and ridiculous rumors, particularly about Madison, that I could help clear up. I had no qualms about answering any question they could ask. I wanted to get this over with and have Whitewater out of my life.

Pat and I briefly flirted with the idea of having him represent me at the meeting, but we thought at the time that his having worked at Madison might make him a potential target of the investigation. So we decided to find an Arkansas attorney, preferably one who had ties to the local community and knew his way around an Arkansas courthouse.

The attorney we chose was Bobby McDaniel. A criminal defense and medical malpractice attorney from the northeast Arkansas town of Jonesboro (the town that later gained national notoriety when two schoolboys shot a number of their classmates), Bobby came highly recommended as someone who was a down-home Arkansan as well as a tough negotiator.

Bobby also had a rock-solid sense of what was the right and moral thing to do. He believed very strongly in the judicial system and fought like hell for the rights of his clients, even when it was unpopular to do so. I was lucky to have found Bobby, who even graciously agreed to represent me pro bono, as Pat and I were now financially tapped out by the Mehta case.

The night before the meeting, Pat spent time preparing me for the questions the attorneys might ask. "Just tell the truth," he told me. "Don't let them twist your words." One favorite interrogation trick, he warned, was to ask the same question repeatedly during the course of an interview, phrasing the question just a little differently each time, in the hope that the subject will eventually give conflicting answers that could then be used against them. He also warned me about talking too much. I obviously could answer some questions about Madison Guaranty and Whitewater, but I did not know many of the details about how either business had been run and he did not want me guessing or speculating as to what happened. He ended our session with one final admonition: "Just tell them what you know—you don't have to try and make them love you like you do everybody else."

Bobby and I, along with Claudia Riley, drove to the OIC's office in Little Rock, which was, coincidentally, located in the same building where Jim and I had set up the first Madison Guaranty office. We were escorted into a rather drab conference room with a large rectangular table. The OIC staff members, four attorneys, and two FBI agents were all seated on one side of the table, and when we came in, the lead attorney, Steve Lerman, gestured to Bobby and me to come sit on the same side of the table with them. I assumed it was meant as a friendly gesture to show that we were all on the same side. Bobby smiled and the proceeded to take my arm and seat us directly opposite from the OIC.

After very brief introductions, Lerman started the meeting: "We think that we have come up with what we consider to be a good plan. This is what we do for a living and we are very good at it."

He then placed his hand atop a foot-high pile of documents that had been placed in the middle of the table. "This stack of papers," he said, "represents potential evidence of several crimes Susan McDougal committed while at Madison Guaranty." If their intention was to get my attention, they had succeeded. I had come in thinking that I was going to answer a few questions and was now being told that I was a target of the investigation.

Bobby calmly said, "May I see those papers?"

But Lerman took his hand and pushed the papers to the side, away from Bobby. "We're not here to talk about potential criminal action," he said, his voice slightly lower. "We want to know whether or not your client is willing to make a proffer in this case, and, if so, what information she can give us."

I had no idea what a proffer was, so Bobby leaned over and explained that it was basically a written statement as to what I could testify to about the case, in particular any illegal activity that I might have witnessed. Typically, he said, a proffer is the first step toward obtaining a grant of immunity. The better the proffer, the more likely the person will receive immunity.

When Bobby had finished this thirty-second primer, I remember thinking, *What a dumb system*. If a person is guilty, and he's offered immunity only if he can come up with a proffer, then he'll naturally be inclined to make it as juicy as possible. It immediately occurred to me that under this system, there was no obvious way to prevent a guilty person from simply telling grandiose lies against another person—one who might well be innocent—in order to save his own skin.

The proffer concept seemed flawed, but I was more than happy to provide one if that's what the OIC wanted, and I told Bobby that. In turn, he announced to the lawyers that "Susan's ready to tell you everything she knows about Whitewater and Madison Guaranty." Across the table, six faces lit up with smiles. "However," he hastily added, "we want a grant of full immunity first."

Bobby knew the OIC was unlikely to grant this request, but after a few minutes of discussion, the lawyers said that they were very intent on obtaining my cooperation. In return, they went on, the OIC was willing to consider a grant of "global immunity." Global immunity? What the hell did they mean by global immunity? As if things weren't bad enough, now it sounded like I was an international terrorist. I may not have been a lawyer, but I had a pretty good idea that this was a not-so-veiled reference to the Mehta case, a fact that Bobby confirmed.

"I don't need your help," I snapped. I'd promised Bobby I'd let him speak for me, but this was too much. "Those charges are bogus. I don't need you to take care of anything."

"Susan," Bobby interjected. "Stop!" But it was too late. I was angry at the OIC's attempt to manipulate me, and I wasn't about to sit quietly and listen to it. I was furious with them, but Bobby was furious with me, and for a few moments he and I sat at the table and argued. At last he managed to calm me down, and we turned our attention once again to the attorneys across the table.

Bobby began to quiz them about what concrete information they were looking for. Their response was not at all subtle: "We want to know about the Clintons' role in Whitewater."

"No problem," I relayed through Bobby. "I'll tell you everything I know about Bill and Hillary's role, from beginning to end." Again, everyone on the opposite side of the table was smiling. "There's one thing you should know, though," I went on. "I don't know of anything wrong that either the president or the first lady has done." The smiles disappeared.

Patiently, Lerman explained to me that a proffer would have to be an honest, open statement of everything I knew. If it was later determined that I hadn't told the whole truth, he warned, any immunity deal could be yanked. "No problem," I said. I was ready to give my proffer under oath, on my grandmother's grave, or just cross my heart and hope to die. But, I said again, I didn't know of anything the Clintons had done that was even remotely illegal.

Once again, Lerman gestured to the stack of documents describing my alleged criminal activity. He warned me that, based on the OIC's investigation, I would very likely be facing criminal charges. Lerman was a real pro: he managed to phrase things in a way that accomplished two things. First, he expressed a clear message: if I gave the

OIC something on the Clintons, I would have no fear of criminal charges. Yet he did this in an oblique enough way that Starr and his staff could later indignantly assert that no one had ever made such an offer. But everyone on both sides of the table understood exactly what was going on.

For the third and final time, I told the OIC lawyers, "I don't know of anything illegal the Clintons have done. If you want a proffer stating that, then this meeting is done." And once more, the OIC made a reference to my possible indictment. With that, the meeting was adjourned. I hadn't been asked a single question.

The OIC did have one more request—the press had apparently gotten wind of the meeting and were camped outside the front door. Would I mind going out the back door? After what had just happened, I was not in a very agreeable mood. I strode out the front door and announced to the press that they wanted me to testify against the Clintons even though I had just told them I knew of nothing they had done that was illegal. I then got on a phone and called Pat and told him, "I don't think you have to worry about them loving me."

In retrospect, it's hard for me to remember why I was so unconcerned about a possible Whitewater indictment. One possibility is that I was relatively sure they were bluffing. A few months before, the OIC had threatened my brother Bill, who'd worked at Madison Guaranty—even going so far as to send him a target letter threatening him with imminent indictment. When he told them, in effect, to bring it on, they backed off their threats and never followed through. Another possibility is that I was consumed with preparing for the upcoming Mehta trial.

But the most likely scenario is also the simplest: I knew I had done nothing wrong, so I didn't think anything bad could come of any investigations into Whitewater and Madison Guaranty. I had learned the hard way in California that innocence doesn't always prevent an indictment, but I was sure that, even if I was indicted for Whitewater or Madison-related activities, I would be quickly exonerated.

In July 1995, just before Pat and I left Nashville for California, the Senate was in the midst of hearings on Whitewater. As I settled in to watch the hearings on television, I was amazed at how ridiculously overblown this simple land deal had become.

I remembered an early-morning phone call I had gotten almost three years ago from Pat during the 1992 presidential primaries. Before he even said good morning, Pat blurted out, "Have you seen the morning paper? You are officially a campaign issue."

Still half-asleep, I fought back the temptation to tell him to call back after I had a cup of coffee. Pat could tell that he had not exactly captured my interest so he pushed forward.

"I'm serious. Jim has given an interview to the *New York Times* about Clinton and Whitewater and they are trying to make it sound like it was some type of sinister operation."

With the mention of Jim and the *New York Times*, he now had my complete attention.

"Come on, Pat, how are they going to make a sinister operation out of a land project that lost money, for God's sake?"

Pat replied, "I don't know, but it's front-page news. My mom has already been on the phone with me this morning reading excerpts from the *Washington Post*. You can just imagine her analysis."

Pat's mother, Alice Ann Harris, was the very epitome of American motherhood. She had selflessly devoted most of her life to raising three kids, despite being talented in a number of areas as well as being very intelligent. She had one quirk, though—she had a weakness for conspiracy theories of all kinds, from the assassination of John Kennedy to the entire presidency of Richard Nixon.

When I asked Pat what she thought of the article, he could barely control himself.

"Oh, you know how she is. She thinks that this is going to be a big story that is going to erupt into a huge national scandal. Can you believe that?"

We both had a good laugh.

Watching the congressional hearings, I kept thinking back to that phone call and how ridiculous the whole idea of Whitewater becoming a scandal seemed. For me, watching the Whitewater hearings was akin to staring at a car wreck on the highway—you don't want to do it, but somehow you can't tear your eyes away. At times I would be laughing at the absurdity of the "revelations," many of which were touted as blockbusters, and all of which turned out to be duds.

At other times, I'd get angry as I listened to a parade of politicians trying to explain to Americans how "complicated" Whitewater was and that was the reason that they had been unable to come up with anything illegal. I'm sure half of Nashville could hear me when I would be in the living room screaming, IT WAS A STUPID LAND DEAL THAT WENT BAD! YOU KNOW DAMN WELL THAT THERE IS NOTHING COMPLICATED ABOUT IT!

During the hearings, it was incredible to hear the politicians and the media offer insight as to what really went on in Whitewater and why the Clintons, the McDougals, and everyone else had acted as they did. The most commonly accepted theory was that, through Whitewater, Jim was buying access to the Clintons so that he could influence them in the future. The theory might have been a little more plausible had it not overlooked one small detail—Jim already had access to the Clintons! We were seeing them several times a month before Whitewater and, after Jim went to work in the governor's office, he had twenty-four hour access to Clinton.

Another popular theory passed around was that Jim and Bill were using Whitewater to launder donations to Clinton for his political campaigns. This scenario also presented problems. Anyone who saw the Whitewater records, especially the checking accounts, knew that there was no money going through the account—that was the problem! No sales meant no money. Having seen my share of gangster movies, it always seemed to me that money-launderers generally try and have an actual money-making business as their front. If we were going to launder money, we would have opened a dry cleaner.

The worst part was listening to an endless parade of politicians and pundits look into the camera and earnestly explain why they couldn't find a smoking gun in the Whitewater affair. After prefacing their remarks with how complicated the entire matter was, they would then explain that the reason no smoking gun could be found was that the Clinton White House were masters of covering up evidence. This was truly the perfect, irrefutable argument. They could accuse Clinton or anyone of an illegal act and then, when no evidence could be found, simply nod knowingly at the camera and complain about how the facts were being covered up. Joseph McCarthy would have been proud.

Running a close second for worst moment was when Sen. Alfonse D'Amato of New York called me sleazy. Being called sleazy by Al D'Amato is a little like being called inarticulate by George W. Bush. You know you have really hit rock bottom when Al D'Amato tries to take the moral high ground on you.

As planned, Pat and I moved to California shortly after the hearings, but it wasn't long before the OIC came calling again. This time they wanted me to come back to their Little Rock office to provide handwriting samples.

I found it a bit strange that they insisted I come to Arkansas, as there was a perfectly serviceable FBI office in Los Angeles. But they offered to pay for the flight and a hotel, and the trip would give me an opportunity to see my family, so I didn't quarrel over the details. Also, I wanted to demonstrate that I was still willing to cooperate, and this was a harmless way to do it. It seemed so harmless, in fact, that Bobby didn't even bother to drive down from Jonesboro the day I went to give the samples. This would prove to be a major mistake.

My flight from Los Angeles to Little Rock was particularly bumpy, and I didn't get to the hotel until well after midnight. After a mix-up at the desk, I finally got a room and fell into bed, exhausted.

The next morning I waited in the lobby for two hours for the FBI agents to come pick me up. When they finally arrived, they explained that they had gone to the wrong hotel. It was a little disconcerting that the top law-enforcement agency in the country could not figure out what hotel I was in when they were the ones that booked the reservation, but I chalked it up to a simple oversight. When I met the FBI agents who would be obtaining my handwriting samples, I was tired and still stiff from the plane ride the night before. And as it always did after a lengthy trip, my back was giving me trouble. After listening to me whine about the trip, the agents were courteous enough to take me to breakfast before we headed back into the office. Once inside, I figured I'd write my name and a few words down and that would be that. Instead, the agents asked that I perform a series of basic writing exercises—and then repeat them over and over again.

Because of my back problems, whenever I write for any length of time, I suffer sharp pangs in my arm, and my fingers experience some numbness. I continued to write, per the agents' directions, but soon found myself wondering just how long they planned to go on. One hour passed, and then two, and my pain and difficulty increased. I explained my problem to the agents, and they let me rest briefly. But then we started up again. Soon we were in a pattern: I would write, complain of pain, be allowed to rest briefly, then the cycle would start again.

Finally, after three hours of writing, I was allowed to stop. I was relieved, but that quickly vanished when one of the agents looked at me and accused me of attempting to disguise my handwriting. I had also, he declared, refused to follow instructions. "I'm sorry," I said, "but I'm in a lot of pain. And I'm exhausted." I assured him that I had no intention of disguising my handwriting, and made a suggestion.

"Do you want me to try again tomorrow, after I've had a chance to rest?" I asked. The agents said no, that wouldn't be necessary. Frustrated and tired, I did what I always did in such situations. I called Pat.

Pat listened as I described what had happened, then offered a simple solution that he figured would satisfy everyone. "Have Bobby call the OIC's attorneys," he said. "Tell them what happened, and deny that you were attempting to disguise your handwriting."

"Then," Pat said, "have Bobby tell them that you'll redo the samples, provided that the FBI will videotape the whole thing." This was a no-lose proposition for all involved. If I was indeed trying to disguise my handwriting, the FBI would now have a videotape of me doing it. And if I wasn't disguising my handwriting, they would know they had an accurate sample—the thing they were supposedly looking for. Bobby called one of the OIC attorneys, explained the situation and offered the proposed solution. But after a short conference, the OIC rejected it.

It was not until my trial a year later that I realized the OIC had already gotten what it wanted from my three-hour handwriting sample: They now had two FBI agents who'd be willing to testify that I had purposefully tried to deceive them.

I flew back to L.A., worried for the first time about the Whitewater investigation. And as the miles went by, my fear began to change into something new: anger. I'd agreed to cooperate with the OIC, trusting that the agents and lawyers were being above-board with me. Now I'd discovered that I'd been naive. Initially, I hadn't had any real opinion about Ken Starr and his OIC attorneys, but the more I thought about what had just happened in Little Rock, the more I began to loathe the OIC. I was about to find out they were not too crazy about me either.

In August 1995, a couple of months after my trip to Little Rock, I was temping as a receptionist at an office in Los Angeles when Chris Vlasto, the ABC producer, suddenly showed up. "Hi, Susan," he said. "How do you feel?"

"I feel fine," I said, confused by the question—not to mention why he was there in the first place.

"Oh," he said, eager to be the bearer of bad tidings, "I guess you haven't heard," and he handed me a sheaf of papers. I looked at the top page and froze: the OIC had indicted me on eight criminal charges relating to the David Hale loan.

I read the words, "United States of America v. Susan McDougal."

I was stunned. My hands shaking, I read through the documents as quickly as I could. Then, when I could speak, I called Pat. "You're not going to believe this," I told him. "I've become the reincarnation of Ma Barker—a one-woman crime spree."

10

ET TU, MCDOUGAL

SINCE FEDERAL TRIALS TAKE PRECEDENCE OVER state trials, the Mehta trial would have to take a backseat to Whitewater. But even though it would come first, I refused to focus on the Whitewater trial, instead choosing to stay in California to work on the Mehta case. I told my family and friends not to worry about the Whitewater indictment and asked them not to bring it up with me. I did not want any of them involved in the trial. It was as if I thought I could make it go away by simply ignoring it. Or maybe I was just so embarrassed about the mess my life had become that I was unable or unwilling to acknowledge what was going on.

I would stand trial with two other people the OIC had indicted: Jim McDougal and Jim Guy Tucker, who was at the time the sitting governor of Arkansas. Five years after Jim and I had divorced, and seemingly a lifetime since we'd lived and worked together, we were about to be thrown together again.

Though I'd left Arkansas and started a new life with Pat, Jim and I had stayed in frequent contact. We spoke often by phone, and I dropped by to see him whenever I was in Arkansas. He was living in Arkadelphia, in the same house on Claudia Riley's property where he'd been living when we first met. Bob had died a year or two earlier, leaving Claudia with one request: "Take care of Jim and Susan," he'd told her. "Stick with them. They need you." So she'd agreed to let Jim live in the same little house he'd rented before.

By the time our divorce was finalized in 1990, I had every reason to seriously distrust Jim McDougal. During the settlement process, I discovered that he'd hidden numerous things from me—including concealing business assets and manipulating the stock in our jointly owned companies so that my shares were diluted. He'd even become a secret partner in several land deals, hiding them from me so I couldn't claim any share of the proceeds. Even worse, he had left many people who'd trusted him—employees, friends, and members of my family included—high and dry when Madison Guaranty collapsed.

Yet I managed to overlook all that when it came to our relationship. I still felt a lot of guilt over how our marriage had ended, especially since Jim's health hadn't been good and had continued to decline after the divorce. When I left Jim, I'd gone on to a better life. But he had proceeded to sink about as low as he could go: he was broke, in poor health, and, worst of all for him, he had no one—even his parents had both died. He was still surrounded, as always, by perky teenage girls, but it seemed to me there was no one he could really talk to, who I thought would understand what he was going through.

Often when I talked to Jim, he would tell me he was just marking time until his death. And I felt like I was the one who had left him to die. I owed it to him, I believed, to make things better for him, however I could.

In facing a trial together, I felt like I now had a chance to show Jim the loyalty he deserved. Despite the fact that Pat, my friends, and my family urged me to distance myself from Jim, I decided to do just the opposite. Jim was facing many more charges than I was—his nineteen to my eight—and I didn't have the first idea of what the truth was behind them or how Jim planned to refute them. But I did know one thing—I was innocent of the charges yet I had been indicted. If they could say I was guilty when I knew I was innocent, why shouldn't I assume that Jim was also innocent?

I also believed that hooking up my defense with Jim's wasn't nearly as dangerous as others seemed to think. Six years previously, shortly after the collapse of Madison Guaranty, Jim had been indicted on a conspiracy charge in connection with the S&L. I had come to that trial to support him, and I never forgot what I'd witnessed there.

Despite the fact that he was already in ill health, Jim had taken the stand in his own defense. He'd delivered an absolutely virtuoso performance, testifying so eloquently and so thoroughly that no one in the courtroom could have doubted his innocence. When the jury came back quickly with a verdict of not guilty, I saw it as further proof of Jim's genius and his basic honesty. Now, with the Whitewater trial approaching, I remembered that performance—and fell right back into my old habit of believing that no matter what we were up against, Jim McDougal could somehow make everything come out all right in the end.

Pat was furious with me. He had studied the evidence the OIC had turned over and had concluded that Jim was guilty of at least a few of the charges against him. "If you align yourself with Jim," he said, "there's a very good chance you'll be taken down, too." Pat urged me just to tell the truth: that Jim had controlled the finances in all our dealings and in all his partnerships. But if I did this, I knew I'd be setting up Jim for a much greater likelihood of conviction—and I wasn't willing to do that to him. I was convinced that I could adequately defend myself without hurting Jim.

"Pat," I protested, "Jim is sick. He's broke. He's been abandoned by everyone he counted on. I'm not going to pile on while he's at the lowest point in his life. Besides, who are you to say that he is guilty?"

Pat pleaded with me to reconsider, but I'd made up my mind. Angry, frustrated, and now frightened at what I was setting myself up for, Pat put an end to our relationship. He'd given up his job in Nashville and put his life on hold to protect me and give us a chance to have a family—and now I was, in his eyes, selling myself down the river for a guilty man. It was just too much for him to take. I saw it differently. This was about having trusted a man for most of my life and not turning my back on him when he was in trouble.

The Woman Who Wouldn't Talk

I went to Arkansas to prepare for the Whitewater trial, and Pat stayed in California. For the first time in nearly a decade, I'd be without my best friend and confidant.

The Whitewater trial got under way in March 1996. Hundreds of reporters descended on Little Rock, and the scene at the courthouse soon resembled a huge traveling circus. Everywhere you looked there were satellite trucks, klieg lights, television cameras, and hordes of people. At least part of the reason for the press barrage was based on the theory that the smoking gun in Whitewater would finally be revealed at the trial.

The glare of the national media spotlight was like an elixir to Jim, who'd been living in semianonymity on Claudia's property. Suddenly, reporters from major newspapers across the country were fighting to hear what he had to say. Just when he needed it, here was a whole new audience he could entertain with his stories about Arkansas politics and impress with his combination of intelligence and eccentricity. The fact that the trial could result in his imprisonment did not deter his enthusiasm in the least.

Jim relished playing the role of the eccentric Southern character, and he dressed the part, wearing white suits and Panama hats and carrying a gold-tipped cane. He also loved playing games with the reporters. "I can't believe how easy it is to fool them," he'd say. And the reporters loved Jim, who was highly quotable and frequently provocative. At virtually every breakfast, lunch, and dinner for the length of the trial, Jim would regale groups of reporters with stories of his past life in the glory days of Arkansas politics. Ever the showman, he knew how to pass along just the right kind of current tidbit that would keep them coming back for more.

My relationship with the press was generally good as well. Most of the time I met reporters together with Jim, and he tended to dominate the conversation. Just as they had done in Nashville, the reporters generally treated me with courtesy and were respectful of my privacy. They would often invite me to dinner or drinks and I would politely decline, telling them I just wanted to go back to the hotel and go to bed.

However, one night after dinner I was walking alone back to my hotel room when I bumped into Bob Franken of CNN. He invited me to join him and some friends at the Capitol Hotel bar, and I thought, *What could be the harm?* So I spent about thirty minutes with the group, exchanging stories. During that time, I sipped a rum and Coke, ultimately drinking about half of it. I hardly ever drank and I wasn't about to make an exception while I was on trial.

Several months later, after the trial was over, that half glass of rum and Coke would end up coming back to haunt me. On a court questionnaire I had to fill out for my probation officer, one question asked whether or not I drank alcohol. Assuming that the question meant on a regular basis, I answered that I did not. Even today, if someone asked me, "Do you drink?" I would answer the same thing.

But the OIC attorneys didn't see it that way: they would later present this answer to the judge as proof that I was a liar. Their evidence came in a sworn affidavit from a witness who'd seen me in the Capitol Bar that night. This would serve as a further reminder that it was difficult, if not impossible, to beat the OIC at a game it was very, very good at playing.

The trial took place in the courtroom of U.S. Federal Judge George Howard, a man who had a unique story of his own. The son of an African-American sharecropper, he had grown up in abject poverty in the Arkansas Delta country. Through sheer force of will, he'd put himself through college and law school, then become a well-regarded attorney in the Little Rock-Pine Bluff area. In the early seventies, he was elected to a seat on the Arkansas State Court of Appeals, and from there he was selected by President Carter to become the first African-American federal judge in Arkansas—and one of the first in the South.

In his mid-sixties, Judge Howard was a diminutive man who couldn't have weighed a hundred pounds soaking wet. But what he lacked in size, he made up in presence, aided by a robust, lyrical voice and a pronounced Southern drawl. A deeply religious man, Judge Howard preached at a church in Pine Bluff on Sundays, and he spoke with the rhythmic cadences of the pulpit. The Little Rock legal community generally regarded him as being a very fair-minded jurist who enjoyed a good scholarly argument and the give-and-take of an intelligent debate—but not someone who looked kindly on a lot of histrionics or silliness in his courtroom. This judge expected both parties to be polite and to conduct themselves in a formal manner suiting the seriousness of the occasion.

The OIC arrived in court with a cadre of lawyers from all over the country. Leading the effort were a short, heavyset U.S. attorney from San Antonio named Ray Jahn and his partner and wife, Leroi Jahn. Ray Jahn had made his reputation by successfully prosecuting the father of actor Woody Harrelson for threatening to kill a federal judge. He was an "aw-shucks" kind of prosecutor, a lawyer who used a down-home demeanor to convince juries that he had nothing against the defendants—he just had a job to do.

Away from the judge or jury, however, Jahn quickly dropped his homey persona in favor of his true aggressiveness. One example is the response he gave when defense attorneys asked the judge for permission to interview the OIC's key witness, David Hale, before the trial. With a straight face, Jahn stood before the court and said that the OIC had no idea where he was or how to find him. As we later discovered, not only did the OIC know exactly where Hale was, but they were the ones who'd provided for his living arrangements, including providing him with regular checks.

The third member of the OIC's team was Jackie Bennett. In contrast to Jahn's down-home amiability, Bennett's style was all "bad cop": in front of the jury, he made no pretense that he was anything but a complete son of a bitch—a fact he appeared to be proud of. Tall and lanky, Bennett had a flattish head and an odd inability to bend his knees when he walked. For obvious reasons, we began referring to him as Frankenstein. The fourth member was Amy St. Eve, a young, pert, button-nosed attorney from Chicago. For the most part, she walked around with a tight-lipped smile glued to her face that looked like the Joker from *Batman*. As we'd find out, St. Eve was extremely ambitious and saw the Whitewater case as her own personal career stepladder. For her, justice was not the issue—a conviction was all that mattered.

My parents' wedding day in Liège, Belgium, October 11, 1945.

My own wedding day, May 23, 1976. Jim McDougal is in a mint green Yves St. Laurent silk suit, and I'm wearing my ice cream cake gown.

(Above) Jim expounds to Claudia Riley, the attorney general-elect, Bill Clinton, his wife, Hillary Rodham, and Bob Riley. They had all come to celebrate our marriage.

(Right) The incomparable Bob and Claudia Riley, my second family.

The newly remodeled Bank of Kingston, with the antique ball safe on the customers' side of the tellers' windows.

(Left) On the surface, I was all smiles, but Jim's decision to run for Congress in 1982 soon threw our lives into chaos.

Elect
SUSAN McDougal
City Board

Above) In 1985, I ran for the City Board n Little Rock. Though I didn't win, I had he best television ad, produced by a political operative named Jim McDougal.

(Right) A drawing by the well-known Arkansas political cartoonist George Fisher, spoofing the then-youngest governor in the country. Governor Clinton wrote to us in the margin, "With thanks for your long friendship and your generous support of my campaign for Governor. Bill Clinton 9/23/78"

BILL CLINTON

May 5, 1976

Mr. James B. McDougal
P.O. Box 351
Arkadelphia, AR 71923

Dear Jim:

Thank you for your contribution. With it, and your
voice, our campaign will reach the people of Arkansas.
Please continue to ask everyone you can to support
me. I will always be grateful for your help. Thank
you.

Sincerely,

Bill

Bill Clinton

bk

*You are a great American
who will live long in the
hearts of your countrymen,
your words carved in stone
by devoted followers and members
of the prison work gang —
Thanks*

BILL CLINTON

October 10, 1976

Mr. James B. McDougal
Route 3, Box 308-B
Little Rock, AR 72211

Dear Mr. McDougal:

Thank you for the contribution. It will be a great help in
my efforts to retire my campaign debts before taking office
in January.

In the next few months, I will be preparing myself to be your
Attorney General. Please keep in touch with me from time to
time. I will always be glad to have the benefit of any suggestions or criticisms you might make.

I will always be grateful for your help in this effort, and I
will try to prove worthy of your trust.

Sincerely,

Bill

Bill Clinton

bk

*British Bill didn't
think much of my
idea to have him
endorse Carter — I was
mildly surprised but at
least amused to have him
giving me hell again —*

There was no more beautiful couple than the Mehtas. They wrote me, "To our sweetest friend. Lovingly, Nancy and Zubin."

DON'T LAUGH~ I JUST MAY GET UP AND CHARGE YOU AGAIN

KEN STARR

SUSAN McDOUGAL

CAMPBELL

People sent me political cartoons from all over the country when I was in jail. I put them up on the walls, where they provided me with humor and solace.

My brother, Jim Henley, and my dad, James, got some great publicity when they protested in front o Kenneth Starr's Little Rock office. Wearing a button that read, 'Susan McDougal Political Prisoner' Jim told the press, "We are angry and we're defiant."

Outside Federal Courthouse in Little Rock, Pat defends me one more time.

It's all over now! After the second Whitewater trial, at the end of a very long road, Pat and I can finally relax and smile.

A month after the Mehta verdict, we had a dinner with some of the jurors; on my right is Rufus Gifford, jury foreman. Pat has his back to the camera.

My first Thanksgiving after my release from prison in 1998. Members of my family pictured here are (from left to right, standing) Brian Henley, Jill Henley, James Henley, Belinda Henley, David Henley, Ben Henley, Royce Ann Henley, Jim Henley, John Henley, me, Gini Henley, (front row) Karlee, Krystina, David, Jr., Walt, and Brandt.

With Mom and Dad, the night of our victory party at Little Rock's Capitol Hotel. We were photographed by Pat's mom, Ann Alice Harris.

When I invited the entire state of Arkansas to our victory party, a lot of supporters showed up from all over the area.

One look at my brother Bill Henley's face shows his single-minded determination to never quit until the fight with the OIC was finished.

Mark Geragos (right) receives the Jerry Geisler Award as Los Angeles attorney of the yea
for his brilliant defense in the Mehta trial

All four of them would crowd around the OIC's table at the trial, along with two FBI agents, a paralegal, and one or two secretaries. The sheer numbers at the prosecution table were a fair indicator of how overmatched we were, especially in the art of creating a paper blizzard to bury the opposition. The OIC attorneys were experts at "papering" the defense, filing numerous motions that the defense must spend time and money answering. Whenever we filed a motion, the OIC answered within a day with three of their own. At one point, my lawyer made a courtesy call to Amy St. Eve to tell her we'd be filing a motion with the court and would fax her a copy. It didn't matter what we filed, she replied laughing, they could answer anything we put together in twenty minutes.

The paper blizzard reached a point where Bobby—who ran a small law office and was working pro bono—went to Judge Howard to complain. Bobby told the judge that he couldn't possibly do all the research needed to answer the voluminous paperwork the OIC was generating. He even weighed the documents on a scale to show the judge just what he was up against. In response, Judge Howard appointed the local federal public defender, Jennifer Horan, to help in the preparation of my defense. Jennifer was willing to help and even turned over her entire caseload to another attorney in the office for the next three months. We still couldn't get all the necessary investigation and research done, but the help at least lightened the burden on Bobby and gave us some hope of fighting back.

But ultimately it wouldn't matter how our numbers compared to those of the OIC. I had single-handedly eliminated my one effective defense by refusing to offer any testimony about Jim's control of the finances. Yet even though this decision put our defense at a huge disadvantage, I still went into the trial believing that if we all stuck together, we would all walk away free.

When Bobby rose to deliver his opening statement, I wasn't even sure what he was going to say—in all the confusion, he and I hadn't had a chance to go over it. As it turned out, we should have.

Bobby was describing the meeting back in 1986 where I signed the $300,000 loan and picked up the check from David Hale. He declared,

"She had on a tennis dress when she went in to sign the papers, signed them, was given the check." At this point, Bobby kicked up one leg and making an exaggerated face while imitating me, he said, "Gee, this is fun! Can I come back tomorrow?"

I cringed when I heard these words come out of Bobby's mouth. For the most part, he'd gotten everything right: I had come to Hale's office in a tennis dress, and the whole process of signing the papers and picking up the check had taken about ten minutes. I remember that I made some smart-aleck remark about how easy it was, and said something like, "Maybe we could do it again sometime." But Bobby's flippant suggestion that I'd exclaimed, "Gee, this is fun!" was jarring. And sure enough, this was the one line from the opening that appeared in the newspapers the next day. From that point on, certain reporters referred to our strategy as "the bimbo defense."

That $300,000 loan was the cornerstone of the prosecution's case against me. The documents I'd signed that day in Hale's office had stated that the loan was to be used for marketing—specifically, that it would be used by the "Master Marketing" marketing company. Master Marketing was a company Jim had formed to advertise and promote our various properties, and he'd appointed me as the chief officer. Before Jim had sent me to Hale's office, however, he'd told me that the loan was to purchase and market some property south of Little Rock; it was this property that he had proposed to me was to be my divorce settlement. Jim had prepared all the documents, so I never actually saw what the loan was for. Jim had just asked me to go down and sign for it—something I'd done for him hundreds of times before with no problems—and I'd done just that. Then I took him the check.

But the $300,000 check hadn't gone into a marketing account, or even a separate business account for purchase of the land. Instead, it was deposited, without an endorsement, into Jim's and my personal account at Madison. Since there was no endorsement, I assume Jim just told one of the tellers to put it into our account. Since he owned the S&L, it was not likely they would have questioned it. Following that, a number of checks were drawn on the account, by Jim, me, and Kirby Randolph, the wonderful, hardworking woman at Madison who balanced the checkbooks of all our business accounts and wrote checks on Jim's instruction. The checks were written for things like credit card bills, medical bills, and groceries.

Because none of the $300,000 had gone into the marketing company—the stated purpose of the loan—I was charged with misapplication of loan funds, conspiracy to defraud a financial institution, wire fraud, and mail fraud. The mail fraud count seemed especially ludicrous, as I hadn't even mailed anything. But apparently, the fact that Hale had eventually mailed some of the paperwork to Washington sufficed to tack this on to my indictments as well.

The crux of the OIC's case against me was this: because I'd written checks out of Jim's and my personal account, I must therefore have known that the $300,000 was being used—and known that it was being used fraudulently. To the jurors, this no doubt was a very convincing argument. After all, how many people get $300,000 deposited in their account and don't have a clue what it's for?

But in the context of my life with Jim McDougal, it wasn't strange at all. We had separate checking accounts for each real estate development, and Jim was constantly shifting large amounts of money back and forth from these accounts to our personal account. I had carte blanche to write checks below $500, and on those occasions when I wanted to write a check for more than that, I simply asked Jim if it was okay. One of the things that I liked about having Jim handle the finances was that I didn't have to keep up with those kinds of details. All I cared about was that if I wrote a check, it was covered.

At any given time, I had no idea how much money was in our personal account. In fact, when the prosecution called Kirby Randolph to the stand to testify about which checks she had written, Bobby McDaniel asked her if I had ever inquired about the balance on the account. Under oath, she replied, "Susan wouldn't have known if there was three dollars or three million dollars in the account."

As the trial progressed, the OIC seemed to focus its efforts on nailing Jim. Witness after witness went to the stand and described how Jim had exercised total control over Madison Guaranty as well as whatever personal dealings with him they might have had. In effect, the OIC was making my defense argument for me: their own witnesses were testifying to Jim's fanatical desire to control all the financial details of every transaction. And these were people who knew a lot more about business than I did. The OIC's list of witnesses against Jim included several investors—a college professor, an attorney with an M.B.A., the former head loan officer at a major bank, and a very successful local businessman. One by one, they described how they'd only done what Jim had asked. For example, Larry Kuca, an attorney and businessman who loved to brag about his business background and expertise, got on the stand and testified that while working for with Madison on Campobello, he did nothing without Jim's permission. When each of these witnesses was asked why they were so willing to just follow orders, their answers were always the same: because they trusted him. Jim had never done anything to raise their suspicions about his honesty.

As the OIC painted it, Jim McDougal was a consummate con artist, capable of fooling even experienced businesspeople. Yet somehow, the OIC insisted that it was inconceivable that Jim had pulled the same thing on me. This had nothing to do with the fact that I'd been married to Jim. It was simpler than that. All of these men had promised to testify against Jim. I had not. Since I'd refused to help the OIC, went their reasoning, I couldn't possibly be an innocent victim—I had to be a part of the scam. It was spectacularly jaded, and deeply flawed, reasoning. And I had no idea whether the jury was buying it or not.

In the first few weeks of the trial, my name rarely came up. Whole days would go by without a single mention of my name—if the trial had been a movie, I wouldn't have had enough screen time to qualify for best supporting actress. The reason was that most of the early part of the trial was focused on another transaction that even the OIC conceded I knew nothing about. It involved an intricate and bizarre financing plan, once again arranged by Jim McDougal and featuring financing by David Hale, but this time involving Jim Guy Tucker instead of me. I had a lot of trouble following the details of the labyrinthine transaction and assumed that the jury was too. Regardless, I was not going to complain about the lack of attention.

There was one time, however, that my name did come up. The OIC had called to the stand a former Madison Guaranty accountant named Greg Young, who was testifying about some of the transactions involving Jim. At the end of his testimony, as he prepared to leave the stand, one of the OIC attorneys asked if he had any recollections of me at Madison.

There was one thing, he said. He remembered me shouting "I own this fucking place!" one afternoon in the bank. In eliciting this important detail, the OIC had accomplished two things. First, the quote made me seem like a power-crazed madwoman, which dovetailed nicely with the OIC's charges against me. Second, it also painted me as a foulmouthed heathen, which was bound to sit poorly with a jury comprised mostly of self-professed Christian women.

Did I say it? Probably, although I have no specific recollection of it. But it sounds like the kind of broad, off-the-wall, loud remark I would make in trying to get a laugh. My natural talent at cursing has always been a weakness of mine but I continued to do it because it usually got a laugh. But no matter what kind of language I used, it was obvious to everyone at Madison that I was no power-crazed lunatic. In fact, the criticism most frequently leveled at me was that I didn't take enough interest in what was going on.

Our days in court were for the most part routine, if not boring, but outside the courthouse things began to get strange. Most nights I made the one-hour drive back to Arkadelphia to stay with Claudia Riley. But once or twice a week I'd get a room in the hotel where Jim was staying during the trial, right across the street from the courthouse.

Occasionally I'd stop by Jim's room to check on how he was doing. He was often busy with his latest Twinkie, and sometimes they were engaged in his new hobby: smoking marijuana. This didn't seem like a very bright idea, but I said nothing. Jim was in one of his manic phases, and I wasn't about to get upset over something that actually calmed him down.

When the prosecution finally got around to my case, the first witness they called was my former assistant and friend, Lisa Aunspaugh. Most of the questions they asked Lisa were about Jim, and, in a way, it was amusing to watch. After I had left for Dallas in 1985, Jim and Lisa had had a short fling (Lisa was twenty years old at the time—right up Jim's alley) and he had given her a few gifts, including a Mercedes with a hefty payment and a building with a heavy mortgage.

The OIC wanted to interrogate Lisa about the building, but the lawyers were hampered by a "sex clause" both sides had signed before the trial. Jim's attorney and the OIC had agreed that two subjects were off-limits: Jim's dalliance with Lisa, and David Hale's affair with his secretary. This agreement put the OIC in an uncomfortable position: it was nearly impossible to ask Lisa questions about the terms of the building without referring to her relationship with Jim. At one point, the OIC attorneys became so exasperated that they wanted to call off their end of the deal. Judge Howard refused.

Lisa's testimony about me was fairly harmless. She said only one damaging thing, claiming that I had coached her what to say when the bank examiners planned to interview her in 1986. This was partially true. I had driven her to the interview, and because she was so scared that she was in trouble over Jim's dealings, I gave her some advice. "Just answer yes or no to the questions," I'd told her. "Don't go into any details unless they ask you." This was the same advice my own lawyers had given me (and which I routinely ignored), so I saw nothing wrong with passing it along.

The next witness had been called specifically to testify against me. This struck me as odd, as I had no idea who she was. Even when she gave her name, I had only a vague recollection of having heard it before. As it turned out, she had worked for Madison Guaranty for a brief time after I had returned from Dallas in the fall of 1985. Despite the fact that we had no relationship of any kind, and that she'd been around me far less time than any of dozens of other people at Madison, this woman had decided that I needed to be closely watched.

First, based upon her incredible powers of observation, the woman reported to the jury that I was loud. This took a real Sherlock Holmes to come up with. If the prosecution had just asked, I would have agreed to stipulate to that. Then, she further testified that I seemed very secretive, not in the secret agent good-guy way, but more in the tradition of all the great secretive villains over the years. This immediately struck me as being rather odd. How did I manage to be both loud and secretive? Was I being loud in order to secretly throw her off the trail? Was this a whole new strain of arch villain: the loud, secretive criminal? These insights, which made no sense at all, were the extent of her testimony against me.

So far, the OIC's case against me was ridiculously weak. I was, according to one witness, power hungry. According to another, I was loud, but secretive. And according to Lisa, I had inappropriately advised her on how to respond to lawyers' questions. None of these things had anything to do with the eight charges against me.

The real drama in the case came with the testimony of the government's star witness, David Hale. In addition to the $300,000 loan to me, he had also made other loans that formed most of the basis of the charges against Jim and Jim Guy. We knew Hale's performance on the stand could turn the case.

Hale had become a government witness the good old-fashioned way: he did it in order to save his own rear end. As a Small Business Investment Corporation operator, Hale had been empowered to grant loans, partially funded by the federal government, to small businesses. In 1992 FBI agents had raided his office and discovered that he was loaning money to dummy corporations he himself had set up—a direct violation of federal law. As it turned out, that was just the tip of the iceberg.

By the time the FBI agents finished going through Hale's documents, they had enough evidence to charge him with crimes that could have put him away for life. Faced with the possibility of spending decades in jail, Hale got desperate. He had been caught red-handed and had no defense—his only hope was to shoot for leniency by giving the U.S. attorneys information on supposedly illegal activities of others, preferably someone more high-profile than Hale.

In 1992, you couldn't find anyone more high-profile than Bill Clinton, the Democratic presidential nominee who just happened to come from Hale's home state. Hale began circulating a story, first to the media and then to the U.S. attorneys, that the $300,000 loan to me was actually for Bill Clinton. It was, he said, an illegal way to funnel money to Clinton to help him clear up some political debts. In fact, he claimed to recall being summoned to a meeting with Jim and Bill Clinton at one of our sales offices one night to discuss it. According to his original story, Clinton had jogged down to the sales office. He changed that story, however, when it was determined that Clinton, while an avid jogger, was not likely to have jogged ten miles down and ten miles back, on an interstate highway no less, unless he was training for a marathon. That story changed to Bill dropping by in the governor's limo. But Hale's story had other problems, specifically, the fact that the checking account records showed that none of the $300,000 had been used to benefit Clinton in any way. Hale had an explanation for that too.

Hale told a reporter for the *Washington Times* that he'd been shopping one day at a large Little Rock mall when he looked up to find a red-faced Bill Clinton charging angrily toward him. According to Hale, Clinton yelled, "Do you know what that fucking bitch Susan McDougal did? She spent all the money. The bitch took all the money." This, Hale suggested, explained everything. Why didn't the loan intended for Clinton ever make it into his hands? Because Susan McDougal supposedly kept it for herself.

There was one major drawback to Hale's story. At the time of this supposed encounter, Bill Clinton was the governor of Arkansas. As a general rule, the governors of Arkansas are usually very recognizable in large, public places. As a result, they tend to try to avoid running around in crowded, enclosed structures screaming phrases like "fucking bitch." Incidents like that would likely place them squarely on the front page of Arkansas newspapers. The story was so ludicrous, it was actually funny. It was inconceivable to me that no one would recognize the governor of Arkansas cursing loudly in a mall. Unless perhaps, Bill, like me, was just good at being both loud and secretive.

Not surprisingly, the U.S. Attorney's Office found the stories ludicrous as well. After investigating his claims, they declined Hale's offer of assistance. But Hale was not done yet. He took his story to such right-wing publications as the *Washington Times,* the *American Spectator,* and the *New York Post,* and they dutifully printed his allegations. Combined with the furor over Vince Foster's suicide, the Hale story started an avalanche of accusations all over Capitol Hill, eventually forcing Clinton to ask for a special prosecutor.

Initially, however, that did not help David Hale. The original special prosecutor, Robert Fiske, did not find Hale any more credible than had the regular U.S. attorneys. But Hale's luck was about to change as Kenneth Starr took over the investigation.

With Starr in charge, overnight Hale went from being an indicted scam artist to being the government's pampered star witness. Up until this point, Hale was telling everyone he was broke and having a hard time meeting his bills. But with the OIC as his new best friends, Hale was given a free place to live, transportation, and a little "walking around money" that eventually came to over $50,000. Also, Hale was in desperate need of an attorney. Starr and the OIC made sure he got one of the most well-known attorneys in the country. Hale was suddenly represented by Washington heavy-hitter Theodore Olson, who was a former law partner of Starr's and, according to Olson, one of Starr's best friends. An attorney of Olson's stature generally charges between $400 and $500 an hour. Yet, in court documents, filed by Hale, he claimed to have been broke at the time. When my attorneys asked the OIC to turn over any documents as to how Hale was able to pay for Olson's services, they refused.

It was later shown by several news organizations that the money for Hale was funnelled through the right-wing, Clinton-hating billionaire Richard Mellon Scaife's nefarious "Arkansas Project."

Starr's loyalty to Hale knew no bounds. At one point before the Whitewater trial, Hale had to make a court appearance in Arkansas before a federal judge to discuss several matters including his finances. At least two OIC attorneys accompanied him to the hearing. Under oath, Hale lied to the judge about an aspect of his assets. A sharp reporter for the *Arkansas Democrat-Gazette* caught the lie and printed an article about it in the paper a few days later. When questioned about Hale being caught lying under oath, Ray Jahn was quoted as saying that Hale simply "misspoke." I always loved this quote because it came from the same group of people who continuously preached to the country about how lying under oath was such a terrible offense because it violated the "rule of law" and the "sanctity of the court-room." Apparently, the same rules did not apply if you were on their team. In that case, lying under oath was considered an art form.

Before the trial I had assured Pat that if David Hale got up and told the story about Bill Clinton and the $300,000, my attorneys would be able to crucify him on cross-examination. That is one reason I was so confident about the outcome of the trial. But Pat was not so sure. He explained to me that the OIC did not need David Hale to testify about the Clinton story—Bill Clinton was not on trial, I was. The most likely scenario was that the OIC would limit Hale to talking about Jim's and my role in the $300,000 loan and what the documents actually showed. He said that it would be stupid for the OIC to even mention Bill Clinton's name at this trial, especially through a major con artist like David Hale. Pat went on to explain that most federal investiga-tions are like a pyramid. They proceed up the pyramid one level at a time, getting the person or persons directly below the next level to tes-tify against the person right above. David Hale was not being used to get Bill Clinton. He was being used to convict Jim and Susan McDougal. If the plan worked the way it usually did, it would be Jim and Susan McDougal accusing the Clintons, not David Hale.

I understood this method of investigation from books I had read about Mafia figures and drug dealers in which underlings were "flipped" by the authorities, who could then get at the kingpins, the ones directing the criminal activity. But Starr's people had turned things upside down. Even by the OIC's own admission, David Hale had com-mitted far more crimes, and more serious crimes, than Jim McDougal, Jim Guy Tucker, Hillary Clinton, Bill Clinton, and myself combined were ever alleged to have committed. Yet, he was the one being given the free ride to go after the smaller fish. Of course, we all knew this was not about politics. After all, the OIC had one of their attorneys go out-side to the press every day and repeatedly tell them that this trial had nothing to do with politics.

When David Hale finally took the stand, he was so pale he

appeared almost invisible. Even his carefully combed hair looked beige instead of brown. Hale was a short, rotund man who bent over both when he walked and sat. He talked in very hushed tones—at times it was almost impossible to hear him.

Throughout his testimony, Hale was very low-key. He would hang his head a lot, admit to having regularly broken the law, and, his eyes moist with tears, reiterate how sorry he was about everything he'd done. In return for his public atonement, his sweetheart deal included a promise from the OIC to ask the judge for leniency in Hale's sentencing. As a result, David Hale would ultimately spend less than two years in jail, despite having admitted (*after* being caught) to stealing millions of dollars from the U.S. government and committing numerous felonies.

Hale's testimony, soft-spoken and underplayed, must have delighted his handlers as much as it frustrated our lawyers. It was like trying to punch the Pillsbury Dough Boy—you were never going to do any real damage. As he testified, Hale admitted freely to having broken the law and humbly asked for forgiveness. At times he spoke like he was at a religious revival, preparing to come to Jesus. He sought redemption, he said—he just wanted to come clean and let the truth be heard at last. When defense attorneys asked him about all the perks the OIC was providing in exchange for his testimony, he talked about how these good men and women were helping him rebuild his life. When asked about the $50,000 he'd been given, he smiled and acknowledged that it was true, but he said he needed the money, as he'd never be able to work in Arkansas again because of his stand against Bill Clinton.

Although Hale's performance was extraordinary, he doesn't deserve all the credit. According to his own testimony, he met with the OIC attorneys more than fifty times to work on his testimony. One would think that simply telling the truth wouldn't require quite so much preparation.

David Hale's testimony about me was brief but deadly. He remembered distinctly, he said, that when I came to his office to sign the loan papers, I took the time to read them over carefully. He went on to say that he didn't recall me asking any questions—but by then the damage was done. The prosecution would now claim that I would have known what the loan was for.

This was a bald-faced lie but there was still one point that undercut the prosecution's charges. In order for me to have defrauded a federally backed financial institution, I would have had to have known that the loan was coming from a federally backed financial institution—and not just a company owned by David Hale. There was no evidence at all that I'd known that, because I hadn't.

The OIC considered this a minor obstacle, however, as David Hale once again demonstrated how willing he was to change his story to give them exactly what they needed. Having apparently caught this oversight, the OIC attorney asked Hale whether or not I'd asked any questions. Yes, Hale responded, I had actually asked one—where was the money coming from? Whereupon he'd replied that it had come from his federally backed financial institution.

First, this was a direct contradiction of Hale's testimony, and second, it was ludicrous to suggest that if I'd asked only a single question of David Hale that day, that would have been it. But Hale's last-minute addition never became an issue, as for some reason our lawyers didn't go after it. After the trial, I always felt that was one of our major mistakes.

Normally, cross-examination on a witness like Hale would be devastating. But in their fifty-plus meetings, the OIC had done a great job preparing him, not to mention that he had the benefit of years of being a con artist. Because he so freely admitted to his lapses in judgment and character, our attorneys couldn't gain any leverage on those points. Hale not only owned up to every terrible thing he'd ever done—he elaborated on them all. As I watched our attorneys struggle, I kept thinking of an old Eddie Murphy routine about two guys in a boxing match. Before the bell rings, one guy starts punching himself in the face repeatedly. So the other guy says, "I'm not gonna fight that guy. If he's willing to do that to himself, what's he gonna do to me?"

When the prosecution rested its case a few days after Hale's testimony, I was getting my confidence back—partly because numerous reporters covering the trial kept assuring me that I was home free and partly because there had been so little testimony even mentioning me. It seemed unimaginable that I would be convicted of anything, especially after Judge Howard, responding to a defense motion, threw out four of the eight counts against me, stating that the prosecution hadn't introduced even one piece of evidence to prove any of those charges.

In April 1996, the trial shifted to Washington, D.C., where Bill Clinton had agreed to be deposed on videotape as a potential witness for the defense. Jim, our lawyers, and I would travel up to Washington and watch the deposition, which was scheduled to take place at the White House.

Jim had arranged a ride to the White House with a society reporter who'd been wanting to interview Jim about his unique fashion choices. I tagged along for the ride.

As he drove us toward the White House, he asked Jim about what labels he was wearing, and Jim rattled off the answer. This struck me as particularly absurd, considering where we were going and why, and I had to laugh when the reporter asked me the same thing. "I have no idea," I said.

The reporter changed the subject. "Well," he asked, "how do you feel about Ken Starr?"

Because I was uncomfortable talking about Starr during the trial to a reporter I had never met, I decided to make a joke out of the situation. Borrowing a line from the movie *The Untouchables*, I told the reporter, "I want him dead." I said, "I want his children dead. I want his dog dead. I want his house burned to the ground." It was a weak attempt at being funny that left the puzzled reporter unsure what he had just heard. Although I assumed he might not know the movie reference, I was sure he understood I was joking. The next morning I picked up the newspaper to see those words featured prominently in an article about the trial—with no reference to the fact that it was a quote or that it had been made in jest.

I'd never been to the White House before, and under normal circumstances I'd have been excited about going. But Jim and I hadn't seen Bill Clinton since the mid-eighties, and I had absolutely no idea how he'd react to us now. The whole Whitewater fiasco had started thanks to an interview Jim had given a *New York Times* reporter in the early spring of 1993. I would not have been surprised that when he saw us, he'd just ignore us, or at best he'd be polite but chilly.

Everyone turned to look when the president strode in. Bill's face immediately lit up when he saw Jim, and he came right over and pulled him into a warm embrace. As he did, he looked over Jim's shoulder and mouthed three words to me: "Are you okay?" I nodded and said, "Yes." When he pulled back from hugging Jim, he promised to give us a personal tour of the Oval Office after the deposition was done.

I was immediately struck by how different Bill was now. Whether it was the trappings of the White House or the gravity and power of his position, he now seemed truly presidential. Having known Bill at the very beginning of his political career, I couldn't help but picture him as a slightly nerdy, baby-faced Arkansan. But Bill now carried himself with total confidence—he almost seemed larger than life. You could see vestiges of the old Clinton—the hug, the wink—but this was someone else entirely.

The OIC's deposition of Bill Clinton lasted several hours. It should have taught me a lesson on how to conduct myself. He was cool and unruffled, and he answered the questions simply, without elaboration. He kept saying that he knew very little about the details of Whitewater, that the details had always been Jim's responsibility, and that he'd always known Jim to be a fair and honest man. Somehow, Bill was able to make the point that Jim ran the show without seeming to put any blame on Jim for the problems. By the time Bill's deposition was over, Jim felt that his testimony might turn out to be his saving grace.

An odd footnote to this story emerged two years later, when Jim declared in an interview that, following the deposition, Jim had privately taken Bill aside and asked that he pardon me if I was convicted. According to Jim, Bill had agreed. This was vintage Whitewater Jim McDougal—in other words, a flat-out lie. First of all, Jim was absolutely convinced I was going to be found innocent, so there was no reason for him to have made the request. Second, I was with Jim every minute he was at the White House, and I was close enough to hear everything he said to Bill. Like so many of the stories Jim later told, this one just did not happen.

By the time the deposition ended, I just wanted to get out of the White House as soon as I could. I was embarrassed to be in this position and wanted to crawl into a hole and never come out again. I walked out of the White House, flagged down a taxi, and went back to the hotel.

My "I want him dead" comment to the society reporter wasn't the only time I put my foot in my mouth during the trial. When I get frustrated, I've been known to turn perverse, and as the tension in me built, that seemed to be happening more often.

One prime example is my response to a reporter's question when we returned from Washington to Little Rock to resume the trial. The reporter asked how it felt to have had the judge dismiss four of the eight counts against me. I knew the "right" answer was to bow my head humbly and talk about how grateful I was to the judge for his wisdom, but I was in the mood for a little Henley "Big Talk." I launched into a ranting diatribe about how glad I was that he hadn't dismissed the other four counts—because I wanted to be around when we kicked the OIC attorneys' asses up to their shoulder blades. The quote made all the national newspapers and ran with some frequency on CNN. By now, it must have seemed to the reporters and half of the American public that I was losing my mind.

As we resumed the trial, Bobby, Jennifer, and I were still on the fence about whether or not I should testify. We decided to give it a trial run and see how I sounded. The verdict was unanimous: not good. The truthful answer to virtually every question was "Jim did that" or "Jim made that decision." Many of the questions scared me, as for the most part I didn't even know what they were asking about. When I finished my mock testimony, no one said a word, but I went straight to the bathroom and was sick. I realized that if I testified, I was likely going to end up burying Jim.

And there was another reason I was reluctant to testify. Compared to the lawyers, the judge, Jim McDougal, and Jim Guy Tucker, I felt uneducated and unsophisticated. The OIC prosecutors were aggressive, highly educated, savvy lawyers whose sole purpose at the moment was to put me in prison. I kept thinking that there is no way that I know enough about any part of this trial to withstand cross-examination. Jim Guy had decided that he was not going to testify and that also made me believe that it was the right move. For all these reasons, the decision wasn't hard to make: I wouldn't testify.

The real question then became whether or not Jim McDougal should testify. In the beginning of the trial, I had memories of Jim's bravura performance at his previous trial and assumed he'd be able to repeat that accomplishment. But the past two months had changed my mind completely. Between popping Prozac, smoking pot, and taking a wide assortment of prescription medications, Jim was in no position to defend himself. Some days he was his old self; other days he was lost in the ozone. I became adamant that he should not testify.

At first Jim agreed. The best defense for all of us, he believed, was just to play back Bill Clinton's deposition for the jury and then rest our case. Although some of the evidence against Jim was damning, there was a strong chance that the jury would simply not be able to decipher the screwy transactions that the OIC had presented during the trial. Furthermore, much of the prosecution's case against Jim relied on David Hale's testimony, and none of us could believe that any jury could overlook his past history as a con man—despite the impressive performance he'd turned in on the stand.

Incredibly, we were all in agreement: none of the three of us would testify. We would stand on our innocence and dare the jury to believe Hale. When I went to bed that night, I got a good night's sleep for the first time in months. Unfortunately, in his hotel room, Jim was awake, thinking rather than sleeping.

The following morning, Jim announced that he'd changed his mind. He now wanted to testify. I was beside myself.

"Jim, we agreed last night!" I yelled at him. "None of us is going to testify! This could mess up everything."

Jim drew himself up and responded haughtily, "My people expect to hear from me, Susan. They've heard the allegations, and now the people expect me to respond."

"Your people!" I shrieked. "Your people! Exactly which people are you talking about, Jim?"

Jim maintained his irritating calm. "A lot of people have been closely following Whitewater," he informed me. "Not just the public. Journalists. Historians. They want to hear from me."

I begged Jim to let Bobby McDaniel talk to him about his testimony. Bobby was extremely nervous about Jim testifying and I was hoping that maybe he could talk some sense into Jim or, at the very least, find out what Jim was going to say. Jim never gave Bobby the time of day, instead brushing him off by saying, "By the time I'm finished, Susan will look like Mother Teresa." When Bobby tried to pin him down on how exactly he'd do that, Jim just kept referring back to his previous trial and reminding us that he'd "kicked their asses." Unable to get a straight answer, Bobby finally gave up.

The morning of Jim's testimony, I sat with him at breakfast and watched as he popped so many pills it looked like he would overdose. "I've had fifteen Prozacs in the last twenty-four hours," he confided with a smile.

"Jim," I said, "you need to be careful. And please be careful how you answer questions on the stand today."

This enraged Jim. He stuck a finger in my face and shouted, "They're the ones who had better be careful!" His eyes wild, he shouted about how the prosecution better look out for him and how he was going to bring them all down. With a feeling of dread, I realized that if Jim's testimony was going to bring anyone down, it was almost certainly going to be one or both of us.

Jim's testimony on direct examination wasn't great, but it wasn't horrible either. He explained the transactions in question and told the jury that if there were any problems, he was the one to blame. He also testified that he'd never seen me do a dishonest thing in my life. Although his testimony was uneven—and although he seemed to be acting sicker and frailer than he was—I felt a bit more confident after he finished.

On cross-examination, however, it was Ray Jahn who destroyed Jim. He dissected him like a biologist guts a frog. At first Jim tried to engage Jahn in a battle of wits, but it was soon clear that Jim was overmatched. Jahn produced document after incriminating document that

Jim couldn't explain—and whenever he tried to, his explanations sounded ridiculous. At one point Jim accused the OIC and a U.S. congressman of forging his signatures.

Things went from bad to worse, and the worse they got, the more Jim feigned illness. At one point, he even began faking a heart attack. It was equal parts pitiful and ridiculous—even the most naive observer could see that he was faking. At one point I saw two jurors actually laughing at him.

By the second day of his cross-examination, Jim knew he was going down, and he was barely even putting up a fight. I'd tried to talk to him the night before, but he was angry and refused to talk about the trial or his testimony. Now, sitting helplessly at the defense table, all I could do was watch as he self-destructed.

The cross-examination on the second day started out innocuously enough, with Jahn asking Jim questions about our relationship and my role in it. Jim began by saying that I had always played an important role in the success of our business. In fact, one of the things that he had insisted on upon our marriage was that we run our business like his mom and dad did their general store for forty years. He explained that they never made a decision without the other's approval and that was how our marriage had been as well. This cute little anecdote further cemented the point in the jury's mind.

But Jim wasn't finished. He told the jury that I was very smart when it came to business and that he had relied on my judgment heavily. Furthermore, I was intimately involved in all aspects of the developments—including the financial end. He reiterated how smart I was and praised me for my business acumen. Not only was he bolstering David Hale's testimony, he was embellishing on it.

I sat frozen at the defense table, unable to believe what I was hearing. *This can't be happening,* I thought. Not only was Jim lying, but he was telling lies that had no possible purpose other than to hurt me. I had always thought the phrase "Your blood runs cold" was just a metaphor, but that day I literally felt like ice water had been pumped into my veins.

This was more than just damaging testimony. It was an absolute and complete betrayal. For years I had been defending Jim McDougal to friends and family, based on my unshakable belief that, despite his faults, he had a good heart. There had been more than enough warning signs that I was wrong, but I had consistently chosen to ignore them. Now, in an instant, I had to face a terrible fact: the man that I'd trusted for all those years, and believed in so strongly, was an absolute fraud.

As soon as there was a break, Bobby said to me, "I have to cross-examine Jim."

Still in shock, I told Bobby, "Jim has already made it clear that he won't let you. He won't stand for it."

But Bobby knew I was in danger of being convicted unless he could get one point across to the jury—and he needed Jim's help to do it. "Tell him I'll only ask two questions: when did Susan leave for Dallas, and was she involved in the business affairs after that?"

I walked over to Jim, struggling to control my anger, and asked him if he'd be willing to answer two questions on the stand. I told him what the questions were.

He stared at me, his eyes cold. "If that hick lawyer of yours asks me even one question," he said, "it will be the biggest mistake of his career."

As calmly as I could, I turned from Jim and walked out of the courtroom. Barely holding it together, I looked for someplace I could go where I'd have a few moments alone. Blindly, I somehow made my way to the judge's elevator in the back of the courthouse and got in. I rode the elevator to another floor, stumbled out, and found a deserted stairwell. I plopped down on the top step and cried for the next fifteen minutes.

The Jim McDougal I thought I'd known was no more. For twenty years I'd always stood by Jim, no matter how he'd treated me or what was at stake. I'd loved him, believed in him, and trusted him for my entire adult life. When he betrayed me in that courtroom, he killed something that I had previously thought would never die.

From that day on, I would no longer be under his power. I never confronted him about his betrayal on the stand. He would have just dismissed me, anyway. I suspected that he realized he was about to be convicted and he did not want to go down alone. But for the first time, I suddenly no longer cared what Jim thought or wanted. When I was finally able to control myself, I stood up and returned to the courtroom.

* * *

The Woman Who Wouldn't Talk

As the closing arguments began, I tried to convince myself that I shouldn't put too much emphasis on Jim's testimony. Only a few days before, after all, I'd been confident that I'd be acquitted, and journalists and court observers were still congratulating me and saying I had nothing to worry about. But I knew Jim's testimony had done considerable damage to me.

The jury was out for several days. I tried to stay upbeat—for others as well as myself—but I was preparing myself for the worst. On May 28, 1996, it came, and it was worse than I'd imagined.

I remember a lot of things about the trial, but no memory burns brighter—or more painfully—than the image of the three jurors who walked back into the courtroom laughing. These people had decided to take away the lives, the very freedom, of three human beings—and they seemed to be having a great time doing it. I will never forget those laughing faces as long as I live.

When the verdicts were announced, Jim McDougal had been convicted on eighteen counts, and Jim Guy Tucker had been convicted on two. And the jury had found me guilty of all four of the counts that the judge hadn't thrown out.

I immediately decided that I wouldn't give the jury and prosecution the satisfaction of seeing my emotions. Though I could see my brother David crying in the rows of spectators, I remained stoic.

For the next minute, I listened as Judge Howard thanked the jury for their service and then, worst of all, thanked them for praying to God each day for guidance, as though God himself had convicted me. All the while, Jim Guy Tucker's young children were in the front row crying hysterically. It was all I could do not to shout out in anger, but I was not going to give them that satisfaction either. I strode out of the courtroom and tried to gather my thoughts.

I was about to begin life as a convicted felon.

11

WHEN YOU DISS UPON A STARR

FOR FOUR SOLID DAYS AFTER THE verdict, I lay in a bed at Claudia Riley's house, curled up in a fetal position. I couldn't get up and I couldn't talk. I was devastated. I had been found guilty of doing something that I was not even aware had happened until ten years later. Guilty! It just kept going through my mind over and over.

As I lay there, I thought back on the number of mistakes I'd made and the incredibly poor judgment I had shown throughout my life. Over and over I came back to the same thought: I had only myself to blame for this mess. People who cared about me had been trying to warn me for years, but I had refused to listen. I was seriously beginning to question whether I even had the ability to function in society.

The immediate future consisted of a sentencing hearing that might send me to jail and a trial in California that could keep me there another seven years. I had run off the man I loved by trying to help a man who apparently couldn't care less if I lived or died. And to top it off, I was dead broke, had no home, and was a nationally known convicted felon.

But perhaps the worst thing was that I was filled with an uncontrollable rage. It's impossible to understand what it feels like to be convicted of a crime you didn't commit. The anger is beyond your control. You desperately want to lash back at the people responsible, but that's not possible. As the frustration grows and grows, it needs a release, anything to relieve the hostility inside. But there is no release.

At Claudia's I did nothing for those first four days. Every time I tried to concentrate on something other than the trial, I would hit a psychological wall that I simply could not get past. I hated the OIC and Ken Starr, and that hatred was destroying my ability to function. I'd never been good at anger—feeling sorry for myself was more up my alley—and I didn't know how to handle it. In nearly forty years of living, I'd been truly angry less than a handful of times.

Claudia finally convinced me to get out of bed, but I wasn't much better off for it. For days I sat around her house in the same T-shirt and shorts, envisioning the cruel ways I wanted my enemies to suffer. "Susan," Claudia would say, interrupting my dark reveries, "you need to get out and do something, even if it's just taking a walk around the block." But I refused.

One day Claudia came to my room with a pen and yellow legal pad suggesting that I make a to-do list. That was how she coped when things got bad. "I feel so good every time I check off one. Now get up and make a list. You'll feel so much better," she told me. I decided that one of us had lost her mind. But her suggestion did have the desired effect: I snuck out of the house later that day and walked down the block to a neighbor's house to complain about Claudia and her stupid lists. The neighbor called Claudia and told her I had run away from home and that she needed to get off my back.

Claudia, however, was not to be deterred. Whenever Claudia was on a tear, Megan, her daughter, used to imitate an announcer's TV voice and declare, "There she is, Claudia Riley, woman of action." My lying around the house whining was not going to be allowed by Claudia Riley, woman of action. She called a friend of hers who was head of the psychology department at a local college and asked if he would see me as a favor to her. He agreed, provided that I came in of my own accord. Though I was still unable to function, I did at least have enough sense to realize that I needed professional help before I ended up on a roof somewhere, taking potshots at strangers. And seeing Claudia's doctor friend would at least get Claudia off my back, even if it accomplished nothing else.

Claudia told me all about Dr. Erwen Janek, building him up as a brilliant man who had incredible empathy for his patients and a sense of humor she thought I'd appreciate. There was one thing she didn't tell me, however, and it was immediately apparent when I stepped into his office.

Dr. Janek was in a wheelchair and was unable to use his legs and one of his arms. He also could only speak in whispers, so I had to sit very close to him to hear what he was saying. His physical problems, which were the result of multiple sclerosis, would have been absolutely debilitating to many people, yet Dr. Janek was sitting there with this loopy grin on his face. He'd been a star athlete in school, he told me, and he'd always been a little uncomfortable around people with any kind of handicaps. So he'd decided that putting him in a wheelchair was God's way of showing him that he needed to lighten up a little. He'd been bitter at first, he said, but he'd learned that the only way to survive on a day-to-day basis was to look at his life and his situation with a sense of humor.

I don't know whether Claudia sent me to Dr. Janek because he was a good doctor, or because she knew that I'd react to his attitude about his own personal problems. I do know, however, that after listening to him talk, I found it very hard to continue to feel sorry for myself. By the time the session was over, I was inviting him home for chocolate chip cookies. I was on my way back. When I left the doctor's office, I felt for the first time since the trial that I might make it through everything.

Just down the hill from Claudia, Jim McDougal was back in the guest house. I asked Megan how he was doing because I had not talked to him since the verdict. She told me he was doing fine—he had not changed a bit.

"Jim has changed," I insisted to her. "He's no longer the man I thought he was."

"Susan," she said, "Jim was never the man you thought he was."

*   *   *

The Woman Who Wouldn't Talk

My favorite movie of all time is *The Godfather Part II*, and one of my favorite lines comes when Michael Corleone quotes his father's advice: "Keep your friends close, but your enemies closer." After nearly forty years of winging it, I figured it was time now to pay attention to what was happening around me.

I suspected Jim was now considering cooperating with the OIC, and I wanted to know what was up their sleeve. Jim could provide that information for me, as long as I just kept acting like my usual self. So I watched what went on down the hill and kept an eye on Jim.

Wasting no time, OIC attorney Amy St. Eve had called Jim to tell him how sorry she was that things had turned out the way they had. She was actually a Democrat, she told him, and had genuinely hated having to prosecute him. Would he be so kind, she went on, to autograph her copy of *Blood Sport*, James B. Stewart's book about Whitewater? Also, she would love to take him to lunch and just talk.

This was right down Jim's alley as the OIC must have expected and he arranged right away for Amy St. Eve to come see him at the WesterN SizzliN restaurant in Arkadelphia where he ate lunch every day. After their lunch, Jim came swaggering up the hill to Claudia's house, blustering about what a fine young woman St. Eve was. "She was just following Starr's orders," he said of her part in our prosecutions.

"That's the defense the Nazis used at the Nuremberg trials," I muttered, before excusing myself and retreating to the back bedroom.

Soon it wasn't just St. Eve coming to visit: Jim was being courted by the OIC like a rich widower at a church social. The traffic flow between the Little Rock OIC office and Jim's house increased dramatically as, one by one, virtually every member of the OIC's office came down to pay homage to the man they'd just eviscerated in court. And every time someone would visit, Jim would come up to the house and tell Claudia and me what nice people they were. "They just want to help," he said. "They know I'm in trouble, and they want to help me. They never wanted us to suffer, anyway! It was the Clintons they were after." From what I could tell, honesty and integrity were in very short supply on both sides of the fence.

I had forever lost my ability to be surprised by anything Jim McDougal did or said. In truth, his deal with Amy St. Eve was predictable—Jim was always scrambling to find a ledge to hang on to. But this time, it was Jim who was in for a surprise. When he told me about his conversations with the OIC, Jim almost certainly expected me to start screaming. Instead, I gave him a hug and told him I understood what he was doing. I knew he was scared to death of dying in jail and I told him I did not want that either.

Inevitably, the OIC circus parade to Arkadelphia came to include the ringleader himself—Kenneth Starr. One sunny July afternoon, Claudia and I looked out the window to see a fleet of government cars pulling into Jim's driveway. Starr popped out of one car, dressed in Sans-a-belt slacks and a plaid workman's shirt, presumably so that he would fit in with the local folks. He was carrying a large bag of M&Ms—Jim's favorite treat. This made for quite a picture: here was the purported protector of the nation's morals, the $500-an-hour Washington lawyer and Supreme Court hopeful, reduced to being a badly dressed bag man for a mentally ill felon.

Apparently the two hit it off, because Starr stayed in Jim's house for quite some time. When Starr finally did leave, Jim, as usual, couldn't wait to come up the hill to tell us about the meeting. Sure enough, Jim launched into a whole recital about how Starr wasn't the beast we'd thought. He was just a regular, down-home guy who wanted to help us. "If Kenneth Starr really wants to help," I said in the most sarcastic tone I could muster, "he can go on TV and say he's a lying bastard. That would help me a lot." Jim dismissed my comment with a wave of his hand and continued on to say how sorry Starr was for all of this.

It took only one more week for the OIC and Jim McDougal to consummate their union. I hadn't heard from him in a few days, but then he called me up at Claudia's and told me excitedly that he was about to make a deal. So I decided to venture down the hill and see what was up.

When I walked in, Jim was on the phone. He waved at me to sit down and be quiet, then continued his conversation. It was obvious that the party on the other end of the phone was someone from the OIC.

Jim listened for a little while, then ticked off his laundry list of requests. He told them he had a lot of "good information"—information that would take them a while to get through. So, he continued, he'd need to have his sentencing hearing delayed for quite some time. Jim paused to hear the response, and after a moment he broke into a grin and gave me the thumbs-up sign.

He continued with his list, warming to the topic as he went along. With all the time he'd be spending in Little Rock, he'd really need to have his own apartment there. Oh, and a driver so he could get around more easily. He hadn't worked in a while, so some walking-around money would be great, especially because he had so many prescriptions to fill.

After describing each item, Jim would sit quivering, listening to the response. And every time, he'd break into a big grin and give me the thumbs-up sign. Jim was writing his own ticket, and he enjoyed having me there to witness it. The next thing he asked for was really the kicker to me—he wanted Ken Starr himself to come to his sentencing hearing and tell the judge that he was a God-fearing man. Jim, who throughout our marriage had made fun of my religious beliefs, was now asking the OIC to tell the judge that he was like Paul on the road to Damascus. Incredibly enough, they had no problem with that either. Finally, Jim asked that, if he did end up getting sentenced to jail, he'd be placed in a federal facility nearby—if possible, a medical facility.

When he got off the phone, Jim was as excited as I had ever seen him. He had really put it to the OIC and claimed he was back in control.

"Did you hear that?" he yelled. "I got everything I asked for. Everything! They've even promised to have Judge Starr come to my sentencing hearing and testify that I'm a God-fearing man. Fuck the lawyers! I'm better than any lawyers!"

So I started my usual—"Jim that was just great. You were wonderful. You really got 'em." But I added, "You need to tell them you won't cooperate unless they get me probation. That would be an easy thing for you to do. After all, they really need you."

"I will, I will," Jim assured me. "I promise, baby. But let me get to know them a little before I bring that up."

This wasn't the answer I was looking for, but as always I didn't push Jim. But there was one other thing I needed to ask him, even though I knew it would spoil his wonderful mood. In order for the OIC to offer all these enticements, they obviously expected that Jim would give them some sort of bombshell information about the Clintons.

"Jim," I said, "you don't know of anything the Clintons did wrong. You've told me that—not to mention the entire country—over and over."

Jim exploded. "Fuck the Clintons!" he screamed. "Fuck them! What the fuck have they ever done for us? At the first sign of trouble, they ran like dogs!"

Jim's face flushed red to the top of his head. "They lied to you! They lied to MY MOTHER! Do you think they care about what happens to you? The only thing the Clintons care about is *the Clintons*! Anytime anyone gets into trouble, they just cut them loose. Well, now it's *my* turn to cut *them* loose!"

I didn't doubt that Jim truly felt this way about Bill and Hillary Clinton. Yet I knew that Jim also had an ulterior motive for trying to turn me against the Clintons. Jim was considered eccentric, even erratic. If he did testify against the Clintons, there were plenty of people who would never believe him. But if Jim could convince me to testify to the same things, then he'd be vindicated—and the OIC would be even more indebted to him than it already was.

My feelings about the Clintons were more complicated than Jim's. I didn't share Jim's outright loathing of them, but I didn't feel any great loyalty to them, either. I had never gotten along with Hillary all that well, but I knew beyond a shadow of a doubt that this was a witch-hunt, and I knew of nothing that she or Bill had done wrong.

For the next several weeks, Jim pushed me to cooperate with the OIC. He was now meeting with them regularly, and he'd always come up the hill to fill me in on the details. He'd also test out stories on Claudia and me to see if they sounded plausible before trying them out on the OIC. I knew Jim was beyond arguing about the ethical ramifications of his making up stories, but it seemed to me to be just plain dangerous, so I tried using that argument to convince him not to do it.

"Don't you even realize how stupid this is?" I said to him in exasperation after he'd tried out yet another story. "Don't you think that the president will use all his resources and all his lawyers to rip apart any story you can create? They're going to kill you with these stories that you're making up!"

In response, Jim smiled wide. "You just don't get it, do you?" he said. "I'm not making these things up out of whole cloth. They're giving me the documents to look over so I can make it right! I've got all the documents, Susan. The Clintons don't!"

Suddenly I was the one who felt stupid. All along, I was wondering how in the world the OIC would handle a man who was mentally ill and whose stories were clearly more fiction than fact. Now the answer was obvious: they were helping him create the stories, and making sure that he had all the details just right. Once again, I was the idiot! The OIC wasn't looking for the truth—they wanted to nail the Clintons no matter what.

Each time Jim prepared to meet with the OIC, I would remind him of his promise to inquire about probation for me. Jim kept promising to do it, but every time he came back, he'd say, "The person I needed to talk to wasn't there," or "It just wasn't the right time today." He'd then go on to say that if I'd just cut my own deal with the OIC, I'd definitely walk away with no jail time.

As the days went by, Jim began to ratchet up the pressure. He'd come up the hill to Claudia's and tell me, "You're an idiot if you don't cooperate. Don't you realize you're about to go to jail?" As my sentencing hearing approached, Jim's nagging escalated into screaming, and on one memorable occasion, he began knocking over furniture before Claudia and I could get him out of the house. "All you have to do," he shouted as he left, "is say that Clinton knew about the loan."

Jim was desperate for me to cooperate—so desperate, in fact, that I later suspected he'd promised the OIC he could deliver me as a witness as part of his arrangement. There was no reason for him to think he couldn't, as I had always done what he asked. He never doubted for a moment that I would crack and we'd be partners again. Now I was balking, and he was getting nervous.

Shortly after I told Jim I wouldn't back up any of the lies he was telling the OIC or David Hale's lie that Bill Clinton knew about the $300,000 loan, he met with the OIC and came back with an alternate plan. It involved the head of the OIC's Arkansas operation, a man named Hickman Ewing. As a part-time fundamentalist preacher, Ewing considered the Clintons the antithesis of everything he believed in. He seemed to despise them both and he was at the forefront of the hardliners' crusade to remove Bill from office at all costs.

Because the 1996 presidential election was approaching, Jim told me, Ewing was particularly interested in seamy revelations about Clinton's sex life. If he could just unearth the right tidbit, Ewing apparently believed he could derail Clinton's campaign. That's where I came in.

"If you'll just say you had sex with Bill Clinton," Jim told me, "they'll give you anything you want."

Apparently, Jim and Ewing had decided that if I wouldn't lie about money, maybe I wouldn't mind being the new Gennifer Flowers. After all, I could get a lot of media attention, make a few dollars selling my story to the tabloids, and I would never have to worry about answering questions about messy financial details. Just talk about a few tumbles in the sack—no big deal.

"That's just great, Jim," I told him. "Now you just want me to be a whore, Starr's whore no less! You can forget it. That is one story my mother will never see in print."

But Jim wasn't ready to give up yet. He soon came back with a third option, one that wouldn't involve going after Bill at all, he said. "The OIC thinks you won't testify because you're in love with Bill and trying to protect him," Jim said. Apparently, in the OIC's limited imagination, the most obvious motivator for any woman was the love of a good man. So, to exploit this unrequited passion of mine, they decided to offer me another option. I could testify against the person coming between my supposed lover Bill and me: Hillary.

Jim was sure I would go for this option. It was an ideal compromise—I didn't have to lie about the president, and I'd never cared much about Hillary anyway. What could be more perfect? But even as Jim listed the merits of this option as he saw them, I had to laugh. He made it sound so easy to just get up in front of a group of people and lie about something that I knew nothing about. Just watching the interaction between Jim and the OIC that summer was enough to make me despise them both.

And yet, as my sentencing hearing drew near, I realized that within weeks I would very likely be sentenced to jail. My family and friends kept assuring me that, since I was a first-time offender, the judge might grant probation, but I wasn't so confident. Every day Jim walked up the hill to tell me, "The OIC is ready for you. If you'll just agree to it, there's no way you'll go to jail."

The thought of jail absolutely terrified me, and now it was becoming an imminent possibility rather than just an abstraction. I reassured my family and friends that I could handle it, and that it wouldn't be as bad as the movies made it out to be. But privately I was scared to death; as a person who regularly whined when the bedsheet corners weren't tight enough, or when a scrambled egg wasn't the right consistency, I wasn't sure if I could handle jail. "If the OIC has such a great deal for me," I told Jim about a week before my sentencing hearing, "then they should call Bobby McDaniel and talk to him."

"They have!" Jim exclaimed. "They've called him a bunch of times! He won't talk to them." But when I called Bobby, he told me that the OIC had never called, not even once. As they'd done with Jim, the OIC had consistently tried to get me to meet with them without my lawyer. "Well, let's call them and just hear what they have to say," I told Bobby.

So a few days before my sentencing hearing, Claudia and I made the three-hour drive to Bobby's office in Jonesboro. Shortly after we arrived, Bobby ushered us into his private conference room, called Ray Jahn, and put on the speakerphone so all three of us could hear. Bobby wasted no time in coming to the point.

"If Susan agrees to cooperate," he began, leaning toward the speakerphone, "what are you prepared to offer?"

Jahn's response was immediate and categorical. If my proffer was acceptable, he said, the OIC would go before the judge at the sentencing hearing and recommend probation rather than jail time. They had spoken to the D.A. in California and could also help me with the charges filed by Nancy Mehta in California. And they would help quash new federal income tax charges that were being drawn up against me as we spoke. In one fell swoop, I could have my life back.

Bobby looked at me, then spoke again. "Exactly what is it you want from her?"

"She knows who this investigation is about," Jahn said. "And she knows what we want."

As long as I live, I will never forget hearing those words. Bobby looked at me, but I couldn't respond—I was in a state of shock. He had made it as clear as he possibly could what they expected from me.

As I sat at the conference table, tears began rolling down my face and I fought to control my emotions.

"My client's distraught," Bobby told Jahn. "We're going to have to call you back." Jahn responded that we needed to do so that day, or the deal was off.

Claudia and I left Bobby's office and walked down the street to a small café. By now I was starting to get my emotions under control but I was still unable to face the choice I now had to make. "What do you think I should do?" I asked her.

Claudia looked at me intently, with a mixture of kindness and worry on her face. "If you were my daughter, Susan," she said, "I'd tell you to take the deal. Do whatever they want, say whatever they want. Save yourself."

I thought about this for a moment. "Is that what Bob would have said?" I asked her. "Because I don't think he would have agreed to it."

Claudia sat back and considered my question. "No," she finally answered. "Bob probably would have told you to fight the bastards to the end."

We sat in silence for a few minutes, and then I said, "I need to call Pat."

Pat had stayed in California after we had fought about the Whitewater trial, but we still spoke almost every day and we were slowly beginning to put our relationship back together again. He had been devastated by my guilty verdict. I also knew that he was the one person I could trust to be completely honest with me. I called him and, as usual, tried to make a joke about it.

"The dark side is looking considerably better to me," I told him. Then I went into detail about the phone conversation and what the OIC was offering.

"No one could blame you if you took this deal," he told me. "It's a tempting offer." We talked about what a relief it would be to avoid going to trial in California—especially since any jury would now look askance at me because I was a convicted felon.

"So you think I should take it?" I asked.

There was a long pause before Pat replied, "You can't."

"What do you mean, I can't?"

"Susan," he said, "it may sound simple. You just go into their office and agree to back up David Hale, or say something negative about Hillary, and then go on with the rest of your life. But it doesn't work that way. A lie isn't just for that day. You'll have to spend the next year or more of your life going before grand juries and into courtrooms—and possibly even an impeachment hearing—telling a story you know isn't true and destroying other people's lives the way the OIC has destroyed yours.

"If you do this," he told me, "it will never end. You'll be lying for the rest of your life."

As Pat spoke, I began crying again. "Will you stand by me? Will you be there? And help me? I can't do this by myself."

"I'll always be there for you," he said. "You won't ever be by yourself. Not one day. Not one minute. I promise."

This was just what I needed to hear. Claudia and I went back to Bobby's office, and I announced, "Don't call them back." Bobby, who hated the OIC almost as much as I did, was delighted—but being a good lawyer, he asked me if I was sure that this was what I wanted.

"I'm sure," I told him.

During the three-hour drive back to Arkadelphia, Claudia and I talked mostly about irrelevant subjects, in an effort to keep my mind off what had just happened. But I already knew what lay ahead. For the first time since the trial, I was relatively sure I was going to jail.

I dropped Claudia off in Arkadelphia and drove the hour home to my parents'.

I had no sooner walked in the door than the phone was ringing. It was Jim.

"What's going on?" he demanded. "I just talked with the OIC, and they said you never called them back."

"Jim," I said, trying to keep calm, "I can't do it."

Jim exploded. "When are you going to quit being such a fucking Pollyanna?" he yelled. "How can you have turned that down? Do you understand that you are going to jail? They are going to put you in jail!"

I didn't respond, which seemed only to enrage Jim further.

"Susan, you had better do this thing," he warned, "or I don't believe I ever want to speak to you again."

For the first time since I had met and married Jim McDougal twenty years before, he heard me say the words, "No, Jim. I won't do it."

There was a brief pause, and then Jim slammed the phone down. We never spoke to each other again.

12

THE SILENCE OF THE HAM

FOR MY SENTENCING HEARING on August 19, 1996, the OIC brought out their whole gang of lawyers, including Kenneth Starr himself. This would be the first—and only—time I'd see him face-to-face.

Before the hearing began, Starr saw me standing against the courtroom railing and walked over, his hand outstretched as if to say, "Nothing personal." That may have been true for him—after all, no one had come into his life and destroyed it, as he had mine. For me, it was very personal. As he strode over, an inane smile on his face, I glared at him and said, "Don't even think about it." He turned and retreated to the OIC table.

The maximum sentence I could receive was seventeen years, and the OIC immediately made it clear to the judge that they thought I deserved all or at least a good portion of that amount. The OIC lawyers put on a full-court press, describing me in terms usually reserved for serial killers and asking the court to consider the "gravity" of my crimes. They pulled out my old Occidental Petroleum résumé to show my deceitful nature. My attorneys argued strenuously for probation, but none of us felt very confident I'd get it.

Pat had flown in from California to testify on my behalf, and for almost half an hour he defended me and explained why I'd made the choices I had. At the end of his testimony, as he struggled to explain why I'd stayed so loyal to Jim—the same issue that had finally driven us apart—he broke down crying and had a hard time continuing. After a few moments of silence, he managed to choke out, "She has the best heart of any person I have ever met."

Because we hadn't put on a defense in the Whitewater trial, this was the first time that anyone on a witness stand had said even one kind thing about me. For months I'd been blasted by everyone—the OIC lawyers, their witnesses, the press. The judge and jury had only heard terrible things about me, and I was absolutely shocked at what a relief it was to finally hear something nice about myself in a courtroom. My family was also touched by Pat's testimony, though it was obvious from the expressionless faces of the OIC lawyers and Judge Howard that it had no effect on them. No matter what happened in the future, it meant everything to me that Pat believed I was a good person after all that we had been through.

When the hearing ended, we waited to hear Judge Howard's decision. For a couple of reasons, we all felt there was at least a possibility, albeit a small one, that I would receive probation. First, Jim Guy Tucker—who'd been convicted on the more serious charge of conspiracy—had just received two years of house arrest. Second, I was a minor player in the whole Whitewater drama, a fact even the OIC couldn't dispute.

But it was not going to happen. The atmosphere in the courtroom that day and Judge Howard's voice and face showed little mercy. Judge Howard sentenced me to two years in federal prison. I was surprised, but not in shock. Judge Howard ruled almost immediately that I couldn't stay out on bail while we filed our appeal, but he did allow me approximately forty days to get my affairs in order before turning myself in to the U.S. marshals. Somehow, even though I'd just been sentenced to two years, it didn't seem at all possible that I'd really be going to jail.

My family, however, was not feeling so sanguine. I walked over to where they were sitting—my parents, brothers, sisters, nieces, and nephews—pulled them close, and told them not to worry. "This isn't over yet," I said.

While we were huddled together in the courtroom, one of the FBI agents from the OIC chose that moment to stride over and, with a smile on his face, hand me a document. It was a subpoena to appear before the Whitewater grand jury in two weeks' time. If he had actually said, "Gotcha," I would not have been surprised.

Once again, rage boiled up within me. Whatever the OIC did to me, it never seemed to be enough for them. It wasn't enough that I'd just been sentenced to prison for crimes I didn't commit; they had clearly chosen this moment to shove it in my face. All the things the OIC had done to me over the past two years were piling up.

After the hearing I had lunch with my family and told them not to worry. I was gaining confidence that I would win on appeal because my lawyers explained to me that after Judge Howard threw out the conspiracy charges against me, my trial should have been separated from Jim and Jim Guy. Later that afternoon Pat and I drove to Nashville, the scene of our last happy times together. It was a gorgeous summer day, and even though I'd just been sentenced to jail, I somehow managed to put it out of my head. Pat and I were reconciling from our breakup, and as we tooled down the interstate, we were talking and laughing the whole way. When we arrived in Nashville, it was like old times being with Pat's family again. For a few hours, at least, I was able to forget the reality of my situation.

But the next morning I woke up shaking, and for the rest of the morning Pat held me while I cried. I sobbed for what seemed like hours, until I was literally too exhausted to cry anymore.

This would be the first and last time I would cry about jail. I was all cried out, but replacing the sadness and the fear was an anger that was so all-encompassing, so overwhelming, that nothing seemed beyond the pale to me. I imagined every sort of torture for Kenneth Starr, every retaliation imaginable. My brother Bill has a saying: "You don't mess with a person whose back is against the wall because they have nowhere to go but at you." After that day I decided to go right at Kenneth Starr and the OIC.

My first attempt at retaliation misfired badly. Ever since my name had come up in connection with Whitewater, TV news shows had been hounding me for interviews. I had consistently declined, figuring that if I just kept my mouth shut, everything would work out fine and I could fade back into obscurity. But everything hadn't worked out fine, and now the only story in play was the OIC's version: that they were the dogged pursuers of the truth and I was a criminal they'd exposed.

Chris Vlasto of ABC had been my most persistent pursuer. He'd also been one of the most courteous, always offering to give Jim and me rides or buy us lunch. I'd come close to talking to him back in Nashville, when the Whitewater story first broke, and he'd camped outside our house for hours on end. Now I was ready to talk—and Vlasto was ready with a deal.

He proposed doing a *Prime Time Live* segment with Diane Sawyer about who I was, where I'd come from, and how I'd ended up in this mess. I would, he said, be able to tell my side of the story and explain everything in my own words. I was tempted, but not yet convinced— but then he angled for my weakest spot. "Nobody really has any idea of who you are," and as a result, he said, people had developed negative opinions of me based on what they'd read in the newspapers. Because my most enduring characteristic is wanting to be universally loved, this argument was persuasive.

I called Pat and asked him what he thought. "I think it's okay to do it," he said, "as long as they understand that there are certain questions you can't answer." I was scheduled to appear before the Whitewater grand jury in a week's time, and Pat didn't want me to give the OIC any additional ammunition. When I relayed this to Vlasto, he said it wouldn't be a problem. This was to be a background piece, not an in-depth look at Whitewater. He even agreed to meet with us the night before the taping to determine which questions would be off-limits.

I then called my brother Bill, the family consigliere, and he liked the idea as well. However, there was one catch—he was coming along. I had screwed up enough on my own and he wanted to be there to protect me.

Pat, Bill, and I flew to New York, and the day before the taping we met Chris Vlasto in a restaurant to discuss the ground rules of the interview. Pat explained which areas were out-of-bounds, and again Vlasto didn't hesitate. It wouldn't be a problem, he told us. We went back to our hotel that night and worked on my television image, which Bill was convinced needed a lot of work. He kept complaining that my mouth was doing something funny when I tried to explain something. "For God's sake, Susan, you look and sound like an old woman on the BBC."

The next afternoon, we met Diane Sawyer in a hotel suite near Central Park. True to Vlasto's word, she spent the early portion of the interview focusing on my background and how Jim and I came to know the Clintons. After a couple of hours, we took a break. Bill and Pat, who'd been standing nearby watching, told me it was going well. "Just keep doing what you're doing," Pat said. Bill told me that I had not looked British even once.

But when we started up again, things quickly turned ugly. Sawyer casually dropped in a question we'd specifically designated as out-of-bounds—and I immediately froze. Unsure of what to do, I turned to look at Pat and Bill, who were shaking their heads, signaling not to answer. I stumbled around for a few moments, searching for some kind of answer, before regaining my composure and saying that I didn't think I could respond to the question for legal reasons. But Sawyer persisted, rephrasing the question—and again I looked over to Pat and Bill for help. Again, they shook their heads, and I replied that I couldn't answer the question.

After a moment, we moved on. I assumed that Diane Sawyer had simply made a mistake—but a few minutes later she broached a second subject that Vlasto had assured us would not be discussed. By now thoroughly confused, I again looked around, sat silently for a moment, then stumbled my way through an apology for not being able to answer the question.

Then Bill took charge. He asked for the taping to stop, then walked over to Sawyer. "This is not what we agreed to," he told her. He then reiterated that I'd be facing a hostile prosecutor before a grand jury in a few days and I couldn't risk having this interview thrown in my face. "We kept our word," he said, "and now you need to keep yours." Sawyer glared coldly at Bill, then agreed to move on.

But the same thing happened again. This time, both Bill and Pat began shouting, "Turn the cameras off! That's it!" Vlasto stepped in, suggesting we take a break for a few minutes to let everyone cool down. Bill, Pat, and I went into another room and discussed whether we should continue with the interview or just walk out. After a few minutes, we decided to continue, but we told Vlasto that if it happened again, we were out of there. Once again, I took my seat in front of Sawyer.

The rest of the interview went along without a problem—until we reached the end. At that point, Vlasto approached Pat and pleaded with him to let Sawyer ask me a question about my trial lawyers, Bobby and Jennifer. He wanted to know whether I felt that they'd represented me or whether they were just fronting for the White House. "That's ridiculous," Pat snapped. He told Vlasto he wouldn't let Sawyer bring up some broad accusation against Bobby and Jennifer when they weren't there to defend themselves. But Vlasto kept pushing. He knew they'd been in communication with the White House, he said, and he wanted to blow the lid off it. Again, Pat told him no.

The story was a bombshell, all right—except that it was totally false. As soon as Pat relayed it to me, I knew exactly where it had come from: Jim McDougal. During one of his visits to Claudia's house, he'd tried out that story on us, substituting his own lawyer, Sam Heuer, as the culprit. Jim had liked that particular story a great deal, and after he started cooperating with the OIC, he began spreading it around, adding Bobby and Jennifer's name to the mix to further stir things up.

The interview ended and Diane said good-bye to me and even to Pat, but never said a word to Bill, who was not used to women who don't fawn all over him. Despite the clashes, Vlasto offered to buy us all dinner to celebrate how well it had gone. I'd spoken to Sawyer for the better part of three hours, and for the most part Bill, Pat, and I felt good about it. We were wary about the parts that we'd fought over—but

Vlasto assured us that those would be edited out. So we headed for dinner with Bill still questioning how Diane Sawyer could not have said good-bye to him. Pat and I were howling down the streets of New York as Bill continued to contemplate this turn of events.

By the time we had finished dinner, Vlasto was in high spirits, thanks largely to the number of drinks he had downed. He began telling us funny stories about his work, and we all began to relax and enjoy the conversation. When Hillary Clinton's name came up, Vlasto's mood took a sudden turn.

Vlasto launched into a diatribe about how Hillary had cost him a position at the White House and how she'd specifically called ABC and had him blackballed during the early days of the Clinton administration. She was a "bitch" who'd tried to torpedo his career and he was determined to pay her back, he said. Vlasto's outburst sounded like the delusional rant of an egotist, but we all caught the gist of what had just happened—Bill, Pat, and I looked at each other with the same thought: we've been screwed.

As the liquor kept flowing, things got worse. Vlasto began pushing me hard to cooperate with the OIC. It was obvious that I was protecting the president from some deep dark secret, he said, and I needed to realize that I could save myself if I'd just rat out Clinton. To make his point as clearly as possible, Vlasto began describing his own past experience with legal trouble. He told us he'd been caught selling drugs when he was in prep school and that he'd faced expulsion and possible imprisonment. But the police weren't really after him—they were after his best friend. So they offered Vlasto a deal: if he turned in his friend, he would walk free. Vlasto proudly told us that he'd done exactly that, and he'd never looked back. He told us that he'd never have gotten where he was today if he hadn't been willing to screw over his best friend.

By the time we left dinner that night, it was obvious we were about to be waylaid. We had been foolish to think *Prime Time Live* was bringing us to New York to let me tell my side of the story. They wanted what everyone else wanted: dirt on the Clintons. Everything they'd promised was just a setup—and Diane Sawyer's line of questioning was no accident. This was the only time someone in the media bla-tantly lied to me, and it was devastating. Pat and Bill tried to comfort me by saying that I hadn't said anything horrible or damaging. "The worst they could do," Pat said, "would be to try and edit it in a way that makes you look suspicious."

Which is, of course, exactly what happened. Vlasto and his *Prime Time Live* crew put together a piece that was so convoluted even I had trouble following it. It was so bizarrely edited that Larry King later remarked on how strange it was. Despite the fact that I'd spoken for nearly three hours on a whole variety of subjects, the interview was edited such that viewers of the program would come away with one damaging impression: that I was hiding something about the Clintons.

The questions that Vlasto had promised to cut out became the cor-nerstone of the segment. Viewers were treated to shots of Diane Sawyer earnestly asking me the out-of-bounds questions, followed by close-ups of me frantically looking to one side, at someone unseen off the set. A voice-over from Sawyer duly noted that, whenever I was asked tough questions, I turned to my fiancé and brother for guidance rather than simply answering the questions. The implication was obvious, and Sawyer's voice-overs drove it home more than once.

This was tabloid journalism at its worst—and not at all what I'd expected from *Prime Time Live*. Fortunately, because a few anxious looks were the most noteworthy things to come out of the interview, the show provoked only a small amount of media hoopla. But I'd learned a valuable lesson. From now on, I would stick to live television, where selective editing couldn't be used to create a false impression.

It was during that trip to New York that I began to seriously consider refusing to answer questions at my upcoming grand jury appearance. The interview with Diane Sawyer had unnerved me. Just telling the truth had not worked so well during the interview—what would happen with the OIC behind closed doors without anyone to halt the proceedings if they tried to twist my words? On the plane ride back from New York, I began to warm up to the idea of not testifying and, for the first time, I asked Pat about it. Specifically, I wanted to know what the legal ramifications would be.

"You'd almost certainly be held in contempt of court," Pat said. "And you could be taken immediately to jail." Civil contempt, he went on to explain, is an oddity in the U.S. justice system: it's the only offense for which you can be jailed without any of the normal safeguards such as bail, a trial, or appeals. The rationale behind this is that civil contempt is not a punishment, but rather a means of coercing someone to testify. There's no set sentence for civil contempt; basically, you're supposed to stay in jail until one of two things happens: either you give in and testify, or the judge decides the coercion technique isn't working and releases you. In rare cases, the judge will keep someone in prison for the maximum allowable time for civil contempt—eighteen months.

Why not just testify and tell the truth? As I considered this question in the late summer of 1996, I couldn't have known that it would soon become the defining question about Susan McDougal, the question that would be tossed around on talk shows and in newspaper editorials for the next two years. There was a whole slew of reasons why I chose not to testify, any of which I felt were argument enough. The whole of them combined together made it almost impossible for me to make any other decision.

First, I'd tried to tell the truth in my original meeting with the OIC, back in 1993. As Henry David Thoreau once said, "It takes two to speak the truth—one to speak it, and one to listen." When Steven Lerman opened that meeting by issuing a veiled threat unless I offered information on the Clintons, it became apparent that the truth held little value for the OIC. I had tried to tell the truth in that meeting, but they had no interest in listening.

Second, my experience with *Prime Time Live* had just shown me how easily my words could be twisted. These were supposedly "neutral" journalists, and they'd managed to turn a three-hour interview into ten minutes that depicted me as hiding something sinister. I was afraid of what the experts at the OIC—aggressive, experienced lawyers who were after just one thing—could do to me.

Furthermore, the OIC would be interrogating me on its home court. I couldn't bring my attorney into the grand jury room; I'd be alone, facing people who were experts at manipulating witnesses. I feared them so much that I wouldn't even testify on my own behalf at my trial—and that was out in the open, with my own lawyers there. There was no way I felt safe going into a grand jury room, where there was no judge to keep an eye on the proceedings and Ray Jahn would be the ultimate authority.

Third—and the ultimate irony—was that I feared being accused of perjury if I told the grand jury the truth. The OIC had accepted David Hale's lies as the truth. They were also now relying on Jim McDougal's lies, which they'd carefully helped him construct. If I came in and directly contradicted these two—whose testimony had been used to convict me of four felonies—I feared the OIC would next accuse me of perjury.

When I first mentioned this as one of the reasons I refused to testify, a number of journalists scoffed at the idea—if you tell the truth how could you ever be charged with perjury? A few months later, my point was made perfectly when Kathleen Willey's friend, Julie Hiatt Steele, testified before a Starr grand jury in Virginia. Willey had accused President Clinton of groping her, and she claimed she'd told her friend Steele about it at the time. Steele, knowing Willey hadn't told her anything at the time, contradicted Willey's testimony and, as a result, was later charged with perjury. She had dared to go before a Starr grand jury and not back up the story that the OIC was promulgating. That was exactly what they were asking me to do. Simply telling the truth cost Steele everything she had, almost landed her in jail, and jeopardized her custody of her adopted son.

Fourth, those who tell the truth in grand jury proceedings sometimes learn the hard way that prosecutors have other ways of eliciting perjury charges. A common tactic is to ask the same question over and over, sometimes only slightly rephrased. If the witness slips up and gives a slightly different answer, he or she can be charged with perjury. And there's nothing to stop the interrogators from being very aggressive and intimidating in their questioning, in hopes of tripping up or confusing the witness.

All these reasons were ample enough motivation not to testify. All of them affected my ultimate decision. But I'm not a calculating person by nature, so I can't claim that I acted in a logical, well-thought-out manner. Bobby had warned me about the perjury issue, and my own experiences in the OIC meeting and with Diane Sawyer had given me pause. But there were other factors that affected me even more than these.

One was that I despised the OIC and all its hypocrisy. It seemed to me that Ray Jahn, Jackie Bennett, Ken Starr, and Amy St. Eve didn't care at all that they were wrecking the lives of decent men and women. They kissed up to one of the most crooked men in Arkansas, David Hale, then went after me with tactics designed to humiliate, embarrass, and intimidate. It made my throat choke up with anger to think of aiding them in their witch-hunt in any way. And it was even worse to imagine that if I told the truth, they might twist my words and still use them against me or other innocent people.

Equally important—and something I'm not sure I fully understood until later—was that in refusing to testify, I could finally regain just a little bit of control in a situation that had gotten wildly out of hand. Throughout my life, I had surrendered control to stronger personalities—to Jim and Nancy, foremost—and now things were crumbling all around me. The Whitewater trial, the Mehta charges, the grand jury, and the press frenzy over them, had put my life on a runaway train that was screaming recklessly forward.

How could I put the brakes on? In choosing not to testify, I could at least temporarily silence the madness around me. And it would be the first real, up-front choice I'd made since things started coming apart two years earlier.

Finally, for those who wonder how I could choose to go to jail for contempt rather than simply testifying, there's another answer that makes sense only in the larger context of what was happening. By now, I'd reached a breaking point in my life. I'd been convicted of felonies, sentenced to jail, I was facing another trial, and my reputation had been smeared in the national media. My relationship with Pat had been broken up, I'd been forced to face the fact that my ex-husband wasn't the man I thought he was, and I was also broke, homeless, unemployed, and paralyzed with fear.

The Woman Who Wouldn't Talk

My daily life consisted of looking into the faces of my family and friends and seeing their sadness and fear. It was excruciating to realize that I was the cause of that pain and that I was helpless to fix it.

My back was against the wall. I had nothing left to lose—except perhaps my own self-respect. And this was my last opportunity to save it. I could either cooperate with the OIC and continue my downward spiral—or I could refuse and try to salvage the little self-respect I had left. I realized that if I did not choose the latter, there was very little hope for the rest of my life.

I had made my decision. But there was one more thing I had to do before I went in front of the grand jury. The family (my army, as my friends always said) had to join the fight.

The night before I was scheduled to testify, I went home to Camden. With my parents, brothers and sisters, and their families gathered together in the living room, I told them what I planned to do and explained what the ramifications would likely be. I walked them through the entire story—much of which they already knew—and explained why refusing to talk was the only decision I felt I could make. As I spoke, my thirteen-year-old niece Gini was on her knees in front me, crying uncontrollably and begging me to lie, to do anything to stay out of jail. The room was quiet except for sniffling when my mother finally spoke.

"Isn't there something . . ." she began. "Isn't there *anything* you know on the Clintons that you can tell them?"

"Mom," I said, "I don't know anything they did wrong. Anything I would say about them would be a lie."

As I looked at my seventy-year-old mother, I couldn't bear to see the worry in her eyes. "Mom," I said. "They want me just to make up something. They figure I'll do it to save my own skin, but I won't. I just can't."

At that point, my mother's expression changed. "It sounds like what happened during the war, families turning against families, children informing on their own parents so that they would live. If I could live through that, I can certainly live through this."

With my mother now backing my decision, the mood in the room changed. I went around the room, asking each of my siblings what they thought I should do. And all of them, without hesitation, echoed my mother's words. My father, the old drill sergeant, stood up from his chair and said, "We're with you, baby! We'll stand with you, no matter what!"

I left my parents' house that night feeling stronger than I had in a long time.

The next morning, September 4, 1996, I arrived at the courthouse and broke the news to Bobby. He knew I'd been thinking about remaining silent, but he had apparently thought that the closer jail got, the weaker my resolve would be.

Before I went into the grand jury room, Bobby took me aside. "You understand what this means, don't you?" he asked.

"Yes," I told him. "I do."

He then issued a warning that showed he was a much better lawyer than psychic. "Susan," he said, "it is not inconceivable that the judge might make you go to jail immediately—for several days, maybe even a week. I'm not sure you can make it that long."

I nodded and told him I was ready. Although I saw no reason to forewarn the OIC of my decision, Bobby insisted that professional courtesy required that he tell them that I wouldn't be answering any questions. After briefly talking to Ray Jahn, Bobby returned to tell me that they had decided to take a wait-and-see attitude. They apparently assumed that no matter what my decision was now, I would crumble once I got into the grand jury room.

Leaving Bobby in the hallway, I entered the grand jury room and was pointed to an old, wooden chair on a slightly elevated platform. The room was spacious, with chairs arranged in rows, like in a classroom, and the grand jurors scattered among the seats. Up until now, I had been relatively calm. But that changed when I walked through the door. Sitting and staring directly at me were twenty-three ordinary Arkansans whose faces registered expressions ranging from intensity to boredom.

I walked to the front of the room, carrying a prepared statement that I hoped to make about refusing to testify, and was sworn in. Ray Jahn stood in front of me and launched right into his questions.

"For the record," he began, "would you state your full name, please, for the court reporter?"

"Susan Carol Henley McDougal," I replied.

The grand jury transcript tells the story of what happened next.

> Q. Can you tell us, ma'am, where were you born?
> A. I'd like to read a statement before we begin, if that would be okay.
> Q. You can read it at the end of the appearance.
> A. I would like to read it before we begin. I think the foreman can let me do that, if he will. Will the foreman allow me to do that?

This irritated Jahn, who was ostensibly in control of the proceedings. Clearly annoyed at having a witness try to impose her own schedule on things, he became testy.

> Q. Ma'am, ma'am, ma'am, you will be given ample opportunity—
> A. May I ask the foreman if he'll let me read this statement before I begin?
> Q. No, ma'am. No, ma'am. You are here to answer questions. You will be given ample opportunity—
> A. I'd like to read the statement. The foreman has the right to let me read the statement.
> The more Jahn insisted I couldn't read my statement, the more I became determined that I would. Finally, he changed tack.
> Q. Ma'am, where were you born?
> A. [No response.]
> Q. Ma'am, where were you born?
> A. [No response.]
> Q. Where do you reside today?

A. [No response.]
Q. Are you employed?
A. [No response.]

At this point, I was scared to death. Still holding the statement in my shaking hand, I no longer knew if I was doing the right thing. Irritated, Ray Jahn continued.

Q. For the record, are you refusing to answer any questions, ma'am?
A. I'd like to read the statement.
Q. Yes, ma'am. And you'll be given an opportunity before your appearance is over. But right now, we need to ask you some questions, ma'am.
A. I need to read it before we begin.
Q. May I see the statement, please?
A. No. I would like to read it.
Q. Then I'm afraid that—well, if you would, we're going to ask you to step outside, ma'am.

I was asked to leave the grand jury room while Jahn conferred with the other OIC attorneys. He then walked outside the grand jury room to speak with Bobby McDaniel. As he approached them, Bobby later told me, Jahn was physically shaking and literally chewing on his mustache. After a few moments, Jahn stomped back into the grand jury room. The grand jury conferred, and about a half hour later I was brought back in and placed under oath again.

The deputy grand jury foreman informed me that, after discussion, they had decided that I did not have a right to make my statement. Then Ray Jahn stepped up to ask me three more questions.

Q. Ms. McDougal, I am going to ask you a question. Did you ever discuss your loan from David Hale with William Jefferson Clinton?
A. Will you let me read my statement?

Q. Ma'am, the question has been posed to you. Will you answer the question?

A. I need to read the statement.

Q. Ma'am, did you ever discuss Lorance Heights with William Jefferson Clinton?

A. Again, my answer would be the same for any questions that you ask me.

Q. Well, one more question. To your knowledge, did William Jefferson Clinton testify truthfully during the course of your trial?

A. My answer would be the same for any questions you ask me.

Q. And you will not answer those questions?

A. I need to read my statement.

MR. JAHN: Okay. Thank you. Mr. Foreman, if you would, we'll notify the judge.

I had no idea why they'd dragged me back in to ask three more questions after I'd already made it plain that I wouldn't talk. But it became clear the next day. The newspapers' accounts of what had happened in the grand jury room were virtually identical: Susan McDougal had refused to answer questions about Bill Clinton.

The OIC had known exactly what it was doing. By asking those three final questions, they could now report that I'd refused to answer questions about Bill Clinton—rather than just saying I'd refused to answer any questions at all. The newspaper reports left the clear impression that I'd been happily answering everything, when suddenly Bill Clinton's name arose and I clammed up. Though Starr's supporters always claimed he was a novice at the spin game, he certainly managed to get the upper hand in it often enough.

After we left the grand jury room, Jahn insisted that Bobby come with him to the courtroom of Susan Webber Wright, the supervising judge. When I tried to follow along, Jahn shook a finger in my face and said, "You aren't going anywhere."

"You don't tell me what to do!" I growled back at him. A few reporters were also following along, trying to ascertain what was going on, but

Jahn wanted nothing to do with them right now. He snapped to Bobby that the hearing with the judge should be closed to the press. "What are you trying to hide?" I interjected. "Are you so ashamed of what you are doing to me?" Jahn just glared at me, but wisely did not respond.

Upon hearing that I'd refused to testify, Judge Wright calmly and deliberately made sure that I understood what could happen. Her manner was not at all threatening, but she did make it clear that if I continued to refuse to answer questions, she would have me locked up. I responded that I understood, but I didn't trust the OIC and I wouldn't cooperate.

Just as Judge Wright was about to have me taken away, Bobby interceded. He asked if he might have a few days to talk with me about what was happening. Bobby had appeared in Judge Wright's courtroom many times, and they'd developed a good relationship. Based on her confidence in Bobby, the judge ordered that I be allowed to come back in five days to see if I had changed my mind. If not, she warned, I was going to jail.

The news of my refusal to testify hit the wire services almost immediately, and within minutes a producer from *Larry King Live* was on the phone wanting to book me as soon as possible. Jennifer Horan, the public defender assigned to help Bobby with my case, was dead set against the idea. "When Judge Wright finds out you've used the time she gave you to go on a TV talk show," she said, "she'll be furious." But Bobby said, "I can talk to you just as well on a plane to Los Angeles as anywhere else. Let's go, if you want to."

I was extremely happy to get to fly to L.A. and see Pat and Bill and talk with them about everything that was happening. I quickly agreed to make the appearance. We booked the tickets and flew to L.A., where Pat and Bill picked us up at the airport.

The possibility that I'd go to jail within in five days' time sent Bill and Pat into a frenzy of activity. Pat was calling every sympathetic lawyer he could find, discussing possible ways to delay the sentencing and keep me out of jail. And Bill was talking with his political contacts in Arkansas, trying to get public sentiment behind me and hopefully get Judge Wright to change her mind.

Shortly before we left for the CNN studio, Pat appeared to have hit paydirt. He'd reached an attorney in Washington who specialized in working with independent counsels (apparently a growth industry) and who believed a compromise could be reached. Pat had spent the better part of two hours on the phone with her and, as we drove to the CNN studio, there appeared to be a glimmer of hope. "But you need to be careful," Pat warned me. "If a compromise is going to be reached, Kenneth Starr will probably have to be a part of it. So don't go blasting him and the OIC on the show."

When we pulled into the parking garage at the CNN studios, I was actually fairly calm. By now I realized that I was going to jail and I was at peace with that decision. The three other passengers in the car—Bill, Pat, and Bobby—were going around and around about how to handle the various questions Larry King might throw at me. I just nodded in agreement with whatever was being said, lacking any real enthusiasm to analyze anything by now.

At the studio, I was taken into makeup, where I was alone with my thoughts for the first time in several days. Everything had been such a whirlwind for the last few weeks that I hadn't had a chance to really think about what was happening.

An assistant came to take me to the studio, but first I ducked into the "green room" for one last word of advice from Bill and Pat. Pat was on the phone with the Washington, D.C., attorney. Bill gave me one last hug, said, "Knock 'em dead, Susan," and then took me by the arm as I turned to leave. "Remember," he said, "Don't burn any bridges tonight."

"Okay, okay, I won't," I said. And then I was ushered to the set to meet Larry King. The interview was held on a large, dark soundstage that looked like a partially vacant warehouse. There was nothing glamorous about it. King's desk was at the back of the soundstage with a picture of the lights of Los Angeles serving as a backdrop.

Larry King was not at all what I had expected. Unlike Diane Sawyer, who had remained aloof during the interview, he was very charming and went out of his way to make Bobby and me feel welcome. But what really surprised me about King was that he was much funnier in person than he comes across on television. During commercial breaks he kept up a steady stream of one-liners that made it hard to keep a straight face when we were back on camera.

The very first question Larry asked was the obvious one: why wouldn't I testify? I began by explaining that a series of events over a number of years had led to my decision not to testify. I recounted how Whitewater had first begun, and how we'd all lost money on it. I then explained that when I tried to cooperate with the OIC, they hadn't wanted to hear what I had to say, but instead only wanted to know what I could tell them about Bill and Hillary Clinton.

The more I talked, the more my anger bubbled to the surface. Before I knew it, I was in full ranting mode. For the rest of the show, I called Starr and his underlings everything but human. The pent-up rage of the past three years came spewing out—making for excellent television but lousy negotiation tactics. Very bluntly, I told America how the OIC had wanted me to lie about the Clintons in exchange for my own freedom.

As soon as the hour was up, I knew I'd dug my own grave but I couldn't have cared less. This was the first time I'd talked publicly about Starr and the sleazy tactics of his investigation and it felt terrific. I wanted to extract a little blood from the other side—God knows they already had plenty of mine. Years later, I would learn from a reporter who was friendly with the OIC that Starr had in fact been watching the program and was incensed by it.

I ran back to the green room to see Bill and Pat. When I walked in, there was a brief moment of awkward silence; I think they were both too stunned to speak. I'd just trashed the most powerful prosecutor in the country and had sealed my own fate in the process. After a moment, Pat walked across the room and silently gave me a big hug. On cue, Bill broke into a grin and said, "Well, thank God you didn't burn any bridges."

Despite the damage I'd done to myself on *Larry King Live*, we left CNN that night feeling giddy. For the first time, I had actually said what I wanted to say about everything that had been going on.

Two days later, I was on a plane heading back to Little Rock. It was a somber flight back, but I spent the hours thinking how much better I felt about my life, a life that was about to include going to jail.

13

AN UNLUCKY FOB

I GOT BACK TO LITTLE ROCK on September 8, 1996. The next morning I was scheduled to report to the U.S. Marshals office, after which I would be transported to the Faulkner County Jail in Conway, Arkansas. I caught a ride from the airport to Jennifer Horan's house where I was spending the night. Jennifer had been more than just a lawyer throughout the trial—she had also been a friend.

That night I found myself wondering exactly what the proper protocol was for going to jail. Do you pack a bag? How much should you bring? I asked Jennifer, and she suggested I call the jail to find out. So I did. "This is Susan McDougal," I said to whoever picked up the phone. "I'm coming to your jail tomorrow, and I was wondering what I should bring." My call seemed to cause a fair amount of consternation, and I was transferred repeatedly before a woman came on the line and apologized for the wait.

"To be honest," she said, "no one has ever called before they came to jail. Usually, they aren't planning on being here."

"I understand," I told her. "But I was just wondering what I might be able to bring with me." There was some discussion on the other end, and eventually the woman told me I should bring nothing more than some white cotton bras, panties, and socks. It only took a second for Jennifer to produce four brand-new pairs of Calvin Klein underwear and two new white cotton bras. She grinned rather sheepishly and said, "It's all I wear." But before she let me take them, she took out a black Magic Marker and wrote MCDOUGAL in block letters on every item.

"Good Lord, Jennifer," I laughed, "I'm not going to summer camp!"

"Well," she said, "this will keep people from taking your underwear."

"Jennifer, if anyone in jail wants my underwear that bad," I told her, "I can promise you that I'm going to be giving it up." As it turned out, her plan would backfire completely. At Faulkner County Jail, the male inmates who did the laundry began stealing my MCDOUGAL underwear whenever it came through, so they could sell it as souvenirs.

The next morning, Jennifer took me to the U.S. Marshals office, where I was to turn myself in. I had refused to let my family come—there was no way I would put myself or them through that. But it was just as difficult for Jennifer, who cried and asked the marshal if she could come with me as I turned myself in. It freaked me out a little because I started wondering what she knew that I didn't.

I said good-bye to Jennifer, and the marshal led me down a corridor to a holding cell that was about ten feet by five feet. It had plain concrete floors and walls, a single bench on each wall, and the inevitable toilet with no seat. When he put me in the cell, I was struck by one thought: *I can do this.* I stretched out on the concrete bench and closed my eyes.

Everything in my life had been moving at warp speed for so long, and the noise and stress had been so constant, that the cell seemed peaceful by comparison. Just then, the marshals brought in another prisoner—a young girl dressed in a dirty orange jumpsuit that was ripped from hip to ankle down one pant leg. She was wailing when she came in, and gave no sign that she even noticed I was there.

After a few minutes of listening to her sob, I sat down next to her and put my hand on her shoulder. "Don't worry," I said quietly. "It'll be okay." She managed to regain her composure long enough to gulp out her story: She had just been sentenced to a very long prison term. Her brother, she said, had been growing marijuana at their home, and they'd both been arrested on charges of conspiracy to distribute it. Her brother was in the holding cell next to ours and periodically she would scream obscenities at him and then start crying again.

I could not believe that this young girl had been forced to go to her sentencing hearing with dirty, stringy hair and a torn orange jumpsuit. According to her, she had not even been allowed to shower for a week. As soon as she said that, my confidence in my ability to make it took a major nosedive. Not showering for a week! I was used to taking a minimum of two baths a day. I knew that I was not going to be taking any luxurious bubble baths, but I least thought I would be allowed to shower daily.

After I'd been in the holding cell for a while, two marshals came to transport me to Faulkner County Jail. I assumed I'd be handcuffed, but I was surprised when they pulled out waist chains and leg irons as well. The marshals dropped the leg irons onto the concrete floor with a loud clang and then bent over to clamp them around my ankles. They handcuffed me and then chained my hands to my waist.

"Let's go," they said, and I shuffled out of the cell behind them. The chains were so short you could only take half-steps and, with your hands chained tight to your waist, it meant that there was nothing to break your fall but your face. I kept thinking, *Oh man, I am going to fall over and kill myself.*

As I shuffled past the other cells, I could feel the handcuffs digging into my wrist and pinching my skin. The marshals were on either side of me, and no one spoke a word. It was humiliating, but, I figured, at least no one would witness my hunched over, lurching struggle to get to the jail van. It was the only consoling thought I could muster.

Directly behind me were two big men in the same cuffs and chains. I had only glimpsed them for a second, but it looked like either one could have passed for a pro football player; their hands and forearms looked enormous stuffed into the handcuffs, which were visibly cutting into the skin. One of them had a baby face, and I guessed he was no more than seventeen or eighteen. The other was older, but he seemed more frightened. It was obvious that this was his first time in custody. Down the long corridor you could see a light shining around the edge of a door. We shuffled together down the hall toward the metal door. Suddenly I realized that I'd seen this door from the outside many times, whenever I'd stopped at the post office across the street or driven by it on my way to a downtown restaurant. I'd always assumed that it led to offices or courtrooms. Once we reached the door, one of the marshals told us to stop there and he stepped forward and opened the door.

I was immediately blinded by camera lights. A swarm of cameramen and reporters was hovering at the door. As soon as I appeared, the reporters began screaming questions all at once. From all sides, I could hear, "Susan!" "Susan!"—and I could see the familiar faces of the reporters whom I had gotten to know over the past few months.

I heard a voice from behind me shout out, "What the fuck did you do?" I didn't have to turn around to know that it was one of the other prisoners—and he sounded equal parts shocked and scared at all the commotion I'd raised. He must have assumed he was chained to a madwoman. At that point, he would not have been far off the mark.

As soon as I saw the camera lights, I instantly knew that everyone I loved would see this on the evening news. I'd assumed that the marshals would transport me to jail in secrecy. Now the entire world would get to see that Kenneth Starr had beaten me. My natural reaction was to duck my head and hide from the cameras, like I'd seen so many people do on television. But another thought hit me—no way would I give them that satisfaction.

Mustering as much dignity as I could—which, given my metal accessories, was not much—I threw my head back, jutted my chin out, and walked out like I didn't have a care in the world. The marshals escorted me into a van, and my two fellow prisoners followed behind me. We pulled out of the parking lot, the reporters still shouting questions, and made the half-hour drive to Conway and my new prison home.

When we arrived at Faulkner County Detention Center (FCDC), I was taken into a holding area, where the first person I met was a heavyset, intimidating matron, Zoe Ann Hudspeth. Meeting Zoe Ann right off the bat did nothing to allay my worst fears about jail—she looked as if she could snap me in two with her eyelids. But looks can deceive, and in this case they did—I would soon learn that Zoe Ann was one of the more caring authority figures in the prison.

After about an hour in the waiting area, I was taken to the women's wing of the jail. It wasn't a series of separate cells, like you'd see in the movies, but rather a "pod"—a twenty-foot by forty-foot room with steel dining tables in the middle and concrete walls all around. Two doors on either side of the pod led to the sleeping areas. These were small rooms—one had six beds mounted on the wall like bunks, and one had four; each room had one toilet. With up to thirty inmates at a time housed in the women's pod, and only ten beds, more than half the women were forced to sleep on gym mats laid on the floor.

When I walked in, I saw a small group of women sitting near the television. They'd just been watching news clips of my exit from the U.S. Marshals office which were running over and over on both CNN and the local Arkansas stations. I took my first step into the jail pod, balancing my dinner tray in one hand and one sheet and one blanket in the other, with my gym mat tucked under my arm. As I walked in, there was a chorus of "Hey Susan" and "It's her." I had no idea what kind of reception I would receive, but they all seemed happy to see me. Then, as I was about to find a place to put my stuff down, the replay of my leaving the courthouse came on the tiny overhead TV. It was the first time I had seen it and as I stood there staring, tears began to well up in my eyes. Suddenly, I heard a voice yell out above the noise.

"I *know* you didn't *buy* that outfit!"

"What the hell were you thinking, wearing that thing?" another screamed, and all the women started laughing.

I started yelling back, "Hey, lay off! This is the first time I've been arrested. Next time, I'll try to dress more appropriately." That got everyone howling. I had just gotten there, but I was officially in.

What they didn't realize was that trash-talking was an art form among my siblings. Growing up in the Henley household, you had to learn how to do it, or else it would escalate exponentially (a true trash-talker smells weakness). Holidays at the Henleys had always been more like a Spike Lee movie than a Waltons family Christmas.

The women at FCDC never gave me time to be scared, mostly because they never quit talking. In order to come to terms with the lives they'd led, they would talk about anything and everything. No topic was off-limits: physical appearance, intelligence, sex, husbands, boyfriends—everything was fair game.

On the morning after my first night in jail, I made a few phone calls to let everyone know that I was okay. The first call I made was to my mother. Her favorite TV station was CNN, so I knew she would have seen repeated news clips of me being led away in shackles the day before. When she answered the phone, her voice was trembling.

"I saw those pictures of you in chains," she said. "It was more than I could bear. After seeing that, I had this picture of you being thrown in a dark hole, all alone."

"Mom, please stop watching TV," I said, trying to think how I could console her. "Listen to me, it's not that bad. We actually had a lot of fun last night—it was kind of like a bunking party." My mother knew that I'd spent my life sugarcoating things, so she wasn't buying. "It's not like what you see in the movies at all," I continued.

"Really?" she asked. "What's it like?" Before I'd gone to jail, I had reminded my mother about a segment she'd once seen on *60 Minutes* about U.S. prisons being like country clubs, with televisions in every room and golf courses. Even though the show was largely baloney, my mother believed that *60 Minutes* wouldn't put something on the air if it wasn't the gospel truth. She was, therefore, open to the possibility that jail could be like summer camp without the s'mores. I saw my opportunity and seized it.

"So far, everyone's been really nice," I told her. "This morning they took us out into a little garden with concrete benches, and we stayed out in the sunshine and we got to plant flowers and take care of the garden. After that, we went back inside for lunch. They have a really nice salad bar."

I'd overdone it just a tad with the salad bar—I could sense she was still skeptical. To ease her suspicions, I told her about a few things I didn't like about prison—none too serious—and this seemed to satisfy her uncertainty. By the time I hung up the phone, she was laughing.

Next, I called Pat because I needed to hear his voice. Whenever I would get upset, he would become very calm and reassuring. I loved the way he reacted to a crisis. But when I reached him, he could barely talk. As a public defender, he was used to going into jails, and he knew exactly what the conditions were like. Nothing, however, had prepared him for the television clips of me being led away in shackles. His voice was cracking as we talked, and that really scared me. In the twelve years we had been together I had rarely seen him cry or even get shaken. "I'm all right," I kept telling him. "It's not that bad." He didn't believe a word of it and when I told him that we were not allowed any books or reading material in the jail other than the Bible, I thought he was going to flip out. "No books at all? How in the world are you going to make it?" I told him again that it would be okay, but he hastily made arrangements to fly to Arkansas and visit me and the jail.

It didn't take long for me to adjust to jail life, mainly because I didn't have any other options. By the third or fourth day, I was bitching about the food, sleeping until noon, and telling stories all night. I learned quickly that my celebrity stature carried little weight with the women: from the moment I arrived, they'd begun to look for any imperfection they could rag me about. It didn't take long before they found a perfect one.

Every night the TV in the pod would blare music videos, and we'd all sit around critiquing the singers' clothes, voices, bodies, and whatever else we could think of. One night I convinced everyone to get up and dance. Since several of the girls had made their livings as strippers, this made for an impressive show. But when I got up and began to dance, the women broke out in hysterical laughter.

"What's the matter, McDougal?" shouted one. "Are your hips frozen?"

"You look like you're drowning, not dancing! What are your arms doing?"

"In the South," I explained with exaggerated politeness, "girls are taught not to move their hips when walking or dancing, or else they'll be considered to have loose moral character." This brought additional howls of laughter, as well as several assurances that I'd never be able to keep a man.

Laughing, I tried to imitate the hip movements of a woman near me, but it was hopeless. Several of the exotic dancers, however, saw me as pathetic but redeemable, and they decided to make a project out of me. Whenever there was music, they'd drag me out of my bunk and show me how to move my hips in a figure eight. "This move," they told me, "will get you any man." Unfortunately, my attempts at a figure eight always came out looking more like an X, much to their screaming delight.

After a while, they gave up trying to teach me anything and instead just lured me into dancing for the humor value. Anytime somebody wanted to break the tension in the pod, or just get a sure-fire laugh, the cry would go up, "Let's get McDougal to dance!"

Life at FCDC was also made easier by the women who ran the floor. At FCDC, the matrons seemed to understand that the women there were already beaten down and didn't need further humiliation. The women's jail was run by the aforementioned Zoe Ann, who could be tough but was extremely fair and evenhanded in her dealings with the prisoners. She employed matrons, women who were not in law enforcement, to work the three daily shifts. For the most part, these women were terrific, especially the older ones who had enough sense to know that these women already had enough misery in their lives without uselessly adding more. Everyone's favorite was Jo Ann Putoff, affectionately known as Mama Jo, because for many of the women inmates she was the mother they never had. She would listen to any inmate, counsel them, even cry with them, but she never let anyone get out of line because, as she was fond of saying, "I'll be watching you."

On one occasion, the officer in charge of the shift before Mama Jo's had prohibited the dispensing of Benadryl because it made the women sleepy. For most of the women who were taking it, that was exactly the point: they wanted the medicine to help them sleep through the nights. I didn't help matters much when I sarcastically suggested to the matron that it would probably be okay if the women got a little sleepy since I did not anticipate any of us operating heavy machinery in the near future. But the officer refused to budge, so we just waited till Mama Jo arrived for her shift and told her what had happened. Mama Jo just shook her head and called for the nurse's office to bring up the Benadryl.

In sharp contrast to the jail matrons were the administrators, whose sole concerns appeared to be pinching pennies and avoiding bad publicity. I had the opportunity to meet one of them, the sheriff, when he called me into his office less than a week after I arrived at the jail. A lifelong politician and avid Clinton-hater, he couldn't resist the urge to offer me some advice.

"Now that you're in here," he told me with a smirk, "the Clintons would be more than happy to let you rot in a cell for life."

"Well, I didn't do this for the Clintons," I said, annoyed.

Apparently determined to get a rise out of me, he went on. "If you think anybody out there really cares that you're in here, you are mistaken. There's nobody out there waiting for you."

I looked at him with as much disdain as I could muster and quietly replied, "Well, I don't see anyone else in here but me so I don't guess it really matters, does it?"

I knew Pat and my family would always be there for me, but I assumed the sheriff was right about everyone else. Why would anybody care or understand why I'd chosen to go to jail? I was well aware that my notoriety fell into the "fifteen minutes of fame" category—and that they'd about ticked down to the zero hour already.

That same night, while I mulled over the sheriff's words, I watched the guards come into the pod lugging two huge sacks. "This is for you," one of them said.

I opened one of the sacks to find literally thousands of letters. Several of the women gathered around, and we began going through the first sack, letter by letter. I could hardly believe what I was reading. Total strangers from all over the country were writing to express their support of my decision—and they were writing in such emotional terms that it was almost difficult to read. The women around me were going crazy, exclaiming, "Listen to this!" or "You won't believe this one!" And I couldn't. I was overwhelmed.

Nearly every letter was from someone writing to say that they understood exactly why I was refusing to cooperate. Over and over, people wrote about how sick they were of Starr's partisan investigation, and numerous letters compared it to McCarthyism. Most surprising was the large number of letters that began, "I'm a Republican, but I'm sick of Kenneth Starr."

I'd seen up close how the Starr investigation operated. I'd seen how the OIC had convinced a jury of Arkansans that I was a criminal. And I'd read the newspaper articles and seen the TV reports that painted me as an unrepentant felon. All these things had led me to the rather myopic viewpoint that I was the only one who understood what was really going on. These letters showed me how wrong I was.

It was clear from these sacks of mail that there were a lot of ordinary Americans sick of seeing an American president being stalked by his enemies. And many of them were outraged at what they saw as Starr's need to humiliate me by dragging me around in chains and shackles. Perhaps Starr didn't think I'd be photographed in that state—or maybe he thought it would be a good "tough on crime" image. What he obviously didn't realize was that it would backfire on him completely. For many Americans, the picture of me walking in shackles would serve as a lasting image of the insanity of the investigation. It was evidence of the OIC's out-of-control need to punish anyone who crossed them. Most harmful to Starr, it forever marred his carefully created image as just a calm, decent fellow doing his job without rancor or vindictiveness.

I read every single letter in those bags and tried to answer some of them. Writing a letter in jail is not easy because you do not have access to pens, only pencils, and writing paper is in short supply. But I tried to answer as many of them as I could because they gave me a huge boost and, more important, they gave me the confidence to strike back against the OIC and Ken Starr.

Though I'd done very few interviews up to this point, I decided to speak out. Energized by the letters, I agreed to speak to nearly every television or radio reporter who wanted an interview, no matter how small their audience.

My brother-in-law, David Cochrane, helped by setting up radio interviews around the country. I'd then place a collect call from the jail phone (usually while sitting on top of a nearby trash can) and tell the interviewer exactly what I'd seen and been through. I no longer worried about being articulate; now I just wanted to get my story out. I blasted Starr at every opportunity, repeating as often as I could the story of how the OIC had wanted me to lie.

The question that everyone wanted answered was why I had refused to testify. As I discovered in the interviews, there seemed to be four main theories.

The most popular theory was that I'd had an affair with Bill Clinton and was covering for him. This was apparently the view of the OIC, and even in 2002 Hickman Ewing is still claiming it as fact. The first, most obvious flaw is that I never had an affair with Bill Clinton. But even if I had, I hadn't seen or spoken to him since 1985 or 1986. Why would I go to jail to protect someone I hadn't even spoken to in a decade? Besides, have you seen the way he looks in a pair of running shorts?

Another popular theory was that Clinton, or someone associated with him, was giving me a big payoff in return for my silence. But this theory is obviously flawed as well. No matter how much Clinton could have paid me, I could have gotten far more for implicating him in something. Not only had Whitewater broken me financially, most of the people who aligned themselves with me are still struggling to make up for the costs as well. And I could have made hundreds of thousands of dollars from tabloids, TV shows, and book publishers by offering dirt on the Clintons during that time.

The flip side of the "protecting Clinton" story was that I was hiding something because I was scared of what he might do to me. A whole cottage industry developed around the idea that Clinton had some kind of Arkansas Mafia (dubbed "La Bubba Nostra" by L.A. Times reporter Ann O'Neill) that went around killing anyone who crossed him. Let's assume, for just one moment, that such a thing existed. Why would I be afraid of it, when David Hale and Jim McDougal had flat out turned on

Clinton and were still living? You'd think the Arkansas Mafia would have made quick work of Jim, especially. After all, he lived alone, in an unlocked house, and ate at the same WesterN SizzliN at about the same time every day. Even Fredo Corleone could have taken care of him.

Finally, some people were simply convinced that, whatever reason lay behind my decision, I was a liar and a con artist. Yet if that were true, why was I sitting in a jail cell? After all, wouldn't a con artist simply tell the OIC what they wanted to hear? That's what David Hale and Jim McDougal had done—and although they'd admitted to or been convicted of far more crimes than I had, they'd been rewarded with housing, a healthy living allowance, and the opportunity to choose their favorite jails. Why wouldn't I simply follow their lead? At any time, I could have made up a lie about Bill or Hillary Clinton and gotten out of jail, out of trouble in California, and earned a big sum of money for a tell-all book. If I was a con artist, I was clearly not a very good one.

Talking about the OIC and Starr to the media helped me release some of my anger. It also helped my family, who were watching television religiously, just in case they might see me, no longer beaten down but defiant and, at last, defending myself. And the interviews also provided a more mundane side benefit—one that the other women in FCDC could enjoy as well. Whenever TV shows would come to film me, the production assistants would smuggle me lipstick, eyeliner, and mascara. Makeup was cherished in jail, since inmates weren't allowed to have it. Taking care with our looks was a way to boost self-esteem, so we'd sometimes make our own fake cosmetics by melting the prison-issued colored writing pencils in hot water, then dabbing the liquid on as lipstick and eyeshadow. We also learned to roll our hair with toilet paper holders and rolled-up brown paper sacks.

Whenever I was preparing to do a show, the women would all pitch in and help me with my hair and makeup. In turn, I'd run back to the cell after my interview, clutching the smuggled cosmetics and calling, "Look what I got this time." The best haul came after a Larry King interview, when Larry, upon hearing of our need for cosmetics, ordered everyone in the crew to empty their purses and pockets and fork over whatever they had.

The press barrage sent Starr into the stratosphere. He began railing against me at his speaking engagements, always taking pains to remind everyone that I was a convicted felon. His depiction of me greatly contrasted with the stories he told of his own life. He once described, for example, his habit when jogging in the mornings. When he reached a stoplight, he related, he'd say a little prayer while waiting to cross the street. The message he presented was clear: In one corner, we have the God-fearing servant of the people, whose only mission is finding the truth. In the other corner is the lying, self-interested, convicted felon. To Starr, it was a good versus evil world, and he'd long ago decided which side he wanted people to believe he was on. For my part, I was up against an adversary so out of touch with everyday life that, according to his mother, his favorite hobby as a youth had been shining shoes on Saturday nights.

With Starr now railing against me, it didn't take long for the jail officials to clamp down on my access to the media. In the beginning I was told that the jail would accommodate a reasonable number of television interviews each week. Within a few days the definition of "reasonable" went from six a week to one or two. One day a jail matron told me that the sheriff had gotten an earful from the OIC about the interviews. Within a few days I was denied access to television interviews altogether. My press barrage had lasted less than a month.

After only a month in FCDC, I found myself settling into life in confinement. Since the jail didn't allow us to have any books other than the Bible, I spent most of every day talking with the women. We told each other all the details of our lives and spent hours analyzing our mistakes and talking about what we'd do differently next time. When we already knew everyone's How Did I Get Here story, we switched to a new game for at least one night: What's the Worst Thing a Man Has Ever Done to You?

The game started with one woman describing how her man had knocked her teeth out when she'd refused to give him oral sex. Then another woman described how her husband had pimped her to his friends for crack money. When my turn came, I was too embarrassed to speak because I couldn't think of anything that had happened during our marriage that could compete. But everyone was yelling that I had to play. So I told the women about the time Jim got mad after I'd ruined a couple of his favorite shirts while ironing them.

"He slammed the bedroom door so hard," I said, "he broke it right off the hinges." The women stared blankly at me, waiting for more. "I know it doesn't sound like much," I said, "but I thought I might have to divorce him."

That busted them up. They pounded the walls and rolled on the floor laughing. They loved this picture of marital strife—I couldn't even come up with a single black eye!

"McDougal," one of the women said when the laughter died down, "you can't play anymore if you can't come up with anything better than these weak-ass stories."

There was a real camaraderie among the women at Faulkner County, but even as much as we enjoyed talking, we needed some other kind of stimulation. With no books allowed and no jail-sponsored education or rehabilitation programs, we decided to make up our own programs.

We decided that getting physically fit was the first step toward a better life. Despite the fact that I'd been largely averse to physical exercise for all of my forty years, I nevertheless agreed to lead a twice-a-day workout. Dubbed the McDougal Workout, it would never be confused with the Jane Fonda workout—it was more like a Henry Fonda workout. At my barked instructions, the women would contort their bodies in a variety of uncomfortable ways with no consistent relationship and limited aerobic value.

"Okay, reach over and touch your right hand to your left ankle," I'd call out. "Now swivel your hips to the right! Put your left arm behind your head! Now bend at the waist! Breathe in rhythm!" The "workout" resembled nothing so much as a giant game of Twister, but no one seemed to mind. It was semiproductive and wasted at least two hours each day.

The workout was not the only organized activity that we had put together. One night shortly after I arrived at FCDC, I had retreated to my bunk to get away from the constant noise of the WB network on the TV. Lying there in the dark, I was still overwhelmed by my feelings of absolute hatred and bitterness toward Starr and his staff. I decided that if I was going to have to do this jail time, I was going to hang on to these feelings and let the anger get me through it. Later that evening, as I lay there fuming, a group of women came and stood by my bunk. One of them asked if I would mind reading the Bible to them. Instantly, thoughts of the pious Kenneth Starr came to mind—I hated his very public Christianity and the hypocriscy of how he practiced his religion. At the time, I was about as far from any spiritual feelings as I could get— no way could I do Bible study. The women sensed my reluctance because one of them leaned over to me and said, "We can't read it ourselves."

Three or four times a week, we would sit in a circle on the concrete floor and I would read stories from the Bible. The overwhelming favorite was the story of David and Bathsheba. King David had fallen in love with Bathsheba, who was married to a soldier in David's army. He arranged for the soldier to be sent to the front lines where he was killed, so he could have Bathsheba to himself—but he would be punished severely by God for his deed. The part the women loved, however, was the part where God said David was a man after his own heart—that was pretty strong forgiveness. Most of these women felt unloved and unlovable. Talking about being forgiven, or just forgiving themselves, was a concept that was not believable. Yet here was God forgiving David even after he had arranged to have a man killed. The story struck a chord with several of the women and they would ask me to read it over and over again.

My biggest fears about jail had diminished, but still, jail life was no picnic. I would eventually spend time in seven different facilities— both federal and local—and every one was overcrowded, filthy, loud, and designed for discomfort.

Most nights, the food at FCDC was close to inedible. The sole exception was the time a guard hit a deer with his truck, after which we had venison for several nights. However, for the most part we could not depend on the providence of suicidal animals. Mealtimes reminded me of Woody Allen's old joke: the food's terrible, and there's never enough of it. The portions were so tiny, in fact, that the lack of food was our chief topic of conversation, with sex running a distant second. On Fridays, if you had $7 on your account, you could order a hamburger after the regular meal was served. Very few of the women could afford to get one. But when the mail started coming in from all over the country, some people would enclose $10 or $20 for me to put on my account, and eventually there was enough money to pay for a hamburger for everyone.

The drinking-water situation was even worse. The only fluid of any kind we ever received was the water from a spout at the top of the toilet. Just looking at the toilet with no seat on it could make you never want to drink again. Equally bad, the water that came out of the spout was warm and we were not allowed ice. I mentioned during a morning radio interview that several of the women in jail, including myself, were having health problems that had been diagnosed as being dehydration-related. I also mentioned that the problems arose because the water from the toilet spout was tepid and we had no ice. That afternoon, a huge bucket of ice was brought in and set on a table. Evidently, people in the community had called the jail and complained. I will never forget the women running to get a glass of ice, thrilled at the possibility of tasting cold water again.

I also began having increasingly serious problems with my back. We slept on thin mattresses and sat on concrete benches. And because the floors were concrete, every step I took was breaking my back down. One day, as I struggled up from my seat on the floor for an inspection, Zoe Ann saw that I had to have help to get up. After talking with me about my back trouble, she was kind enough to arrange weekly appointments for me with an osteopath, so at least I got some care for my back. But the longer I stayed in prison, the worse the problem became.

A lifelong and avid reader, I was also very frustrated that we couldn't have books. I'd read the Bible before, I told the prison officials, and I knew the ending already—weren't there *any* other books we could have? I asked if I could substitute another religious book, such as the

Koran or a book on Hindu deities, so I could at least learn about other religions. Not too surprisingly, my request was refused. There were no copies of the Koran in Conway, I was told.

In the weeks I was in FCDC, the women prisoners became a close-knit group. Just about everyone got along well—though there were a few incidents that served to remind us that we weren't one big happy family.

One day during a random search, the guards discovered that one of the women had gotten hold of some crack cocaine. She refused to tell the guards how she had gotten it, and in response the jail officials declared that they were taking away the privileges of all the inmates—including visitation, TV, and commissary privileges—until she confessed. This was a very serious matter—most of these women would wait all week just so they could see their children for twenty minutes. It didn't take long for some of the women to decide to take her into one of the side rooms and beat the information out of her. Because she was new to the jail, and not very well liked, this seemed to be the obvious and quickest solution to the problem.

"Wait, don't do this," I said. "Why don't you let me just talk with her first? I'll try to reason with her." The women agreed, not because they thought the other inmate would see the light of reason, but because, as one person said, "McDougal will talk her to death." With this enthusiastic backing, I approached the woman and tried to appeal to her better instincts. When that failed, I turned to plan B: I explained to her that if she didn't cooperate, she was about to have her head bounced against the wall several times by some very unhappy women, with the full complicity of the guards. This proved a much more convincing argument, and she soon gave up the information.

Proud of the fact that I'd successfully neutralized the situation without violence, I began to lecture the women on solving problems without resorting to force. I was midway through my speech when one of the women said, "Okay, so you got her to tell without violence. But she only did it because of the *threat* of violence." Unable to respond to this logic, I cut my lecture short and dutifully shut up.

On another occasion, a woman was brought into jail with hepatitis, a highly contagious disease. This set off a furor, as nobody wanted to have to share the shower and toilet facilities with her. We complained vigorously, but the jail officials refused to isolate her. And the situation was made worse by the woman's careless hygiene in our crowded space; among other things, she continuously coughed onto the telephone. It seemed to us that she was going out of her way to spread her disease.

Three days after her arrest, the woman was taken to court, where her lawyer begged the judge to release her without bail so that she could receive proper medical treatment and rest. He also cited her problems with the other jail inmates as a hindrance to fighting her illness. When the judge seemed prepared to ignore her pleas and send her back to jail, the woman tried a last-ditch effort. She cried out, "Even Susan McDougal wants me released!"

I could have explained to her that, as a general rule, dropping my name in court was more likely to get her the death penalty than early release. But for whatever reason, this particular judge thought her outburst was hilarious and subsequently granted her request.

There were many sobering moments in jail as well. Perhaps the most difficult moment for me came one night when a new girl was brought in. Painfully thin, with dirty blond hair and a tattoo on her shoulder, she apparently had been running a local marijuana ring in a manner that would have been the envy of a Fortune 500 company. I was especially curious to hear her story and how she had gotten to this point in her life. After giving her a couple of nights to adjust, we put her on the hot seat in the How Did You Get Here? game.

In a matter-of-fact tone, with no hint of self-pity, she drew us a picture of a harsh, wrenching childhood. She'd grown up in a lower-income middle-class family near a midwestern city, with most of the normal childhood experiences you'd expect—save one. By the time she was nine, her father had begun molesting her on a regular basis, while her mother pretended not to know what was going on. The abuse was difficult to take, she told us, but she managed to endure it for three or four years by not fighting him. But she reached a breaking point when she turned thirteen—that was when she began to hear the cries of her little sister as her father began raping her as well.

Unable to stand hearing her sister's cries, she began sneaking out at night, most often sleeping in a rest room at an abandoned gas station three blocks from her house. Within a few days, word had gotten out around the neighborhood that she was sleeping there, and one night she was attacked and gang-raped by a group of teenage boys. Faced with either returning home to her father or further subjecting herself to the neighborhood boys, she chose a third option: she ran away from home.

Up to this point, she had tried to keep going to school, but now she could no longer cope. She took up life on the streets, and ended up selling first her body, then a variety of drugs, before setting up her marijuana ring. By the time she was incarcerated at FCDC, she'd been in and out of jail most of her adult life. The only thing that differentiated her from the majority of the women in jail was that she wasn't abusing drugs herself—she just used them as a profit mechanism.

The woman's story was remarkable, but even more remarkable for the nonchalant, detached way she told it. And most amazing of all was the ho-hum reaction from the women gathered around in the circle. I was near tears as she described the story of her lost youth; the rest of the women reacted like she'd just told us about a family vacation to the Grand Canyon. After she finished her story, I approached Lucy, one of the more kindhearted and sensitive women, and asked her, "Why didn't anyone respond to that story?"

"Susan," she said, "every girl in here could tell that story, or knows someone who's gone through what she has. It's not that we don't care. It's just that things like that are a part of our life."

In the two and a half months I spent at FCDC, I came to realize this was true. Many of the women I met were victims of physical and sexual abuse, and most had been through the jail system already. Nearly all were addicted to alcohol or drugs, with the drug of choice being crack cocaine.

The way the women described it, crack was at once the most fantastic and most horrific substance on the planet. In trying to describe its appeal, they all agreed that, in the throes of a crack cocaine withdrawal, you'd gladly sell your baby, steal from your mother's purse, or have sex with the smelliest man alive to get your fix. It didn't matter what your background, education, or family situation might be—once you fell under the spell of crack, you could never give it up. Even in the relatively small FCDC prison population, the women who had at some time been addicted to crack ran the gamut of race, education, and socioeconomic class.

For these women, jail was the ultimate withdrawal program. Being locked up 24/7 was forcing them to get clean, and as they did, many of them vowed to get their lives in order. These were, for the most part, caring, good women, but they had one emotion in common: self-hatred. They hated what they'd done to themselves and their families— and they also had a fatalistic sense that, once they were out of jail, they would slip back into the same behavior. And for the large number who had been sexually abused, the self-loathing ran even deeper.

I can recall one night when a drunk woman named Althea Britten was dumped in the pod. She collapsed against the wall and we all just decided to steer a wide path around her because she smelled so horrific. For days she would awaken from her stupor and she would "see" things on herself and slap at them or "throw" them. After a few minutes of this, she would collapse back into a deep, snoring sleep.

Althea was a desperate drunk, a one-case-a-day beer drinker. She had eaten very little in weeks but had instead been living off beer. Essentially, she had been left to detox on our floor. She had positioned herself right under the phone and, since no one wanted to touch her, they would roll her as far from themselves as possible with their feet. After spending almost two weeks in a drunken coma, Althea woke up starving. She begged for food constantly and would eat whatever scraps anyone had left on their tray, oftentimes even licking the tray for the last little bit. It took a long time before Althea was physically able to join the How Did You Get Here? game, but her story proved to be one of the most remarkable.

Growing up in the hills of Tennessee, Althea was raised by two alcoholic parents. They would buy groceries for their five children, then open the cans of food and dump the contents on the floor. The kids would get down on their knees and, like animals, begin grabbing for the food. Until she left home, she had never seen a table or a plate. When each kid got old enough, they would just wander off. When Althea left home, she began to steal to eat and ended up in jail time and time again.

Susan McDougal

Amazingly, Althea began eating in jail, and made a remarkable recovery and started painting and writing poetry. One morning, I awoke to find this poem under my pillow.

She Makes Us All Feel Free
We can't see any wrong she's
done
But we know just why she's
here
God has sent this woman of
courage
To help calm our fears

We're grateful every morning
when
We rise and see her shine
We feel it's such a pleasure
To sit with her and dine.

She makes us feel worth-
while
As she gets us through the
day
She speaks of a brighter
future
In a special sort of way.

Every day I thank God
For introducing her to me
It doesn't matter that the
door is locked
She makes us all feel free.
To: Susan McDougal
—Althea Britten
Faulkner County Jail

251

The Woman Who Wouldn't Talk

I posted the text near the telephone and overnight everyone's perceptions of Althea changed, even her own.

One thing that surprised me about life in jail was how much of a relief it was. Unlike my life outside, which had been a nonstop parade of stressful events and emotional upheaval, I had nothing to worry about as a prisoner. I was clothed, fed, and housed, and I had a community of people I was growing to care about. Inside the jail walls, Ken Starr, Whitewater, and the Mehta trial didn't exist in any real way for me. For the first time in my life, I could see what a gift my whole life had been and how much love and support I've always had and continued to have, now from all over the world.

For that reason, visitation was always a time of mixed emotions for me. I wanted to see my family, of course, but every time they'd come, they brought the stress of the outside world with them. It was gut-wrenching for me to see the worry on their faces, knowing there was nothing I could do to ease it. Because he was an attorney, Pat could see me just by setting up an appointment, and he frequently flew in from L.A. and did that. But the rest of my family was limited to a single thirty-minute visit per week—and only three people could come at once. So there was constant juggling over who would get to come each time. In addition, Camden was two hours from FCDC and it was often difficult to rearrange work schedules to get off work long enough to make the trip.

The list of potential visitors was pared down by one, however, when I forbade my youngest brother John from coming. John has a bigger heart than anyone I've ever known, and he can't stand to see anyone suffer, much less his own sister. Whenever he came to visit, he was so torn up that I'd spend the entire time consoling him. I often went back to the cell feeling worse than I had before the visit. So I called Mom and told her to give the family the word—either they come to laugh and visit or they would be stricken from the list.

During family visitation, we were separated by a thick wall of glass that required us to practically shout at each other, and since my father had lost much of his hearing during World War II and the Korean War, he couldn't hear me. On the days he came, the entire visit was taken up trying to help him understand what was being said. One of the prison guards witnessed the problem and actually called Judge Susan Webber Wright to see if she'd allow me to have contact visits—where we could sit side by side, with no glass wall—with my parents. She refused.

Judge Wright's refusal to grant contact visits wasn't surprising. She became increasingly antagonistic to any requests, possibly because she was beginning to take criticism about keeping me in jail when it was obvious that I wasn't going to testify. She reportedly said at one point that she couldn't go grocery shopping without someone coming up and asking why she wouldn't release Susan McDougal.

According to the laws governing civil contempt, she should have let me go. The laws state that a judge must release a recalcitrant witness whenever the judge reasonably believes that the witness is not likely to respond to the coercion of being jailed. In most cases, a few weeks or perhaps a few months are generally considered sufficient time to discern this. The notable exceptions to this pattern are Mafia cases, in which witnesses often refuse to testify because of fear of reprisals. In these cases, witnesses are often kept for the entire eighteen-month maximum allowed by law.

Since I'd gone on virtually every television and radio show available, loudly proclaiming to anyone who would listen that I had no intention of ever cooperating, it should have been clear that I wasn't going to change my mind. But Judge Wright and the OIC chose to ignore that. My attorneys filed several motions over the course of the first year asking for my release, but the OIC vigorously opposed them. They would state in their opposition papers that it was still likely that I would give in and cooperate even though they knew that there was not a chance in hell.

As my second month of incarceration came to an end, I believed even more strongly that I'd done the right thing in refusing to testify. Thousands of letters of support were pouring in from all over the world, and the discussion groups and exercise classes we'd set up at FCDC seemed to be having a beneficial effect on all the women—including me. At one point, a jail matron took me aside and told me that in all her years as a matron, she'd never seen so little trouble in the women's section.

Although I badly wanted my freedom back, I now began to believe that I could do the whole eighteen months if I had to. I felt I was doing some actual good in Conway and that was a feeling I'd never had on the outside.

One night, while talking on the phone with Pat, I shared these sentiments. "If it came to it," I told him, "I believe I could do the whole eighteen months here." Pat's response surprised me. He told me to be careful about what I said over the phone, since every jail conversation may be taped. If the OIC felt I wasn't suffering enough, he warned, they could easily arrange for me to be moved to a worse jail.

Just days after that conversation, a federal marshal showed up. "Roll up your things," she said. "You're out of here."

"Where am I going?" I asked.

"Just shut up and get moving," she responded.

"I need a few minutes to say good-bye to everyone," I said. But the marshal was in no mood to wait for any farewell tour; she ordered me to get everything together and be ready to move out in five minutes. "I'm going to take a few minutes," I said. "These women mean a lot to me, and I am going to say good-bye to them." By now the others had caught wind of what was going on, and they'd begun gathering around the marshal and me. The marshal didn't like it but, realizing she was in a difficult position, she grudgingly agreed to let us have our farewells.

Leaving FCDC was extremely hard. Not only was I leaving women I'd grown to care for—guards and prisoners—what lay ahead scared me to death.

The marshals drove me from Conway to Little Rock, where they then loaded me onto a chartered prison plane. There were two other prisoners onboard with me, both from Florida. Before we took off, a marshal warned me to keep my distance from one of them because she was mentally ill and considered dangerous. Upon our arrival at Carswell Medical Prison in Fort Worth, Texas, I was promptly placed in a closet-sized room with the woman who was then given a sharp instrument: to wit a large, sharpened pencil for the purpose of filling out her registration form.

Within minutes, the woman began ranting about prison and the "need to be tough." She then got up off the floor and came at me with her pencil clutched tightly in her fist shouting that she was going to plant it in my eye. I never took my eyes off of her, but I also never moved. I had no illusions that, if push came to shove, this woman could kick my ass rather easily. Fortunately, the woman got within a couple of feet of me and then turned around and walked away.

When the guard came to take the forms, I whispered to her to get me away from the woman immediately. When she took me outside, I told her what had just happened and she got very upset—at me! She snapped at me for not having told her that the woman was dangerous. Silly me, I thought—I'd assumed the marshals who'd dropped us off might have at least mentioned it in passing. This was yet another valuable lesson learned: never assume anyone in the criminal justice system has any idea what's going on or, in many cases, gives a damn.

At FCDC, I'd heard stories about how much cushier federal prison is than local jails. Although I was now ensconced at a federal prison, I wouldn't find out whether that assessment was true; I was placed not in the regular prison facilities, but in the attached medical facility. More specifically, I was placed on the floor reserved for inmates who were being observed for possible mental illness. Nicknamed the Almond Joy floor ("sometimes you feel like a nut, sometimes you don't"), it housed women who had pled to some type of mental incompetency in their crimes.

From the start, I felt out of place and frightened on the Almond Joy floor—not to mention confused as to why I'd been put there in the first place. As I would discover, most of the women there were serving lengthy terms (the majority for drug conspiracy charges), and many felt they had little to lose. My first day on the floor, a woman ripped a telephone off the wall and beat another woman senseless with the receiver. The tension in the facility was palpable, with fights breaking out on a regular basis. A misunderstood word, a perceived slight, a little good-natured teasing—any of these could result in a severe beating.

Shortly after my arrival, I had a quick lesson in Carswell prison etiquette. While talking on the phone with my brother Bill, I complained,

"I don't belong on this floor. They need to move me to another one, or over to the prison." When another woman on the floor overheard, she and several others quietly "escorted" me to the shower, shoved me up against the wall, and demanded to know whether I thought I was too good for the rest of them. After some hasty clarifications, I managed to end this impromptu group therapy meeting by assuring the women that I considered myself the lowest of the low. From then on, I kept my mouth shut.

At FCDC, I'd had many friends, but at Carswell I had only a few. In the beginning, my only close friend was a young woman who was in for bank robbery. In an act of incredible naïveté, she'd gone up to a bank teller, declared that she had a gun (which she didn't), and demanded $432—the exact amount of her mortgage payment. She'd recently lost her job, but had decided she could get back on her feet again if she could just make it through the month without losing her house, so she set out to get exactly the amount she needed.

When the bank teller tried to give her all the money in her drawer, she politely declined and just took the amount requested, figuring that even if she was caught, the amount was so small that she wouldn't go to jail. What she didn't realize was that, even without a weapon, the mere threat of violence in a bank robbery would send her to prison for six to eight years. I made her tell me the story twice because I had such a hard time believing it.

The atmosphere at Carswell was completely different than at FCDC, and I found it very hard to integrate. Part of this was because of the floor I was on, and part of it was because the long-termers were so hardened. And part of it came from a very unexpected source: the evangelical Christian movement in the prison.

Started by ex-Watergate felon Charles Colson, the "born again" movement had metamorphosed from a very worthy project to a kind of gang—the Christian Crips of prison. Led by a few strong, outspoken women, the Christian converts habitually told other prisoners when they could eat, when they should pray, and with whom they should socialize. They were unabashedly intolerant of anyone who disagreed even slightly with their views, and they seemed to reserve special contempt for the Jewish women on the floor. Routinely harassed, the Jewish women tended to keep their mouths shut and kept themselves separate from everyone else.

Having been raised a Christian, I was angered by this perversion of Christian principles. I never could stand the hypocrisy of those who claimed to be religious yet acted in profoundly un-Godly ways. It was one of the things that I had grown to despise about Kenneth Starr.

After meeting with the Jewish women, I came to enjoy spending time with them and they accepted me with no questions asked. We spent many hours talking, and the more I learned about the teachings of Judaism, the more I liked the humility of the religion and the peace it offered. I attended Shabbat services regularly, and even registered with the prison as Jewish so I could take part in other activities with them. I had my first Jewish Hanukkah at Carswell and learned how to bake challah bread in the prison kitchen. Because of their kindness to me, I gained an appreciation of a culture I knew little about. And there was another benefit I gained from the Jewish women: as I watched them lay low, trying to stay below the radar screen of the Christian Crips, yet resolute in their desire to quietly practice what they believed, it gave me strength to go on.

Although I was having a harder time at Carswell, federal prison did have its charms. In addition to the mandatory yoga classes and the one prisoner–one bed concept, Carswell had a cafeteria that actually served recognizable variations of food. And instead of having to wear dirty prison uniforms, each inmate was issued a clean pair of khakis and a nice cotton shirt, kind of a Ralph Lauren at the Hamptons look. Much to my delight, there was also an ice machine on my floor, and a couple of vending machines.

If the conditions were better in Carswell's medical facility than at FCDC, they still weren't as good as in the actual prison itself—where I should have been placed to begin with. From my first day at Carswell, I agitated to be moved, and pushed for an explanation as to why I was being housed with mentally ill prisoners. After a couple of weeks of whining, I finally got an answer: the authorities apparently feared that if I was put in the prison camp, I would be more susceptible to a helicopter rescue!

On hearing this theory, I was too stunned even to laugh. Who exactly would pull off this operation, an Israeli commando group? They certainly could not have suspected my family of plotting a rescue because they had trouble even finding Carswell. Maybe they suspected Clinton was going to use an air force helicopter, but I doubt he had much interest. Breaking convicts out of federal prisons is rarely viewed as a good political strategy for a sitting president.

Besides, the whole idea of escape—of any sort—was absurd on its face. First, pictures of me had been beamed around the world in the last two months; where was I going to hide? And if I did get a sudden urge to escape, I could walk out the door at any time just by agreeing to tell a story about the Clintons. Hearing about the prison officials' fears of a Great Helicopter Escape did serve as a kind of reminder that decisions about my incarceration were either being made by Starr's people or by idiots, not that the two groups were mutually exclusive.

I was disappointed at being kept in the medical facility, but as things turned out, it may have been a blessing. During a routine medical examination, a nurse discovered a large lump in my breast and noted in my records that I needed a biopsy. The lump worried me, but the nurses assured me that it was probably nothing. But from that point on, I felt some degree of relief that I was living in a hospital.

I should have known better than to get too comfortable. Just days after my breast lump was discovered, and only two months since I'd been moved to Carswell, I was told to pack up my things. I thought this meant I was moving into the Carswell prison, but when I arrived downstairs I discovered otherwise. I was surprised to find Detective Ignacio Gonzalez, the Los Angeles police officer who'd been assigned the Mehta case, waiting for me. I'd met Iggy (as he was called by his fellow officers) once before, nearly two years earlier, during my arraignment in California. He'd escorted me from my cell to the courtroom, and I remembered him well because he had a hard time concealing his contempt for Nancy Mehta. I learned later that she was giving him quite a hard time, throwing tantrums and complaining that he wasn't giving her case proper attention.

Iggy's appearance at this juncture could only mean one thing: I was headed to Los Angeles. Sure enough, he and a female officer transported me to the Dallas–Fort Worth airport where we would catch a commercial flight. I didn't know what the jail would be like, but I was very happy about one thing: because Pat and Bill lived in Los Angeles, it would be much easier for them to come see me.

Iggy draped a jacket over my handcuffs as we walked through the airport. Although I was the one in handcuffs, he was the one who seemed embarrassed. I tried to bait him into discussing the Mehta case and his dealings with Nancy, but he grunted and refused to comment. His female partner did mention that Iggy had taken a lot of crap during the investigation. I actually found myself feeling sorry for him. I might be in prison, but if he was dealing with an angry Nancy Mehta, he was in hell.

As we walked through the airport, I noticed that Iggy and his partner were getting dirty looks from people at the airport. People started coming up to me and saying, "I'm so sorry this happened to you" or "Hang in there, Susan!" My face had been plastered on CNN and in newspapers just as I'd been sent away to jail, so I wasn't used to being recognized. It was strange enough to suddenly be in the world again after being in prison—but having total strangers walk up and speak to me was really wild. All I could think of to reply was, "I'm all right." But heading off the Los Angeles, to my third jail in less than six months, I was anything but all right.

14

IF IT'S TUESDAY, THIS MUST BE SYBIL BRAND

WHEN WE ARRIVED IN LOS ANGELES, I was put in a van and taken to my new home, the Sybil Brand Institute for Women. Named after a legendary champion of prison reform, Sybil Brand seemed designed to showcase in one place all the reasons prison reform was needed. Housed in a creaky old building apparently erected sometime during the reign of William the Conqueror, it had gained a well-deserved reputation for being one of the most notorious women's facilities in the country.

At Sybil Brand, I was thrown into a cramped cell with five other women who had evidently been arrested for prostitution or for wearing too much spandex. The mere fact of finding myself in a jail cell was no longer the shock it once had been, but I was unprepared for the squalor I found here. The floor and walls were covered in grime, the toilet was overflowing, two cigar-size roaches were playing on the floor, and it was so cold I could see my breath. To top it off, the nonstop clamor in the cells and hallways resembled the decibel level at a Beatles concert. The guards seemed incapable of speaking below a roar. They screamed every request, command, and question and, in addition, they physically shoved the women up and down the corridors—a potentially dangerous situation, since handcuffed inmates can't break their fall if they trip.

The Woman Who Wouldn't Talk

Over the course of my first four months in jail, I'd come to believe that the horror stories about prison were just that—stories. The jails I'd been in so far hadn't been nice, but they weren't hellholes. In this freezing cold, squalid cell, however, I began to wonder for the first time if I could survive.

As I talked with the other women in the cell, a guard soon came for me. Once again, it seemed that prison officials weren't quite sure what to do with me, so they decided for the time being to move me to a private room on the medical ward. This was an improvement, but by now I'd gone a while without food, so I flagged down a passing guard. "Can I get something to eat?" I asked him. "Maybe something out of the vending machines?"

The guard cocked his head and peered at me, apparently trying to assess just how crazy I was. "I've just been in federal prison down in Texas," I told him. "They let you get something from the vending machines if you miss a meal."

"Well, McDougal," the guard replied, breaking into a grin, "it looks like you finally found yourself a *real* jail."

Sybil Brand may have been a real jail, but the wardens still were having a hard time figuring out what to do with a not-so-real prisoner. They kept me on the medical ward for the first few days, then finally settled on a unique solution: since my stay was generating a fair amount of publicity, they would assign me to the jail's special "high-profile" wing.

My first reaction to this news was a positive one—this being L.A., I had visions of kicking back with other high-profile inmates like Charlie Sheen and Robert Downey Jr. But high-profile at Sybil Brand had a whole different meaning: it referred to cases where the inmate's crime had received some degree of publicity. In most cases, this meant murder. It took me approximately one day on the high-profile wing to realize that I had been placed on what the guards and other prisoners affectionately called Murderers' Row.

Murderers' Row consisted of ten cells, lined up side by side and facing a gray brick wall. Between the cells and the wall was an eight-foot-wide walkway, where the women were allowed out to socialize, go to the showers, and make phone calls. In addition, once a day they were let into a nearby recreation room that had an exercise bike, a television, and a vending machine.

Two women occupied each cell, which consisted of a bunk bed, toilet, and sink. Since murder trials frequently take a long time to get to court, most of the women had been there for a year or more and expecting to be there a lot longer. Once they went to trial, they'd be moved to state prison—where most of the women on this cell block would spend the rest of their lives.

Being on the high-profile ward meant getting special jailwear. Everyone on Murderers' Row was forced to wear a bright red prison gown—the same color gown that was reserved for those charged with child molestation. Our red gowns alerted the rest of the prisoners to our "special" status, ensuring that whenever we left the wing to meet with attorneys or go to the medical unit, we'd be subjected to as much verbal and physical abuse as possible from both the guards and the other prisoners. Anyone wearing the dreaded red dress was considered the lowest form of life—no mean feat in a place like Sybil Brand.

For my first three days on Murderers' Row, I was allowed out of my cell with all the other women for ten to twelve hours a day, giving me access to the hallway, the showers, the rec room, and, most important, the telephone. I didn't have a cellmate, so these hours were the only time I could get to know other women on the cell block. But on the fourth day, even that little bit of relative freedom was abruptly taken away when I was notified that I was being put on K-10: lockdown status. In simple terms, this meant I would be kept in my cell all day and would only be let out once or twice, for about an hour each time—and then only while the other women were in lockdown.

I was devastated—this was like being in jail within a jail. I couldn't believe they intended on keeping me locked up twenty-two to twenty-three hours a day in a cell. But when I vehemently protested, I was given what I soon recognized as the standard line: "It's for your own protection." This was the strategy the jail officials had settled on—they would do whatever they wanted with me, no matter how twisted the logic of it, and the rationale was always the same. Being put on Murderers' Row, being locked up in my cell for twenty-three hours a day, being forced to wear the red dress—everything was for my "own protection." It was hard to argue with people who purported to have my interests so close to their heart.

Right away I embarked on a campaign to overturn the ruling. It was obvious that the women on Murderers' Row weren't a threat to me—most of them, in fact, weren't a threat to anyone. For the most part, they were women who had killed in the heat of passion, usually a husband or other relative—essentially, they had just snapped.

I made this argument to the sergeant, telling him I was willing to take my chances. His reply was definitive. "McDougal," he told me, "the K-10 status order comes from way up. You can complain to all the people around here you want, but nobody can change it. Jesus Christ himself," he concluded, "could not get you off lockdown status."

The sergeant's statement proved to be prophetic—in the eight months I was at Sybil Brand, I was kept on lockdown status the entire time. It was tough asking to be let out because whenever I was out, it meant the guards had to lock all the other women in their cells. If the women hadn't wanted to kill me before, this was about enough to push them over the edge. So mostly I shut up and tried to make conversation from behind bars.

From the time I arrived at Sybil Brand, I struggled constantly with the prison officials and, to a lesser degree, with the guards. The approach to management at Sybil Brand was at least as antiquated as the deteriorating facility itself—everything was accomplished by yelling, threatening, and pushing the women around. All inmate requests, no matter how basic, were met with immediate rejection. Rules varied from shift to shift, depending on the mood of the deputy in charge that day. And the prevailing attitude was that the inmates were animals and should be treated as such. Many of the deputies, in fact, took a perverse pleasure in seeing how far they could push the women before one of them exploded.

The inmates' reactions were predictable. The more the officers applied pressure, the more the women chafed. Challenges to authority were commonplace, and the anger level was palpable. The relationship between the inmates and the guards was almost always hostile, bordering on explosive.

Having spent time at Faulkner County Detention Center (FCDC) in Arkansas, I could see how stupid the Sybil Brand approach was. At FCDC, the officials tended to grant most simple requests—and when they didn't, they offered an explanation as to why. Rules were consistently enforced so it was always clear exactly what you could and couldn't do. I never saw physical force or verbal abuse by guards at FCDC. Neither the inmates nor the guards at FCDC were happy to be there, but they did their best to get along and make a bad situation tolerable. In contrast, the women at Sybil Brand woke up every morning to the sound of screaming and went to bed every night still being yelled at.

Part of the difference was that correctional officers at FCDC and at Carswell were professional guards. At Sybil Brand, the guards were sheriff deputies who were trained for street patrol. In addition, it could not do much for the deputies' self-esteem to be assigned to work at a dark, roach-infested facility. Though I never heard any of the guards complain, I was relatively sure that being assigned to Sybil Brand was not a sign that you were on a fast track to success.

Despite what seemed to be earnest efforts, the staff at Sybil Brand was never able to keep the place very clean. They were constantly at war with the army of roaches that had infested the jail, and it was obvious that the roaches were winning. Often, when I was lying in my bunk at night, I'd suddenly get whacked on the face by a roach falling from the ceiling. We tried several approaches to stop the roaches, from applying hair gel to the wall to washing the walls with undiluted green floor cleaner, but nothing worked.

At mealtime, when the guards scooted a food tray on the floor under the bars of a cell, you had to snatch it up quickly before the roaches suddenly materialized to swarm all over it. And for anyone unfortunate enough to accidentally sleep through a meal, it pretty much guaranteed that the food—never very good to begin with—would be covered within minutes.

The jail also had a healthy population of rats, but having lived at the Mehtas' rat resort in Brentwood, Sybil Brand actually represented a decrease for me in the number of rat encounters.

The conditions at Sybil Brand were miserable, but it was the trips to and from jail that were the real nightmare. On days that I had to appear in court for procedural matters relating to the Mehta case, a guard would appear at my cell door at 4:30 A.M., shine a flashlight in my eyes, and yell, "McDougal—court!" At the appointed time, I'd be led down to a waiting room and then put on a large black-and-gray passenger bus—like a Greyhound bus, only with a tall metal cage built in at the front. The guards would shepherd me into the cage, chain my arms to the rail, and we'd be off.

The bus would then make a tour of various men's jails, picking up male prisoners for their day in court. I found that my time with the men on the bus was invariably two hours of hell. For the duration of the drive to the courthouse, the men would yell obscene remarks at me, expose themselves and pretend to masturbate while the bus driver and guards looked the other way. On one horrific occasion, an inmate sitting directly behind me did masturbate. I heard the sound of chains—*clink, clink, clink*—over and over. I finally turned around only to have the guy stick his penis up to the cage and ask me to play with it. Everyone was laughing and cheering him on. A few weeks later, I received a letter from the man, in which he apologized and asked if I would send him an autograph.

Upon arrival at the courthouse, I'd be taken to a holding cell. Once the guards actually chained me to a toilet. I would then have to lie down on a filthy concrete bench until my name was called. The pain in my back was so intense from being handcuffed that when they took them off, I couldn't move my arms from behind me.

After what usually amounted to a thirty-second appearance in court on some procedural matter, I would then be returned to the holding cell and would stay there for the remainder of the day before being loaded back on the bus. By the time the bus dropped off the male prisoners at their various jails and I was returned to Sybil Brand, it was usually past mealtime. I would then be ordered to get off the bus and told, "Shut up, turn around, and face the wall!" The guards would then do a cursory pat-down to make sure that no one had slipped me a gun. Then I would be led off to a concrete room and strip-searched, with the female officers doing a very thorough cavity search. It was a fitting ending to a truly disgusting day.

On the days I went through the ordeal of being dragged to court, I fully understood why so many women are willing to plead to crimes they did not commit, just to avoid having to go back to court. There were days that I would have pled guilty to the Lindbergh baby kidnapping.

On one particularly memorable trip back from court, a female guard took it upon herself to teach me a lesson in humility, a recurring theme between Sybil Brand's guards and inmates. As I stepped off the bus, she yanked out of my hands the manila envelope I was carrying, then dumped its contents—my glasses and some court documents—onto the sidewalk. My glasses broke and the guard, unapologetic, then refused to remove my handcuffs, as was required. Instead, she put me in a locked waiting room with several other women—none of whom were hand-cuffed. As she left, the guard loudly announced that I had just told her I shouldn't be placed in that room, as I was better than the other women there. The guard was clearly expecting the other women to administer a first-class beating, but thankfully, no one took her seriously and they just ignored her.

There was one other reason that I hated to go to court—I no longer had a California attorney. Leonard Levine had done a very good job of representing me to this point, but he told me he couldn't continue as my attorney without a minimum of another $50,000. He might as well have been asking for $50 million. By this point I had nothing, and I couldn't continue to ask for help from my family, or from Pat and his family, all of whom had already gone to the wall for me.

Several high-profile attorneys made noises—and in some cases, even promises—about handling the Mehta case for me pro bono. But whenever they talked to D.A. Jeffrey Semow, he'd tell them that the case might take six months or longer at trial. It was extremely hard for any attorney, no matter how much they wanted the publicity or believed in my innocence, to commit to suspending their income for six months.

Bill and Pat got busy following up every possible attorney lead, frantically trying to find someone with a California license who'd be willing to handle the case for free. All I could offer in return was the publicity the case would generate and a promise that I was not guilty. I wasn't looking for Johnnie Cochran—in fact, I wasn't even looking for anyone to actually prepare the case. Pat could do that. We just needed an attorney with a California license, an I.Q. above 100, and a willingness to work for free.

It turned out to be virtually impossible to find all these elements in one person. Among the lawyers Bill and Pat interviewed was a veteran attorney who assured them he could handle the case and any media attention it produced. When Bill told him that we needed someone as early as the next Sunday for a session on NBC's *Meet the Press*—the longest-running show in television history—the attorney replied, "Don't worry. I'm great on radio!"

Another attorney, a Yale graduate no less, asked to see the documents related to the trial before deciding whether or not to represent me. After reading Nancy's interviews, he met with Pat and not so politely declined to take the case. "I'm sorry," he said abruptly, "but the case appears to be unwinnable."

"Don't you even want to talk about the defense?" Pat responded. "You've only looked at one side of the story."

"It doesn't matter," the attorney said. "The alleged victim is the wife of a well-known and respected L.A. figure. The jury will believe her over a convicted felon. I told you I'd only take the case if we could win it, and I don't see that happening."

After about ten such frustrating meetings, I came to a decision: I would represent myself. With Pat handling the legal side, and Bill working with me on strategy, I believed we could do everything ourselves. Neither Bill nor Pat took me seriously, and they continued the attorney search—but I was dead serious. I was so tired of the whole thing, especially the trips to the courthouse, that I decided I'd just get up at the Mehta trial and tell my story. If the jury believed me, great. If not—well, I'd already learned I could survive in jail.

One Friday night shortly after I made this decision, the guard yelled out, "McDougal, you got a visitor. Your lawyer is here."

Since I'd just gotten off the phone with Pat a few minutes earlier, I knew it couldn't be him. My first reaction was to turn down the visit, thus avoiding the cavity search I'd have to undergo after the visit. But my curiosity got the better of me, and I decided to go downstairs and see exactly who "my attorney" was.

When I was escorted into the attorney room, I was greeted by a tall, angular man with a thick mustache and a very mischievous half-grin who I had never seen before in my life. "I'm Mark Geragos," he said. Mark told me he'd been an attorney in L.A. for more than fifteen years and said that he ran a small firm with his father and brother that specialized in criminal defense work. He went on and on about his background, but I was having a hard time concentrating on what he was saying. Instead, I was fixated on the gorgeous black leather briefcase that he had brought with him. I kept thinking that any lawyer with that kind of briefcase had to be good.

After a while, Mark got to the point. He had been sent by a mutual friend who knew I was not represented and had been asked to come to the jail and talk with me. After we talked for a few more minutes, he looked at me and said, "I would be willing to represent you if you want to retain me."

"Why?" I asked.

"I have been following your legal problems for a long time and I think what they have done to you is a travesty. My father was a long-time prosecutor in Los Angeles before he began to practice defense work," Mark said. "He knows how a prosecutor is supposed to act and he believes that what Starr is doing is criminal. I told him that I had been asked to talk to you, but I also warned him that if we agreed to represent you it could cause the firm enormous financial problems. He told me, 'After what she's done standing up to that bastard, someone should stand up for that girl.' We agreed that someone should help you."

The Woman Who Wouldn't Talk

As a general rule, I've come to believe that anything in life that sounds too good to be true usually is. We'd hit numerous dead-ends looking for a marginally acceptable attorney, and now an articulate, well-dressed, intelligent young attorney had walked in unannounced to tell me that he understood what I'd done and wanted to help. There had to be a catch.

But the more we talked, the more comfortable I became. We talked about cases he had won, including one that was eerily similar to the Mehta trial. I told him that I'd like him to represent me, but only on one condition: he could never, under any circumstances, ask me to plead guilty to stealing from the Mehtas.

"Just remember, Mark," I told him, "you can never make a mistake with me as long as you fight. No matter what you say or do, I just want someone who's willing to fight back."

"It's a deal," Mark said. "I will never push you to plead."

Near the end of the conversation, Mark asked me if I had any money at all. I looked at him and said, "I have less than no money." He laughed and said, "That's what we figured. I do not need a down payment, but I want a signed retainer agreement right now. I won't leave here without it."

"Well," I told him, "I have to clear it with my fiancé and brother first."

"I won't be dragged along while they shop for other attorneys," Mark said, looking intently at me. "Do you want me to represent you or not?"

I knew that simply taking him on, without Pat and Bill's input, might be a huge mistake. I knew nothing about Mark Geragos and his background—or even if he was telling me the truth. Where had he come from and why was he willing to help me? For all I knew, he could have been sent by the OIC. But there was something about him I trusted. When he told me he could help me, I believed him. "As long as you're sure you know what you're getting into," I told him, "then I want you as my lawyer."

Later that evening, I called Pat and broke the news to him. "I hired an attorney tonight."

"What in God's name are you talking about?" he asked, clearly surprised.

I tried to explain to him about Mark's visit and that he had made me feel confident, but I was having a hard time putting it into words. Finally Pat asked me, "What was it about him that you liked so much?"

I told him the truth. "I loved his briefcase."

Pat was getting a little exasperated by this time and blurted out, "You have to be kidding! You liked his briefcase. That was it—that is how your going to choose your attorney."

"Well, actually I liked his shoes, too." I replied.

But Pat was not about to let me choose an attorney on the basis of nice footwear and executive accessories. The next day he set up an appointment to meet with Mark and find out what was going on. In the meantime, he had begun telling me not to get my hopes up and that he did not like the way this had taken place. This was all too good to be true—he was going to expose Mark as a fraud. An hour after the meeting, I called Pat at home to find out what had happened. But before I could ask any questions, Pat very quietly said, "I think you found yourself one hell of an attorney." That would prove to be an understatement.

Because I was on lockdown, it wasn't easy to get to know my fellow inmates on Murderers' Row, but one day two women were brought in and put on lockdown in the cell next to mine. I wondered if maybe they were also in jail on civil contempt so I struck up a conversation with them, although the logistics of the cells made it impossible for me to see them while we talked.

They began telling me about their religious beliefs—a code of conduct that made David Koresh look mainstream. After a time, I found out that the women were in jail for having killed a little girl—by stomping her to death. According to the arrest report, the girl, a member of their church, had been something of a hyperactive child—a sign, these women believed, that she was possessed by demons. They decided to stomp the demons out of her, then watch as she, like Lazarus, on the third day would rise from the dead. To their great surprise, the little girl simply stayed dead. The little girl's mother was later brought in for being an accomplice in the murder and she was placed in the cell on the other side of me. She told me she believed the women until the second day when the little girl did not come back to life. At that point, her young son began screaming, "Momma, she's dead, she's dead!" This apparently snapped her out of her trance because she then began calling for help. Unfortunately, it was too late. The two crazy women then told the mother that she had killed the child by not waiting until the third day.

At first the women on Murderers' Row were not quite sure what the story was with me, especially since I was being kept in lockdown all the time. Gradually, curiosity got the better of several of the inmates, and they began to hang out on the walkway in front of my cell whenever they were allowed out on their own. Before long three or four women started to gather regularly in front of my cell to play cards or Scrabble through the bars.

One of my new friends was a short, heavyset woman named Butch. Though she was in her forties, Butch could easily have passed for sixty—she had the kind of face that collects lines and crags for every hardship endured in life. And Butch had certainly experienced her share of hardships.

When Butch was nine, she'd stood up to her religious fanatic mother, refusing to try speaking in tongues and attend church every day. Her mother responded by throwing Butch out of their upstate New York home, but not before giving her a lasting memento—a punch in the mouth that knocked out Butch's front teeth. For the next several weeks, Butch lived in a lean-to in the woods, still going to school and eating scraps out of trash cans. Fortunately, a classmate told her parents how Butch was living and they invited her into their home to finish fourth grade.

That was the end of Butch's childhood—assuming she'd ever really had one. By age twelve, Butch was working two jobs and renting her own small place above a garage. By sixteen she'd dropped out of high school and was abusing alcohol and drugs. By the time I met her, she had an arrest record that was longer than she was tall, almost all for drug possession.

Although Butch wasn't educated, she had an advanced degree in street smarts, and a truly wicked sense of humor. She was also the only other person on Murderers' Row for something other than murder.

After having dealt with lawyers for years, Butch had decided she could do a better job representing herself, so she got a court order allowing her to use the law library. She'd been placed on our wing because it was the closest to the law library and she'd have easy access to the law books she needed to represent herself.

Having spent much of her life in jails, Butch knew how the system worked. She also understood exactly how far she could push it—and she never hesitated to push it as far as she possibly could. Butch was always coming up with wild ideas to fight the boredom of prison life. One night she hatched a plan to make homemade wine out of our leftover food: if we would all save our fruit from dinner, Butch would store it for several days in a cool, dark place while it fermented.

Unfortunately, the most obvious cool, dark place was also the worst: the toilet. Butch somehow procured a plastic bag, packed it with leftover prison-meal fruit, and stashed it inside her toilet. Like an alchemist on a divine mission, she carefully measured a few sugar packets and other ingredients into the mix, and then left it to age for a week or two.

It didn't take long for the plan to run into problems. After a few days of rotting, the fruit was exuding a smell that threatened to overpower everyone on the wing. The guards quickly grew suspicious, but no one seemed sure as to exactly what the smell was—and considering the place it seemed to be emanating from, no one really wanted to ask. But as the musky scent of moldy fruit grew thicker by the day, the guards began to snoop around, and we realized it was only a matter of time before Butch's toilet would reveal its secret.

Where could we put the bag to keep it safe from the guards until it had aged properly? Someone offered what all quickly agreed was the ideal solution: "Let's put it in McDougal's cell—they'll never suspect her of doing something like this." Though I wanted to help, I protested that I just couldn't keep the bag in my toilet. All I could think was that, if I got caught, the headlines in the newspapers would read, "Hillbilly McDougal Busted for Running Jail Still."

But after a fair amount of arm-twisting, I finally relented. I told the women I would keep the wine for a maximum of two days, which was when it was supposedly going to be ready for consumption. At this point,

The Woman Who Wouldn't Talk

I must confess, I wasn't so sure it would ever be fit for drinking—it was the only thing I'd ever seen the roaches at Sybil Brand run *away* from.

With the bag safely stowed in my toilet, excitement about our "wine-tasting" grew. But at the end of the second day, one of the women who'd been integral to the plot was hospitalized for a short time—and we didn't think it would be fair to indulge without her. By the time she arrived back on the wing, the wine had passed its peak and was fast headed down the other slope—but this did nothing to deter the festive atmosphere on Murderers' Row.

One by one, each woman surreptitiously gulped down a mouthful of the black liquid before passing it down the row. By the time it reached me, the odor was so powerful that I refused to take a drink—the smell itself was enough to make me gag. But the women on the row would not hear of it. Exercising the kind of peer pressure that leads eighth-graders to begin a lifetime of smoking, the women convinced me I had to take my turn. Their insistence, and my always wanting to be "one of the gang," finally led me to give it a taste.

I scrunched my eyes shut and took two quick swigs—and within a few moments, I was so dizzy I couldn't sit up. A half hour later I had passed out. By all accounts, the night that followed the "wine-tasting" at Sybil Brand was one of the wildest and funniest in the storied history of the jail. I'm kind of sorry I missed it. But now Butch was on a roll: as a follow-up to the fruit wine, she came up with a scheme to create Japanese "sake" from our leftover dinner rice. Surprisingly, this process not only went much more smoothly, but the drink itself was actually not bad. And on sake night, I managed to last a full hour before passing out.

Butch was one of several inmates who came to spend a lot of time in front of my cell. Another was Sveta. They'd grown up in completely different circumstances, but a few key elements of their stories were depressingly similar.

Sveta was a beautiful, talented nineteen-year-old Russian girl who'd grown up in privileged circumstances, the daughter of a successful businessman. They seemed to be the family that had everything—but under the surface, things were considerably bleaker than they looked. Sveta's father had an alarming inability to control his drinking and his temper. As a toddler, he would punish her by picking her up by a leg and bashing her face into the wall. She told me that her mother would put toilet paper in her ears so that she couldn't hear the screaming.

In her teenage years, Sveta rebelled. She began running with a tough crowd, doing heroin and other drugs, essentially trying anything that kept her away from home. She'd found herself a new home at Sybil Brand thanks to one terrible incident.

One night when she was eighteen, Sveta and her boyfriend decided to steal a car to get money for more heroin. The car they chose to steal, however, belonged to a police officer and, as they took off, he ran across the street and stood in front of the car with his legs and arms in a shooting stance. The boyfriend panicked and went straight at the officer. He hit the officer, seriously injuring him, and although Sveta hadn't been behind the wheel, she was charged with being an accomplice in an attempted murder. When I arrived at Sybil Brand, Sveta had been languishing there for almost two years. She rarely saw her lawyer, who told her only that she was facing thirty years to life for being there that night.

Like Butch, Sveta was very funny and had a wonderfully creative streak. At Christmas, for example, she melted down M&Ms and used the colors to paint pictures on the walls and windows of her cell. But sadly, Sveta's creativity was matched by her cynicism. She was very bitter, not only about her upbringing, but about the world in general. Once, when I was encouraging her to explore her Jewish background, she interrupted me to say, "Susan, if I was God, I would never let happen to anyone what happened to me. I can't believe there is a God." And on another occasion, she told me, "Your problem is that you trust everybody until they screw you over. I take the opposite approach. I don't trust anybody until they prove to me they won't screw me over."

From time to time our group was joined by Amy, an inmate who looked at first glance to be a member of the junior-high glee club. Although she was actually nineteen or twenty, Amy looked much younger, and in fact she was still very immature.

Of all the women I would meet in jail, Amy was perhaps the kindest and most gentle—a demeanor that contrasted starkly with the life she'd come from. By the time Amy was ten, both of her parents were gone and she was being passed around from relatives to foster homes and back to relatives, none of whom seemed to care too much about what happened to her.

The only people who seemed to care about Amy were members of a local street gang. When they promised to take care of her and always be there for her, it seemed to Amy that she'd at last found the family she'd always wanted. Eager to please and anxious to belong, Amy took part in a shootout as part of her gang initiation—and when a young child was left dead in the crossfire, she soon enough found herself on Sybil Brand's Murderers' Row. Whenever Amy sat outside my cell, talking in her girlish voice and fishing for my approval and acceptance, I always found myself staring at her, trying to imagine how this shy, sweet young girl could possibly be a gun-toting gang member, complete with a tattooed tear falling from one eye—the gang symbol for a killer.

As difficult as prison life was, I found that getting to know these women made it bearable. Some of my favorite memories of my time at Sybil Brand are of working with Butch on her upcoming trial. At first glance, her case seemed to be a lost cause. Butch had been arrested more than twenty times for drug possession and now she was facing similar charges. But Butch was absolutely convinced that, since this time she was innocent, she could get herself off. All the other times, she told me, she'd pled guilty because she was in fact guilty—but this time she'd been framed. And this arrest was particularly galling because she'd finally made up her mind to get off drugs and had been clean for a while.

Butch had been working at a car wash near her Long Beach apartment when a police officer who'd arrested her a couple of times before spotted her and stopped his car. At her last arrest, Butch had been belligerent to the cop, and he had apparently decided to exact his revenge. Either that, or he just wanted Butch, a known drug user, off the street, and saw no harm in accomplishing that by framing her. It's the kind of thing that happens a hundred times a day across the United States in the war on drugs. The cop sidled over to the drinking fountain where Butch had just taken a sip of water and produced a rock of crack cocaine that he claimed he saw Butch drop.

After Butch told me about her case, I called Pat to ask his advice. He came up with a novel suggestion. Rather than run from her previous arrest record, he told me, Butch should embrace it. She should explain to the jury that, in every previous instance—all twenty-three of them—Butch had willingly pled guilty and accepted responsibility because she was in fact guilty. Though Butch was admittedly a convicted criminal, she had her own unique code of honor, and she'd always been honest about her drug problem. Butch clearly had her faults, she should tell the jury, but lying wasn't one of them. We worked furiously over the next few weeks to prepare her defense, drawing up more than a hundred questions to ask the police officer during cross-examination and going over Butch's testimony repeatedly.

The prosecutor on the case was young and inexperienced, and she likely viewed this case as a slam dunk. After all, who was the jury going to believe—a twenty-time loser or a police officer? But Butch, wearing a new suit my brother Bill had bought her, stuck close to the script during her cross-examination of the police officer, and she actually caught him in several lies. She embraced her record as evidence that, when she was guilty, she had never been afraid to admit it. After the two-day trial, the jury returned with a unanimous verdict: not guilty. Butch was ecstatic, electrified. It's probably no exaggeration to say that hearing that verdict was the highlight of her life—a life that had, since its very start, been unfairly marked by more than its share of lowlights.

But sadly, Butch's victory turned out to be short-lived. She was released from jail and did manage to stay clean for several months. And she even became a minor celebrity when NBC's *Dateline* interviewed her for a piece they were doing about my time in jail. But the years of hard living had taken their toll on her not only psychologically but physically, and, less than a year after she'd been released, Butch died of a heart attack.

15

DEATH OF A SALESMAN

BY AUGUST 1997, I HAD BEEN in jail on the civil contempt charge for almost a year. Judge Wright could, by law, keep me in for another six months on civil contempt—though she could, at least in theory, choose to release me at any time. We were still appealing the two-year sentence for my conviction and had a certain degree of hope that it would be overturned. And I could, of course, get out of jail at any time, if I was willing to cooperate with Starr.

Although I'd had my share of bleak and depressing moments in jail, I had never seriously considered giving in and testifying. I'd proven to myself that not only could I survive in jail, but in some ways I could even thrive. That would change, however, when I was moved from Sybil Brand to a new facility in L.A. called Twin Towers. At Twin Towers, I would endure the single worst experience of my life—a nightmare that made me question whether I could survive jail with my sanity intact. It lasted seven weeks, and by the end of that time I would have done almost anything to end the ordeal.

Located near downtown Los Angeles, Twin Towers was the pride of the Los Angeles County Sheriff's Department. It was a state-of-the-art building, a technological wonder with every computer-enhanced, electronic gadget imaginable, and not a soul at the jail who knew how to operate them—certainly not the deputies who were in charge of our lives. Although it looked like a high-rise hotel from the outside, the inside was standard-issue American jail: stark white concrete walls, the constant sound of slamming steel doors, and the ever-present smell of Lysol and rotting food.

As I prepared for the move to Twin Towers, I found myself becoming increasingly nervous about the transfer. Sybil Brand, where I'd spent the last eight months, was a hellhole compared to some of the jails I'd been in, but it was at least a hellhole I knew. One way prisoners learn to survive in jail is by adapting to a regime; change of any kind, even a cell change, will adversely affect a longtime prisoner. While I was still at Sybil Brand, Lieutenant Moltman, one of the sheriff's deputies, dropped by to give me a sneak preview of my future. Laughing, he told me that he had seen my new cell and that it looked a lot like the glass cage where Hannibal Lecter was housed in the movie *Silence of the Lambs.* In fact, he said the deputies who had seen it were already calling it the Hannibal Lecter cell. I immediately called Pat and Bill and told them about my nervousness over the move. Though they tried to calm me by suggesting the new facility had to at least be better than Sybil Brand, I found my sense of apprehension growing as the transfer drew near.

My instincts were not only correct, the experience was far worse than I had imagined. When we arrived at Twin Towers, the guards placed me in the special cell, in the middle of one of the four square pods on the floor. Unlike any other cell I'd been in, this one had a thick sheet of Plexiglas that extended from ceiling to floor, rather than bars. The Plexiglas wall allowed me to see what was going on in the pod, but it was so thick I couldn't hear anything that was going on outside of my cell.

Since my K-10 lockdown status was still in effect, I was locked in this cell for twenty-three hours a day. I'd been in lockdown at Sybil Brand as well, but at least there I'd been able to talk to women through the bars of my cell. Here, not only did the Plexiglas wall prevent that, but the jail officials even hung a sign outside my cell warning, that "If McDougal is seen talking to anyone while entering or leaving her cell, she is not to be allowed out until further notice."

For twenty-three hours a day I could observe the other women eat, play games, watch television, and talk, but I could hear nothing. It was a bizarre, surreal feeling. For the first few days I lay on my bunk and watched in frustration as the women laughed and joked together. Inmates, when they weren't being watched closely, would come to my cell, but despite their shouting for my benefit, I could not hear them. Up to this point I'd been able to deal with jail because of the women I met and our interactions. I did not have even a watch or a radio. Now I was as alone as I'd ever been, and I was starting to panic.

I sat silently in my glass cage for hours on end unable to hear anything or speak to anyone. Amid the stark silence, the one hour a day I was let out was hardly a relief: I was escorted by a guard to the basketball court where I could either lie on the floor and look through a wire net that was about fifty feet high, or I could stand and use the phone. I usually chose the latter. The phone calls were the only thing that I had to look forward to. My hands would shake as I pushed the numbers to call Pat or Bill or Mark.

In the two years that I spent in jail, there was only one time that Pat was not at the other end of that phone. This was the night he had been hit by a bicycle on a jogging path and taken to the hospital. I didn't sleep the entire night. I knew something must have happened because he never let me down. Bill also kept up constant contact with me by arranging for his answering service to accept my collect calls and connect me to him anywhere in the world. I desperately needed that security—I needed to know that no matter what, I could reach either of them at any time.

My only other diversion at Twin Towers was reading—unlike FCDC, Twin Towers allowed inmates to have books—and with all this time on my hands I was going through a book a day. Friends, relatives, and even strangers were sending me books, everything from Pulitzer Prize–winning fiction to self-improvement books, and I was reading them all. The prison did not provide newspapers or magazines and most of the books in the prison library were ten or twenty years old.

The Woman Who Wouldn't Talk

There was only one television on the pod and, of course, I could not see it.

Since I wasn't let out with the other women, my meals were delivered to my cell. This was apparently difficult for the guards to remember, and they frequently forgot to do it. Frustrated and hungry, I'd ring the buzzer in my cell, but that was ignored as well. Though each cell was equipped with such a buzzer, to notify the guards of problems, they were routinely ignored—largely because each floor had only one guard, who couldn't respond to everyone. The lone guard would sit at a control panel high above the four pods, where he or she could regulate everything on the floor—temperature, cell doors, lights—by pushing various buttons. In retrospect, I have doubts that the buzzers were even hooked up since mine was never answered, not even once.

As I sat in my cell, watching the silent movie going on just beyond the wall, I found that it was easier just to turn away. It was too hard to watch everyone laughing and talking. It was particularly hard to see the chaplains, many of whom had become my friends, come for the different services and barely even acknowledge me. They would give me a sad wave, but even they had been told to stay away.

When I would talk to Mark, Bill, or Pat on the phone, I increasingly had trouble concentrating and often couldn't focus on what was being said. When Pat visited me, he told me my eyes were glazing over even when I was talking.

As disoriented as I was outside the cell, I soon felt just as disoriented inside. When I'd wake up in the morning or after a nap, I often didn't know where I was. I completely lost track of time. I'd read about sensory deprivation before, but I'd had no concept of what it felt like. Now I was beginning to understand why it was such an effective form of torture. I'm convinced that reading was the only thing that kept me from losing my mind—and by this point, I wasn't sure how much longer even that would sustain me.

After three weeks I didn't think I could go on any longer. In the deathly quiet of my cell, I began experiencing panic attacks. Anxiety pulsed through my limbs and I found it hard to breathe. The only relief I got was while sleeping, so I began to sleep all the time.

Finally, one afternoon, I got let out of the cell by accident. A guard who didn't know how to use the high-tech control panel accidentally pushed the buttons that opened my door. When it clicked open, I rushed to sneak out before the guard realized the error. I hurried to a phone and called Pat.

"Pat, I need to see you," I said, rushing to get the words out before I was caught and returned to my cell. "You need to get down here right now."

"Okay," he said, calm as usual. "I'll just finish up what I'm doing and be there in an hour or two." As an attorney, Pat could visit any time from eight in the morning until eight at night. He had been dropping by regularly but at Twin Towers, even attorney visits were restricted by a glass window. It was awkward trying to talk with him without being able to at least touch his hand.

"You don't understand," I told him, my panic rising. "I need to see you now. Right now! Please get here as soon as possible." As I spoke, it scared me to hear my own voice.

Pat arrived within a half hour, and he talked soothingly to me, trying to get me to calm down. But it was no use. I couldn't stop talking—it was almost as though I was afraid that, if I stopped, the silence might consume me. "I can't keep my thoughts together," I told Pat. "I think I'm losing my mind."

As soon as he realized the condition I was in, Pat did something he hadn't done the whole time I was in jail. He asked me, "Do you want to give this up? It's okay if you do. Everyone will understand. We can have you out of here tomorrow." Though Pat's manner was calm, he would later tell me that he was frightened at what he saw in my face.

"I don't know," I said. "I really don't. I can't tell you how hard this is. All I know is that I'm scared of what's happening to me."

"We'll take care of it, Susan," Pat said. He succeeded in calming me down, but he later told me that when he left the jail that day, he was as scared as he'd been throughout the whole ordeal.

Pat had been able to calm me down, but as I was led back to my cell, it was hard not to feel utter despair. Mark had already tried to get me moved to federal jails in and near Los Angeles, but every time it seemed that an arrangement had been worked out, the Sheriff's Department would create an excuse to turn down his request. Mark even had a judge sign an order demanding that I be placed in a federal facility, but even the judge's order was ignored. L.A. County sheriff Sherman Block was notorious for running the county jail system the way he wanted and he apparently couldn't care less what some judge thought. This seemed odd since, at the same time, the sheriff's office kept insisting they wanted me out of their system.

Because I had been sentenced to civil contempt in a federal court, I should have been kept in a federal prison—not a county facility like Twin Towers that fell under the state system. Someone was obviously responsible for keeping me in a jail I wasn't supposed to be in, but Kenneth Starr insisted it wasn't he. Starr's staff regularly asserted that they had nothing to do with where I was housed and no idea why I was still being kept in the state system. With Starr and the Sheriff's Department both passing the buck, it was impossible for Mark to know whom to confront to get me out and into another facility.

I was about ready to give up hope, but help suddenly arrived from an unlikely source. A few months earlier, a New York journalist named Elizabeth Kaye had interviewed me for an article she was writing for *George* magazine. We'd become friends, and she'd been sending me books in jail, as well as keeping in touch with my progress through my brother Bill. When he told her what was happening to me at Twin Towers, she became incensed. She called a friend who worked for the ACLU and demanded to know why they weren't doing something about my situation.

The ACLU, led by Mark Rosenbaum and David Schwartz, leapt into action. In conjunction with Mark Geragos, they called a press conference and announced the filing of a motion in federal court to have me moved to a federal facility. At the press conference, Mark and Bill spoke publicly about the conditions I was being kept under and condemned the Sheriff's Department for allowing this to happen. The motion, they announced, was being sent overnight to a federal judge for an emergency hearing.

All I was really hoping for was that the judge would take me off K-10 status so that I could be treated like all the other prisoners.

But two days later I was notified to pack my bags—I was being moved to a federal facility. Block was running for reelection and he clearly didn't want a full-blown hearing into how his jails were being run. He'd apparently been willing to go along with what the OIC had wanted, as long as there was no great outcry. But now that we'd filed a motion, he wasn't going to put his own neck out on the block.

After the press conference, Kenneth Starr and his staff suddenly found themselves having to respond much more frequently to reporters' questions about why I'd been housed in Sybil Brand and Twin Towers, when I belonged in a federal prison. Starr and his supporters dismissed as hogwash the idea that they had any influence whatsoever over where I was jailed. They challenged anyone making that assertion to prove it— even though they knew very well that any proof would be in documents that no one outside the OIC could ever hope to access.

Initially I had trouble believing that Starr was responsible for where and how I was jailed. I've always doubted conspiracy theories. But two separate incidents convinced me that, despite their assertions that they had no control over prison placement, Starr and the OIC were in fact able to dictate where people were jailed.

The first involved Jim McDougal. Back when he was living on Claudia's property, he'd told me that as part of his deal with the OIC, he'd be placed in the federal prison of his choice. And following his sentencing, Jim was sent exactly where he'd told me he wanted to go— an unlikely coincidence.

The second involved Chris Wade, the northwest Arkansas real estate agent who had originally contacted Jim about the Whitewater property. Chris had been hounded and investigated by the OIC for more than two years, and the FBI questioned nearly everyone in the small town of Flippin, Arkansas, where he lived. At one point, there was a growing suspicion in the town that Chris was actually the Unabomber. Unable to find anything wrong with Chris or Whitewater, and desperate to turn him into a cooperating witness, the OIC found a small violation in Chris's recent bankruptcy petition—an infraction so obscure that his attorneys couldn't find a single other instance of previous enforcement. They indicted Chris on bankruptcy fraud, and then, when he refused to plead, they threatened to indict his wife. He gave in and agreed to plead and he was subsequently sentenced to eighteen months in a federal prison.

Although Chris submitted to numerous FBI interviews, he refused to implicate either the Clintons or Jim in any wrongdoing. The OIC, growing frustrated, then threatened to have Chris shipped to one of the worst prison facilities in the country. When Chris's wife called to complain about this treatment, she was told that the better his memory, the better his jail location would be.

As insistent as Starr was that the OIC held no sway over prisoner placement, the cases of Jim McDougal and Chris Wade seemed to belie that notion. At any rate, it was clear that someone somewhere had been determined to keep me in Sybil Brand and Twin Towers for as long as possible—even though it clearly violated the law and a judge's orders.*

There was one final absurdity to the whole saga of getting me out of Twin Towers. Whenever Mark or I had asked why authorities didn't move me to a federal facility, the standard answer was that it would be "logistically difficult" and a "waste of manpower" to arrange for the special escort needed to move me. As it turned out, the facility I was moved to, the Metropolitan Detention Center (MDC), was a grand total of three blocks from Twin Towers. They could have literally walked me down the street or dropped me off on a doughnut run.

MDC was a federal facility with an unusual purpose. While most jails house convicted criminals, MDC housed men and women who'd been indicted but hadn't gone to trial yet—and who didn't have the money to post bail. Essentially, like the other jails I'd been housed at, MDC was primarily a dumping ground for the poor.

At MDC, the guilty and innocent were jailed together, to be sorted

---

* This is why in the course of this writing this book, we have decided to file an official request for information about the conditions of my imprisonment from the OIC.

out whenever their trials came up. I found it incredible that potentially innocent people were forced to stay in jail just because they couldn't afford to pay their way out, but this didn't appear to cause anyone in the judicial system any sleepless nights. As I finally figured out, despite our judicial system's supposed presumption of "innocent until proven guilty," the prevailing mentality seemed to be that people don't get arrested if they haven't done anything wrong. The fact that many of the MDC inmates were later proven innocent didn't seem to matter. If they were found not guilty, the deputies would say it was because they "beat the system," not because they were actually innocent.

In some ways, my move to MDC was like a return to the Faulkner County Detention Center. MDC was a relatively clean facility, with the women on one floor and the men on the other eight. Each cell was exactly alike, with four concrete walls, a toilet, a sink, and two bunks.

At MDC I was finally taken off lockdown status and treated like all of the other inmates. After my isolation at Twin Towers, this was a huge relief, and I quickly got to know some of the other women on the floor. I also took part in group activities, such as crowding around the television every day to watch *The Jerry Springer Show*.

In MDC, the Springer show was much more than just a viewing party; it was the springboard to numerous philosophical debates, largely because the issues often hit close to home for many of the women. I was amazed to learn how many women's boyfriends had slept with their mothers or impregnated their sisters. In the first ten minutes of each show, the women would choose up sides, and when the televised brawls got started, we'd cheer on our favorites like a mob at a Roman Coliseum. Even after the show was over, we'd keep talking about it through lunch and into the afternoon.

Apart from the Jerry Springer hour, the television was always tuned to the WB network, as this was the only network that had shows with African-Americans as anything other than bit players. For the most part I wasn't a fan of the WB shows, but I did become a devotee of *Buffy the Vampire Slayer* during my time in MDC, mostly because I would have killed for her wardrobe. I also got to be a fan of *Dawson's Creek* and became very upset when Katie had sex with James.

The Woman Who Wouldn't Talk

Beside television, the women had one other major form of entertainment: talking to the men on the floor below us. This would have been a lot more fun if the method of communication hadn't been so disgusting. The only way to speak to the guys was through the toilets. I still don't fully understand the physics of it, but because the toilets on each floor shared pipes that ran vertically up the building, they acted as conduits for sound. Talking through the toilet pipes was expressly forbidden, but by switching off on lookout duty, the women were able to stay up all night talking to the men on the floors below them. Given the content of these conversations, it was highly appropriate that they were conducted through a toilet. I didn't actually participate in the conversations, but I did serve my time as a lookout. I doubt I could have carried on a conversation anyway—half of the language they were using was way beyond even the army drill sergeant vocabulary I had grown up around.

Even more disgusting, however, was the fact that inmates actually passed food to one another through the toilet system. By wrapping things up tightly, draining the toilet's water, and setting up a hooking system to catch things within the pipes, the women were able to send things down to the floor below. One of the most popular food items transported was tamales, which some of the Mexican women fashioned out of ingredients they'd collected from various meals.

In return, the guys would send down contraband such as prescription drugs or stamps from letters that had drugs mixed in the glue. One of the great urban legends at MDC was that a woman prisoner had gotten pregnant from the sperm of a man that was sent down through the toilet. No matter how much I argued against the plausibility of this story, the women at MDC vehemently insisted that it was true.

Although MDC was similar to Faulkner County Detention Center in many ways, it did differ in one dramatic way: inmates were allowed to have contact visits with their spouses and family once a week in the large visiting room downstairs. Because it had been almost a year and a half since I had touched any member of my family, their first visits with me at MDC were beyond incredible. The first time Bill came, he swung me around and kissed me on both cheeks. Pat and I had to be more careful. As an attorney he was allowed in on visits, but it didn't look too good if you were in the attorney room making out with your lawyer. Most of the time, the guards knew the situation and did not hassle us if we hugged and kissed.

Under the rules, "contact" consisted of a hug and a kiss on the lips on greeting and departing. But because there weren't enough guards to police the activities—especially on busy visiting nights—the rules were largely ignored. As a result, Friday nights in the MDC visiting room tended to resemble a scene from *Caligula*. Even when the guards did witness the numerous groping sessions, they usually ignored them as long as no one started rolling around on the floor.

Late one afternoon not long after I arrived at MDC, one of the friendlier guards pulled me aside and asked if I would do him a favor. A wealthy young woman from Beverly Hills had been arrested on some type of tax charge, he told me, and because she couldn't make bail until the next day, she'd have to spend the night at MDC. Although I wasn't supposed to have a cellmate, he wondered if I wouldn't mind sharing my cell with her and making sure she got through the night okay.

This turned out to be a much bigger job than I'd expected. From the moment the woman arrived, it was clear she didn't really understand the whole jail concept. She treated the guards like bellhops at the Four Seasons, constantly barking orders at them and becoming irritated when they didn't jump in response. When she went to take a shower, she came strolling back to the cell with just a towel around her, asking to borrow my hair conditioner. I tried to explain to her that these kinds of amenities did not exist in jail, but she chose to ignore me. I think she viewed her time in jail as similar to being a pledge living in a sorority house while a little good-natured hazing was going on.

She made it through the night without a major meltdown and the next morning awoke late and staggered out to the common area, where several other women were hunched over breakfast trays, lapping up some very runny oatmeal. She took one look at the gruel and proclaimed, "I can't eat that stuff. I'm on a high-protein diet. Where can I get some granola?"

By this time I'd given up trying to explain to her how jail worked, so I just sat back and let the women have at her.

"Granola!" exclaimed one. "Granola! Let's see . . . I think the granola is being served out on the veranda."

"No, wait," said another. "We may be out of granola this morning. Maybe we could interest you in some Eggs Benedict? Or a nice double cappuccino with some scones?"

To her credit, the Beverly Hills woman seemed to take the teasing in stride—though I wasn't sure whether this was because she was good-humored or because she didn't get it. I suspected it was the latter. Regardless, by late morning word arrived that she'd been bailed out—not a second too soon as far as I was concerned.

For the most part, relations between the guards and inmates at MDC were smooth. On one occasion, however, things threatened to break down when a guard tried to carry out a particularly absurd order from the prison authorities.

It started shortly before lunch one day, when a guard walked in as a few of us were playing cards. We watched as he walked toward an Asian woman sitting quietly by herself in a corner; although this woman didn't socialize much, she was unfailingly polite and was generally regarded as one of the least troublesome women on the floor. So it came as a complete shock to us all when the guard told her, "Get up. You're going to isolation."

As he led the woman toward the stairs, she started to scream—the first time I'd ever heard her raise her voice. I walked quickly over to the guard and asked, "What's this all about?"

"This doesn't concern you, McDougal," he said. "Go back to your card game."

At this, several other women came over as well; everyone wanted to know why the woman was being taken away. With a crowd now gathering, the guard—one of the best at MDC—apparently decided he should head off potential trouble by taking me aside and explaining the situation.

"Her cellmate accused her of sexually assaulting her last night," he said. "We're taking her down to isolation until either the matter gets cleared up or charges are filed."

I couldn't believe what I was hearing. "But her cellmate is psychotic," I said. "You know she's a liar. She's accused everyone here—including most of you guys—with some kind of assault. I can't believe that on her word alone, you're going to put this woman into isolation for what could be weeks!"

"I don't believe her, either," said the guard, "but there are procedures that have to be followed. Anytime an accusation is made, we have to take the person down to isolation until it can be cleared up. It's policy."

This was outrageous. Unsure what to do, but furious at what was developing, I quickly explained to the other women what was going on. Then, without really thinking it through, I suddenly came up with an idea.

"Sir," I announced to the guard, "I would like to make the accusation that the alleged victim sexually assaulted me." The guard looked at me blankly. "I expect to see her taken into isolation."

Within seconds, the other women picked up on what I was doing. One yelled, "I want to accuse Susan of sexually assaulting me!" Another said, "I want to accuse Carlotta of sexually assaulting me!" Soon, every woman on the floor had been accused, and all were demanding to be taken to isolation.

The guard grabbed my arm and pulled me aside. He was clearly unhappy with me, but he also knew he was on the verge of a major incident. "Look, McDougal," he said, "if you'll calm everybody down, I'll promise to see what I can do about getting this processed and getting her back up here by tonight. Okay? Is that a deal?"

"That seems more than fair," I told him.

I went back to the women with the guard's offer and convinced everyone to hold off causing any more uproar, at least until the evening. True to his word, the guard brought the Asian woman back up that night—and nothing was ever heard about the alleged assault again.

I didn't get off quite so easily, however. A woman administrator who I greatly admired, Linda Thomas, called me down to inform me that I'd come within a hair of being charged with inciting a riot in a federal institution—a charge that carried a term of up to twenty years.

"We're going to keep a close eye on you," she said, "and if you do anything remotely like this again, we're filing charges."

Since MDC was a federal facility, the vast majority of women were there on drug-related charges, most commonly for conspiracy to distribute drugs. As I talked to the women, I heard the same story over and over: a husband or boyfriend had been either selling drugs or working for someone who was, and they'd gotten the women involved. It's very common for drug dealers to recruit women as couriers—or "mules," as they were known—especially on overseas deliveries, because women were less likely to be searched. Unfortunately, because these wives and girlfriends often weren't used to acting as drug couriers, they'd become nervous and arouse suspicion.

Many of the women who were caught and arrested were given the option of "flipping": if they told on their boyfriends or on some higher-up in the drug ring, they might get out of prison in just one or two years. The problem was, most of these women didn't know anyone higher-up in the drug-selling hierarchy, so their only option was to finger their husbands or boyfriends. This wasn't much of an option: If a woman remained loyal to her man and refused to turn him in, she could get ten to fifteen years in prison. If she turned him in, it was usually the case that she'd be putting away the father of her children.

This was exactly the scenario faced by Carlotta, the woman who became my best friend and eventual roommate at MDC. Carlotta was from Manchester, England, where she'd been raised in an upper-middle-class family and educated at some of the best private schools in the U.K. In college, she had fallen in love with a man named Paul, and they'd decided to get married and open up their own business together.

Neither had the cash to support the new venture, and after several unsuccessful attempts at getting financing, they settled on an alternative course of action. Paul had an acquaintance from college who had become a wealthy and well-known drug dealer. He needed women to act as mules in delivering the drugs, especially to the United States. Paul volunteered

Carlotta to deliver a large number of Ecstasy pills, in exchange for the amount of money the couple needed to start their business.

The results were predictable. When Carlotta arrived in Los Angeles with her illegal stash, she was so nervous that she was pulled aside almost immediately. Within about twenty minutes of her arrival, she'd already been arrested. Federal agents pressed her to tell them where they could find the drug dealer, but she had no idea how to locate him.

So Carlotta was hauled off to jail, facing ten to twelve years for possession of drugs with intent to sell. But this was only the beginning of her problems. Within two weeks of her arrival, Carlotta discovered she was pregnant.

Carlotta and I quickly struck up a friendship. Her droll British wit stood in sharp contrast to the over-the-top buffoonery the rest of us dished out. She was quiet and thoughtful, and read a great deal—and she mostly kept her distance from the rest of the women on the floor. Although I was allowed to have a private cell, after a few weeks I requested that Carlotta become my roommate. She was scared and needed somebody to talk to, especially late at night. Her greatest fear was having her baby in the jail hospital, and then watching authorities take it from her. This was a realistic scenario, and all I could do was keep reassuring Carlotta that she'd somehow get out of prison before her baby was born.

By the time she reached her sixth month of pregnancy, Carlotta felt desperate. She told Paul over the phone that he'd better find out where the drug dealer was hiding—and fast. Paul had been cooperating with the police but had made little progress in locating the dealer—until one day there was a breakthrough in the case, and the dealer was found. Even though it was risky, Paul agreed to testify against the dealer in return for Carlotta's release. The prosecution agreed to this deal, and less than two months before she was to give birth, Carlotta was out of jail and on her way back to England. I knew I'd miss her, but it was an incredible relief that she'd managed to get out—not just because she was my friend, but because it was such a rarity for any of these women's cases to end well.

The Woman Who Wouldn't Talk

There was another category of crime that was very common among the women of MDC: bank robbery. California not only leads the nation in bank robberies, it actually has more than all the other forty-nine states combined. Perhaps it is because knocking over a 7-Eleven lacks panache or maybe it is just because so many Californians will do anything to be on camera.

Two things struck me about the women who had robbed banks. First, they were almost all under the age of twenty-five. Second, they didn't appear to be overly intelligent. I was no expert on the subject, but it seemed strange to me that these young women often seemed to have robbed banks in their own neighborhoods—often banks where they had accounts. There's something to be said for living near your work, but I couldn't help but think your chances of getting away with bank robbery would be improved if you weren't on a first-name basis with the tellers.

The bank robbers also seemed, on the whole, not to have planned their escapes very well. One young girl explained how she and her boyfriend had planned to flee the bank after robbing it, immediately dump their outer layer of clothes, and then walk down the street as if they were out for an afternoon stroll. For some reason, in the excitement of the moment, she discarded her shoes as well—a particularly unwise move, as it was a blazing hot day. She hadn't gotten very far before her feet began sizzling on the sidewalk, and she ran back to get her shoes. Upon her return to the scene of the crime, she was promptly arrested.

I'd been in jail for a year and a half now, and even if I stayed in for thirty years, I don't think I'd ever get used to how very innocent, naive, and young most incarcerated women are.

One of the major benefits of returning to a federal facility was that I'd get far better medical care than I had in state jails like Sybil Brand and Twin Towers. At Sybil Brand, for example, I had gone immediately to a doctor to check on the breast lump the nurse had found at Carswell. But the Sybil Brand doctor claimed he couldn't find anything and simply declared that I was okay. This was not reassuring in the least, and I spent the next few months worrying constantly about the lump. As soon as I arrived at MDC, I requested that it be checked out thoroughly.

When the doctor at MDC did a breast exam, he found the lump and recommended that I undergo further testing. Because the tests weren't available at the jail facilities, he arranged for two U.S. marshals to take me to a nearby hospital.

The marshals took me to the hospital in full handcuffs and leg chains. As I shuffled and clanked down the hospital hallway, mothers grabbed their children and shrank against the wall. The marshals then led me into the examination room, and after I climbed with difficulty up onto the examination table, they chained me to that as well. I felt like a cross between Frankenstein's monster and a wild, dangerous criminal—but at least I was now safe in an exam room, temporarily free of the stares in the hallway.

When the marshals turned to leave, however, a nurse that had come into the room suddenly went pale with fear. "Wait!" she exclaimed. "Don't leave me alone with her!" At that moment I realized that no matter what a prisoner is really like, the mere fact that you're wearing prison garb is enough to frighten ordinary Americans half to death. Whenever people think of prisoners, images of Willie Horton or Charles Manson come to mind. The truth is that the vast majority of people in prison are nonviolent criminals; as I learned, prison populations pretty closely resemble a Saturday afternoon crowd at Wal-Mart.

The medical tests were run, and a few days later the marshals brought me back to hear the results. There was a mass in my right breast, the doctor told me, and I needed to have it removed right away. He told me to prepare to have surgery that day, but before I signed the waiver form I wanted to talk with Mark, who had specifically told me not to let anybody operate before talking to him.

I called Mark, who told me, "Don't sign the waiver. Don't have this operation before we get a second opinion." He wanted me to go to Huntington Memorial Hospital in Pasadena, where his father-in-law was a doctor. The hospital had apparently just purchased state-of-the-art equipment for detecting breast cancer, and his father-in-law wanted the opportunity to examine me before any surgery. Since the idea of having surgery shackled to a gurney didn't appeal to me anyway, I took Mark's advice and declined to sign the waiver.

When I was returned to MDC, Mark asked the jail officials to have me transported to Huntington Memorial Hospital, a twenty-minute drive, so I could have the tests run. The officials declined, citing the fact that it would mean tying up a marshal for the day. This was a disappointment, but Mark then came up with something better. He filed a motion with Judge Wright back in Arkansas to allow me a forty-eight-hour medical furlough. I would be released from jail for two days, on the basis of Mark's assurances that I would get full medical treatment and then return to jail.

The OIC's reaction was predictable. They opposed the motion, as they'd opposed pretty much everything I'd ever requested. But after initially opposing the motion outright, someone in the office must have figured out that it didn't look good to be fighting a woman prisoner over treatment of a lump in her breast. They came back with an alternative suggestion that I just be taken by the marshals to another hospital nearby and have the same tests run. This made little sense, as it would still tie up a marshal. And besides, we had asked specifically to go to Pasadena because of the hospital's new, state-of-the-art equipment.

Despite the OIC's opposition, Judge Wright, who had a history of breast cancer in her family, granted the furlough. For forty-eight hours, I would be allowed out of jail.

The idea filled me with mixed emotions. On the one hand, I was excited about being able, for the first time in a year and a half, to feel the wind in my hair and the sun against my face. On the other hand, the idea of being outside filled me with a crushing sense of pressure. Even though much of the time would be taken up at the hospital running tests, I knew that it would be very hard to see everyone I wanted to and not hurt the feelings of anyone I missed seeing in this very short time period.

On a Wednesday afternoon in March of 1998, Mark, Bill, and Pat came to pick me up in the lobby of MDC. I walked out of the prison, excited about the prospect of two days of freedom, but before we even got across the street to the car, I felt anxious. In jail I was always in cramped, confined spaces; there's something secure about being surrounded by walls, and the wide-open space around me left me feeling disoriented and a little uneasy. Just crossing the street to get to our car was a problem.

We drove to Pasadena, where Mark had arranged for a suite at a Ritz-Carlton near the hospital. Pat and I checked in, and I went straight to the bathroom for a long, luxurious bubble bath—a treat I'd missed for almost two years. That evening Pat and I met Mark and his wife, Paulette, and Bill and his girlfriend for dinner at a small Italian restaurant.

I was happy to be out, but I was also a little shell-shocked. It just seemed impossible to take in everything that was happening around me. Nothing outside the jail walls seemed real to me anymore. I had reached a point where jail seemed more normal to me than being out. Though I'd lived in prison for less than two years, and outside prison for thirty-eight, I found it almost impossible to adjust to this "new" environment. In part my reaction may have stemmed from the knowledge that I wasn't really free; in fewer than forty-eight hours, I'd have to report back to jail. But it was also because I'd been so successful in blocking out all my outside problems while I was in jail. Being out in the world forced me to recognize them again.

As the evening wore on, I became increasingly quiet as the rest of the party tried to keep me cheered up. I'd smile and laugh along with everyone else, but it still felt as though none of this was really happening.

The next morning I went to the hospital. The tests took all of the morning and most of the afternoon, but when the doctor brought the results, the news was good. I did in fact have a mass in my breast, but it wasn't cancerous. The doctor even recommended against removing it. I was relieved about the lump—but still, my health news wasn't all good. In undertaking the tests on my breast, the doctor had noticed that my back was causing me pain, and he wanted to run tests on that as well. We'd need another day to complete those, so Mark called Judge Wright and explained the situation. She granted me an additional twenty-four hours.

Relieved at the good news about my breast lump, Pat, Mark, and Bill suggested ways we could go out and celebrate. All of Los Angeles was available to us, and the three batted around suggestions: boat rides, dancing, a concert, a seaside restaurant. "We'll do anything you want to do, Susan," Pat told me.

I hated to disappoint everyone, but there was only one thing that appealed to me: I just wanted to go home with Pat and be very, very quiet. One of the worst things about jail is the constant noise—guards and inmates yelling, the television blaring, and cell doors slamming. Even late at night the noise continues, dropping to a low roar. Also, you're never really alone in jail, even when you're in your cell. The last thing I wanted on this rare night of freedom was crowds and noise. My fantasy was to spend a nice, quiet evening watching a video and cuddling with Pat on the couch.

Pat took me home, then offered to bring in dinner from any place I wanted. "We could get seafood, or pasta, or steak," he said. "Whatever and however much you want. Just tell me."

I thought for a moment, then said, "How about a cheese pizza, from Pizza Hut?" I knew it sounded perverse, with the whole galaxy of cuisine I could choose from, but for some reason a greasy cheese pizza was all I wanted. Later on, when I told the women back in jail I'd chosen pizza for my big night of freedom, they were disappointed that I had deprived them of a much better food story.

The next day the doctor's news was not as good. My scoliosis had gradually worsened with age. I'd always managed to keep it under control through chiropractic visits, ice packs, and special chairs and pillows. Unfortunately, none of those remedies was available in jail. In addition, being handcuffed in different positions and lying on numerous concrete surfaces had severely aggravated the condition. At one point my back had gotten so bad that my right hand had gone numb, and I had to wear a neck brace for pain and a sling to support my arm.

The longer I was in jail, the more my back was hurting—but I still had no idea how serious it had become. I found out when the doctor showed me an X ray of my spine: it was curved so severely, it looked like the letter *c*. At some point, he said, I should consider back surgery. But for now, all he could do was give me a prescription for pain medication and an order for physical therapy.

With that, my seventy-two-hour sojourn outside the prison walls was over. As Mark and Pat drove me back to jail, we happened to tune in to a local radio station that was playing a game called "Where's Susan McDougal?" The deejays were taking calls from people reporting sightings of me around Los Angeles over the previous few days. Most callers had me in places I'd never even heard about, much less visited, but a couple were right on target.

I said good-bye to Mark and Pat in the MDC lobby and went back upstairs to join the women, who crowded around me, eager to hear every detail of my time outside. Most of them were disappointed that I hadn't done anything thrilling or exotic, but I told them without hesitation, "I did exactly what I wanted."

In March 1998, with seventeen of the maximum possible eighteen months for civil contempt completed, the OIC made one last-gasp attempt to obtain my testimony. It would have been pathetic had it not have been so laughable.

The OIC had recently hired a U.S. attorney from the Los Angeles office named Michael Emmick. According to Mark, Emmick's primary reputation in the L.A. legal community was as a lawyer whose suave sex appeal in the courtroom supposedly left women swooning. When he was assigned to the Susan McDougal file, it had been months since the OIC had tried anything new to get me to cooperate. But Emmick came prepared with a plan. He wrote Mark a letter explaining that he was new on the job, held no preconceived notions or prejudices toward me, and would like permission to just come out and talk with me face-to-face.

When Mark told me about the letter, I pictured in my mind the OIC meeting that had spawned this idea. I could just see a group of clueless middle-aged male lawyers all sitting around a table discussing what to do about the Susan McDougal problem.

"Let's see," one might say, "she's served seventeen out of a possible eighteen months for civil contempt, she's shown no signs of relenting, and, in fact, whenever she gets the chance to say something to the media, her criticisms of the OIC have grown stronger. She's endured roaches, body cavity searches, and sensory deprivation. We've repeatedly called her a con artist and a liar, and still she hasn't broken."

"I know, let's send a cute guy to talk with her. I bet she'll break then!"

The ego and idiocy that it took to come up with this plan was mind-boggling, even by OIC standards. It showed an incredible lack of understanding of women by a group of middle-aged men who had been watching way too many James Bond movies. I begged Mark to let me talk to Emmick. I really wanted to hear exactly what persuasive tactics he planned to employ—especially from the far side of a two-inch-thick Plexiglas wall—that would somehow cause me to change my mind and cooperate with the OIC. I desperately wanted the opportunity to tell him face-to-face that I would never be that hard up. Personally, I felt that any day I could help lower the individual or collective ego of the OIC was a worthwhile day. But Mark and common sense eventually won out, and I never did meet the charming Mr. Emmick.

As a footnote, it turned out that the Emmick sex appeal was highly overrated. In December 1998, the OIC had sent Emmick to the Ritz Carlton hotel room into which they'd dragged Monica Lewinsky for questioning. Though the OIC apparently thought Emmick might be able to charm Lewinsky into ratting out Bill Clinton, this plan worked about as well as it had with me. Part of Ms. Lewinsky's eventual deal with the OIC was that Mike Emmick was to be kept as far away from her as possible.

There are many prison experiences that stand out in my mind: helping Butch win her trial, for example, or playing How Did You Get Here? But no experience was as strange or as emotionally conflicting as learning that Jim McDougal had died. It began with a horrifying mix-up and ended with a strange blend of sadness and relief.

I was sitting in my cell when a guard notified me that the Catholic priest, Father Santo, needed to see me. Father Santo was an example of God working in the best possible way: he was selfless in his dedication to the men and women he ministered to and he focused on making their lives better in more than just a spiritual sense. I had attended all of Father Santo's Sunday services and loved to hear him talk. He never looked down on any prisoner. I had been to Father Santo's office before to visit with one of the nuns from Sybil Brand, so it wasn't strange for him to call me to his office. But when I arrived and saw the look on his face, I knew something bad had happened.

"Please don't hold me in suspense, Father Santo," I said, sinking into a chair. "What's happened?"

"Susan," he said, "I'm very sorry. Jim has died."

It had been two years since I'd last spoken with Jim McDougal, and I almost never thought about him. In jail, especially, he just seemed like a character from some feverish dream. On the other hand, I spoke often with my oldest brother, Jim Henley—so that's who I thought Father Santo was referring to.

"Oh my God!" I exclaimed. "I have to talk with my mother. She must be devastated!" I just couldn't believe that my brother, who I'd just spoken to a few days earlier, had died. "Can I use your phone?" I asked.

Father Santo seemed a bit puzzled, no doubt wondering why my mother would be so crushed at news of Jim McDougal's death. Nevertheless, he handed me the phone without comment. I couldn't reach my mother, so I called my brother Bill. Before I could get the words out of my mouth, Bill asked, "Have you heard about Jim?"

He asked it in such a detached way that I was surprised. He didn't seem to be nearly as torn up about the passing of his eldest brother as I'd expected.

"Bill," I said, "how did it happen?"

"From what I heard it sounds like a heart attack."

"Have you talked with Mother?" I asked, growing upset at the thought of her grief. "Is she okay?"

Now it was Bill's turn to sound bewildered. "Well, I guess she's okay. She may not even know."

At times I can be remarkably dense, but with that remark, it finally dawned on me that Bill and I were on two totally different wavelengths. I thought for a moment, recounted in my mind what Father Santo had told me, and suddenly realized that he had been talking about Jim McDougal. I explained this to Bill, who assured me that it was in fact Jim McDougal, not my brother, who was dead. I hung up the phone, now feeling a tangle of feelings rather than the simple grief of a moment ago.

In 1996 Jim had offered up one compelling reason for why he was making a deal with the OIC: "I have to do it," he'd said, "because I don't want to die in jail." In the ultimate irony, Jim had made his deal with the devil—and then he'd died in prison anyway. The OIC had delayed his imprisonment, and then let him choose his facility, but from there on, the treatment of him apparently went downhill. Jim's many physical ailments had gotten worse quickly. He had a prostate problem that made it hard, if not impossible, for him to urinate and he was instructed to urinate on demand for drug testing. When he couldn't, he was put in solitary confinement. He had a heart attack and died there, at age fifty-seven, alone on the concrete floor of a prison cell.

Mark asked me if I wanted him to file a motion so I could attend the funeral. I considered the idea, but decided that my presence in chains and shackles would turn the funeral into even more of a media circus than it was already going to be. When I later saw reports of the funeral, I was glad I didn't go.

In an unbelievable display of gall, Hickman Ewing, the OIC attorney who had helped put Jim in jail, delivered the eulogy. In the speech, he declared that although Jim might have done some bad things in his life, he'd come clean in the last two years—even at great personal sacrifice. For an evangelical minister like Hickman Ewing, cooperating with the OIC was the political equivalent of being saved or born again, and he shamelessly bestowed that status upon now-deceased Jim McDougal.

I wasn't sure how I felt about Jim's death. The Jim I'd known had died years earlier, and I had already mourned that passing. I was sad now that he'd actually died, but I couldn't pretend to be devastated.

Jim McDougal was a very complex man, made even more so because of the manic-depressive illness that he never overcame. He was capable of unbelievable acts of generosity, and equally unbelievable acts of perversity and deceit. I'd come to loathe the man he was—the man who threw away every principle he believed in (or claimed to believe in); the man who cared about no one but himself and who seemed to take pleasure in hurting others. But for every bad thought I had about Jim, there were also numerous good memories of the Jim I'd married, the man who so effortlessly gave whatever he had to those in need.

Whatever sins Jim committed—and he certainly committed his share—he didn't deserve to die lying on a concrete prison floor, pleading weakly for help. I later learned from Claudia Riley that Jim had been calling Hickman Ewing in the weeks prior to his death, begging him to help him get sent to a prison hospital, the way Ewing had for David Hale. He told Ewing that he wouldn't survive much longer in jail. But Ewing never responded to Jim's pleas, though he was more than happy to later stand over Jim's dead body and talk about him like they were close friends.

16
FREE BIRD

MY MAXIMUM EIGHTEEN-MONTH SENTENCE FOR civil contempt expired on March 6, 1998. Despite reassurances from just about everyone familiar with the case that Judge Susan Webber Wright would never make me serve the maximum sentence, she had remained steadfast in her refusal to vacate the contempt.

It had been obvious to everyone after a month or two of my being in jail that I wasn't about to cooperate—no matter the circumstances. By the time a year had passed, it was ludicrous to suggest that another six months of incarceration might suddenly change my mind. But Judge Wright had refused to release me. I believe she took my refusing to talk as a personal affront; she seemed determined to prove that she could be every bit as stubborn as I.

I got a hint of her personal feelings toward me in a February 1998 *Washington Post* article about her husband. After bragging to reporter Lois Romano about his role in writing her opinions and how much he influenced Judge Wright's decisions, Robert Wright responded to the suggestion that his wife's decision to keep me in jail for seventeen months on contempt so far was vindictive. "Susan McDougal is a liar.

The Woman Who Wouldn't Talk

She is still in jail because someone has persuaded Susan Wright—maybe Ken Starr—that she still might talk."

Although I had finished serving my contempt sentence, I had still more jail time ahead of me. On March 7, 1998, I began serving the two-year sentence I'd received for my conviction in the Whitewater trial. My appeal of the conviction had failed, so I would stay in MDC to do the time.

At the same time, the Whitewater grand jury term was ending (grand juries usually serve a term of no more than eighteen months). The grand jury had produced no indictments, despite almost daily rumors that either Bill or Hillary Clinton, or some White House higher-up, would be charged. Possibly sensitive to the perception that the grand jury's time had been wasted, Kenneth Starr and Hickman Ewing came up with a plan: they would indict me again. I always had this mental picture of Starr and Ewing glumly sitting around the OIC office depressed because they just couldn't find any evidence to indict either of the Clintons. Ewing would suggest, "Hey, why don't we indict Susan McDougal or Webb Hubbell again?" This would at least temporarily cheer everyone up so that they could continue on their business of investigating the president's sex life.

The pending indictment was for criminal, rather than civil, contempt. Like the civil charges, it arose from my refusal to testify back in September 1996. But unlike civil contempt, which is meant to coerce a reluctant witness, the purpose of criminal contempt is to punish. I was not sure that anyone in the prison system cared whether I was in jail to be coerced or punished or both. I thought that, as long as I was in jail, it was more impressive to at least be incarcerated for something that was criminal. It had always been a continuing source of embarrassment for me among my jail peers that I was in for something as wimpy as civil contempt.

The law leaves open what the penalty should be, so the OIC—leaving nothing to chance—decided to add a count of obstruction of justice, which carried a prison term of up to seven years. Criminal contempt, unlike civil contempt, also carried with it all the safeguards of the criminal justice system. I would get a full-blown jury trial in Arkansas with all the rights of a normal defendant.

I was still being held in the Pulaski County Jail when Mark and Pat came to break the news to me about the upcoming indictment. They were both acting very somber—Mark could barely even utter the word indictment. It took me a minute for the news to soak into my brain. I knew that being charged with criminal contempt was a possibility, but everyone connected with the case had been assuring me that the OIC would never be stupid enough to actually do it. Even my brother Bill, my most paranoid supporter, kept telling me that the mood of the country was turning against Starr and he would not want to be seen as piling on. After collecting my thoughts, I looked at Mark and Pat and said, "I have an idea. Can we just respond that, while I appreciate their interest, I regret to inform them that I will be unable to attend their indictment?"

Mark and Pat had been afraid that the news of the new indictment and the idea of even more jail time would possibly send me over the edge. But it actually had the opposite effect—I saw it as a great opportunity. Before they left, I hugged them both and told them, "Wouldn't you have been disappointed if they had not indicted me? This is going to be our chance. They are not going to put me on trial . . . we are going to put them on trial!"

The OIC also planned to subpoena me to appear again before the grand jury in Arkansas before their term expired. Ordinarily, the law prevents bringing a person repeatedly before a grand jury, unless there are new circumstances or new evidence in the case. The OIC had that covered: they told Judge Wright that they had new information they wanted to ask me about.

The OIC's plan to bring me before the grand jury a second time was a farce. It wasn't enough that they were already planning to file criminal contempt and obstruction-of-justice charges related to my 1996 refusal to testify; they still wanted more. If I again refused to testify in front of the grand jury—which was clearly what I planned to do—then they could charge me with yet another count of criminal contempt.

With these new charges, and their insistence on dragging me back in front of the grand jury, I despised the OIC even more. In addition, I was angry about being subjected to "diesel therapy"—the time-honored prosecutorial tradition of hauling defendants around the country and placing them in different jails along the way. In mid-April 1998, I was transported from MDC in Los Angeles to the Oklahoma City transfer center, and then on to the Pulaski County Jail in Little Rock, Arkansas, to go before the grand jury again.

The night before my second grand-jury appearance, I lay awake in my cell for hours. I decided that this time, rather than simply refusing to speak, I'd try and explain to the grand jurors why I had refused to testify back in 1996. These were fair, decent Arkansas citizens, I reasoned, who, during their eighteen months of grand jury service, must have read at least some of what I had been saying in the media. I would describe why I'd made my decision, and convince them that they were being misled by a politically motivated prosecutor. Exactly how I planned to convince them of this without getting into specifics about Whitewater was not quite clear; my thought process did not extend beyond the initial idea.

The next morning, April 23, it became clear quickly enough that the grand jurors didn't care what my reasons might have been. When I walked in, I was stunned to hear a few of them begin hissing at me, and I looked at them in shock as several glowered openly at me.

Suddenly, all my carefully thought-out arguments flew right from my head. In their place was one all-consuming thought that kept going around in my head—these people hate me! I couldn't believe it. As someone whose sole goal in life was to be universally loved, I was now officially in hell.

My questioner was a new recruit to the OIC team, Julie Myers. She appeared to have been cloned from the same genetic material as Amy St. Eve: she was short, peppy, and looked a little like a feminine version of a Chucky doll. In a syrupy, almost babylike voice, she opened by telling me that no one in the room wanted me to lie. She then asked me my name, which I stated for the record. Then, she attempted to pick up where the questioning had left off in September 1996:

> Q. Ms. McDougal, the last question pending was, do you understand that Judge Wright ordered you to come today and testify before the grand jury?

A. I will not answer any question you make to me because I believe you're conflicted and you have no right to ask me.

Q. Do you understand that Judge Wright considered that argument yesterday and rejected it?

A. You do not have any right to ask me questions. You are totally conflicted.

Q. Do you understand that, Ms. McDougal?

A. You are conflicted and you should not ask me any questions.

Q. Ms. McDougal, do you understand my question?

A. Mr. Starr should resign. That's my only answer to you.

Q. Ms. McDougal, are you refusing to answer my questions?

A. I have told you I won't answer your questions.

Myers then offered up the OIC's "new evidence" against me: a check made out to Madison Guaranty in the amount of $5,081.82, dated August 1, 1983, and signed by me. In the memo space in the bottom left-hand corner, I had written "Payoff Clinton." This was, the prosecutor implied, evidence of secret payments Jim and I had made to Bill Clinton.

This was their big new evidence—a check that said "Payoff Clinton"? I had no memory of the check, which certainly appeared to be in my writing—but the idea that Jim and I would pay off Bill Clinton by writing him a check and then making sure to take care to record the bribe on the front of the check was absurd. I half-expected the OIC to present a few more checks as evidence, with "Hush Money for Hillary" or "Bribe Money for Chelsea's College Fund" on them.

To this day, I have no idea what that check was for. It might have been money to pay off a portion of the Clintons' Whitewater loan, or to make an interest payment on a loan. The most likely scenario, however, is one I can't prove without access to records that the OIC had taken from the bank. Jim and I had once bought land in northeast Arkansas, near a town called Clinton. It's very possible that this check was part of paying off the loan on the Clinton, Arkansas, property, and had nothing to do with Bill Clinton at all.

When the OIC presented the check as evidence, I asked to be excused so I could speak with Mark and Pat, who were waiting outside the grand jury room. When I returned seven minutes later, the grand jury foreman reminded me that I was still under oath. Myers continued her questioning, but my response remained constant.

Q. Ms. McDougal, what did you mean by the notation "Payoff Clinton," on the check that's been marked as Grand Jury Exhibit 1892?

A. I don't believe your office has the right to ask me any questions.

Q. Judge Wright rejected that argument yesterday, Ms. McDougal. You've been ordered to come in here and testify truthfully today. What did you mean by the notation, "Payoff Clinton"?

A. I think because you are so conflicted, it would be the honorable thing to do to get someone else to investigate this. It would be honorable and right.

Q. Ms. McDougal,—Ms. McDougal, I understand—

A. If you really believe there's a crime, let somebody investigate it who might not be so prejudiced.

By now, a few of the grand jurors had begun hissing at me again. Myers tried another tactic, turning the questioning over to them. I began trying to respond, to explain to the grand jurors how they were being misled by the OIC.

GRAND JUROR: Can you tell us exactly what that check was for? It does say, "Payoff Clinton."

A. I would love to tell you. I would love to tell you everything I know about it, but not with these people running the investigation. I don't believe they're interested in the truth. I really don't.

GRAND JUROR: Do you know who makes the ultimate decision of whether this is correct or not correct? Do you think it's Judge Starr or do you think it's the twenty-three members that are in here?

A. I went to trial believing that that was true, and I was convicted and I was not guilty. And I can't believe that again because they brought prejudice[d] testimony up at my trial that was untrue. They put on David Hale, who lied at my trial.

Q. [By Ms. Myers] Ms. McDougal—Ms. McDougal, the point the Grand Juror, I believe, is trying to make is, they make the decision. We won't make any decision about how any of this information is —

Desperate for the grand jurors to understand how skewed the OIC's presentation of the facts was, I addressed them directly, my voice rising.

A. But they only tell you what they want you to know. You don't know everything.

GRAND JUROR: You are the witness. You are going to tell us what we want to know.

A. But they only show you what they want you to see. That's what I'm afraid of. And they believed David Hale and they believed Jim McDougal, and they both lied to you.

Q. (By Ms. Myers] Ms. McDougal, so you are refusing to answer the Grand Juror's question regarding what—

A. They lied to you.

Q.—the statement, "Payoff Clinton," means?

A. I want you to know they lied to you.

Q. Ms. McDougal, so you are refusing to answer the Grand Juror's questions?

A. I told you I would not answer you. If you want to resign and you want to get an independent counsel to investigate this, I will answer their questions. But not this man. He has, from the first day, decided that he would do this. And it's been a long road for me, and I'm sorry to be so nervous and so scattered in what I'm trying to say to you. But I have to tell you from the first day with these people, all they wanted was something on Clinton.

Q. Ms. McDougal—

A. From the very first day.

Things got more tense as the questioning continued. I kept hoping that someone—anyone—in the grand jury would hear and understand what I was saying. But it seemed impossible to get through to even one of them. When I had gone out to talk to Mark and Pat, I told them in utter disbelief, "They hate me!"

Mark started laughing and said, "What did you think was going to happen—they were going to give you a standing ovation? Of course, they are going to side with the OIC. Who do you think is bringing them doughnuts and coffee every day and telling them what an important part of the process they are? Grand jurors always love the prosecutor!"

After a moment, a new OIC attorney named Mark Barrett stepped up to ask questions. A heavyset redhead in his early forties, Barrett had been a U.S. attorney in Colorado for a number of years where, legend had it, he had never lost a single trial. With his rotund build and scraggly beard, he resembled a rumpled Santa Claus. He would turn out to be the one OIC attorney that I actually had trouble disliking. In addition to his genial, laid-back manner, he seemed actually to have a sense of humor—something his colleagues uniformly lacked.

My exchange with Barrett during this questioning, however, was no less hostile than the one with Myers.

MR. BARRETT [Associate Independent Counsel]: Mrs. McDougal, excuse me. You were just posed questions by two members of the grand jury. And if I—

A. You know very well what you've done.

MR. BARRETT: May I please finish?

A. You know very well what you have done.

MR. BARRETT: May I please finish? Earlier in the proceedings you said you'll answer questions from you—all, [indicating toward the grand jury]. When Ms. Myers was unsuccessful in getting you to answer any questions, she turned it over to the members of the grand jury. Two members of the grand jury asked you questions. Are you refusing to answer?

A. Resign and I'll answer all their questions.

MR. BARRETT: Are you refusing to answer the questions from—

A. If Ken Starr will admit he has a conflict—

At this point, the transcriber interjected.

THE REPORTER: Ma'am, if you'll just wait until he finishes his question before you answer, so I can write it down.

A. I shouldn't have to listen to his sermons, though: do you think?

THE REPORTER: I just have to write down everything.

A. Please. What?

GRAND JUROR: We're listening to your sermons and we've got some questions to be answered.

With this interjection, I remembered that the grand jurors were probably as frustrated as I was, so I tried to calm my agitation and back off slightly. But the next thing the grand juror said set me off completely.

A. You're right. I'm sorry, You're absolutely right. I'll listen to it.

GRAND JUROR: This has been going on for two years, too, for us.

A. It's been since 1985 for me. Okay? You think I don't want it over? You think I don't want to answer your questions? You think it's not serious for me? These people are wrong in what they're doing. They have been on this. And from the very first day when I told them, "Let me just answer—let me tell you what this check is about," they said to me, "Susan, we want a proffer from you. We want something on Bill or Hillary Clinton." That was at my very first meeting with them. And they have done this investigation exactly the way they wanted to do it.

I just couldn't believe that the jurors didn't see how patently unethical the OIC had been all along. I wanted to explain that first meeting with the OIC, and if I had time, I'd have gotten into their manipulation of my handwriting samples, their shameless courtship of Jim McDougal, and their flat statement that "you know who this investigation is about, and you know what we want." But I couldn't, and the grand jurors just didn't seem to want to hear it anyway. Defeated, I stopped answering the questions.

MR. BARRETT: You have been posed questions by three members of the grand jury that you refused to answer: is that correct?
A. [No response.]
MR. BARRETT: Let the record reflect the witness is not answering the question.
A. Get another independent counsel and I'll answer every question.
MR. BARRETT: Mr. Foreman, may this witness be excused?
GRAND JURY FOREMAN: Yes, you may.

Before I left the room, I spoke to the grand jurors one more time. "I'm sorry," I said. "I'm sorry to all of you. I know you've put in a lot of time, and I have, too. And I'm sorry."

During my time in Little Rock, I stayed in the Pulaski County Jail. This was the seventh prison facility I'd been placed in, and I found myself thinking that if I ended in any more jails, I could write a book on the jails of America—sort of a Zagat guide for career criminals.

The worst part of going to Pulaski County Jail was the processing into the facility. As usual, I was asked to remove my prison-issue shirt and pants and white underwear. After a very thorough cavity search, the deputy told me to put my hands above my head and slowly turn around. She then pulled out a DDT gun with a double-barrel mosquito sprayer on the front and starts pumping spray all over me. It was extremely humiliating, but the humiliation was just beginning. I was given the normal orange jumpsuit, but was told that there were no panties.

"No panties!" I screamed. "This can't be possible. Women have to have panties. If you don't want to give me any new ones, just give me back my old ones."

The deputy just smiled and shook her head. But by this time I was out of control. I may have been starving and wet from insect spray, but I was not giving up my panties without a fight. The deputy started getting a little nervous and went to look for backup. I grabbed my old panties and put them on, figuring that it would be a lot harder for them to get them off of me once they were on. I was right. When she returned, the deputy said that she had checked and I could now keep my panties. Furthermore, if I wanted, I could have someone from the outside bring me a fresh supply. This was a small but significant victory.

Pulaski County was a pretty run-of-the-mill jail, but my time there was anything but ordinary. In my eighteen-month odyssey through the American criminal justice system, I'd met many interesting women and seen some incredible things. But nothing could match the stories of two women I met at Pulaski County.

The first was Debbie, an attractive nineteen-year-old woman who never should have been in jail to begin with. A week before I arrived, Debbie had gotten into a disagreement with another young woman over their mutual boyfriend, which culminated in the other woman running Debbie over with a car. As is often the case in fights, the police were unsure who was to blame, so they arrested both of them and left it to the courts to sort the situation out.

The problem for Debbie was that she was sent to the hospital first, before going to the jail—she'd been seriously injured when the other woman drove over her and ended up having her leg amputated. But going to the hospital first wasn't the procedure the jail and courts were used to, so Debbie ended up having her case lost in the system. She'd never been in trouble before and had no idea that she was supposed to be arraigned, have an attorney assigned, and make court appearances at certain times.

When she arrived at Pulaski County Jail, Debbie was confused and in total denial about her situation. She was a scared teenager who had not only just lost a leg, but had been put in jail for being run over by a car. Debbie obviously needed counseling, but the jail provided none. In the short time I was there, I made an effort with several of the other women to try to help her adjust. At first she was in a complete daze, but gradually she seemed to respond, eating meals regularly and practicing how to walk on crutches. After I'd spent two weeks in Pulaski County Jail, I was sent back to Los Angeles, but I felt Debbie was doing pretty well considering the circumstances.

Back at MDC, however, I received a letter from Debbie that was frightening in its madness. Very little of what she wrote made sense, although she seemed to be saying that someone was trying to poison her. I wrote her back, but I was frustrated that there was nothing else I could do for her. As it turned out, I would soon get another chance to see her. I was sent back to the Pulaski County Jail just a few weeks later for a hearing before Judge Howard.

When I arrived at Pulaski County, however, I found Debbie in terrible shape. She had slid from denial of her situation into full-blown paranoia. She was now being kept in the lockdown cell—a room with nothing but four concrete walls and a hole in the middle of the floor where she could relieve herself. Debbie was wearing a paper gown as a suicide precaution, because a previous inmate had nearly managed to strangle herself with a regular jail uniform.

Debbie was refusing meals and medicine because she was absolutely convinced she was being poisoned. She'd wasted away to skin and bones and had begun peeling off the skin on her dried-out lips and eating it. The jail officials had taken away her crutches after she'd swung one at a water sprinkler and caused it to spray all over the unit. Without her crutches, Debbie had given up trying to walk; she spent her days hunched alone in her cell, murmuring over and over, "They're trying to kill me."

One morning I stopped the prison doctor by yelling out the window in my cell door. He was kind enough to stop and talk with me, but when I asked him what he could do for Debbie, he told me that they were not allowed to force her to take antipsychotic drugs. He had tried to give her something to help with the paranoia, but she believed he was trying to poison her. The deputy in charge of our unit said she would have been glad to send her to the state mental hospital, but she was told that the hospital had too few secured beds for incarcerated patients.

That night, at the prison church services, a woman from a nearby church who came into the jail to lead our services asked me why I seemed so depressed. I relayed Debbie's story to her. Unsure whether to believe me—after all I was a convicted felon—she contacted the sheriff who ran the facility. When he confirmed Debbie's situation, the woman sprang into action. She must have had her entire church call the Sheriff's department to complain. In addition, I called Rick Holiman, a terrific lawyer who I knew in Little Rock, and told him the story. Within forty-eight hours, Debbie was released to her family on a sheriff's bond so she could get the help she needed. Whenever people ask me what they can do to help women in jail, I tell this story. It's a clear example of how concerned ordinary people can make a difference in the lives of prisoners.

Even more gut-wrenching than Debbie's situation was the story of Christina Riggs. Christina had become one of the most reviled people in all of Arkansas when she committed the unthinkable crime of killing her two young children in late 1997. A nurse by training, Christina had injected each of them with a lethal dose of potassium chloride. The shock and horror stemming from a mother's cold-bloodedly murdering her children kept the story on the front page of Arkansas newspapers for weeks. To make matters worse, police reports showed that just two nights before the killings, Christina had been in a local bar, dancing till late in the evening and even winning a karaoke contest.

Christina was the perfect villain for a society that craves simple, black-and-white, good-versus-evil stories. Here was a woman who had not only committed the most heinous of crimes—she appeared to have been living it up right before doing it. The public outcry was enormous, and the prosecutors immediately announced that they would seek the death penalty. Christina appeared to be the ideal argument for the pro-death-penalty lobby.

When I was first sent to Pulaski County, Christina had not yet gone to trial, and so she was still allowed to mix with the general prison population. At first, like most of the other inmates, I steered clear of her. But eventually I had a few conversations with her, and I learned several things about her that hadn't seemed to make it into the news stories. One weakness of our criminal justice system is that up until trial, the press usually receives its information about charges against a person only from the prosecution. Typically, the defense keeps quiet, so as not to give away any of its strategy. Thus, the public receives a very one-sided view of any case. In talking to Christina, I learned, even in a case that appeared to be open and shut, there are still two sides to the story.

At her trial, the prosecution had portrayed Christina as having killed her children so she could more easily pursue men. But Christina had actually tried to kill herself along with her children. She'd written a suicide note, arranged for her last paycheck to be sent to her mother, and injected herself with the same poison as her children. In fact, she had injected so much poison into herself that it had eaten through her vein and the flesh. You could actually see the hole in her arm where the poison had burned through. But she did not get enough poison in her veins to kill her. Her mother found her in bed unconscious and called paramedics. The prosecution would later argue that she had conveniently arranged the timing of the poisoning so that her mother would arrive in time to save her, but not the kids.

Christina had a troubled childhood, which included being sexually abused by a relative. She'd then endured a series of difficult personal relationships, as well as financial hardships that had left her struggling to make ends meet. She had always wanted children because she'd hoped to give them a better life than she had known. She had been married twice and both husbands had just walked out on her, leaving her with the children and no child support. She could not find anyone to babysit her son, who had been diagnosed with attention deficit disorder. Shortly before the poisoning, her car had broken down and her utilities had been shut off—she felt she had reached a dead end.

With rising dread, Christina saw her children's future turning even bleaker. A deeply religious woman, she believed she could spare the children the pains of the kind of life she had endured, and take them immediately to the better place they deserved.

Nothing I can say or write can ever make what Christina did that night any less wrong. But by killing her children in the misguided hopes of sending them to a better place, Christina displayed mentally disturbed behavior rather than the actions of a monster. And her actions in the Pulaski County Jail were evidence of her essential decency: in the short time I spent with her there, she performed innumerable acts of kindness for other inmates. Whenever another inmate was hungry, Christina was the first to give up some of her food. Whenever she was able to buy a few products from the jail commissary, she always took them directly to the women who had nothing.

Christina never tried to defend her actions or blame anyone else for what had happened. From the very beginning, she told me that she welcomed the death penalty; when the jury convicted her of the two murders and sentenced her to die, she was not upset except for the pain it caused her mother. Her attorney begged her to let him appeal her conviction so he could fight for life imprisonment, but Christina steadfastly refused. She declined all avenues of appeal and in fact asked the state to hurry up the execution so she could be with her children in the afterlife.

Christina's story haunted me, and after I was released from jail I spoke with her on the phone several times, begging her to reconsider and appeal her death sentence. "Even though you'd be spending the rest of your life in jail," I told her, "you could tell your story to other women, and maybe prevent something similar from happening. You can do so much good, Christina."

The last time I spoke with her, Christina very quietly, but in a firm voice, told me not to interfere. I had promised her I would go to the governor—I would consider it an honor to beg for her life. She told me not to do anything, including going to the media with her side of the story. She felt it would only drag out the inevitable and, at this point, she welcomed death. Two weeks later after our last phone conversation, on May 3, 2000, she was executed by the state of Arkansas, the first woman to be executed there in more than a hundred years. I pray that somehow, somewhere, she has been reunited with her children.

One Sunday afternoon, while I was in Pulaski County Jail awaiting my transfer back to Los Angeles, I was notified that I had visitors. Since none of my family had said they were coming, I had no idea who it could be. I went upstairs to the assigned visiting room and looked through the glass partition to find a handsome couple accompanied by a young boy—none of whom I'd ever seen before. Under normal circumstances I would have been wary of them, but because they were wearing "Free Susan McDougal" T-shirts, I assumed they probably weren't there to try to lecture me on my evil ways.

The couple, Cindy and Fred Mann, had driven twelve hours from Wichita, Kansas, with their six-year-old son, Elliott, for one reason: they'd heard I was being kept temporarily in Little Rock, and they wanted to tell me face-to-face to hang in there. I found this incredible, as well as very moving—and what made it even more remarkable was that the jail doesn't ordinarily allow visits by anyone, not even relatives, without prior notice and a great deal of paperwork. But Cindy, Fred, and Elliott had just waltzed right in. I couldn't believe they had done it. I called Pat and told him that this stunning couple just drove from Wichita, Kansas, to see me and, if I was ever going to orchestrate a jail break, they were the people to call.

A few days later, during my transfer back to Los Angeles, I was again taken to the Federal Transfer Center in Oklahoma City. Under normal circumstances, my stay there (while further arrangements were made to take me to Los Angeles) would have been brief and uneventful, but this time there was a bureaucratic mix-up and I was classified as a suicide risk. "There *are* a few people I'd like to kill," I explained to them, "but I'm not among them." But no amount of cajoling or insisting could keep them from dressing me in a paper gown, putting me in a lockdown cell with paper sheets, and forbidding me from making phone calls. Once again, I was in solitary, and my meals were slid under the door.

As frustrating as this was, it might have been little more than a minor irritation but for one thing: Because I couldn't use the phone, Pat, Bill, and Mark had no idea where I was. Not only that, no one at the Bureau of Prisons would give them any information when they called, so it wasn't long before they became frantic. After approximately a week, I convinced a sympathetic guard to let me use the phone for a few minutes, so I could at least alert them to where I was being kept. Pat made a plane reservation for the following day to fly to Oklahoma and get me out of lockdown, but before he arrived I was picked up and moved back to Los Angeles.

Back at MDC, I once again fell into something of a routine, which came to include calling Pat first thing in the morning before he left for work. One morning he greeted me with, "You're not going to believe this one! There's an article in the *L.A. Times* alleging that Bill Clinton had an affair with an intern. Apparently it has some merit, and Starr is already investigating it."

Within hours, Mark and Bill were besieged with phone calls from the media, wanting to know my reaction to this revelation. For once, I declined to comment. The reason was quite simple: I was so conflicted about this news that I didn't really know how I felt. One minute I found myself furious at Clinton for not having the self-discipline as the leader of the free world—not to mention as husband and father—to resist some schoolgirl's flirtations. The next minute I was angry that the president's personal life was now the center of the OIC's investigation. Kenneth Starr's people could declare all they wanted that the investigation wasn't about sex, but fact of the matter is this: the OIC's investigation was always about finding something on Bill Clinton. And anyone who knew him would know that the best place to look was at his sex life, so that's where they looked.

I was also frequently asked how I felt about Monica Lewinsky. Monica doesn't deserve a free ride in this affair, as she freely chose to participate in an affair with a married man. But I tend to give Monica a break. She's frequently described as immature, but most of us could have been fairly described that way when we were in our early twenties. It's certainly not uncommon at that age for people to act in their own self-interest.

That said, I do believe Monica displayed a great deal of courage and integrity in her dealings with Starr and the OIC. From day one, she told them the truth, including the fact that neither Clinton nor Vernon Jordan obstructed justice or asked her to lie. Even though she was consistently offered immediate immunity if her story changed, she steadfastly refused to change it.

I know from bitter experience how hard it was for Monica Lewinsky to face being criminally charged, and possibly going to jail, rather than just changing her story a little bit and walking away absolutely free. For months the OIC refused to grant Monica immunity while she continued to insist that Clinton had never obstructed justice. It wasn't until months later, when the OIC basically had no other choice but to give in, that they offered her a deal. Monica knows what it's like to be pressured to change her story. To this day, she says she still fears the OIC, but she has never wavered on her story—even though it would have benefited her personally. In the frequent criticism of her actions, her willingness to stand by the truth is often overlooked.

In May 1998, Mark submitted a Rule 35 motion to Judge Howard in Arkansas asking for my early release on a number of grounds, including time already spent in jail, exemplary behavior, and medical reasons. This was a long shot, even though by now I'd spent more time in jail than any other Whitewater defendant—including the admitted multi-count felon David Hale. The OIC naturally opposed it. We were very surprised when Judge Howard sent a reply granting a hearing on the motion even though he was limiting it strictly to medical issues. He set the hearing for June 25, two days before my forty-third birthday.

In the last few months, my back condition had deteriorated to the point where I had trouble bending at the waist or sitting upright for even short periods of time. The pain was severe enough that I could no longer write letters because my right arm and the last two fingers of my right hand would go numb. As my scoliosis worsened, a hump gradually appeared on my back, thus providing the women of the jail with a wealth of new comic material. By now, I was referred to more frequently as Quasimodo than McDougal.

In anticipation of the hearing, we hired Dr. Ron Fisk, one of the pre-eminent neurosurgeons in the country, to evaluate my condition and serve as an expert witness. From the beginning, Dr. Fisk told us that he wouldn't lie or exaggerate my condition: if we asked him to take the stand, he would testify to the truth of my condition, and that was that. He even seemed skeptical about testifying, apparently figuring this was nothing more than a last-ditch scheme to get me out of jail.

When Dr. Fisk had a look at the X rays and examined my back, however, he changed his mind. He told me that not only was my condition rapidly deteriorating, but that I was in danger of incurring some permanent damage if I didn't start getting serious treatment. He also told me that one eye was now bigger than the other. This was great news. It was bad enough that I had a hump, a numb right arm, and two very sore legs; now I was getting bug-eyed.

Even though Judge Howard had granted the hearing, Mark and Pat told me not to get my hopes up. "The best scenario you can hope for," Pat told me, "is that Judge Howard will take the matter under consideration and maybe cut your sentence a little." Given their pessimistic outlook, I wasn't too excited about being dragged back to Arkansas, through the Oklahoma City federal transfer center, and back to Pulaski County Jail once again.

Dr. Fisk's testimony was the key to the hearing, and he proved to be a compelling witness. His testimony about my medical condition was easily understandable, and it was obvious to anyone present that he was a true expert—he simply knew what he was talking about. He explained how important it was that I start receiving immediate treatment beyond what the jail could provide. I didn't envy the OIC attorney who had to cross-examine him.

That turned out to be Julie Myers, and from the very beginning it was a total mismatch. Although it was rumored that she had been a medical malpractice attorney, Myers seemed lost when her questioning veered into anything scientific. Over and over, Dr. Fisk had to correct her assumptions and explain how she wasn't looking at the right data. If their matchup had been a boxing match, it would have been stopped after the second round.

The highlight of the cross-examination came when Myers questioned Dr. Fisk about something that had seemed to have been weighing heavily on her mind. A few weeks before, during a phone conversation with Mark Geragos, Julie told Mark that she thought I was a "complicated woman." Apparently seeking a medical opinion on this, she asked Dr. Fisk, "Do you consider Ms. McDougal to be a complicated woman?"

The puzzled neurosurgeon, unsure of what the question meant, replied, "Do you mean complicated medically?"

"No," Myers replied. "I mean complicated in the normal sense of the word."

"Actually, Ms. Myers," Dr. Fisk said patiently, "I'm a medical doctor, not a psychiatrist. I would have a hard time giving an expert opinion on that."

Myers went on to other areas, seemingly satisfied with the answer.

In rebuttal to Dr. Fisk's testimony, the OIC called their own doctor, a well-credentialed Atlanta physician. He explained that, although he generally agreed with Dr. Fisk about the severity of the injury, he felt that certain medical procedures, if available in the federal facility, could solve the problems. On cross-examination, Mark got him to further expound on the seriousness of my condition and to admit that, if particular complications arose and I couldn't be immediately treated, I could end up permanently paralyzed.

The final witness for the OIC was an officer from the Federal Bureau of Prisons, who had come to testify that the medical care necessary for my back was indeed available in the federal prison system. But bringing this officer to the stand would prove to be a major mistake by the OIC.

The officer was very adamant, bordering on cocky, about the federal prison system's ability to handle cases such as mine. He dismissed Mark's questions about jail medical facilities in a condescending manner and seemed to suggest that this entire hearing was unnecessary. But as soon as his testimony ended, Judge Howard spoke up.

In an agitated voice, he began to ask the officer about a previous case that was similar to mine. The year before, another Bureau of Prisons official had taken the stand in Judge Howard's court and testified that the bureau could handle a severely handicapped man that the judge was debating whether to sentence to prison. The judge had accepted the bureau official's assurances, and a few months later the prisoner had died while in custody—apparently from a lack of proper medical treatment. As Judge Howard detailed this prior incident, it was clear he no longer trusted the bureau's arrogant assertions that they could take care of everything.

After Judge Howard had his say, we took a short break. Mark and I decided that I would testify next, to describe to the judge how my back problems affected my daily life. During the break, one of Judge Howard's clerks came over and asked if we were going to put on any more witnesses. "Susan's going to testify next," said Mark.

The clerk said nothing, but she looked Mark in the eye and shook her head slightly. This movement, slight as it was, wasn't lost on Mark. When the judge returned from the break and asked if there were any more witnesses, Mark stood up and announced that we would rest. My fate was now in Judge Howard's hands, and because Mark and Pat had warned me that he probably wouldn't make a decision for two to three weeks, it was time for me to head back to jail.

Judge Howard, however, had other ideas. As the hearing ended, he turned to look at my parents, who were seated in the front row of the courtroom. He asked them to step up to the bench. Both were now in their seventies, and they walked slowly to the front, unsure what the judge wanted with them. My father stood at attention, hands to his sides. My mother, who is a little over five feet tall, couldn't even be seen by the judge in front of his bench.

When they stood before the bench, Judge Howard spoke. "Would you be willing to accept responsibility for Ms. McDougal if I were to place her into your custody?"

My dad bellowed out, "Yes sir!"

Neither of my parents really knew what the judge meant by custody, or what exactly he was asking them to do, but fortunately they had the good sense to answer yes.

"Then I'm going to release her forthwith into your care," he said, "with the understanding that she will be under home detention for the next ninety days in the care of her parents."

The courtroom erupted. Several members of my family were there, and they jumped to their feet, crying and hugging each other, trying without success to keep twenty-one months of emotion from spilling out loudly enough to incur the judge's wrath. The reporters present, in a scene reminiscent of a fifties movie ("Stop the presses!"), scrambled out of the courtroom to call in the story. As for me, I was too stunned to say anything. I hugged my parents while Mark asked the judge if I could have a day or two before I began the home detention.

A marshal stepped forward to ask the judge if I was to be taken back to the jail and released from there. Judge Howard said, "No. When I say I want her released forthwith, I mean forthwith. She is free to leave this courthouse."

I raced into the spectators' seats and began hugging everybody I could find. Then Mark handed me a cell phone and I began calling the family members who hadn't been able to come to the hearing. When I reached my younger brother, John, and told him that I'd been released from jail and would be spending the next ninety days in Camden under our parents' supervision, he didn't miss a beat. "Can't you appeal that last part?"

As we prepared to leave the courthouse and face the mob of reporters outside, I realized that I was still wearing my jail uniform. My release had been completely unexpected—no one had thought I'd need any clothes to change into. I didn't care: I walked out of the courthouse into an enormous media circus with Mark on one side, Pat on the other, and me in the middle wearing a huge grin and an orange jail jumpsuit. I was absolutely overwhelmed. In my wildest dreams I had never expected that the judge would release me, especially in such an abrupt manner. I was walking around in a daze, holding on to Mark and Pat because I had no idea what to do next. After Mark answered a few questions, Pat and I slipped away to the hotel where he was staying, while various members of my family went to buy me some clothes.

That night we all met for dinner at my favorite Little Rock restaurant: the Capitol Hotel. "The chef's been watching the reports of your release on TV," the waiter told us, "and he wants to prepare something special for your first meal." Shortly thereafter, the waiter presented me with a beautifully prepared plate of Chicken Kiev and proudly announced that the chef was calling it his "Free Bird" special.

For the first few hours of my freedom, everything moved so fast that I had no time to think. When I returned to the hotel after dinner and plopped into a bubble bath, it suddenly occurred to me that I hadn't had a chance to say good-bye to the women at the Pulaski County Jail. So the next morning I made a call to the jail administrator. "This is Susan McDougal," I told him. "I was wondering if it would be possible to come by the jail later so I can say good-bye to the women."

I could tell he was confused by this request because he kept referring to the visiting hours and explaining how I could meet with any single prisoner during those hours. I tried to explain that I didn't want to see one at a time—what I really wanted was to be allowed back into the unit where I'd been staying so I could talk to everyone one last time. Finally, he seemed to understand what I meant.

"You want to be let back into jail?" he asked, a bit incredulous.

"Yes," I said.

"I'm sorry, Ms. McDougal," he said. "I don't think we can do that. I've never had anybody ask to get into jail." Just as in the classic O. Henry story, I couldn't get put in jail.

17

SHE THINKS SHE'S SUSAN MCDOUGAL

I WAS OUT OF PRISON AT last, but being housed at the James Henley Detention Center for Wayward Daughters presented its own set of problems. I was placed on electronic monitoring, a process that involved setting up an electronic device in the house and outfitting me with an ankle bracelet. If I went outside the radius of the signal emanating from the monitor, a distance that barely allowed me to go into the backyard, the monitor would notify the local police and I would be in violation of the court order and could be placed back in jail. My father, however, was not clear on the concept. When the judge had told him that I was being placed under his care, he interpreted that to mean that I was literally not to be out of his sight. Thus, when he went to the store or took the dog for a walk, he kept insisting that I was supposed to go with him. When I told him that I couldn't, he kept threatening to call the judge and tell him that I needed to have the rules explained to me. After a few days, he grudgingly gave in, but no matter where I was in the house, he still kept a close eye on me. When Sergeant Henley was given an order, he was going to follow it to the letter.

The judge had ordered me to do ninety days at my parents' home, but circumstances in California quickly changed that. The Mehta case was now the oldest untried case in the entire L.A. court system, and the new judge assigned to the case was determined to rectify that problem. He refused to agree to any more continuances and ordered me to start trial in mid-August, approximately forty-five days after I had been put on house arrest. I received Judge Howard's permission to transfer the house arrest to Los Angeles for the last forty-five days, and, since I would be going back and forth to court, I would not have to be under electronic monitoring. Instead, I was put on the honor system. I was to go to court and go right back home.

Pat and I had long since reconciled so I went to live at his house near the ocean in Redondo Beach, a distance of approximately thirty minutes from the courthouse where the trial would be held. As the trial approached, I was scared to death. I knew that this trial would be one of the defining moments of my life. Although the Whitewater affair had made me a nationally known felon and had sent me to prison for nearly two years, it still never seemed as real to me as the charges leveled by Nancy Mehta. Whitewater was a political issue, but Nancy's charges were personal, and they cut deep.

Now that the trial was near, my mind wandered often to the details of the case. Why hadn't I seen this coming? It wasn't like I hadn't had warnings. I had seen what could happen to the people who had fallen out of favor in Nancy's life. In my head I would replay all the people's voices who had tried to talk with me about Nancy. I remembered my brother David grabbing my arm one night so hard that it hurt, trying to get through to me. "Susan, you have got to get the hell out of there! No one in their right mind would stay in that situation for five minutes!" he had yelled.

"But she needs me, David," I had answered. Finding that someone I cared about was in deep trouble, physically or emotionally, had always been a catalyst for me. When I was younger, I remember a friend saying, as we drove by a homeless person, "There's Susan's dream date—no home, no car, no job."

That was why the news articles about my relationship with Nancy hurt so much. A few of Nancy's friends had spoken to reporters, characterizing Nancy as a kind, generous, wealthy woman who'd bestowed gifts and friendship on a scheming young woman who then betrayed her. Not only was I being branded a thief; according to them I was a disloyal, ungrateful thief.

The accusation of disloyalty hurt almost more than anything else. I knew I was capable of carrying loyalty to a ludicrous degree. Now, even though nearly five years had passed since I first heard of Nancy's charges, I felt stung every time I thought about them. And I thought about them all the time.

The Mehta case took most of my attention for another reason: I was genuinely scared of losing. A year and a half earlier, while I was imprisoned in Sybil Brand and before Mark was representing me, prosecutor Jeffrey Semow had made me an offer: if I would plead guilty to several of the counts, he'd recommend that I get just six months in jail, to be served at the end of my current sentence. On the one hand, this was not much of an offer at all. I was completely innocent of the charges, so why would I plead guilty and accept jail time? But, I'd been innocent of the Whitewater charges, too, and I'd still gone to prison. Although I knew pleading guilty in exchange for a light sentence would be a cowardly way out, it was a way out nonetheless. If I went to trial in the Mehta case and lost, I faced the possibility of being sent to prison for another five to seven years.

So when Semow made this offer, I seriously considered it. But as he'd done before, Pat refused to let me give in. He'd worked for Nancy and witnessed many of the events that had led to the charges, so he knew just how preposterous they were. He couldn't stand the idea of Nancy's baseless accusations putting me in prison. And besides that, he still had enough faith in the legal system to believe that truth would prevail in the courtroom. I had no such faith, having been burned so badly by the system in the Whitewater trial. But I did have faith in Pat's judgment, so I had sent word from Sybil Brand that I would decline Semow's offer of a plea bargain.

Now, just before the trial, Semow called Mark Geragos to reiterate his offer—but with a new twist: instead of six months in prison, I wouldn't get any jail time at all. He told Mark that, although he personally couldn't wait to kick my ass, the Mehtas didn't want to go through a nasty, prolonged trial. He told Mark they were pressuring him to convince me to plead to a couple of counts and get it over with.

This was even more tempting—no trial, no jail time, and then I could just go on with my life. It wasn't as if I hadn't already been labeled a convicted felon by the Whitewater conviction. By this point, I was frustrated, worn out by my twenty-one months in jail, and desperate never to set foot in a courtroom again. I dreaded the idea of going through a new trial, battling someone who'd been a good friend, and possibly being convicted yet again of a crime I didn't commit.

I would have gone ahead and pled just to have it over with, but Pat kept insisting we could win. I had no such faith—in my mind there was no way that a jury was going to believe a convicted felon over an icon like Zubin Mehta, in whose name the charges had been filed. Eventually, I made the decision to go forward, even though I was scared to death.

Although Bobby McDaniel and Jennifer Horan had done a good job in my first Whitewater trial, they'd been vastly outnumbered by the OIC's crowd of lawyers and their unlimited resources. Now I'd be going to trial with a legal team that matched up far better against the prosecution.

I'd never seen Mark Geragos perform at trial, but he handled all the pretrial hearings beautifully. He exuded confidence and, despite the fact that this was his first high-profile case, he was also handling the media extremely well. Also, unlike the Whitewater trial, when Pat was in California, he would be with me throughout the Mehta trial, assisting Mark. In addition, my brother Bill was living in California, and for the nine weeks of the trial he put his life on hold and came to the courthouse every day. Bill was not just there to offer support; he intended to make absolutely sure that I would not be convicted. His advice was extremely helpful and usually right on the money.

Finally, Mark enlisted the best investigative firm in Los Angeles, John Brown and Associates, to help us with the trial. The founder and namesake of the firm, John Brown, was an old-style liberal and political activist who was willing to commit incredible resources to preparing my case, even though we could pay him very little. He commissioned his best investigator, Clara Solis, to work on my case full-time, and pushed his firm to the brink of collapse to give us the support we needed. His partner, Larry Frank, had every reason to complain about the financial burden we were putting on the firm—but he, too, chose to support me unconditionally.

Leading up to the trial, Bill and Pat told me to prepare for a bitter, nasty fight. I still wasn't convinced it would unfold that way. It was difficult for me to imagine either Nancy or Zubin trying to attack me on the witness stand—Nancy, because I believed she still cared about me, and Zubin because he simply wasn't the attacking type.

But what I didn't expect was the hostility aimed at me from prosecutor Jeff Semow. He'd shown signs of antipathy toward me before—most notably when he called me a fucking bitch after one hearing—and I knew he had a reputation for being arrogant. Some of the district attorneys in his own office even disliked him so much, they'd told Mark they were rooting for us to rip him apart. Despite all this, I believed Semow would be objective when it came to my case. But he repeatedly proved me wrong on that score.

One afternoon a few weeks before the trial, I mentioned to Mark that Nancy seldom threw away anything, including years-old paperwork. Mark immediately asked whether I thought she might have any records squirreled away at her house that could be helpful to us for the trial. I told him it was possible.

The next day, Mark called Semow and requested that he be allowed to go the Mehtas' house and search the office where I'd worked with Nancy. "Sure," Semow told him, "knock yourself out." His only requirement was that the investigating police officer in the case, my old friend Iggy Gonzalez, had to be present. So one afternoon shortly thereafter, Mark met Iggy outside the Mehtas' gated entrance, and they proceeded up the hillside to the house. Nancy was out of town, but her latest assistant ushered them into the small office where Nancy and I had worked.

It didn't take Mark long to hit pay dirt. In the bottom drawer of Nancy's desk, tucked under other documents, were six MasterCard receipts from 1989—all bearing Nancy's unmistakable signature. This was the very same MasterCard that Nancy claimed I had acquired under false pretenses, saying she had no knowledge of its existence. These receipts represented proof that not only did Nancy have knowledge of the card, but she had been using it herself! Perhaps most damning, it appeared she had deliberately removed these receipts from the other evidence she'd turned over to the D.A.

Thrilled with his discovery, Mark turned the receipts over to Iggy, who remarked, "If that's her signature, I guess this puts a hat on the case." Mark then called Pat and me, assuring us that no D.A. in his right mind would proceed with the case now.

But Semow was apparently not in his right mind over this case. He expressed some concern over the receipts, then a day later offered Mark a bizarre story that supposedly explained their existence. These receipts, he told Mark, simply proved that as far back as 1989, I was already developing my elaborate scheme to steal from the Mehtas. Since I knew it would later be important to demonstrate Nancy's knowledge of the credit card, I must have slipped the MasterCard into her purse when she wasn't looking. Because Nancy had so many credit cards, she would have used this one inadvertently—not even realizing it wasn't one she normally used. I then, according to Semow, slipped it back out of her purse and began my crime spree.

The great irony of my journey through the justice system was the prosecutors' repeated insistence that I was able to mastermind elaborate long-range schemes. All my life, I'd been told that my biggest problem was that I lived day to day and never had the foresight to plan beyond my next meal. But in the eyes of prosecutors, I somehow metamorphosed into the ultimate scheming, calculating thief.

On August 18, 1998, jury selection began in *The People of the State of California* v. *Susan McDougal.* The trial was being held in a drab, two-story concrete courthouse about three blocks from the ocean in the seaside city of Santa Monica.

The presiding judge, Leslie Light, was a short, bespectacled man in his mid-sixties with a full pompadour of graying hair. Judge Light was, in a word, cantankerous. He never smiled, was quick to anger with both the prosecution and the defense, and had a very low tolerance for listening to anyone other than himself talk. He possessed a remarkable vocabulary, which he would demonstrate during sudden ten-minute soliloquies on topics only marginally related to the trial. In addition, he seemed to enjoy interrupting attorneys during cross-examinations so he could begin questioning the witnesses himself.

As the trial got under way, Judge Light announced that he didn't appreciate any shenanigans in his courtroom and declared that he wouldn't allow this case to be turned into a circus. He went on to tell us that after many years on the bench, he'd seen and heard everything, and he intended to control his courtroom. Despite his pronouncements, he would very soon be reduced to little more than the ringleader of the Mehta trial circus.

Jeff Semow went out of his way to project confidence in the courtroom. He would frequently rise from his chair and swagger back and forth behind Mark and me, even when Mark was addressing the court. There was a constant smirk on his face and, in contrast to his diminutive stature, he appeared to be trying to portray himself as the ultimate tough guy. Unfortunately for Semow, some early events in the trial would make his apparent confidence seem very misplaced.

During his opening statement, Semow announced to the jury that he would prove that not only had I illegally obtained and used a fake credit card, but that I had written numerous checks that Nancy Mehta never authorized. He would introduce these checks during the course of the trial, he said, but he wanted to give the jury a sneak preview.

Semow pulled out a large white poster board and propped it up for the jury to see. It showed a blown-up photocopy of a check, written to Wells Fargo Bank for more than $5,000. On the check's memo line were the words *Danish Krones*—the currency of Denmark—written in my handwriting. Semow then produced a copy of the Mehtas' travel schedule and waved it at the jury, explaining that the evidence would show the Mehtas had never set foot in Denmark and would therefore have absolutely no use for Danish Krones. The evidence, he went on, would demonstrate that I had simply cashed the check at the bank and kept the cash for myself. I had written

Danish Krones in the reminder line, he said, because the Mehtas often needed foreign currency when they traveled abroad—so this check wouldn't draw any undue attention.

As I sat at the defense table, I couldn't believe what I was seeing and hearing. Had Semow even asked Nancy about this check, or had he simply jumped to this conclusion? Whatever the case, he'd just made a huge, easily avoidable mistake.

I whispered to Mark, "That's for their Flora Danaka china." I then went on to explain: As a wedding present, Zubin had bought Nancy a very expensive brand of china, Flora Danaka, that was manufactured in Denmark. Nancy had acquired a manufacturer's price list and over the years when a piece of china broke or she wanted to add a piece, she ordered it directly from Denmark because it was cheaper. The manufacturer wanted payment in Danish Krones. While I worked for her, a piece of the china was broken by a caterer and she had asked me to arrange for a replacement piece.

When court had adjourned for the day, Mark went back to the office and checked the computer records the prosecution had been required to turn over to us. He looked at the Mehtas' accounts to see how the check had been itemized. He found the check, and next to it in the computer ledger were the words *Flora Danaka*. The next day, in his opening statement, Mark explained how the evidence would show that I'd written the check to pay for the Flora Danaka china—and that I'd done it at Nancy's request. He then showed the jury the computer records itemizing the purchase. Semow's Danish Krones poster board disappeared, never to be seen again.

Mark seized Semow's mistake to cast doubt on all the evidence the prosecution would produce. He went on to taunt Semow and tell the jury that this was exactly the kind of slipshod evidence they could expect to see throughout the trial. He urged the jury to take a close look at each check or credit card charge Semow produced and then withhold their judgment until after we had an opportunity to respond. By the time the opening statements were done, the jury already had plenty of reason to doubt the credibility of Semow's case.

*   *   *

In the first three weeks of the case, Semow introduced a succession of witnesses whose testimony arguably helped my cause more than his. Under his questioning, most would testify to one or two marginal issues that bolstered the prosecution's case—but then under Mark's cross-examination, they would give numerous answers that contradicted the story Semow was trying to weave. From the outset, for example, Semow had tried to characterize my relationship with Nancy as one where I was stalking Nancy in order to fleece her out of money, while she tried to keep me at a distance. But several of his own witnesses testified that Nancy and I were extremely close and that Nancy, in particular, seemed to pursue the relationship.

As his case kept stumbling along, it was clear that the pressure was getting to Semow. His once-confident smirk turned into a tense grimace, and he began spewing out sarcastic comments. While questioning witnesses, he paced the courtroom nervously, and during arguments over evidentiary matters his already sunburned face turned even brighter shades of red. He knew his case was going badly, and the tension betrayed itself in numerous ways—which didn't help his presentation before the jury.

Like a drowning man, Semow began grasping for anything to keep him afloat. He began complaining about minor matters—everything from where I was sitting in the courtroom to facial expressions that spectators were making. At one point my sister Paula gave me a thumbs-up signal from her seat. Semow didn't see it, but when he heard about it, he went into a lengthy rage about how we were deliberately trying to sabotage his case in front of the jury.

Seeing that Semow was rapidly losing his composure, I decided to try to aid that process. I had discovered that, from where Mark and I were sitting, I could make comments to Mark that were loud enough for Semow to hear, but inaudible to Judge Light. So several times a day I'd make disparaging comments to Mark about Semow's voice, mannerisms, clothes—whatever I thought might rattle him. Occasionally I'd repeat Semow's own words in an exaggerated, whiny tone.

After a week or two of this, Semow snapped. With the jury out of the room, he began complaining to the judge about some minor matter. As soon as he sat down, I leaned over to Mark and began to mimic his complaint in a whining voice. Semow jumped to his feet and objected. A very puzzled Judge Light, who'd heard nothing, asked him what exactly he was objecting to.

Semow immediately realized the position he was in. He could announce to the judge and the packed courtroom that he was objecting to my making fun of him, but that would only make him look silly—especially if the judge asked him to repeat what I'd said. Instead, Semow took the wiser option, which was just to sit down and shut up. After a few seconds of tense silence, Judge Light asked, "Is there a problem?"

Still seething, but now unsure how to respond, Semow muttered under his breath, "The problem is, she thinks she's Susan McDougal."

After three weeks of testimony, Semow brought in his main witness, Nancy Mehta. Upon entering the courtroom, she was forced to wait near the railing by the jury box while the attorneys argued over something at the judge's bench. I hadn't seen Nancy in seven years, and as I looked over at her, I found myself having an unexpected reaction.

I was angry at Nancy for what she'd done, but when I saw her waiting nervously by the jury box I found myself feeling sorry for her. She looked lost, and even a little scared. I had a sudden urge to walk over and tell her that everything would be all right. Despite all that had happened, I still cared about her. Seeing her now, for the first time in years, I found myself wanting to help her to the jury box.

Owing to an agreement between Nancy's lawyers and mine made later (the result of a malicious-prosecution suit I brought against Nancy in 1999), I'm legally constrained from revealing anything about Nancy's or Zubin's testimony at the trial. Suffice it to say that, at the end of her testimony, Semow's case was no stronger than it had been.

With Nancy's testimony failing to bolster his case, Semow now apparently decided he had only one other chance to sway the jury: he would try to make them hate me. The evidence against me was weak, but if he could convince the jury that I was a conniving, scheming thief, perhaps they would vote for conviction out of sheer disgust with me. Semow had prosecuted cases involving murderers, rapists, and child molesters, so demonizing the defendant was not a new approach for him. With this, the trial took a decidedly nastier turn.

Semow's character assassination started out with an old standby: my falsified 1989 Occidental Petroleum résumé. We spent the better part of one morning going over it point by point, with Semow asking me to explain to the jury exactly where I had lied. As soon as he started the questioning, I held the document up, looked straight at the jury, and said, "Not much of anything on this résumé is true. I needed a job and I was not applying to be a brain surgeon. I just wanted to be a secretary and to start a new life." But Semow was not going to let it drop that easily. He continued to go over each individual section where I had changed names or lied about my job duties. It may not have been relevant to the trial, but it did force me to sit on the stand for an entire morning and admit to lying.

Following the résumé, Semow produced a financial statement from 1986. The statement showed that Jim and I had done well financially and showed that we owned a house valued at more than $400,000—a sizeable amount in Arkansas. According to Semow, this demonstrated that I was a small-town girl who'd schemed to marry an older man in an effort to get rich and live an exorbitant lifestyle (never mind the fact that Jim had bought the house as an investment, and I'd never actually lived in it). When Jim and I had lost everything, Semow implied, I had then latched on to Nancy Mehta, so I could continue my lavish lifestyle.

Finally, Semow began questioning my loyalty—specifically, my loyalty to Pat. He hinted that whenever Pat was out of town, I more or less ran wild in the streets. Semow was really reaching now, but in some ways these implications were the hardest thing for me to deal with, as it would be almost impossible to refute such vague rumors and indirect allegations. Mark decided it was best not to respond to Semow's personal attacks because it would just give them credence, so I was forced to simply sit there and listen as my character was impugned on a daily basis.

Day after day of listening to personal attacks began to take its toll.

Pat kept reassuring me, reminding me that the prosecution's evidence had been torn apart, but soon I couldn't focus on the case itself—all I could think about were the horrible things Semow was saying about me. I hated having to sit silently and listen to his attacks, and I especially hated the fact that the members of my family who'd come to Los Angeles to support me had to listen to them. Soon I began to have trouble sleeping, and I'd often find myself wide awake at 2 A.M., filled with dread about the next day in court. For four or five hours each night, I would wander around the house like a ghost.

One night near the end of the trial, I finally broke under the pressure. It had been a particularly nasty day in court, and I was once again wandering the floors at 2 A.M. As I paced around the house, I grew more and more frantic—fearful of conviction, upset about Semow's attacks, worried about my family, and depressed about my future. After weeks of being vilified publicly, attacked by my former best friend, and pilloried in the press, I suddenly couldn't take it anymore.

After pacing for about an hour, I felt my panic rising until I could hear my heart pounding in my ears. I went into the bedroom and shook Pat awake.

"I have to get out of here!" I said "I want you to take me somewhere—to a mental hospital—anywhere. Now! I can't take this anymore."

Pat sat up in bed, groggy with sleep. I pulled at his wrist. "Call Bill and tell him. He'll help us find a mental hospital. Come on, Pat. Let's go!" At that moment, all I wanted was to be checked into a mental ward somewhere and given a quiet, empty room where I could just sit—a place where I'd never again have to hear another word about Whitewater, Nancy Mehta, courtrooms, trials, lawyers, and jails again. There was too much pain in all of this and I just couldn't listen anymore. I couldn't sit there quietly while this man who knew nothing about me characterized my entire life as evil. And I had to just sit there and take it with a smile on my face so that the jury would not see how it was killing me.

Pat could see I was distraught, and at first he thought I was just being dramatic. But as I sat on the bed, crying uncontrollably and begging him to take me away, he realized I was serious. For the next hour he talked to me in quiet, reassuring tones, asking me questions and listening to all my frustrations. It was as though he was a negotiator talking a person down from leaping off a tall building: slowly I began to calm down. I was still crying, and my misery was far from over, but my panic finally subsided.

As difficult as it was to control my emotions in general during this period, it soon became equally difficult to control them in the courtroom. One afternoon as I was sitting at the defense table, I became angered at a question that Semow had asked one of the witnesses. I slammed my hand down so hard on the table that it could be heard in the next courtroom. Judge Light was not amused. He excused the jury from the courtroom and then began to loudly berate me for my outburst.

His voice rising, Judge Light threatened me with several types of sanctions, culminating in the ultimate threat: "Ms. McDougal," he warned, "if you cannot control yourself in this courtroom, I will have no choice but to find you in contempt of court—and perhaps even put you in jail overnight."

As the judge's words echoed in the courtroom, someone began snickering. At first it was just one or two spectators, but the sound quickly spread; within seconds, most of the courtroom had begun to laugh. It didn't take long for Judge Light to recognize what was going on. For a woman who'd just spent eighteen months in jail for contempt of court, the threat of an overnight stay didn't seem like much of a deterrence.

The judge put his head down, and I couldn't tell if he was laughing or crying. Mark, looking to defuse the situation, suggested to the judge that he could provide the bailiff with a cattle prod, and then every time I opened my mouth the bailiff could just zap me. Mark was joking (I think), but I could tell from the judge's face that the idea held some appeal for him.

After two and a half months of testimony, the Mehta trial finally wound down. The attorneys prepared to give their closing arguments: Semow would be up first, then Mark, and then Semow would be allowed to rebut Mark's argument.

For Semow, this was it. He had to know how weak his case was—not only had many of his witnesses inadvertently bolstered my defense, but numerous checks that were allegedly forged were proven to have been written for the Mehtas' benefit. In addition, the existence of signed receipts for the disputed MasterCard in Nancy's files showed that Nancy had known about the credit card. This was Semow's last chance to somehow gain a conviction, so as he had done during the trial, he resorted to trying to convince the jury I was so sleazy that I just needed to be in jail regardless of the evidence.

For two days Semow stood before the jurors and delivered a hate-filled, deeply personal attack on me. I can't begin to describe how painful it is to sit silently in a courtroom, with friends and family watching, while someone spends two days saying every cruel, hurtful thing about you they can think of. More than four years have passed since Semow delivered that closing statement, and to this day I have nights where I wake up replaying some of the worst parts of his closing in my mind.

Though the evidence was clearly in my favor, I began to fear I would be convicted as I listened to Semow's closing argument. If the jury believed even half of what he was saying about me, I figured they might vote to convict me just on principle. Mark was very confident, and Bill and Pat were reasonably so—but then, everyone around me had been confident at the end of the Whitewater trial, too.

When the closing arguments were finished, I was as worried as I'd ever been. I wasn't scared by the thought of going back to jail because I already knew I could survive that. I could not, however, live with the idea of being falsely convicted of stealing from Nancy. One night Pat and I walked down to the ocean and I noticed some freighters out in the distance. "Maybe," I said, "I ought to just black out my two front teeth, put on a wig, and hop a freighter to the West Indies." I was only half joking.

The jury began its deliberations on a Thursday afternoon and they weren't able to reach a decision by the time they recessed on Friday. That whole weekend I slept less than four hours.

The following Tuesday, at around noon, we were notified that the jury had reached a verdict on all twelve counts and that the decision would be read in thirty minutes. The next half hour was a total blur. I remember seeing CNN bring cameras into the courtroom, but I didn't realize they planned to carry the reading of the verdict live. I also recall seeing Nancy reappear for the first time since her testimony. She strode to the front row of the courtroom and sat as close to the jury box as she could get. The thought crossed my mind that she wanted to be near the jurors so that after the reading of the verdict she could personally thank them all for convicting me. However, I didn't dwell on Nancy for long—her presence didn't really matter. I knew that what was about to happen would change my life forever and I was focused on my own situation.

I watched the faces of the jurors as they filed into the courtroom. Legal lore holds that if jurors returning from deliberations look a defendant in the eye, it means they've reached a not-guilty verdict. If they refuse to look at the defendant, it's supposedly because they're uncomfortable looking at someone they've just condemned. As the jurors took their seats, not a single one looked me in the eye.

The jury foreman handed Judge Light the twelve-page verdict form—one page for each count. The judge read over each page for what felt like an eternity. He then flipped back and forth through the pages, never registering a single facial expression that would indicate what the decision might be. Finally he handed the forms to the court clerk and asked her to read the results aloud. As she faced the courtroom and prepared to read, I felt too choked to breathe.

"As to count one," she read aloud, "we the jury find the defendant, Susan McDougal, not guilty." One down, eleven more to go.

"As to count two, we the jury find the defendant, Susan McDougal, not guilty."

"As to count three, we the jury find the defendant, Susan McDougal, not guilty."

Down the list she went. After the fourth or fifth consecutive "not guilty" verdict, I began to feel my breathing returning to normal, but I was not yet ready to celebrate. At last, she reached the final count.

"As to count twelve," she announced, "the jury finds the defendant, Susan McDougal, not guilty."

My mind went blank. I simply shut down, overloaded with emotion and exhaustion. I remember nothing of the first few moments following the verdicts other than putting my head wearily on Mark's shoulder. Later that evening, I watched CNN's clips showing my reaction after the last verdict was read. The courtroom erupted, but it looked like I was moving in slow motion and had no emotional response to what I'd just heard. In the background, you could hear a lot of yelling—but on-screen, I appeared oblivious to it all.

When I was finally able to think, one thought kept running through my mind: "It's over. It's over. It's finally over." The Mehta case had hung over my head for almost five years, and it was at last gone forever. But I couldn't celebrate yet. I'd just been given my life back, and it would take longer than I ever expected for that to sink in.

The verdicts were a huge victory, but what happened next was even more remarkable. The jurors requested the opportunity to address the press directly. "Is this normal?" I asked Mark. He just laughed and said, "Most jurors, especially after a two-and-a-half-month trial, can't wait to get away from the courthouse."

The TV crews set up a long table and microphone in a nearby empty courtroom, and the jurors came in. Foreman Rufus Gifford, a young writer who lived in nearby Venice Beach, began by making a statement about how the majority of the jurors felt the entire trial was ludicrous. At no time, he announced, did any juror cast a single "guilty" verdict on any count. They had deliberated for three days, carefully going through each accusation and making sure not to rush the process, but at no time could they find any evidence that I had stolen from the Mehtas.

One by one, the jurors blasted the prosecution and questioned why this case had even been allowed to go to trial. Reporters began asking whether the jurors had discussed Kenneth Starr. Did they believe Starr was behind this prosecution? All the jurors denied that Starr's name had ever come up, but Nancy Nieman, a Spanish professor from Santa Monica College, said it was hard to imagine any other reason why this case had been prosecuted.

I stood there in utter disbelief. I could not have personally choreographed an ending this ideal. While I sat in jail, I had convinced myself that there was no possible way we'd be able to get twelve people to understand my relationship with Nancy. I didn't even understand it myself! But not only had they understood it—they showed terrific insight as they discussed the case. At the end, I was so blown away by their remarks that I had trouble going up and thanking them. For one of the few times in my life, I was at a loss for words. Somehow, a handshake and a thank you just didn't seem sufficient for twelve people who had just saved my life.

The jurors were particularly critical of Jeff Semow. Several mentioned how unnecessarily cruel his closing argument had been. Others said that they'd been turned off early on by Semow's lack of compelling evidence, and commented that his personal attacks on me had done nothing to salvage the case.

I hardly had time to thank everyone and let the victory sink in when the reporters mentioned the next trial on my agenda. My second Whitewater trial—this one on criminal contempt and obstruction of justice—was scheduled to begin in less than four months, and the reporters had plenty of questions about it. Though I wanted to have a few moments of savoring this victory before having to consider the next battle, I answered a few questions about the upcoming trial.

Finally, as I was wrapping up the interviews, one reporter asked, "Are you scared of Kenneth Starr?"

I looked at the reporter and with my best Clint Eastwood imitation sneered, "He had better be scared of me."

18

STARR WARS

THE VERDICTS IN THE MEHTA CASE changed my life overnight. For five years I'd lived under the cloud of Nancy's extremely personal allegations, and I'd worried about this trial and its outcome more than I had ever worried about Whitewater.

The impact of the Mehta victory went beyond my wildest dreams. In an instant, the media's and public's perception of me changed completely. Prior to the Mehta trial, every article about my ongoing battle with Kenneth Starr included the phrase, "McDougal is also accused of embezzling $150,000 from world-renowned conductor Zubin Mehta." Even people sympathetic to my refusal to talk with the OIC had been leery of openly supporting me because they were disturbed by the Mehta charges. But now, that all had changed; with my complete vindication, several writers even began openly questioning whether Starr had pushed the Mehta case in order to pressure me to talk.

After the verdicts, I began hearing from dozens of old friends, all of them calling to say that they'd been behind me all the way. Likewise, a huge number of new friends contacted us, offering everything from financial support to inside information on the personal lives of Starr and his staff. Lawyers from prestigious firms in New York and Washington,

D.C., suddenly wanted to offer legal help, and a few Hollywood agents called, wanting to buy the movie rights to my life. I appreciated the interest, but I never followed up with any of the agents, partly because it just would have felt cavalier to turn around and hire an agent. I felt that I had made my choices out of very strong personal beliefs and it just felt wrong to try suddenly to capitalize on those decisions.

Pat and Bill were ecstatic with the verdicts; all those years of hard work in the face of huge obstacles had finally paid off. Mark Geragos, too, was riding a wave. In the national spotlight for the first time, he had risen to the occasion magnificently—not only in his trial work but in dealing with the media. In fact, his performance in front of the cameras had been so strong that he was now becoming a hot commodity on the TV talk-show circuit. His career was about to take off into the stratosphere, a distinction he had earned by having the guts to stand up for me when no other lawyer would.

By contrast, Starr and his staff seemed to be reeling. The September 1998 release of the Starr Report had confirmed what I had been saying for the past two years: the president's pursuers were a bunch of middle-aged, moralistic morons who were obsessed with sex. Much of the public seemed to agree with me. The impeachment hearings revealed the Starr investigation for what it was—a witch-hunt to get Bill Clinton—and with Clinton's approval rating hovering near the 80 percent mark, it had obviously backfired.

Even so, Kenneth Starr wasn't finished yet. In March 1999, just four months after the end of the Mehta trial, I'd have to face the OIC once again in a courtroom, fighting two counts of criminal contempt and one count of obstruction of justice related to my refusal to testify in front of the grand jury.

In December 1998, a few weeks after the end of the Mehta trial, Pat and I moved back to Arkansas to prepare for Whitewater II.(You know you're a true serial criminal when your trials are numbered like Super Bowls.) In some ways things were better than they'd ever been since that fall day five years earlier when I had first heard about the Mehta charges. But in other ways I was having a hard time adjusting to what my life had become.

For the six months since I had gotten out of jail, I hadn't had even a single day of normalcy. I had gone straight from house arrest at my parents' home to attending trial every day for three months. The national media attention had been intense and, because I'd been in jail for so long, I still felt skittish around crowds. I desperately needed some downtime just to decompress, and I even found myself missing the simplicity of jail life.

I was also having trouble forgetting Jeffrey Semow's vicious closing argument from the Mehta trial. Some nights I would wake up at two or three o'clock in the morning and remember some part of his closing that I just couldn't get out of my mind. Other times I didn't think of anything in particular. Sometimes I couldn't even remember anything specific, as though I'd blocked it all out. I simply remembered and relived the sickening feeling of hearing someone tear me apart for two days, in front of my family and friends.

Despite the hectic pace and the occasional nightmares, it was a great holiday season. My whole family was together for the first time since I had gone to jail, and we rehashed all the old family stories over and over again, pretending like we were hearing them for the first time instead of the fiftieth. Pat and I also drove across the country to see his family, and wherever we stopped, people went out of their way to offer a word of support and to tell me they were rooting for me against Ken Starr.

Things between Pat and me were still good, despite the strain of the trials. He and I would be together in Arkansas for the length of the Whitewater II trial, but we hadn't really discussed what would happen after that—partly because it was entirely possible that I'd be going to jail again. At this point, where our relationship was concerned, we simply took each day as it came.

As the trial approached, I was still hearing from people all over the country who wanted to know how they could help. Several people drove from as far away as Florida and New Mexico to attend the trial and lend their support. One of the people who called to offer us help was an elderly gentleman named Fred Darragh. Fred had been the charter member of the ACLU in Little Rock, and though I'd never met him, he was anxious to help me out as I prepared to face the OIC once again. Fortunately, he offered me the one thing that I believe saved my sanity during this period: the use of his beautiful country home just outside Little Rock.

Fred's place sat on twelve acres of idyllic, unspoiled land, and I'll never forget how relaxing it was to wake up in his house, look out the window, and see deer milling about in the yard. Best of all, he had a heated pool where I could swim for hours, even when it was so cold that there was frost on the ground. If it hadn't been for Fred's generosity, I might have been stuck in a hotel in Little Rock in the midst of the media frenzy.

Ensconced at Fred's country house, with Pat, Bill, Mark, and my family in Little Rock to support me, I felt as ready as I ever would to face the OIC once again. At last I would have my chance to put Kenneth Starr's prosecutorial misconduct on trial.

As the Whitewater II trial geared up in March 1999, the press was still in full Clinton feeding frenzy. Monica Lewinsky was still around, but with the impeachment process over, press interest in her was fading fast. Reporters were looking for a new whiff of scandal wherever they could find it, and several cable shows, including *Geraldo* and *Burden of Proof*, broadcast live from Little Rock for a week or two, hoping something juicy would come out of the trial. Several of the jurors from the Mehta trial actually flew out to Arkansas to offer their support, even holding a press conference at the courthouse to reiterate their belief that there had been some kind of political motivation behind the Mehta charges.

When I walked into the Little Rock courtroom, I felt almost like I was at a family reunion—albeit of a very dysfunctional family. The OIC trial attorneys were Mark Barrett and Julie Myers, the two prosecutors who had handled the medical hearing that led to my release from jail. On their witness list were two holdovers from the first Whitewater trial, Ray Jahn and Amy St. Eve. And, for the third time in three years, the judge overseeing the proceedings would be the Honorable George Howard. Although I never felt Judge Howard liked me very much, I was glad to have him presiding because I did believe he bent over backward to be fair and impartial.

The OIC had charged me with two counts of criminal contempt (once for each time I had refused to testify) and one count of obstruction of justice. The general consensus among media experts was that the OIC would have a hard time making the obstruction of justice charge stick, but the criminal contempt charges should be a slam dunk for the prosecution. After all, I had publicly and blatantly defied the OIC's subpoena, and that was essentially all they had to prove.

The only real chance I had of winning was a strategy that lawyers aren't allowed to bring up: jury nullification. Jury nullification occurs when jurors hear the evidence and see that it fits the elements of the crime, but refuse to convict the person for other reasons. Though it's rarely acknowledged publicly, this happens fairly often within the judicial system.

Jury selection is important in any trial, but in a high-publicity, politically charged trial, it is critical. Because Judge Howard knew it would be difficult to find impartial jurors, he had each prospective juror fill out a lengthy questionnaire. There were questions about what TV shows and newspapers the jurors watched, what newspapers they read, what they had heard about the case, and how they felt about key characters in the upcoming trial. The questionnaires were then provided to the lawyers on each side.

When reading the potential jurors' answers, I was struck by how obvious it was that most of them actually *wanted* to get on this jury. Many had realized that if they expressed any specific political belief, they'd get booted by one side or the other. So more than half of the jurors professed indifference to Bill Clinton, Hillary Clinton, and Kenneth Starr. That was absurd: in a state where Bill Clinton had been the major political figure for two decades, you could count on one hand the number of people who had no opinion about him or about the Starr investigation.

The would-be jurors' lack of honesty in filling out the questionnaires made jury selection very difficult. It was obvious that people were deliberately trying to get on the jury, but the tricky part was trying to determine *why*. The OIC tried to overcome that problem by using taxpayer money to hire a professional jury consultant. Mark and Pat had a different approach: they used my unerring ability to totally misread people as a barometer of how *not* to choose the jury.

Pat and Mark made this decision after the first day of jury interviews. When the first twelve people from the jury pool were brought into the jury box, I watched each face carefully, looking for clues. The judge explained to them that they'd be taken three at a time into the judge's chambers, where lawyers from each side would question them. Before the questioning began, Mark asked if I had noticed anything in particular about any of the jurors. I didn't hesitate.

"The red-haired older woman in the front row to the right is giving me horrible looks," I told him. "I don't want her anywhere near my jury."

As it turned out, that woman was one of the first to be brought into the judge's chambers to be questioned. The judge had barely opened his mouth to speak when the woman started to cry. "I'm sorry, your honor," she said, "but I have to be honest. I can't be fair and impartial in this trial. I love Susan McDougal and what she did—I think she is a hero!" The judge thanked her for her honesty and quickly dismissed her from jury service. From that point forward, Mark and Pat would only ask my opinion about a juror whenever they couldn't agree between themselves. My vote was the tiebreaker—whichever way I voted, they'd go with the exact opposite position.

We knew going in that we would never get a perfect jury, but when the selection was finished, we felt confident there weren't more than one or two Clinton-haters in the group. Keeping the Clinton-haters to a minimum was very important. Jury studies show that three or four people on a jury with strong opinions can often drive a jury to a particular verdict. But it is very difficult for just one or two people to take over a jury and engineer a result.

The night before the trial began, Mark, Pat, and I went to a Japanese steak house in Little Rock, the kind where groups of people sit around a large, flat grill and watch while a Japanese chef prepares the food. We were joined at our table by four or five young men who looked like they had just posed for the cover of *Redneck Weekly*—exactly the demographic that typically comprised the biggest percentage of Clinton haters.

For most of the meal, I sat where they couldn't really see me, but I could hear them talking—especially as the drinks kept coming. About halfway through the meal, the topic of Bill Clinton came up, and it was clear that they were not supporters. These young men despised Clinton—and here I was, the woman famous for supposedly "protecting" him with my silence, sitting right near them. Afraid they'd recognize me and make a scene, I tried to keep my back turned toward them.

But near the end of the meal, they started whispering to each other—and finally one of them leaned over and asked Pat, "Is that Susan McDougal you're sitting with?"

"Yes, it is," Pat replied. And with that, three of the men got up from their seats and walked over as I shrank down into my seat. To my surprise, each man reached out to shake my hand. One of them told me, "I hate Bill Clinton, but I admire you for standing up for what you believe in. I hope you kick Kenneth Starr's ass!" Not only did they all offer words of encouragement, they even insisted on paying for our dinner. We left the restaurant ecstatic. If even the Clinton-haters could support us, this trial might be the beginning of the end for Ken Starr.

Though I was exhausted from the media attention and the frenzy of events since I'd gotten out of jail, I also knew that this trial would be much easier on me than either of the first two had been. In the first Whitewater trial, I had been so worried about harming Jim in some way that I had compromised my own defense. And Jim had been so unpredictable and volatile that I was on edge the entire time. At the Mehta trial, I had been accused by a former best friend and had been forced to listen as my character was torn apart by a vitriolic prosecutor. In both cases I was scared of being convicted of something that I knew I had not done.

But now I was facing trial for something I knew I *had* done—and not only that, it was something I would have done again. Also, unlike during the first trial, I now didn't fear the possibility of going to jail. I didn't want to go, of course, but in many ways my time in jail had been a very good experience and I knew I could handle it. In the end I simply wasn't as emotionally invested in this trial as I had been in the others.

From the beginning of the trial, the OIC made its strategy clear: they would show the jury that Kenneth Starr and his staff had simply been disinterested lawyers seeking the truth, no matter which way it came down. The grand jurors were the ones tasked with making the decisions, and I had illegally refused to cooperate. At every turn the OIC tried to take the emphasis off themselves: in their version of events, it was the grand jury—a hardworking group of patriotic, middle-class Americans—that I had thumbed my nose at, not the OIC.

The OIC had selected Mark Barrett and Julie Myers to represent them, apparently because they were more able to project a nonthreatening, just-doing-our-jobs demeanor than Amy St. Eve and Jackie Bennett. In his opening statement, Barrett portrayed the OIC as a big, happy family, with Kenneth Starr as a kind, paternal figure. The only reason they were upset that I wouldn't testify, Barrett implied, was that it prevented them from quickly wrapping up their investigation and letting President Clinton get on with the business of running the country.

In order to lay the foundation for this strategy, the OIC called as witnesses three of the grand jurors. The first was a sweet-looking woman in her late thirties who testified about how nice all the OIC attorneys were and how they had no agenda but were simply seeking the truth. She emphasized that it was the grand jurors who made the ultimate decisions and the OIC was simply providing them all the information they needed to make informed judgments. But she quickly learned that perhaps the grand jury had not been getting all the information. Under cross-examination, Mark asked her whether the OIC had ever told them about the criminal history of their star witness, David Hale. The woman seemed genuinely surprised at the mention of this and answered no. Mark then went through a list of things the OIC was aware of that were either positive about the Clintons or damaging to the OIC investigation. After each one, he asked the woman if the supposedly neutral OIC attorneys had presented any of this evidence to the grand jury. In virtually every case, the woman said no. By the end of Mark's cross, she looked like she was having a severe crisis of faith.

The second grand juror was much better prepared to answer Mark's questions. She asserted confidently that the OIC represented the epitome of honesty. Her own honesty, however, soon came into question. Mark asked her if she had met with the OIC before taking the stand, and she said no. On redirect examination, Mark Barrett gently reminded her that she had spent the last hour's lunch break discussing her testimony with members of the OIC team. Apparently she had assumed this would never be brought out—and she turned beet red in suddenly "remembering" that meeting.

The third grand juror was a tall, stately-looking man from eastern Arkansas who had been the grand jury foreman. He was an absolute gentleman and testified that he had very much wanted to hear what I had to say. He made a perfect witness for the prosecution because his sincerity was obvious and he seemed like he had no ax to grind. Wisely, Mark limited his questioning of the man and moved on.

The prosecution then brought in Ray Jahn as their next witness. Jahn's purpose was twofold: first, he was there to deny my allegations that the OIC had ever wanted me to lie. And second, he was there to talk about my first Whitewater trial—a strong reminder to the jury that I had already been convicted once.

As an attorney, Jahn always played the part of the "aw-shucks" down-home charmer in front of juries. He did the same thing as a witness, starting with the story of his hiring by the OIC. According to Jahn, he was working happily as a U.S. attorney in San Antonio when someone in Starr's office called to ask him to interview for a job with the OIC.

OIC attorney Mark Barrett asked, "What did you tell Starr?"

Jahn answered, "I told him that I had been through the Department of Justice throughout the Watergate investigation . . . I told him that it was my hope that we would be able to clear the president, that at this particular stage in our country we did not need to be in a position where we were losing confidence in our government and I thought it was very important for us to do the best we could to clear the president."

I still can't believe Jahn was able to tell this story with a straight face.

Jahn then tried to ingratiate himself with the jury by invoking the state religion: University of Arkansas sports. He claimed that after the job interview, he and Ken Starr had gone to a local restaurant to cheer for the Razorback basketball team in the national championship game. This declaration was carefully calculated to enhance the image of the OIC lawyers as having become just good old regular Arkansans.

With this latest story, I thought Pat was going to have a heart attack. He grabbed Mark and told him that there is not a Texan on the planet who would root for Arkansas in anything. They have been bitter sports rivals for years. Furthermore, in the national championship game, Arkansas was playing Duke, which just happened to be Starr's law school alma mater. In his cross-examination, Mark asked, "Are you telling me Mr. Starr was down there as a Duke graduate rooting for Arkansas during that day?"

Jahn answered weakly, "I don't remember. We were rooting for Arkansas."

"Yeah. Is that common?" Mark asked.

"Mr. Geragos, that is true, we were rooting for Arkansas," Jahn insisted.

By the time he finished, several of the jurors were openly laughing at his claim that he had indeed been rooting for Arkansas. It may have seemed like a small detail, but with that one little attempt at ingratiating himself with the jury, Jahn actually lost a lot of credibility.

Of much greater importance, Jahn verified under cross-examination my account of what he'd said back in 1996, while Claudia and I sat in Bobby McDaniel's office listening to him through the speakerphone. He admitted that, after promising me several incentives, he had told us, "You know who this investigation is about, and you know what we want." He then attempted to explain how his remarks had been misinterpreted. Again, his efforts came across as sounding a little desperate and unbelievable.

By the time Jahn stepped down from the witness stand, I was surprised at how easily he had gotten rattled. As someone who had been in a courtroom hundreds of times, it was amazing that he had lost his composure. I remember Pat telling me before the Mehta trial that it is one thing to be outside a courtroom making accusations like Nancy was, but it is another thing altogether to be sitting on the witness stand under oath with an attorney cross-examining you. It is enough to make even the calmest person's knees shake. I had assumed that Jahn's experience in the courtroom would negate that, but in the end he was as nervous as any witness I had ever seen. It was clear to everyone after Ray Jahn's testimony that, despite his claims to the contrary, he was a man with an agenda.

The OIC then turned to satisfying the technical elements of establishing the crimes of criminal contempt and obstruction of justice. They put on witnesses to testify that I'd been properly subpoenaed, that I'd been given every opportunity to testify, and that I had refused. They also played audiotapes of both of my appearances before the grand jury. Much of the testimony was perfunctory but necessary to prove their case. By the time the prosecution rested, they had explained the definition of criminal contempt, and shown that my actions clearly fell within that definition.

Up to now, the OIC had put on a carefully choreographed case. They had painted their investigation of Bill Clinton as a calm, sincere effort to find the truth. They indicated that they held no personal animosity toward me, but were only bringing these charges because the law required it. But then, instead of resting their case, they just couldn't resist the opportunity to go after me personally, at least a little bit. So they asked the judge for permission to show the jury the taped interview I'd done with Diane Sawyer for *Prime Time Live* back in 1996, before I'd gone to jail. Supposedly, they intended to show that the story I had told in that interview was different from the story I was now telling.

This decision was the OIC's first big mistake of the trial. They set up three large-screen TVs at various spots in the courtroom, then rolled the tape. The effect was dramatic—but not in the way the prosecution hoped.

There on the screen was a very upbeat, fresh-faced young woman who could have passed for about twenty-five years of age. In sharp contrast, the jury could look over at the defense table and see that same woman who, after three years of fighting the OIC, including almost two years spent in jail, looked beaten down and at least twenty years older. It was apparently stunning even for the judge—my sister Danielle told me she watched the judge wipe away tears at one point during the interview.

As I sat and watched the video, I couldn't believe how much I had changed in just three years. I leaned over to Pat and whispered, "I don't even know that girl anymore." It was a point that was clearly not lost on anyone in that courtroom.

Even though I was less emotionally invested in this trial, I still despised the OIC as much as ever. This was especially true when I saw Hickman Ewing, the self-righteous preacher-turned-prosecutor who had so sanctimoniously delivered the eulogy at Jim McDougal's funeral—after having ignored Jim's pleas to get him out of prison before it killed him. At the very beginning of the trial I saw Ewing for the first time in several years, and the mere sight of him was enough to make me sick. At one point I cornered Ewing against a wall, got right up in his face, and said, "I want you to know that I hold you absolutely responsible for the death of Jim McDougal. Why don't you go crawl back under the rock you came out from." Ewing had said nothing, slipping away with a look of shock on his face.

In the weeks leading up to the trial, Mark had been publicly stating he would call Ewing as his first witness. This would be a daring move—Ewing was the head of the OIC's Arkansas operation and one of the major driving forces in their investigation of Bill Clinton. Over the years, the OIC staff had gone through tremendous turnover, mostly in the Washington, D.C., office. But Ewing and a few of the other hardliners had been constants almost from the beginning, and their influence—as well as their determination to get the Clintons— had grown. I remember Jim McDougal coming back from meetings with Ewing laughing about how obsessed he was with the Clintons and how willing he was to believe anything negative about them—no matter how outlandish.

The consensus among observers was that Mark was blowing smoke—he would never put Ewing on as a witness. Not only would Ewing be a hostile witness, but he was a seasoned attorney who would presumably know how to handle Mark's cross-examination. Furthermore, several commentators noted that there were many ways for this move to backfire. If Ewing came across as calm and sincere, for example, it would play right into the OIC's argument that they were reasonable prosecutors simply doing their jobs. On one CNN show, the host pointedly criticized Mark for even considering such a risky move.

One reason that I loved Mark's style in the courtroom was that he was willing to take risks, and he wasn't about to be swayed by the criticism of TV pundits. He also had a sense of humor. He obtained the subpoena for Ewing, then in a move I'll always be grateful for, asked me to deliver it personally. This power shift between the OIC and myself is something that I really enjoyed.

The day the prosecution rested, Ewing, who often referred to himself as "Mr. Hick," was in the back row observing the trial. I took the subpoena and made my way back to where he was sitting. "For you, Mr. Hick," I said sweetly, handing him the subpoena. He looked like he'd been slapped in the face. For someone who'd been handed subpoenas, surprised with indictments, and sent to jail, it was a rare treat. "See you in the morning," I laughed, and walked back to the defense table.

The next day the courtroom was packed, mostly with media, as everyone expected fireworks from Ewing's testimony. They were not disappointed.

Just like Ray Jahn, Ewing had extensive experience in the courtroom, but just like Jahn, Ewing proved to be a terrible witness. He squirmed in the witness chair, refused to make eye contact with anyone, and, worst of all, he gave halting, evasive answers. He also appeared to be sweating.

After first questioning Ewing about a few details of the OIC's operations, Mark came to the point. "Now between the 1995 interview and the date of the conviction of Ms. McDougal, had you at that point already determined in your mind that Mrs. Clinton was guilty of a criminal offense?"

"I wouldn't say that," Ewing answered.

"Had you drafted an indictment on Mrs. Clinton?" Mark persisted.

"Well, sir, when you're a prosecutor, you're always thinking about, when you're investigating, under the mandate. . . . And you're always thinking about—you're trying to disprove whether this actually happened. So whether or not I actually drafted a rough indictment for talking points, I can't say positively that I did. It is possible—I mean, I know I did at some point," Ewing told the court.

Ewing and the OIC had assumed that once I was convicted in the first Whitewater trial, I would immediately flip in order to avoid jail time and would back up whatever story they needed to make the case against Hillary. Ewing's testimony played perfectly into our theory of the case. It showed how desperate the OIC was to get me to cooperate—because if I agreed to lie, they could indict Hillary. Without my cooperation, they had found themselves at a standstill.

Having secured this admission, Mark then ratcheted up the pressure, continuing to probe Ewing about the proposed indictment of Hillary Clinton. Mark asked, "But part of what you had a problem with is that Mrs. Clinton answered 'I don't recall' to a number of questions that you thought, based upon whatever you came to that interview with, she should have answers for, isn't that right?"

"Yes, sir. And the same was true of the president," answered Ewing.

Mark continued, "Did you, after those first two interviews, express the opinion that the Clintons were liars?"

Ewing said, "I don't know if I used the 'L' word or not. But I certainly expressed internally that I had a problem with some of the answers that we had gotten from both the president and first lady." He said all this, despite the fact that Hillary was being asked to answer questions about obscure legal issues that were more than ten years old.

The irony of this, as Mark was quick to point out, was that now, during his own testimony, Ewing repeatedly used the phrase "I don't know" or "I don't remember"—yet for the most part, he was responding to questions about events that had happened just in the last two years. Apparently, Ewing saw no contradiction in that—but then, consistency never was the OIC's strong suit.

The press leapt on the news of Hillary's close call, and for the next few days pundits and reporters speculated endlessly about what might have happened if the first lady had been indicted. Mark's strategy of putting Ewing on the stand was completely vindicated; in fact, the CNN host who had criticized Mark the previous night now hailed it as a brilliant move. For me, Ewing's testimony was sweet revenge. It's hard to describe the satisfaction I got out of watching him squirm and sweat on the witness stand.

The next witness up for us was Claudia Riley. Claudia testified to what she'd heard when she had been with me in two pivotal early meetings—the first with the OIC in Little Rock and the second when Bobby McDaniel had put Ray Jahn on the speakerphone. She'd told me that morning that she was nervous about testifying in court, but with Mark leading her through the questioning, Claudia did a great job of recounting what she remembered—especially the phone call where Jahn had made his veiled but unmistakable references to the real target of the OIC investigation, and made promises to me if I cooperated in their pursuit.

When Claudia finished her direct testimony, the judge recessed for a morning break. We walked out of the courtroom, and Claudia sat on a bench in the hallway while I went to get her some water. Seeing Claudia sitting alone, the OIC's Julie Myers walked over, sat down next to her, and inquired whether she could ask her a few questions. The always-gracious Claudia said, "I think that would be all right." Myers then asked two or three innocuous questions before getting to her real question.

"Did Susan McDougal ever tell you that she had sex with Bill Clinton?" asked Myers.

Claudia, a proper, polite Southern lady in her seventies, was taken aback and was barely able to stammer out a negative response. With that, Myers got up and walked away. Claudia then called Pat and Mark over and told them what had just happened. She was too much of a lady to repeat exactly what Myers had said, however— she told them,

"She asked me whether Susan had ever had a liaison with Bill Clinton."

Myers's ill-advised question was the OIC's second big mistake of the trial. When we went back into the courtroom, Mark asked the judge for permission to briefly reopen his questioning of Claudia.

Mark began by asking Claudia about Myers, "What was she asking you?"

Claudia replied, "I was pretty nervous right then. I'm still pretty nervous but whether or not Jim—Jim had ever said to me something about a liaison with the president or Susan having said that perhaps. . . . "

Mark asked gently, "Liaison meaning sex?"

Claudia answered, "Yeah."

Mark then asked Claudia if she had just had a conversation with Julie Myers in the hallway.

The OIC's other attorney, Mark Barrett, looked like he was going to explode. He had obviously not been aware of Myers's questioning of Claudia, and he immediately understood the damage she had done. With his back to the jury and as quietly as possible, Barrett tore into Myers. On her cross-examination of Claudia, Myers tried to put a different spin on her sex question, but it only served to point out how ridiculous the question had been in the first place.

After we had called two other witnesses to recount their similar experiences with the OIC, it was my turn to testify. From the first time I'd refused to testify to the grand jury, I had stated numerous times that I would answer any questions the OIC wanted to ask, but only in an open forum, with my attorneys and journalists present, so the OIC couldn't twist my words, or lie about what I'd said, or trump up a perjury charge against me. Now it was time to put up or shut up.

I was ready, but nervous. This was finally my chance to have my say, and I wanted so much to come out of it that it was almost paralyzing. Just as I had in the first Whitewater trial, I worried about whether I could handle their questioning. They had all the money in the world and the ability to research everything I had ever said or done in my life. And I worried, too, that they'd start asking me about Jim's financial dealings, which I didn't know anything about.

Mark took me through a basic direct examination. I had told the story of what happened to me numerous times on television and radio, so this part was rather easy. I had been nervous when I took the stand, but the more I spoke, the more relaxed I felt. Yet I knew that when it came time for cross-examination, Mark Barrett wasn't going to let me off so easily.

The OIC staff had gathered a number of interviews that I'd given, and Barrett proceeded to cross-examine me on things I had said over the course of the past two years. He was looking for inconsistencies or changes in my story, but he wasn't going to find any. This was not some car accident or crime scene I had witnessed one day and was trying to recall; this was my life. Not only had I lived through these incidents—I then had almost two years of sitting in a jail cell to think about the choices I'd made.

After getting nowhere with his first line of questioning, Barrett then began asking me the questions that the OIC had intended to ask me in front of the grand jury. In some cases, I was able to give very simple and straightforward answers. But in many cases, I either had no recollection of details he asked me for, or I hadn't even been involved in what he was asking about to begin with. I struggled through these parts of the cross-examination, at times looking a bit confused.

As he approached the end of his cross-examination, Barrett wanted to emphasize to the jury that I had already been in a trial in this courtroom once before and lost.

He asked me, "You were found guilty in this courtroom by a jury of twelve Arkansans, isn't that true?"

I knew exactly what he wanted me to say, but I was not going to give him the satisfaction.

"Your office put on testimony by David Hale that you knew was a lie."

Barrett objected that I was not answering the question and asked the judge to warn me to answer the question as it was asked. Barrett then repeated the question. But I was not about to give in this easily. I started on another David Hale harangue and Barrett began objecting again. The judge upheld the objection and ordered me to answer the question.

But the more Barrett asked about the first trial, the more stubbornly I dug in my heels. Every time he asked the question, I refused to give him the simple yes answer he wanted. Finally, Judge Howard became exasperated with my refusal to answer the question and very sternly told me to answer either yes or no. Grudgingly I gave in, but not before I prefaced my answer with one more attack on the OIC.

As the grand finale to our defense, Mark had a surprise in store. He called Julie Hiatt Steele to the witness stand.

Julie's story was a cautionary tale about the perils of telling the truth to the OIC. Whenever people asked me why I didn't simply "tell the truth" to the grand jury, rather than refusing to testify, I had often replied that I was afraid I'd be charged with perjury if I told the truth. That comment was more often than not met with derision—how can you be charged with lying if you're telling the truth? But Julie Hiatt Steele's story showed exactly how it could happen.

In 1997, Julie's friend, Kathleen Willey, had asked her to help her out by lying to *Newsweek* reporter Michael Isikoff. Willey had accused Bill Clinton of having groped her in the White House, and she wanted Julie to tell Isikoff that Willey had told her about the groping at the time it allegedly happened. Julie agreed that she would, but only if it would be "on background" and never published. Julie knew it was a lie, but she was worried about Willey and wanted to help her.

When the story was published in *Newsweek*, with Julie's supposed "background" information included, Julie stepped forward and admitted that she had lied. Even though she had no connections to Bill Clinton, and hadn't even voted for him, Julie had no intention of letting this lie spin out of control. She faced a dilemma similar to one I had, also realizing that she wouldn't tell this lie once, but would be forced to repeat it over and over.

Many would say that Julie had displayed a commendable sense of right and wrong by coming forward and admitting she had lied, but the OIC saw it otherwise. When Kathleen Willey testified that she had told Julie of the alleged groping at the time it happened, the OIC, for obvious reasons, needed Julie to back it up. But Julie refused to lie and the OIC charged her with perjury.

Not only was Julie indicted, but the OIC launched a thorough investigation of her private life—even asking her sixteen-year-old babysitter if he had ever slept with her. The OIC also raised questions about the legitimacy of Julie's adoption of a Romanian orphan and intimated that the child could be taken from her. Julie was forced to spend her savings and sell her home in order to defend herself, all because she'd told the truth.

Mark desperately wanted Julie to testify at my trial because, as he told me, "You are the theory about the OIC's methods. Julie is the actual practice." Yet for Julie, it would be a dangerous thing to do. Her own trial was just two months away; by testifying now, she'd be giving the OIC an opportunity to cross-examine her and get testimony under oath to use against her then. This was pretty much like showing all your cards in a poker game, then daring the other player to beat you.

I had never even met Julie Hiatt Steele. Everything was at stake for her—she could lose her family or go to prison as a result of supporting me by testifying at my trial. Yet despite all the risk involved, Julie chose to testify on my behalf. It was a tremendously selfless and courageous act. To this day, I feel amazed and grateful that she stuck up for me in that way.

Julie was a very convincing witness. She was petite—around five feet tall, weighing about a hundred pounds—and she was almost dwarfed by the witness box. She spoke quietly, and her demeanor was that of a very gracious Southern lady. For more than an hour, Julie told her story in a composed manner, with only a slight hint of anger. She talked about being called before a grand jury and telling her story—and then being threatened with an indictment if she didn't change her story. When she was called back before the grand jury, she again refused to change her story. The OIC indicted her shortly thereafter.

The OIC chose to let Julie Myers cross-examine Julie Hiatt Steele, which proved to be their third big mistake of the trial. Inexplicably, Myers launched a full-out attack on Steele. She barked even the simplest questions at her, and if she didn't receive a satisfactory answer, she would raise her voice even louder and repeat the question. She phrased her questions in sarcastic tones and launched gratuitous attacks on Julie's character.

It was an amazing performance. For three weeks the OIC had worked very hard to build a façade of reasonableness. Now, at the last hour, they were choosing to bully a polite, diminutive single mother on the stand. Julie handled the badgering calmly, refusing to engage Myers in a shouting match.

When it was over, a veteran Arkansas attorney named Rick Holiman walked over to me and said, "They just lost the case. No Arkansas jury is going to stand for a woman to be treated like that."

As the trial wound down after three weeks, both sides were getting anxious. The jury was giving no clues as to which way they were leaning, and it was hard to read anything in their faces.

As Mark prepared his closing statement, I thought back over the trial and marveled at how different it was from the Mehta case. Then, the courtroom had been suffused with bitterness and rancor. Now, although I still despised Ray Jahn and Hickman Ewing, the tension level in the courtroom was about ten degrees lower. Even the closing arguments by both sides seemed a little flat. Other than Mark referring to the OIC as Nazis—which prompted Barrett, his face reddening, to scream about how his father had fought the Nazis in World War II— there were very few sparks.

When the case went to the jury, however, the butterflies in my stomach started again. This was it: when the jury came back with its decision, I would either walk out of the courthouse able to start my life over again—or I'd be looking at returning to federal prison for several years. I spent the next few days of jury deliberations sick to my stomach.

The ending wasn't going to be without some controversy. After two days, it was discovered that one juror had brought a law book into the deliberations—a serious breach of juror rules. Although Judge Howard determined that the jurors hadn't really used the book during the deliberations, he still had to decide whether the jury pool had been tainted. For several hours it appeared that he might have to call a mistrial—and we'd have to start the whole process over again. Eventually, to my relief, both sides and the judge agreed that the harm was probably minimal. Judge Howard instructed the jury to continue deliberations, with a strong admonition to refrain from using outside sources.

On the third day of deliberations, the jury passed a note to the judge saying they'd reached a decision on one count but were hopelessly hung up on the other two counts. After polling the jury foreman about the likelihood of reaching a verdict on the two hung counts, the judge was satisfied that no decision could be reached.

This was it: five years after my legal odyssey began, it was time to learn whether that odyssey was finally coming to an end. The judge announced to the courtroom that the jury had hung on the two counts of criminal contempt. As for the count of obstruction of justice, the jury had reached a verdict: not guilty.

A cheer went up in the courtroom, and Mark, Pat, and I hugged one another at the defense table. Barrett came over and shook hands and wished us all luck. Ewing, however, who had not missed a minute of the trial, was conspicuous by his absence. He had apparently seen the handwriting on the wall. Unlike the Mehta trial, this time I did not lapse into a semicomatose state after the verdict. And I was loving it. We had taken on the most powerful prosecutor in the country, an organization with an unlimited budget and incredible resources, and we had beaten them soundly. But as much as I enjoyed being a part of the victory, I was not naive enough to believe that the verdict was about Susan McDougal. The entire trial was a referendum on Kenneth Starr and we had succeeded in showing just how corrupt his investigation was.

The media reported the verdict as a total rejection of Starr and the OIC. I had clearly defied the OIC's subpoena, after all, and so any outcome other than guilty verdicts on those counts was considered a huge loss for the OIC. The press also reported that the vote on the two hung counts was 7–5 in favor of acquittal. Starr and his lawyers couldn't even get a majority on those counts.

In interviews with the media after the trial, several of the jurors stated that we had convinced them the OIC was not looking for the truth. Particularly satisfying for me were quotes from the jurors that described Jahn and Ewing as "oily" and "untrustworthy." The jurors said that the deliberations were very nasty, with a couple of jurors almost coming to blows. But despite three days of discussions, for the most part no one changed his or her position from the beginning of deliberations to the end.

That afternoon, in a radio interview, I invited the entire state of Arkansas to come to our victory party at the Capitol Hotel in Little Rock. When we got there that evening, it seemed like much of the state had taken me up on the offer. As one newspaper would later report, I spent the evening "twirling"—turning around every few seconds to respond to people tapping me on the shoulder, offering a hand or a hug.

Although Kenneth Starr could have chosen to retry me on the two criminal contempt counts, he gave in to the inevitable a few weeks later and finally ended the OIC's campaign against me. Given the jury's 7–5 vote in favor of acquittal on both charges, he was left with little choice.

For the first time since November 1993, almost six years earlier, I was facing no criminal charges-*six long years*. As we celebrated into the night, I couldn't help but think back to that day in 1996 when I had been sitting in Bobby McDaniel's office and Ray Jahn had offered to give me my life back if I would just agree to cooperate with the OIC. It had taken three years, seven prisons, and two more trials, but I had gotten my life back without having to give in. As I stood there in the Capitol Hotel reflecting back on those years, I could honestly say that if I had to do it all over again, I would not have changed a single thing.

EPILOGUE

WITH THE LAST OF MY TRIALS over, and my legal troubles behind me, I finally was able to have the down time I so desperately needed. Thanks to Fred Darragh's generosity, I continued living at his home in the country while I started trying to assimilate the events of the last six years. Reflection has never been one of my strong suits, but in the serenity of Fred's country house, I spent a lot of time thinking back on everything that had happened to me.

Uppermost in my thoughts were the women I had met in the seven different jails I'd been housed in across the country. These women formed an incredibly diverse group, from all economic backgrounds, races, and religions, and they had a lot of different stories about how they ended up in jail. But virtually all of them shared one thing in common: a tremendous amount of self-hatred. The self-loathing these women felt for what they'd done to themselves and their families was overwhelming.

Over the past few years, certain politicians and pundits have adopted the mantra that Americans need to step up and take "personal responsibility." It might seem at first glance that women in prison are a natural audience for that message, but during my time in jail I learned that wasn't the case. Not only were the women I met taking "personal responsibility" for their own screw-ups—they were also taking responsibility for what others had done to them. I cannot count the number of times I heard women talk about how, whenever they were hit or otherwise harmed by someone, they "probably had it coming." Even the women who had been sexually abused tended to blame themselves for what had happened.

It always irked me to turn on the television and see one of the blonde bimbo brigade (Ann Coulter, Laura Ingraham, Kelly Anne Fitzpatrick) or some other conservative commentator whine about how people need to take "personal responsibility." These people, whose idea of adversity is getting a bad pedicure, seem to have no problem summarily dismissing people who were unfortunate enough to be born without trust funds. In a recent interview with the *New York Observer*, Coulter stated that "I had a very happy childhood—nothing conflicted." In the seventh grade her beagle, Tiger died. Coulter said, "That was the only bad thing that ever happened to me." It's a good thing that her pet dying was the worst thing to happen to her because she does not have anywhere near the strength of character that the women I met in jail have. She would have never survived there. She was even afraid to go on *Larry King Live* to promote her book when she found out that I was also invited to be on the show to challenge her assertions.

The more I thought about the women I'd met in prison, the more I realized I was in a position to do something for them, and other incarcerated women. As I began the healing process, I started thinking about what I could do that would be constructive.

Meanwhile, I tried not to think too much or too often about Kenneth Starr. The second Whitewater trial had been very satisfying, as I got to turn the tables on the OIC and force them to answer questions about the Whitewater investigation. In a lot of ways, that trial cooled my hatred of the OIC. I was still very angry about what I'd been put through, but I simply didn't want to spend a lot of time reflecting on Starr and the OIC.

Yet wherever I went, I was continually asked about Starr and my feelings toward him. I usually declined to go off on a rant about him—for the most part, I felt that the American public had watched the Whitewater investigation unfold, and that they'd made their own decisions about him; many had chosen to reject Starr and his agenda. But one thing still rankles me about the Starr apologists and the way he's been covered in the media. Despite abundant evidence to the contrary, he is almost always described as an honest man, indeed as a man of real integrity. Any "misstatements" of facts by Starr have always been written off as simple mistakes resulting perhaps from his inexperience as a prosecutor when he became independent counsel. Virtually no one challenged Starr's honesty throughout the investigation, despite the fact that he was caught in numerous lies.

At first, I had a hard time understanding this phenomenon. How could a man who was so frequently caught bending the truth be able to maintain such a reputation for probity and honesty? Finally, one possible reason began to dawn on me: the media continued to describe Starr as an honest man because he was so quick to assure us over and over of his reputation for honesty. Whether comparing himself to Joe Friday or quoting scripture, Starr made sure to constantly talk about his integrity. Sometimes, talking about something incessantly can seem to make it real.

Actually, Ken Starr was the architect of one of the greatest snow jobs of the 20th century. Remarkably, his charade continues even today, with several commentators recently depicting him as simply a naive, in-over-his-head prosecutor who tried to do the best he could with a tough job that was supposedly thrust upon him. Of all the ludicrous stories to come out of Whitewater, this characterization of Starr is one of the most ridiculous. Before he became head of the OIC, Starr was a very powerful Washington lawyer who defended the tobacco industry and other major corporations in multimillion dollar lawsuits. A lawyer doesn't represent clients like that on the strength of old-fashioned country values and "aw-shucks" charm.

Unlike the picture his supporters tried to paint of him, Starr was not some political neophyte who got eaten up by the Washington wolves when he took on Bill Clinton. For years, Starr himself had been one of the head wolves—and he didn't get there by being naive. He actively lobbied for the job as head of the OIC, viewing the position as his ticket to the Supreme Court, and when he found that the rest of the country wasn't as willing to go along with his witch-hunt as his K Street buddies were, he started holding everyone but himself responsible.

The simple truth is that Kenneth Starr had absolutely no compunctions about telling outright lies if they served his purposes. He stood before Congress and stated that Madison Guaranty was one of the most corrupt institutions in America—a blatant example of the S&L excesses of the '80s. He repeated this frequently to the press, and his claim was gullibly parroted in the media.

Starr's dissembling before Congress and in the press about Madison helped him to justify his runaway investigation. The truth is that he spent millions of dollars and assigned many FBI agents to go through every transaction at Madison from the day it had opened. There were all kinds of rumors and wild allegations of check-kiting and loan fraud, and no matter how absurd the charge or how little evidence there was, Starr investigated it. With all this alleged corruption, and with Starr and his staff going through every detail of this "most corrupt" of all institutions, it would be safe to assume that the result must have been numerous criminal charges and a slew of convictions.

But what was the actual result? The final tally was one misdemeanor conviction (of an appraiser who wasn't even an employee of Madison, but who inflated an appraisal on one of Madison's loans), and one fraudulent loan that played a part in Jim McDougal's conviction. After years of investigation and millions of dollars spent, that was the sum of the illegalities found at Madison. I'd challenge anyone to walk into any business that employs over 100 people, put in millions of dollars and numerous FBI agents, and come out with less corruption than was found at Madison.

But thanks to Starr and his willingness to lie, it's now a widely accepted fact that Madison Guaranty was a criminal enterprise. He knew that wasn't true when he stood before Congress and referred to Madison as a corrupt institution. A lot of very good, hard-working people were smeared by Starr's statements and were unable to get work later because Madison was on their resumes. But that was the modus operandi of the entire OIC investigation. They were willing to run over people and ruin lives in order to further their goals.

*   *   *

The questions I'm asked most frequently since getting out of jail are, "Have you heard from either of the Clintons?" and "Did the Clintons ever call to thank you?" The answer to both questions is no. I haven't spoken to Bill or Hillary since about 1990—other than at the deposition in the White House in 1997. We were friends once, a long time ago, but I was never particularly close to either of them. I admire their politics a great deal, and if my refusal to cooperate with the OIC in any way prevented Starr from hurting the Clinton presidency, then I'm happy about it. But that was not the reason why I chose to remain silent. Lots of people thank me for refusing to cooperate with Starr and for helping the Clintons. But I didn't do it for the Clintons—I did it for myself.

I never felt comfortable around Hillary, but I do admire a number of things about her—most notably her willingness to stand up for what she believes in. I think New York is lucky to have her as a senator, because she's a fighter and embodies the great spirit of New Yorkers.

I also have a great deal of respect for Bill. Historians will argue over his legislative legacy as president, but those achievements are not what I find so impressive about him. Bill Clinton grew up without a father in a lower-middle-class family in a small town in Arkansas—yet he went on to become a Rhodes Scholar, the governor of Arkansas, and, finally, the leader of the most powerful country in the world. That's an incredible accomplishment that should not be overlooked. Just look at the 2000 presidential election—both of the major party candidates came from very wealthy backgrounds, and both had fathers who were famous politicians. It may be a long time before we see someone with Bill Clinton's background again make it all the way to the White House.

On his last day in office, Bill Clinton gave me a presidential pardon. I had hoped to get one, but I hadn't really expected to—in fact, I had repeatedly downplayed the possibility in my mind. When I heard the announcement on television, I was surprised at how much it meant to me. I knew that the presidential pardon list was going to be announced on the morning of Bush's inauguration but I did not want to have to listen to the Bush festivities so I kept the sound off on the television. Suddenly, I saw my picture flash on the screen with the word pardon underneath. I actually started screaming. I'm still not sure why I reacted so strongly to the news. Perhaps I felt that this was one more step in showing that I was wrongly convicted in the first Whitewater trial. Whatever the reason, I will always be grateful that Bill pardoned me.

I'm still close to the three people who supported me most strongly through the Whitewater saga—my brother Bill, Mark Geragos, and Pat Harris. The Whitewater affair soured my brother Bill on politics and the criminal justice system, and shortly after the second Whitewater trial, he married and moved to a quiet resort town in the mountains outside of Los Angeles. He now spends his time running his company and playing golf. Despite the distance from Arkansas, Bill remains the family consigliere—his dedication to the Henley clan and his willingness to sacrifice for us is extraordinary. The family never makes a move without Bill's advice and his blessing.

Mark Geragos's career, which was already on the upswing, went into orbit. He has not only become one of the leading attorneys in the country, Mark is now in demand on every political and legal commentary show. When I think back to the days I spent sitting in a jail cell, praying that I would find even a mediocre attorney to represent me, I still can't believe that Mark Geragos walked into my life. From the minute Mark took over representing me, I began a winning streak. This was not a coincidence: his talents as a lawyer are surpassed only by his dedication to fight for his clients.

After the second Whitewater trial, Pat had returned to Los Angeles to work in Mark's law firm, and I stayed on at Fred Darragh's for more rest. When we discussed it, we agreed to decompress a little before deciding where to go with our relationship.

And with that, Pat and I separated for the last time. It wasn't a specific decision we made, but as the weeks went by, it simply became clear that with him in Los Angeles, and me in Arkansas, the relationship we'd held onto for so long, through so much, would simply fade of its own accord.

The experience Pat and I shared cannot easily be expressed in writing. We essentially grew up together, even though we were adults when we met. We became so close that I didn't even have to ask him how he felt about a movie we'd just seen or a political speech we had just heard—I already knew, because 99 times out of 100, I felt the same way.

The most amazing thing was that Pat never stopped believing in me, even when sometimes I had stopped believing in myself. No matter how bad things got, he refused to quit—and he refused to let me quit. There's no way I could have made it through my ordeal without him.

I consider him a great friend. I don't believe I could have gotten through the years that this ordeal lasted without his intelligence, his absolute belief in the justice system, and his willingness to put his life on hold to fight for me. He kept his sense of humor, and helped everyone else keep theirs, too. When the question came down to, do I lie for leniency, or stand up for what was right, it was Pat who made the call. I often think he is the real hero of this story.

Not long after the end of the Whitewater II trial, Mark Geragos began getting phone calls from people inviting me to speak about my experiences. I accepted a few of these invitations, and began making speeches in front of political and legal groups. When I did, a surprising thing began happening.

Though most of the groups seemed to expect me to talk about Kenneth Starr, Whitewater, and the Clintons, I found myself spending the most time talking about my time in jail, and the women I met there. I didn't plan it that way, but whenever I started talking about the things that had changed my life, and the things that had real meaning for me, that was what invariably came to mind.

The amazing thing to me was how people responded to the stories I would tell. Politicians and commentators have demonized the men and women in the criminal justice system to such a degree that people are actually surprised to find that the women I met were not animals. The more I talked about my experiences with women in jail, the more invitations I got to speak around the country on the subject, and to raise money for organizations dedicated to helping incarcerated women.

I now speak two to three times a month to groups all over the country about the conditions in local jails and what they can do to help women that are locked up. It doesn't take much to help these women—they have very little to begin with and even the smallest gesture can make an enormous difference. I remember how just having a large bucket of ice delivered to our pod once a day at FCDC made for a dramatic improvement in the women's lives. I hope to use whatever visibility I have now to continue to shed light on the status of women in prison and to educate the public about their lives.

I am a much different person today than I was in September of 1996 when I walked into jail for the first time. As a teenager growing up in Camden, I would have been voted least likely to defy a government subpoena. But by the time I went to jail, I was angry and filled with a consuming hatred for the people who had unfairly put me there. Jail, quite frankly, was probably where I needed to be. When I left, I still hated them—but my outlook on life had changed.

A horrible thing that happened to me actually turned into a good thing. Being sent to jail was a frightening and sometimes horrible experience. But, being incarcerated actually changed my life for the better. In a strange twist, it was going to jail that proved to be my salvation, and there's no doubt in my mind that I'm a far better person than I was before I went to jail. As the reader of this book knows by now, I've made a lot of mistakes in life and done some foolish things that I'm not proud of. But, during my time in jail, I honestly evaluated the truth about my life, and examined with renewed clarity many of the life choices I had made. That process of evaluation and examination is one I would not forfeit for anything in the world, despite the fact I had to be jailed before I experienced it. Now, just a few years removed from my legal battles, I don't know what my future holds. But I do know that I'll be ready to face it squarely. And I truly believe that the best is yet to come for me.

ACKNOWLEDGMENTS

The number of people who deserve to be thanked would constitute a book unto itself. However, I would like to specifically thank a number of people who deserve special mention. Beginning with my lawyers (in order of appearance) Bobby McDaniel, Jennifer Horan, David Berg, Leonard Levine, and, of course, Mark Geragos who saved my life. My entire family was remarkable throughout the Whitewater ordeal: James Henley, Laure Mathieu Henley, Danielle Dickinson, Bob Dickinson, Michelle Fite, Mike Fite, Lane Hodge, Heath Hodge, Jason Dickinson, Niki Dickinson, Taylor Dickinson, Jim Henley, Sharlene Henley, Brian Henley, Jill Henley, Braden Henley, Ben Henley, Trace Wilhide, Gini Henley, David Guyden Cochrane, Paula Cochrane, David Guyden Cochrane, Jr., David Henley, Belinda Henley, Krystina Gleghorn, Karlee Gleghorn, David Mathieu Henley, John Henley, Royce Ann Henley, Brandt Henley, Walt Henley, Eli Henley, and Robyn Horn who every day make life worth living.

My friends, Ellen Ratner, Veda Morgan, Henry Morgan, and Claudia Riley for your strength. The news media who gave me the opportunity to tell my story, especially Larry King, Stone Phillips and *Dateline,* Geraldo Rivera, Greta Van Susteren and the *Arkansas Times.* Finally, my brother Bill who stormed the gates of all five jails and stood up not only for his sister, but for every woman brutalized by the inhumane conditions of America's jails.

Pat would like to thank his family for their ongoing encouragement and support in every way possible: Eugene Harris, Ron Harris, Carolyn Harris, Sarah Harris, Susan Harris, Charlie Harris, Cheryl Ledbetter, Dennis Ledbetter, Katy Wolfe, Rebecca Wolfe, Bob Pine, and Sue Pine.

In addition, he would like to thank both Lindsey Blenkhorn and Paulette Geragos for their insights and suggestions. Finally, a special thanks to Farima Shahimati for her infinite patience and understanding.

Pat and I would both like to thank our tremendous agent, Deborah Grosvenor, for helping to make this book a reality. Special thanks also go to Lisa Dickey who sacrificed time, money, and peace of mind to help make sure that everything flowed smoothly. Also deserving of special thanks is our editor at Carroll & Graf, Philip Turner, who, from the very first time we met, understood what this book was about and worked extremely hard to make it better.

Finally, we would like to send a thank you to everyone who supported me while I was in jail and through my trials, people like Corky Hale, Marie McGee, Walt and Marie McGee, Lee Kendall, Rabbi Kriegel, Father Santo, Elizabeth Kaye, Clara Solis, John Brown, Cindy and Fred Mann, Margie Shumate, Senator Pryor, Steve Smith, Monique Osby, and the thousands of people who took the time to write or call—you let us know that someone cared and that you were watching. Thank you for believing in me when it was not an easy thing to do. I could not have made it without you.